INVESTOR RELATIONS

INVESTOR RELATIONS
The Professional's Guide to Financial Marketing and Communications

William F. Mahoney

New York Institute of Finance

New York   London   Toronto   Sydney   Tokyo   Singapore

Library of Congress Cataloging-in-Publication Data

Mahoney, William F.
     Investor relations : the professional's guide to financial
marketing and communication / William F. Mahoney.
          p.   cm.
     Includes index.
     ISBN 0-13-691254-0
     1. Financial planners–Marketing–Handbooks, manuals, etc.
     2. Public relations personnel–Handbooks, manuals, etc.   I. Title.
     HG179.5.M34   1990
     658.15'2–dc20   90-46038
                                                                            CIP

This publication is designed to provide accurate and authoritative information in regard to the subject matter covered. It is sold with the understanding that the publisher is not engaged in rendering legal, accounting,
or other professional service. If legal advice or other expert assistance is
required, the services of a competent professional person should be
sought.

From a Declaration of Principles
Jointly Adopted by
a Committee of the American Bar Association
and a Committee of Publishers and Associations

© 1991 by NYIF Corp.
A Division of Simon & Schuster
A Paramount Communications Company

Printed in the United States of America
10   9   8   7   6   5   4   3   2   1

To my mother and father,

who taught me life's most valuable lessons and showed their love
for me every day.

92-29091

ADVISORY BOARD

Contents

Foreword   xiii
Acknowledgments   xv

**Part One   The Capital Market and Its Participants:
              The Role of Investor Relations**   **1**

Chapter 1   The Genesis of Investor Relations   **3**

**Chapter 2   The Two Worlds of Investors: Institutions
               and Individuals**   **7**
Bringing the Capital Marketplace into Focus   9
Dissecting the Investment Universe   12
Profile of the Institutional Segment   14
A Closer Look at the Individual Investor Market   16

Chapter 3   Basic Elements of an Investor Relations Program   **21**
Setting Program Objectives   21
Conducting Benchmark Attitudinal/Knowledge Research   23
Building and Maintaining Market Relations   23
The Information Process   27
Methods of Distributing Information   29
Use of Technology   32
Putting Together a Global Investor Relations Program   33
Value of Media Relations   34
External and Market Forces Impacting Investor Relations   35
Measuring the Investor Relations Program   41

Chapter 4   A Capital Market Profile   **43**
Economics Basic to Process   45
Calculating Return and Risk   47
Role of Analysts   49
Making the Asset Allocation Decision   53
Equity Investment Strategies and Styles   54
Using Futures and Options   66
Short Selling as a Technique   69
Trends in Institutional Behavior   71
Is Indexing Reducing the Amount of Fundamental Analysis?   74

Chapter 5   Why Individuals Should Be Emphasized   **77**
Individuals Hold More Shares, But Impact Is Declining   78
Brokerage Industry Ambivalent   80
Companies Can Lead Individuals Back   82

**Chapter 6   Takeovers Become the Catalyst for Investor
                     Relations to Cook**   **87**
Takeover Wave Covers 1980s   90
Companies Dug in to Preserve Their Independence   92
How Corporations Defended Against Takeovers   96
Investor Relations Gains Respect   100
Investor Relations Role in a Takeover   100
Once the Battle Begins   106
Director Responsibility in a Takeover   112
What Can Be Expected in the Future   114

**Chapter 7   Institutions Involving Themselves in
                     Corporate Governance**   **117**
Takeovers Trigger Institutional Activism   118
Poison Pills Can Raise Takeover Premium   121
Other Key Governance Issues   122
Activist Circle Widening   124
The Progress and Arguments on Both Sides   129
The Corporate Side of the Question   132

**Part Two   How the Essential Parts Fit Together
                     in an Investor Relations Program**   **137**

**Chapter 8   Marketing Becomes the Operative Investor
                     Relations Approach**   **139**
The Purpose of Investor Relations   142
The Value of Investor Relations   145
Basic Investor Relations Duties   148
The Basic Structure of an Investor Relations Program   149
Working With Research as Program Basis   151
Using the Communications Vehicles   154
Two Hypothetical Case Histories   158
Measuring the Program   163

Chapter 9   Valuation as Basis of the Investor Relations Practice   **167**
Negative Views on Valuation   169
Arguments for a Valuation Approach   170
How Value Is Determined   171
Ways of Measuring Valuation   174

Valuation as a Basis of Strategic Corporate Action   174
Key Value Drivers Shown in Investment Behavior   175
Share Price Management as Investor Relations Priority   177
Scientific Process for Selecting Value-Enhancing Activities   181
Experience Rates Investor Reaction to Various Value-
    Raising Moves   183
Value Creation as an Ongoing Process   184

Chapter 10   Building Buy- and Sell-side Relationships   189
How the Relationship Is Evolving   191
Sell-Side Research Contribution Depends on
    Institutional Need   192
Institutions Evaluating Companies as Information Resources   194
Building Brokerage Analyst Relationships   196
There Are Good Reasons to Influence Investors Directly   210

Chapter 11   Marketing to Individuals and Retail Brokers   219
Marketing Approaches Depend on Motivations and Reality   221
Psychology and Demographics: Valuable to Understand   223
The Affinity Group Concept   227
Reaching Individuals Through Brokers   233
Communications Programs to Support Retail Market Efforts   239

Chapter 12   As Markets Globalize, So Does Investor Relations   241
Institutions Diversifying Globally   244
Assembling an Investor Relations Program   247
Plotting the Course   249
Making a Commitment   254
Formats for Meetings   255

**Chapter 13   Annual Reports Are the Leading Printed
               Communications Tool   259**
The 10-K and Annual Report as a Team   260
Positioning the Annual Report   262
The Report's Main Sections   268
Preparation and Production of the Report   279
Summary Reports Haven't Caught On   284
Marketing the Annual Report   286
Positioning Quarterly Reports in the Mix   288
The Value of Other Printed Communications Materials   290
Emergence of Electronic Communication   294

Chapter 14   Well-planned Meetings Enhance Program Results   297
Organizing Meetings around Objectives   298
Plotting the Best Meeting Forums   303

Taking a Programmed Approach   310
Field Trips and Annual Meetings   312
Getting the Most Out of Meetings   317

Chapter 15   Technology and Outside Services Playing
              Beautiful Music In Investor Relations Orchestra   323
Three Leading Roles of Technology   324
Reaching New Horizons as an Information Resource   325
Streamlining Information Dissemination   335
Organizing the Investor Relations Office   338

Chapter 16   Why a Proactive Approach Is Best in
              Media Relations   345
Investor Relations Role in Media Relations   349
The Case for Proactive Media Relations   352
Components of a Media Relations Program   355
Some Tips on Good Media Relations   376

Chapter 17   Debt Relations a Growing Part of the Job   381
Positioning Equity and Debt Relations   383
How Proactive Should Debt Relations Be?   385

Chapter 18   Material Disclosure: The Delicate Role of
              Investor Relations   389
How We Got Here   392
Outsiders Also Must Be Careful   400
Exchanges Push for Disclosure   400
Establishing a Communications Attitude, Policy, and Practice   401
How Companies Are Handling Various Disclosure Situations   406
Disclosure While in Registration   409

Chapter 19   Investor Relations: A Career or Preparation
              for Moving On-High   411
Investor Relations as a Rotational Position   414
Elevating Investor Relations   415
Making Investor Relations a Career or Stepping Stone   420

Index   423

Foreword

Today, as always, securities markets are truly efficient only when they have sufficient and appropriate data with which to price or "value" publicly traded issues. It is obvious, then, that communications must be recognized as a paramount element in creating and maintaining market efficiency and fair valuation.

Skeptics often challenge the value of communications, the heart of true investor relations, on the grounds that "the numbers speak for themselves" or that "stocks are worth what investors are willing to pay." There is no direct challenge to those "theories" here, but those of us who have been in the investor relations business for some time—those who have worked with managements who have recognized that securities are sold, not bought—know that the combination of performance and the effective communication of business and financial objectives and strategies is the real key to maximizing market values. Two companies that have been performing pari passu go their separate ways when one communicates and the other does not.

Investor relations has gone through a long period of incubation, often clouded by the sometimes justified stigma of hyperbole. But look around and talk to the new breed of investor relations manager—sophisticated in the ways of business management, articulate, and financially savvy. Dedicated, knowledgeable people like this make it easy to understand how investor relations has muscled its way into the corporate suite in just a very few years.

Much of the credit for the acceptance and appreciation of investor relations, I suspect, is owed to a most unlikely source—the corporate raider. For it is he, more than anyone else, who has put top managements and boards of directors on notice that they need to take a more active role in creating and sustaining a fair value of the corporation to fulfill their duty as shepherds of their stakeholders' interests.

The result has been a mandate to understand what makes capital markets tick and to merchandise the communicable assets, liabilities, goals, and prospects of the corporation to the global investor village with clarity, consistency, and condor.

This is a tough job, to say the least, but an exciting and rewarding one at the same tøme. It's an interdisciplinary function that touches on a broad variety of business skills and aptitudes. One must gave good business sense, a feel for accounting, finance, corporate law, securities analysis, and marketing *and* be an effective communicator. Nowadays, some very astute investor relations people are proving that a combination of these talents need not be an oxymoron.

Investor relations has been a pioneering effort to date, as well. There really have been no direct pathways through academia or through the securities markets, that offered a well-marked and paved road to success. It has been trial and error on the job— backed by the persistence of a determined cadre of thought leaders, oftentimes with distinct minority positions—that has brought the craft of investor relations to its rising level of respectability and strategic corporate/financial significance.

Until now, there has been no definitive primer on the practice of investor relations, principally because of the continued, dynamic changes on capital market facia. Bill Mahoney certainly goes a long way towards providing that kind of authoritative guide. I invite you to read, save, and reference *Investor Relations: The Professional's Guide to Financial Marketing and Communications*. I have, and I will.

ROBERT D. FERRIS

Acknowledgments

Many people have contributed to the writing of this book. In generously sharing their ideas, they have helped foster the growth of investor relations as an important corporate function. Investor relations is marked by hard-working, dedicated people who enthusiastically share their knowledge in advancing the practice. Their influence is evident in this book, just as it has been in the *Investor Relations Update* newsletter over the past decade.

My appreciation is extended first to the editorial advisory committee set up by the New York Institute of Finance to help shape the content of this book and offer suggestions on the writing. This group of valued advisors consists of Frank Jepson, vice president of investor relations for Bausch & Lomb; Bob Ferris, executive vice president of Gavin Anderson Doremus and Company; Samuel B. Jones, vice president and portfolio manager for Keystone Investment Management Corp.; and Dennis McConnell, professor at the University of Maine, College of Business.

Among the corporate practitioners whose ideas and comments are an integral part of the body of knowledge contained in this book are Roseanne Antonucci, Jim Armstrong, Roger Beidler, Larry Bishop, Vern Blodgett, Bill Brantley, John Budd, Kathy Chieger, Howard Christensen, Charles Cohen, Pete Crawford, Jerry Doyle, Doug Ewing, Gerrie Foster, Jennifer Frey, John Fuller, John Gearhart, Len Griehs, Bill Hartl. Demi Hetrick, Dick Holthaus, Jim Hurley, Jerry Isham, Johnnie Johnson, Debbie Kelly. Marvin Krasnansky, the late Stark Langs, John Lewis, Keith Mabee, Jim Mabry, Barry Murphy, Peggy Moore, Ed O'Meara, Richard Olson, Becky Osterberg, Lee Parker, Marshall Peterson, Jim Powers, Shellie Roth, Glenn Saxon, Jim Simon, Walt Skowronski, Mark Steinkrauss, Jim Stier, Steve Swartz, Ted Swift, Kathy Tarbox, Carol Tutundgy, Frank Vitale, Sharon Vuinovich and Ashley Weare. Several serve as consultants today.

The consulting role is vital to the greening of investor relations. A list of those whose ideas are embedded in this book includes Ken Altman, Bob Amen, Kay Breakstone, Bill Chatlos, Bill Crane, Bill Dunk, John Gavin, Jerry Hanan, Gordon Holmes, Gary Kraut, Mark Leeds, Dick Lewis, Dick Morrill, Al Miller, Gerry Murray, Win Neilson, Steve Nowlan, Ted Pincus, Art Rivel, Carol Ruth, Mike Seely, Diana Shayan, Joe Shenton, Arlen Southern, Carrie Thomas, Des Towey, John Wilcox, and Claudia Zaner.

My list of acknowledgments would be incomplete without including a diverse group of people who have contributed to this book as educators, editors, investors, advisors, consultants, and friends: the late Mark Appleman, Marv Chatinover, Carol Coles, Jim Danowski, Deb Dierking, Charley Ellis, Larry Farrell, Ken Janke, Sr., Ed Kulkosky, John Lafferty, Russ Mason, John McCabe, Don Mitchell, Mary Mitchell, Tom O'Hara, Andy Rothman, Joel Stern, Lou Thompson, and Carol Villecco.

Research for this book also includes references from four books on investing and investor relations: *Managing Investment Portfolios*, by John L. Maginn and Donald L. Tuttle (Warren, Gorham & Lamont); *Creating Investor Demand for Company Stock*, by Richard M. Altman (Quorum Books); *Corporate Communications Handbook*, by Wesley S. Walton and Charles P. Brissman (Clark Boardman); and *Security Analysis* (New York Institute of Finance). Investor relations professionals are encouraged to tap the many valued resources available as books and articles covering investor relations, the capital markets, and investing practice. Bibliographic information is available from the National Investor Relations Institute and the Association for Investment Management and Research. The NIRI Foundation is preparing a comprehensive bibliography at this time.

Readers starting on page 1 and following along to the finish are asked to be patient with the repetition of ideas in various chapters. Each chapter is intended to be complete in covering the subject.

If an enthusiasm for investor relations comes across in this book, it is by design. This is intended as a proactive book about the role and value of investor relations. It seeks to encourage practitioners to take the high road in stretching themselves, to see just how far they can carry the practice. As noted portfolio manager Russell G. Redenbaugh said at a NIRI conference in 1990: The practice of investor relations is moving from "lore" to "discipline," just as the investing practice began to do some 30 years ago.

The Capital Market and Its Participants: The Role of Investor Relations

1

The Genesis of Investor Relations

The metamorphosis of investor relations has been a 25-year process; it is still taking place, but now also taking shape. The "parents" of investor relations are public relations (which gave it birth), and finance. In the early years, investor relations was under the influence of public relations, growing with a promotional flair, as seen in its annual reports and "dog and pony shows"—the euphemism for brokerage analyst and retail stockbroker meetings.

Now beyond the age of impression, investor relations is being nurtured by the principles of finance. This is both logical and necessary: the capital markets have been institutionalized; institutions follow sophisticated financial models in their investing; and thus, the information must be financially driven.

Still, the influence of both parents is vital. While the information is financial in nature, the process always will be communications focused on the quality of information and the effectiveness of the delivery systems.

Quality in this context is defined as two dimensional: what investors want to know in setting up their investment strategies and in working through their investment models; and, additionally, the information companies believe investors should learn in viewing the business favorably as an investment. This gets to what many practitioners believe is the essence of the investor relations contribution, namely helping "close the information gap" in the process investors use to put a value on the companies' securities. The information is designed to help investors realize the full value potential of a company.

The main delivery systems include such communications materials as annual and interim reports, 10Ks and 10Qs, fact books, newsletters, and videos as well as direct contact, in the form of either one to one or group meetings.

As investor relations matures, public relations is giving way to marketing. The result is a broadening of activity to include the components of marketing—audience research and targeting, careful message development and testing, and evidence to support selecting certain communications vehicles. Whether these activities are considered public relations or marketing is a moot point; the investor relations practice calls it marketing.

In any case, the important ingredient is the relevance of the information to investor audiences. Learning what's relevant continues to be a high investor relations priority as well as a target that moves with the changing investing strategies of Wall Street.

Critics contend that investor relations has gone too far in adopting marketing techniques. The investor relations function, they argue, is an information resource, pure and simple, and there's no place for some of the aggressive tactics of today; tactics found chiefly in modern marketing such as self-serving expression, effusive graphics, excessive usage of direct mail, and barnstorming trips to ferret out retail brokers and institutional investors.

The arguments are oversimplified. Heavy-handed communications materials tend to fail anyway. It has been a long struggle for investor relations people in winning some measure of credibility for the informational value of annual reports among securities analysts and institutional investors, for example. At the same time, some promotional-type programs, such as direct mail and broker communications, can be useful to companies—specific types of programs in certain circumstances.

As a two-edged sword, the explosion of marketing-oriented services is enabling the more adventurous companies to be more aggressive in trying new ideas, but it also is elevating the already-present element of uncertainty that exists inherently in the subjective, hard-to-measure investor relations function. That combination challenges corporate investor relations people to really understand their profession so they can evaluate each opportunity intelligently in terms of the company's strategic goals and their own budget. It also is challenging consultants charged with the responsibility of advising their corporate clients on how best to use those precious budget resources.

The profession needs to be questioning itself every day on the wise use of investor relations monies. How are the ultimate objectives of an investor relations program satisfied in the preparation of an annual report, in the conduct of a series of meetings with brokers and analysts across the country, or in a direct mail program? And are the programs cost-effective? Habits are hard to break and have a way of costing more each year, often with little quantitative effort made to measure their value. Many of the habits in the practice of investor relations are well-established and would benefit from new scrutiny.

Now grown and contributing to the success of a corporation, investor relations has two dimensions: the assignments themselves, such as producing annual reports and building relationships with analysts and leading investors; and participation in the strategic decisions and actions that affect the cost of capital, price of the stock, as well as long-term survival and success of the enterprise.

Investor relations people will benefit from performing well in both dimensions. For many, that means advancing from the first, or "duty" level to the higher, "strategic" level, while incorporating both into the function. The two levels are inexorably and intricately linked, with the quality of the first being critical in reaching the value of the second. The ability to advise senior management on the likely reaction of institutional investors to a planned acquisition or stock repurchase and the effect of that reaction on stock price requires close, positive, working relationships with those investors. And, those relationships cannot be built without a good information base, extended in every annual and quarterly report, presentation, and meeting.

The investor relations practice is operating at the strategic level in many companies, with the number rising. Frequently, the credit belongs to the effectiveness of the investor relations person in showing the role and contribution of the function to senior executives.

Consultants also are advising managements on the part investor relations can play. These include investor relations consultants, and in recent years, the emergence of shareholder value consultants. Their focus is on corporate strategies and programs dealing with the entire financial structure such as:

> raising capital in a cost-effective manner on a global basis;
>
> the debt/equity relationship;
>
> best uses of capital in sustaining growth; and
>
> specific actions that will strengthen the company and increase the worth of the securities such as acquisitions, divestitures, partial public offerings of subsidiary operations, share repurchases, dividend changes.

Communicating these moves and their benefits in the overall corporate strategic plan to gain favorable investor response is the most important job of the investor relations function.

Practiced at this higher level, investor relations is becoming an integral part of financial planning; investor relations professionals are advising management on the best sources of low-cost capital around the world, how the leading investors are valuing the company's securities, and specifically, the impact of major strategic decisions under consideration on stock valuation, price, and volatility. Their qualifications are comprehensive understanding of the capital markets and the behavior of investors combined with a thorough working knowledge of the financial and operational structures of the company.

The ongoing task of the investor relations profession is to complete the metamorphosis by qualifying a maximum number of its people to work successfully in both the task and strategic dimensions of the practice.

2

The Two Worlds of Investors: Institutions and Individuals

Investor relations people are forever playing catch-up in trying to keep pace with their two "masters"—the capital markets and their corporations. Mastering them both is essential in managing a quality program. Mastering either isn't easy.

The two come together like siblings—connected, mutually supportive, but frequently at odds. The imperative of investor relations people is to win the respect of their corporate managements and investors. To do so, they must bring something of value to each.

The challenge inside the company (and among consultants serving clients) is to demonstrate a unique knowledge of the capital markets and behavior of investors that can be translated into real dollar benefits in terms of share price and lower cost of capital. With investors, the job is to bring information that will lead to decisions producing higher portfolio returns.

It's probably harder for investor relations people to catch up and stay astride the capital markets. Investor relations people are a step behind by definition. The investing strategies originate with the investors, and have become complex, highly sophisticated and in some cases, proprietary for as long as possible.

For these reasons, investor relations practitioners need to understand the capital markets thoroughly, as well as the investing techniques of institutions particularly, if they are to maximize their value to their companies or clients. The institutionalization of the equity markets, a reality of the last 20 years, has made the task even tougher. Institutional dominance puts pressure on investor relations people to know their stuff. It's much simpler to communicate with individual investors.

However, the opportunity to have impact on share price and cost of capital is greater when dealing with institutions. By virtue of the size of their holdings and tendency to trade actively, institutions set the price, at least in the larger capitalization companies. That's a good reason for investor relations people to concentrate their communication efforts on the institutional side.

Institutionalization and the desire of investor relations practitioners to be more valuable to their companies make for a powerful combination. It's a motivating force in encouraging investor relations people to be students of investing theories and practices.

The situation is especially challenging to investor relations people with communications backgrounds. Their proficiency in communications may not offset their lack of in-depth knowledge of financial statements and investing models when weighed against counterparts with financial MBAs, experience as assistant treasurers, analysts, traders, or brokers. Practitioners coming from the PR/communications side more than ever must work at overcoming their disadvantage if, in the future, they want to *direct* serious, management-supported investor relations programs that include carrying on daily contact with institutional investors and analysts. Financial/investment management courses and a rich resource of academically based information are at their disposal.

Communications and marketing skills also are vital in the credentials of the well-rounded investor relations professional. Practitioners with finance or Wall Street backgrounds don't bring communications talents automatically either. There aren't that many multi-dimensional investor relations people out there. However, the trend favors the finance background, with writing and other related communication services provided usually by the public relations department.

BRINGING THE CAPITAL MARKETPLACE INTO FOCUS

Seeing how all the parts fit into the capital markets picture can help investor relations practitioners figure out which pieces should get the biggest slices of their budgets. It also helps to try to piece together the trends and patterns of the markets, in order to get as clear a picture as possible. Here are some.

- Assets managed by U.S. institutions have grown tremendously. Various estimates put the total at over $5 trillion, counting those managed by pension and mutual funds, insurance companies, and banks. The trend in having more of those assets invested in stocks also grows thanks to liberalized pension rules and high returns compared with other instruments. About half of the institutional assets are in stocks.

- Institutions are taking over the U.S. equity markets, replacing individuals. Institutions are steadily moving toward holding half of corporate America's common stock float and are responsible for about two-thirds of daily stock trading. As a result, institutional impact on companies is growing. They are leading the advances in investing techniques, and in so doing have become the principal users and demanders of corporate information.

- Individuals remain an important part of the equity mix and should not be counted out. In fact, strong arguments are being put forth that individuals should be wooed with more fervor than ever before as an alternate lover to institutions, whose active trading habits combined with large holdings can lead to stock price volatility. Individuals still hold about 55 percent of all shares, and while stocks are less important in their investment mix, their total holdings in stocks has continued to rise. In 1970, the $700 billion held by individuals represented 36 percent of their financial assets. The $2 trillion now in individual hands represents just 20 percent of their total financial worth. They also are the force behind much of the money managed by two large institutional groups—mutual funds and bank trusts.

■ Of special concern to the brokerage industry, which generates considerable commission revenue from stocks, equities are becoming a smaller piece of the investment asset pie even as their numbers have grown. That growth in total equity value, however, also has been stunted, at least for now. Domestically, equities were about 45 percent of the value of marketable securities in 1980 but under 35 percent in 1989 according to the Securities Industry Association (SIA). Interestingly, U.S. securities, mainly Treasuries, have forged into the lead. During the time the impact of equities was declining, however, its total market value was doubling. The gains are seen, as already indicated, in both institutional and individual investor investment.

■ Size of the equity pie has been shrinking dramatically in the United States. It is estimated that some $500 billion worth of stock has left the market in the past few years (the figure being the net between the effects of mergers, acquisitions, takeovers, leveraged buyouts, debt recapitalizations, and new public equity issues).

■ At the same time, the trend of corporations to use debt more than equity in new underwritings was evident in the latter half of the 1980s. In 1989, for example, corporate bond underwritings were $114 billion, severalfold more than new stock offerings.

Debt has taken on two dimensions, one seen as vital and practical, the other as controversial: funding business expansion; and facilitating corporate takeovers and leveraged buyouts. The dramatic rise and fall of junk bonds, the hectic pace of takeovers that were at least partially funded by those bonds, the rise in the number of leveraged buyouts with many involving highly publicized big-ticket numbers, and the subsequent flurry of debt-related bankruptcies came together to ring the alarm that overleveraging was about to undo American business.

However, the debt/equity ratio of corporate America does not appear to be in trouble. It was almost one to one after 1988, the latest year of calculation, and probably hasn't changed that much, despite an active 1989 debt year. At the end of 1988, the Federal Reserve counted $2.77 trillion in corporate debt versus $2.56 trillion in the market value of corporate equity. The ratio has not changed much in a decade. In 1977, corporate debt totaled $898 billion with the market value of stocks being $748 billion. That was before the bull stock market of the 1980s. However, an alarmist might note that the debt/equity ratio among large U.S. industrial companies, as measured by the S&P 400 Industrials, is rising.

Debt is seen by many corporate finance consultants as desirable. It is shown to improve corporate performance by functioning as an incentive to managements. The interest/principal payment obligations are always at hand. Debt also offers tax advantages in the cost of capital equation.

■ The stock market is becoming truly global. Two statistical studies bear this out. In 1980, according to the Securities Industry Association, U.S. equities were 55 percent of total global stock capitalization with Japan holding 17 percent, the United Kingdom holding 9 percent, and the rest of the world holding 19 percent. In 1989, U.S. equities represented 29 percent, Japan 45 percent, the United Kingdom 8.5 percent, and the rest of the world 17.5 percent. Of some $22.2 trillion in a global investable capital market, as calculated in 1988 by First Chicago Investment Advisors, some 13.7 percent was in U.S. equities and 28.4 percent in non-U.S. equities. Dollar bonds made up 20.2 percent, non-dollar bonds 24.1 percent, real estate 7.3 percent, cash equivalents 6.2 percent, and venture capital 0.1 percent.

DISSECTING THE INVESTMENT UNIVERSE

While the players in the investment process continue to wear the same numbers as always, their roles and impact are changing dynamically. The sell-side (brokerage) has three main groups:

research analysts;

brokers who deal with institutional investors; and

and brokers who deal with individual investors—*registered representatives*, as they are called.

Traders, also, are part of the brokerage family but they have not been key investor relations contacts. The investor side consists of institutional analysts, fund/portfolio managers, institutional traders, and individuals.

Within this universe are an overlapping and a mixing of duties. Brokers (and financial planners) take on "buy side" responsibilities, functioning as portfolio managers for individual investors and small corporate funds. Bank trusts are institutions that manage the money of wealthy individuals, as well as corporate trust accounts. And certainly, mutual funds are institutions even though most of their customers are individuals.

Fundamental research is basic to the investing process, but how it is prepared, produced, and provided is being altered dramatically and permanently by the computer. Equity research/analysis has been the foundation of brokerage industry income for decades, but no longer. Its value as the basis of commission income peaked, has dropped precipitously and may never regain its lofty stature.

A little history, brought up to date, shows how the process is unfolding. Research undergirds brokerage commissions; investors like the research and recommendations of a particular firm (that's how analysts become "stars") and use the firm to execute the transactions. The brokerage industry geared its research and trading services to the institutional segment as it began taking charge of the U.S. equities markets in the 1960s and 1970s. While the brokerage commissions are only a few cents a share (fixed rate commissions ended in 1975), the totals are substantial in institutional transactions involving hundreds of thousands of shares. The bulk of the big institutional business has been with the investment banking and New York firms.

Retail equity commissions remained an important income source, both to national and regional firms. The national wire houses established strong networks of brokers, numbering in the thousands across the country. Regional brokerage firms relied even more for revenue on retail market commissions and still do.

Equity commissions were 61 percent of brokerage industry income in 1965, according to the Securities Industry Association. But that figure has been dropping steadily since, and was at under 20 percent for 1989. Institutional and individual investors alike are contributing to the decline in brokerage commission income as a percentage of total revenue. Individuals are inclined to trade infrequently, invest in stocks through mutual funds, and have not been growing sufficiently to maintain the momentum in commission volume that had been rising steadily in years past. Some observers suggest that individuals are leaving the market; one estimate says they took $500 billion out from 1982 through 1989. Individuals remain an important source of income for regional and discount brokerage firms.

Institutions are taking on more of the research role and handling more of their transactions directly. They're tapping the electronic databases for the research and using their models, in effect, for the analysis or as critical information inputs in active investing decisions. Institutions also appear to be trading less for a number of possible reasons:

a desire to lower the cost of transactions;

a rise in use of indexed investing, which results in less trading;

fewer takeover premiums to capture;

a perception by investors and clients alike that short-term trading isn't improving returns; and

a renewed focus on the higher returns that can be achieved from longer-term investing horizons.

PROFILE OF THE INSTITUTIONAL SEGMENT

The two most important groups to the practice of investor relations are institutional and individual stock buyers. The institutional universe is the fastest growing and is also wielding the most influence on companies. The institutionalization of the U.S. equities markets has been the result of an economy that has bumped along rather successfully since the end of World War II with only a few recessionary bruises. Assets have been accumulating steadily, mainly in retirement and savings funds, but also in bank, insurance and mutual fund money pools, all ballooned by successful investing returns.

Trying to get a composite picture of institutional assets under management requires going to a number of sources. The total comes to almost $5 trillion, counting the assets of pension and mutual funds, banks, insurance companies, and bank and savings association money markets.

About 21,000 tax-exempt pension funds manage around $2 trillion in assets, according to the annual "Directory of Pension Funds and Their Investment Managers" published by Money Market Directories, Inc., a subsidiary of Standard & Poor's Corporate Information Company. These include:

corporate pension, thrift, stock, and 401(k) plans;

state and municipal retirement plans; and

union, endowment, and foundation plans.

More than $1 trillion is in corporate plans, with over $600 billion in public funds (the fastest-growing of the group). The numbers continue to rise. More than half of the corporate pension plan assets are in defined-benefit plans, but defined-contribution, ESOP, and 401(k) plans are gaining favor rapidly. Intersec Research Corp. placed total U.S. pension assets at the end of 1988 at $2.1 trillion with $1.475 trillion in private and $675 billion in public funds.

Pensions & Investments and *Institutional Investor* magazines also profile the institutional community every year. *P&I's* 1989 numbers showed a pension fund asset base of $1.875 trillion among the 1,000 top plans while *Institutional Investor* recorded $1.5 trillion among the 500 largest corporate and 232 largest public funds. According to growth patterns and actuarial assumptions, assets managed by the public funds are expected to catch and pass the totals in private pension funds by the turn of the century.

Also in the category of fast growing markets is the mutual fund industry. It surpassed the $1 trillion asset level in January of 1990. Nearly $450 billion of those funds are in money market and short-term municipal bond funds, with some $300 billion in bond and income funds, and just under $250 billion in stock funds according to the Investment Company Institute (the mutual fund trade association).

Banks, savings associations, and insurance companies constitute the other big player in the institutional lineup. The "Directory of Pension Funds and Their Investment Managers" indicated that investable insurance industry assets were about $735 billion at the end of 1988, while bank trust assets under management totaled nearly $730 billion. To these numbers need to be added the money market and savings deposits of financial institutions, totalling some $125 billion at the end of 1988, according to the Federal Reserve System.

Investment management firms also have grown tremendously, especially in the 1980s. Money managers proliferated in the decade, many started by the top portfolio managers and analysts from the bigger institutions—investment firms, banks, and brokerage houses. Often, the successful investing formula for these investment firms flows from an investment model, carved from internal research and computer-generated market and corporate data (critical numbers, research of financial analysts, consensus earnings forecasts), combined with following a certain investment discipline and a proprietary value-add from the firm's founders. Basically, these firms combine quantitative and active management. They use small computer screens but make big investment decisions.

Pension and other retirement funds are a big market for these firms. The "Directory of Pension Funds and Their Investment

Managers" showed some 964 U.S. investment counselors managing tax-exempt pension accounts covering private and public plans plus other types of clients worth $2.322 trillion at the end of 1988. More than 1,000 such firms were listed in the 1989 *Institutional Investor* directory.

The competitive nature of these investment firms, spurred by plan sponsors' interest in maximizing returns, and the temptations of takeover premiums in the 1980s have contributed to the criticism that institutions are transaction driven, turning their portfolios over and over in the interest of achieving the highest comparative performance results possible in the shortest time frame. The wisdom of short-term speculative tactics versus long-term investing strategies is likely to undergo close scrutiny in the 1990s. Institutions appear to be dissatisfied with the results of the short-term approach.

A CLOSER LOOK AT THE INDIVIDUAL INVESTOR MARKET

Persuading individuals to rekindle the spark of enthusiasm for stock investing they had from after World War II until the mid-1980s is considered by many to be a worthwhile investor relations objective. However, investor relations people who believe the institutional market is the center of the action, question the cost-effectiveness of retail programs. Chapter 11 focuses on investor relations for the retail market.

While individuals hold $2 trillion in stocks directly, the trend favors institutional management of individuals' funds. Investors with smaller stakes seem to be relying on the professional management capabilities of mutual funds. The Investment Company Institute estimates that some 87 percent of the total of the nearly $250 billion in stock funds managed by its members at the end of 1989 represented equity holdings by individuals. Conventional wisdom suggests that these "small" shareholders are becoming increasingly reluctant to invest directly in stocks because they can't compete with institutions in terms of information resources and speed in conducting transactions to catch the market at exactly the right time. Institutional program trading is cited frequently as at least one of the culprits in chasing individuals from the U.S. equities market. It is, no doubt, a contributing factor in the larger process of institutionalizing the market.

Individuals also call upon professional management of their discretionary assets by utilizing bank trusts, brokers and certified financial planners for portfolio management, and by investing in the bond and money market mutual funds. Stocks are a serious part of the investment mix of the bank trusts, brokers, and financial planners. U.S. bank trusts are managing some $85 billion in personal trust accounts with about $25 billion of that number invested in stocks. Bank trusts tend to be traditionalists utilizing fundamental analysis in picking good companies with consistent performance that suit portfolio goals involving price appreciation and income from dividends compounding over time.

More than half of total household investment income is staying away from stocks altogether, instead seeking interest-rate returns. Mutual funds in this country are managing over $300 billion in bond funds and nearly $500 billion in money market funds. According to the Federal Reserve, financial institutions are managing about $125 billion in deposits and money markets. Second to stocks, individuals hold more money—$1.9 trillion—in federal interest-bearing securities, primarily Treasury notes, bills and bonds. U.S. government securities, mainly Treasuries, have become the largest domestic security classification, with about $3.2 trillion in assets altogether, the Security Industry Association reports.

Retail brokers and financial planners are direct conduits to individual investors. But they have become much more than stockbrokers and life insurance salespersons in recent years. Brokerage firms have contributed to the change, parrying the competitive thrust of mutual funds and the package of money instruments available from financial institutions by creating a potpourri of products for brokers to sell in their portfolio management approach. Brokers still like stocks, and indeed, many of them favor stocks, but the products they push will always be the ones that sell best and provide the highest income returns to the firm and brokers themselves.

In analyzing the prospects of positive progress in an investor communications effort aimed at individuals, it is useful to break the group into pieces. A 1985 survey of the New York Stock Exchange showed the number of individual investors to be rising (47 million in 1985 versus 30 million just five years earlier). That 1985 figure translates into one in four adult Americans. The median stock portfolio of investors in the survey was $6,600. However, the average portfolio size of new stockholders in the 1980s was only $2,200, according to other studies.

At the other end of the spectrum are wealthy, high-tax-bracket individuals and those who are serious, virtually lifetime stock investors, many of whom have become wealthy as a result of their wise investing. The wealthy individual target group includes the growing number of "millionaires" in the country, each with estimated investable assets of around $500,000. Studies indicate the percentage they invest in stocks is trending down from about 40 percent of their total assets in 1976 to just over 30 percent in 1982. Real estate holdings were the big gain items during that time frame.

The other group—the serious stock investors—are all over the lot in terms of income status. What distinguishes them from other investors is their "approach" to investing it tends to be very professional by the standards of research and analysis. Two "control groups" that can be called representative of the serious individual investor are the members of the National Association of Investors Corporation, and American Association of Individual Investors. They are educational groups that help individuals be better investors. NAIC is an investor club with an emphasis on teaching its members essentially how to be "value" investors with long-term perspectives. A goal of the membership is to double the value of each stock investment every five years. At the end of 1989, there were 700 NAIC investment clubs with 112,000 members whose average stock portfolio was worth $110,000.

Wealthy and serious stock investors (certainly the wealthy investors are serious, too) worry about the same factors that worry institutions—risk, returns, cash flow, and tax implications. NAIC members do their own analysis. So do many of the high-income individuals who execute the trades through their brokers. The discount brokerage business serves many of these investors. Many use brokers and financial planners for stock selection and portfolio management advice. Investors also are turning more to computer software programs for market and corporate data as well as portfolio management tools.

Basic Elements of an Investor Relations Program

While no two investor relations programs are identical, most fit into a framework that contains certain basic pieces. They are outlined here, accompanied by commentary on each.

SETTING PROGRAM OBJECTIVES

There is a tendency to jump into a string of activities that emulates those being done by other companies without thinking through the purpose of the program and how it is best accomplished. The program also will benefit from an upfront analysis of the needed qualifications of the resource team, degree of management participation required, projections of reasonable costs, and estimates of results that can be expected realistically. Getting executive management on the same wavelength with the investor relations team on expectations, timetable, time involved, and costs can avoid disappointment, displeasure, disruption, and discontinuance of the program later.

It also is important for management to agree on the objectives. That may call for some persuasion, or at least, mutual acceptance of what investor relations should do and can accomplish. *Fundamentally*, it should function as a service to shareholders and potential investors—providing information and accommodating certain basic needs, which also tend to be information oriented, such as transferring shares and finding lost certificates. *Foremost*, it can help facilitate the acquisition of capital at lower cost, raise stock price to its warranted value, and keep an even pace of share flow and volume in the markets.

In addition to these broad purposes, there should be specific objectives, which vary by company. These may involve creating higher investor awareness and better understanding of the company, increasing analyst coverage, building stock holdings by institutions, adding to the number of institutions holding the stock, bolstering holdings outside the country, and fashioning a stronger retail base and broker following.

Before the launch of the program in earnest is a good time to hash out attitudes and come to an understanding about what might be thought of as intangible aspects of investor relations that can produce quite tangible results or problems. These are the "soft" areas of communication that end up as the measure of a company's credibility and establish the levels of confidence investors and analysts have in the company as an information resource. For companies, this involves finding that comfort zone, probably deciding what information will and won't be provided. Companies tend to be overly reluctant to be forthcoming, believing they're helping the competition or simply saying too much. The corporate ethic is to wear information close to the vest. It becomes a habit.

Inconsistency in communication can be just as serious a problem. It labels companies as being too promotional—talking profusely when they have something to say and clamming up when things aren't going so well. Managements should come to grips with this issue before beginning a proactive investor communications program. They need to recognize that they need to be open at all times.

In sum, the hallmarks of an effective program are candor, openness, integrity and timeliness. Companies should be prepared to have their programs judged well on these measures.

CONDUCTING BENCHMARK ATTITUDINAL/KNOWLEDGE RESEARCH

It's a good idea to precede the rollout of an investor relations program with benchmark surveys that reveal how much is known about the company and the amount of misconception and bias that exists among investors and their chief influences. A well-informed, objective investor and analyst/broker group is a good thing. A poorly or misinformed, biased group suggests the need for a lot of investor relations work. Most companies are somewhere in between, leaning one way or the other. The benchmark surveys also serve as the basis of measuring investor relations progress in subsequent soundings of the financial community.

Surveys should cover a representative sampling of key people, with and without stakes in the company, in each of these prime groups: research analysts, institutional investors, and brokers. The idea is to gain insight from followers (institutional and individual shareholders, analysts, brokers) and non-followers who have valid reasons to join the ranks, namely brokerage analysts covering the industry, institutions investing in competitors, brokers in the home base of the company.

Companies also should interview present individual shareholders, covering registered and beneficial owners. The research helps a company understand its appeal among individuals and position the attitudes of this important group of investors in the overall shareholder mix.

BUILDING AND MAINTAINING MARKET RELATIONS

Increasing Analyst Coverage

Brokerage coverage is the bedrock of an investor contact program. It sets the stage with institutions and individuals since research is the enticement brokers use in convincing these investor segments to conduct transactions (buy or sell). In this sense, brokerage analysts and their research are part of the investor relations sales team. Indeed, analyst coverage that carries a buy recommendation represents a third-party, objective endorsement of the stock.

Quantity and quality make up the coverage equation. The objective is to be widely covered with the contingent including a number of the leading analysts in the industry. This means investor relations people need to do their homework—not just in identifying the analysts covering their industry and/or peer group, but also those commanding highest respect from investors.

In doing the analysis, investor relations people should get a fix on the brokerage firms with known industry expertise, any regional firms specializing in their industry, and the relative strengths of each firm in serving the institutional and retail segments. Smaller companies, particularly, need to be identifying national houses with strong retail business, in general and in their industry. As of January 1990, the firms with the largest number of retail brokers, in descending order, were Merrill Lynch, Shearson Lehman Hutton, Prudential Bache, Dean Witter Reynolds, Paine Webber, A.G. Edwards, Smith Barney, Kidder Peabody, Bear Sterns, and Piper Jaffrey.

For most companies, being widely covered is a building process. It normally works up from the company's underwriters to regional brokerage, then nationally as the wire houses start to notice the regional coverage, respond to investor relations contact, or pick up the stock through institutional interest, media attention or some aspect of its modeling research process. Investor relations activity helps get a good story recognized and move it along faster. Eventually, investable companies are discovered by investors; many of them anyway, but not all. Another important truth is that investor relations can't create investment strengths where they don't exist, especially in these times of precision investment models interpreting tightly defined financial and performance parameters.

Coverage targets also include local brokerage firms that may not have an analyst covering the company's industry or peer group, but are likely to be responsive because of convenient access to information and management. The regionals are always in the hunt for new investment-worthy companies, trying to find them ahead of their national brokerage competitors.

While being well covered is both crucial and valuable, there also are advantages in not being overly covered. A slit of market inefficiency keeps the analysts searching for insights that enable them to add value to their investor clients' decision making, and leaves room for other analysts to believe there's something left for them to discover.

Reaching Institutions

The company's purpose in marketing to the buy side is to have more say in the makeup of their institutional investor base. Companies are trying to influence and induce certain types of institutions to buy and hold their shares. They're searching for supportive shareholders. Supportive shareholders are defined as those with investing philosophies and methods that are compatible with the strategies of the company—growth investors creating a stock price surge in a growth company, and value investors being comfortable with the management's long-term plans.

Investor relations' opportunity to help shape the company's institutional shareholder base is better now than probably it has ever been. Institutional receptivity to direct contact with companies is on the rise, motivated in three parts—by the declining use of brokerage research, by renewed institutional analysis, and by the ability to plug information right into computer investing models. The role of institutional research/analysis continues to recycle; it was substantial and significant in the 1970s, stripped to the bone in the 1980s, and appears to be regaining stature in the 1990s. Institutional analysts are accustomed to corporate contact. Now, the portfolio managers are engaging actively in dialogue with corporate managements and investor relations people, either attending meetings with their analysts, calling companies, or taking their calls.

For companies to succeed in swaying institutions toward their stocks, the information has to be just what the computer ordered.

To fill the need, companies must be students of those models, following a curriculum that includes being the perfect prefect in satisfying their information hunger. To do that, companies have to
understand themselves and how they fit the investment parameters of the institution's style and model.

The information is built around an appraisal of the value of the
company's stock. It compares present price with potential and real
value, based on full utilization of the assets. Then, it evaluates the
extent to which management is achieving full utilization. Some
companies are properly valued, as reflected in stock price, some are
undervalued at the moment, and some are undervalued in terms
of the assets' potential. Institutions make investment decisions on
the basis of that kind of assessment. Companies emphasizing stock
value (not all companies consider it to be among the highest priorities) are taking actions to enhance it and focusing their investor
communications on those actions.

The picture is completed as investor relations professionals use
their research resources to identify institutions that will support the
company's strategies because their investment characteristics tuck
into the investing prerequisites of the institutions' models. The second source is institutions investing in other companies with like
credentials—same industry or investment characteristics.

Reaching Individuals

First thing for companies to confront and resolve is the degree of
their conviction about the importance of having and keeping individuals as shareholders and expanding the base. It poses a three-
part question. One, do we believe in the value of individuals as
shareholders and are we committed to their being an important
part of our ownership? One person's opinion: the answer should
be yes. Two, what is the practical percentage of our mix that can be
individually held, given the size of the company and stock float,
industry, and trends in institutional interest? And, three, what activities are shown to be the most productive and cost reasonable,

given our profile? The answers direct the thrust of the research and investor relations program.

Cost-minded companies focus on "affinity" groups—those that can be reached directly, inexpensively, and with results that are measurable. They include existing shareholders, employees, customers, suppliers, investor clubs, and communities with a strong company presence. Two key programs for these groups are tailored-share purchase and dividend reinvestment plans that provide incentives for reinvesting by eliminating transaction costs and increasing holdings.

Companies continue to concentrate on brokers because they're still the main link with individual investors. Sophisticated programs seek to focus on the top-producing, stock-driven brokers.

Communications in the retail market is both exacting and "conditioning." It conditions the market, as examples, a mailer to 60,000 brokers or media story seen by brokers and investors. It is exacting when in the form of a fact sheet detailing the company's investable strengths, used to sell brokers and by brokers to sell their customers.

For pursuit purposes, retail brokers divide into two groups: those at regional firms, whose stock selection list at any time is drawn from their own research with input from their analysts; and those from national firms, whose buy list leans on the firm's recommendations but is laced with their own findings.

THE INFORMATION PROCESS

Information is the lifeblood of investor relations. Practitioners can't live without it. It takes two forms: the factual, numbers-oriented information (quantitative) that analysts and investors need to complete their data buildup, conduct their analyses and make their investment decisions based on formulas or judgment; and the qualitative inputs that enable analysts and investors to make those numbers and their recommendations more incisive and meaningful.

Investor relations people need to know what information is basic in investment research and analysis; the specific information beyond the basics required by each analyst and investor; and they need to know and understand their own company as well as any senior executive. That understanding starts with strategy and carries into every aspect of the business, covering every significant detail. Numbers crunching is essential and so is the ability to articulate the company's mission, strategic priorities, and to dissect each corporate program with the precision of a surgeon.

While companies need to be consistent in their message, the specifics and spin on the story are not the same for each investor audience. Speaking with one voice is desirable, but what gets said varies with the information need of the listener. Analysts want numbers detail and interpretation; institutional portfolio managers want to compare companies against their investing criteria; brokers want the salable strengths and assurance that they're real.

Since investors seek to place a stock price value on a company, its management and investor relations professionals are now focusing on the vital ingredients of valuation. Valuation is becoming the basis of communication to investors. Companies are assembling the pieces that make up their value, arriving at their own worth, and then translating it into stock price. Today, many companies have a strong sense of their fair value as reflected in their stock price. The exercise of determining their fair value isn't for the purpose of second guessing investors in calculating worth, but for the benefit of carrying on strong discussion that emanates from the same base of understanding and purpose.

That can lead to dual education—investors and companies learning more about how the other prioritizes the value drivers and calculates the value. It puts companies in a position to better understand how they are being valued and to enlighten investors on the specific impact of the value drivers.

Many companies have taken the next step. They're rolling out programs geared toward boosting value and being very deliberate in communicating these actions to institutions. In this way, companies are participating more forcefully in their valuation, perhaps even starting to control it. Historically, institutions have been the leaders in setting valuation, companies the followers. Certainly, institutions will continue to set the criteria, forever refining their research-based models to enhance return while minimizing risk, but companies are taking charge of the determinants.

METHODS OF DISTRIBUTING INFORMATION

The methods of distributing information and conducting communication should suit the audiences and constitute the best ways of being effective. They combine instruments and dissemination methods and divide into five groups:

1. Proscribed and voluntary communications materials and vehicles emanating from the company—an arsenal that includes the 10-K and 10-Q reports, annual and interim reports, fact books and fact sheets, newsletters, "white" papers, videos and slide shows;

2. Personal contact between the company and investment community players through one-to-one visits, meetings, and the telephone;

3. Electronic distribution of printed information through facsimiles, online computer transfers, information dissemination services, and database retrieval;

4. Mailings, either directly from the company or in campaigns, arranged by outside services to reach predetermined target audiences either broadly or tailored in some manner; and

5. Exposure in the media, expressing specific ideas or portraying the company in a certain way, accomplished through editorial coverage or advertising.

Right down the line, the objective is to make the maximum of these methods and opportunities by loading them up with good information. No effort should be wasted; too many are. The professional opinion of investors and analysts that 10K and 10Q reports are more useful than annual and interim reports says something about the self-serving content of the latter versus the value of the required disclosure of the former. The investor relations mindset in putting together a fact book comes closer to reaching reality. Some companies do fact books to make up for what's missing in annual reports and not required in 10-K reports. The fact books address the specific numbers and information needs of analysts and detail-oriented investors, dictated by the industry and what distinguishes the company.

Information content of meetings ranges from excellent to awful. They are a time for judging management and investor relations:

ability to organize and present information;

depth of knowledge about the industry and company;

command of macroeconomic factors and how they impact the company;

recognition of the needs of investors;

insights into how management is capitalizing on opportunities and dealing with problems; and

the willingness to be open and forthcoming.

Serious analysts and investors want one-to-one discussion. It enables them to get beyond the boilerplate, ask the penetrating questions and rate management on their responses. It provides the opportunity to learn more about the company—critical to an analyst deciding if following the company/recommending its stock will generate revenues for the brokerage firm and personal income; and an investor considering a multi-million dollar decision.

The investor relations game plan analyzes the various meeting formats by deciding which are best with each audience, in each city, taking into account the reason for getting together, interest and knowledge levels. There are five audience groups—brokerage analysts, institutional analysts, institutional portfolio managers, retail brokers, and individual investors. Levels of knowledge and interest—they can be entirely separate or brought together—range from zero to intense. The investor relations opportunity is to build interest and knowledge among investors, analysts, and brokers through information. The process usually runs from having them participate in group meetings to moving to one-to-one sessions as interest and knowledge grow. When a company is able to set up an appointment on a first try, chances are something already is stirring.

Meeting formats to choose from include:

1. Addressing the various analyst/investment manager and broker societies;

2. Addressing industry, trade group and brokerage-sponsored conferences;

3. Hosting meetings by invitation, determining size, location, time, and the specific audience segment;

4. Conducting on-site tours and presentations at the corporate offices, research center, or major production facility;

5. Getting together with several other companies in the industry or business community to host a conference, inviting probably a combined audience of brokerage analysts, brokers, and investors;

6. Arranging appointments with individuals, either at their office or at the company;

7. Holding each quarter what amounts principally to question/answer sessions for analysts and institutions as financial results are announced, concentrating on New York and perhaps Boston, as a way of capturing the largest and most important followers;

8. Talking with brokers of one firm in their main or branch offices.

USE OF TECHNOLOGY

Investor relations efficiency and effectiveness call for arming the department with the latest in computer technology. It has three purposes:

1. The ability to bring in information, quickly, in a working format, with assurance of its completeness;
2. The ability to send out information quickly, in a working format, with the assurance of its completeness; and
3. The ability to run the function at the highest quality and cost-productive levels considering such vital factors as thoroughness of information, efficient dissemination, handling administrative detail, and managing the entire process.

Point one. Information *in* includes lists of targeted investor segments; reports and data from around the company; key market performance data and measures; macroeconomic and industry input; reports, statistics, spread sheets from analysts and institutions with major investments in the company; and anything useful about anything that can be retrieved from the world of electronic databases.

Point two. Information *out* includes quarterly and annual performance releases with tables, charts, a consolidated balance sheet and other useful data; material announcements such as an acquisition or senior management change; letters or statements involving major news or developments; and disks providing numbers for analyst or investor models.

Point three. Program quality and cost control are the chief benefits of a computer-run investor relations department. Computers provide more information, faster; in desired formats, faster. That makes them more efficient in relaying information to investors and in compiling data and reports for management. Computers save time and reduce labor. They produce more mailing lists, invitations, letters, labels, and do all these things faster. Their overall effect is to help the investor relations director better control the gathering and flow of information and manage the entire process.

PUTTING TOGETHER A GLOBAL INVESTOR RELATIONS PROGRAM

The global appetite for capitalism is creating a worldwide opportunity for companies to find capital and investors. Strong economies exist or are building around the world. At the same time, competition is an international fact of life—competition for business, for money, and for investors.

Just as investors are constructing global portfolios, companies are constructing global plans for raising money, pursuing it at the lowest cost. Just as North American companies are making securities offerings and increasing equity holdings among foreign investors, foreign companies are making securities offerings and increasing equity holdings among North American investors.

The tenets of an investor relations strategy that seeks investors on a worldwide scale are:

1. Stronger economies are producing huge investment money pools in Europe, Asia, and elsewhere;
2. Demand for stocks can raise their prices; and
3. Proactive marketing efforts can help create that demand.

Companies need to be deliberate and thorough in their research and implementation of international investor relations programs. The markets for American stocks are less efficient outside of the United States, providing opportunity for investor relations efforts to be effective. But those opportunities need to be qualified company by company and country by country. It is equally important to know how to approach the investors in each country—to understand who they are, what they're interested in, their investment objectives, and their investing styles and methods.

Before embarking on an international program, companies should determine what reasonably can be accomplished, the parts of the world and countries to focus on, which investor groups to target, and how to communicate with them. The decision may be that the effort stands little chance of bringing a payoff. It's tougher, for example, for smaller companies to make headway away from their home base. Foreign investors in American stocks tend to stay with well-known names and bigger companies, or certain industries in favor.

VALUE OF MEDIA RELATIONS

Media visibility can be shaped into something concrete in building investor awareness. Coverage can be applied directly to investor relations efforts by dealing with the company's strengths, strategies, and performance, and by working carefully to have the stories appear in outlets read by investors.

Most managements fear the media, expecting to be hurt rather than helped by it. Being realistic, it is more productive for companies to recognize the media's power, maintain a healthy respect of that influence, and learn how to benefit from it while minimizing the potential for an adverse result. Managements need to get comfortable with the role of the media in a free society, understand its emphasis of negative news and concepts in helping bring about reform or improvement, and accept the reality that its own business isn't perfect. From that attitude can flow ideas that are useful to the media in story coverage and produce a benefit for companies.

The process involves searching for story subjects by analyzing the company in the same way as a business or financial writer or editor. The analysis leads to story themes, which can be outlined and backed up with information for presentation to the appropriate media outlet. Key is selecting stories with true appeal to the audience, assembling the full package of facts and support information to tell the story well, and picking media outlets to contact with interests and formats that fit the idea. These can be business/

financial and investing magazines, newspapers, television and radio shows. Most likely, there will be company and outside interviews. What eventually appears will be balanced, which may mean other companies are included, or everything said about the company isn't totally flattering. However, the investor relations value is there, if the coverage is essentially positive and makes points that present the company favorably—in its operations, management, financial structure, prospects, investment characteristics.

The other part of building media relations is being responsive to the needs of reporters and editors. That can be trickier since the subject may appear to be negative or controversial. The first question becomes what happens if we don't participate. That can produce the worse result. Giving information or comment enables the company to speak for itself rather than having the story filled with what probably will be negative thoughts of others. The participation may balance the story or even color it positive. There also are many examples of openness convincing a reporter or editor that the story idea has no merit.

Not all requests are dangerous. Many involve adding information or expertise to a subject. Companies set themselves up as worthwhile resources in these situations, an excellent way of enhancing relationships.

EXTERNAL AND MARKET FORCES IMPACTING INVESTOR RELATIONS

Takeovers and Proxy Contests

Investor relations' involvement in takeover bids and proxy contests for corporate control can range from intense to invisible. Outside consultants tend to take charge of strategies and activities or, at least, become strong advisors and active participants even when the chief executive officer is the final authority and decision maker. Occasionally, outsiders assume those responsibilities as well. Investor relations counsel frequently carries more clout than internal practitioners. There are a number of investor relations consultant specialists with well-deserved reputations for coming up with hard-hitting ideas, especially in turning aside the takeover.

The investor relations/communications role in control battles grew with the rising number of takeover bids in the 1980s, in both offensive and defensive situations. Investor relations practitioners are in a position to make three important contributions in control contests:

1. Use their knowledge and relationships to help gauge investor reaction and the likely outcome of the bid, track stock movement before and during the offering, and lead the communications effort in gaining institutional support;

2. Develop communications strategies and direct their implementation with each critical audience—analysts, institutions, shareholders, brokers, employees, community and legislative leaders, and others in a position to influence the outcome;

3. Serve as spokesperson with the media and investment community, or at least as a valued advisor and idea/information resource to the spokesperson.

The media role can be crucial. The actions of arbitragers and institutional investors determine how most takeovers turn out, and their evaluation of the deal often is weighted heavily by the offensive and defensive stances put up in stories and the slants and spins of respected writers.

Institutional Involvement in Corporate Governance

Concern over how companies are being run rises with institutions' equity positions. The stakes have gotten high enough for institutions to be activists in corporate governance. The institutional motivation is to protect these now huge investments in individual companies, at minimum, but, more to the point, do what they can to make them grow by maximizing the returns. Companies should be flattered. Institutions recognize the superior returns stocks have earned over the past 60 years. But, apparently, they're not content to continue earning at that pace or to be patient with managements for very long if performance isn't measuring up to their standards. The evidence of that is seen in investing models geared around short-term trading to capture fractional point gains, enthusiasm for takeover premiums.

Essentially, the activist institutions want to put shareholders into the position of making the biggest decisions that affect the price and value of the company's securities—stock and bonds. The assumption is that these shareholders are other institutions of like mind. Those decisions involve who should be managing the company and who should be deciding its fate when the opportunity for a change of control occurs. Institutional investors leading the governance charge see incompetent management that is able to entrench itself as their biggest obstacle. The entrenchment prevents others from managing the assets more productively and blocks a change of control that would put the assets in better management hands. It also runs the risk of losing a takeover premium that is on the table on the basis of a bonafide offer.

Activist investors are attacking the corporate bastion on three fronts. The first is to change the proxy system which, they believe, favors companies. They want to create confidential voting which, they believe, would eliminate any fear of voting against management that may linger with investment managers that have business ties to the companies. They also want to make the shareholder voice authoritative by forcing their voting majority to become corporate law.

Second, activist investors want to remove what they see as impediments to takeovers that don't have the full approval of shareholders. Basically, this means that such takeover deterrents as "poison pills," staggered election of directors, and coming under the protection of stringent anti-takeover state statutes should be approved by shareholders before they can be enacted by the company.

Third, activist investors want to have more direct influence in the selection of board members and corporate management. Institutions' first forays into this arena involve convincing companies to let investors recommend directors for shareholder nomination. The

next step, already taken, has been to have input in the choice of a
new chief executive officer. Institutions say the purpose of this is to
create closer dialogue. They reason that this will come about when
directors are independent of the influence of management.

State, county, municipal, and teachers' retirement funds are
leading the governance activism movement. They're not encum-
bered by business relationships with corporations.

Investor relations people have several major responsibilities to
their companies in the area of institutional activism. The first is to
let management know how serious the situation is. Even many
investor relations people don't seem to understand that. Investor
oversight in deciding the strategies and management of corporations is a very real possibility. There currently is a proposal by the
most active public fund (California Public Employees' Retirement
System) that would vest the bulk of that authority in the hands of
giant funds with the largest equity holdings in the company.

Second, investor relations practitioners can monitor activist
buildup in industry and company by identifying the issues of
greatest interest. Besides proxy reform and anti anti-takeover, the
leading issues likely relate to environmental, product, or social
concerns.

And, third, investor relations people can use their relationships
and communications skills to influence attitudes and actions on
these issues. That's a two-way street. The critical role of investor
relations may end up being that of mediator—helping managements and investors find a reasonable common ground that satis-
fies the objectives of both groups. It would be a noble calling
because so much is at stake. No one is more qualified to fill the role
than investor relations professionals, based on their knowledge of
corporate and investor goals and their sensitivities to both.

Being Careful About Disclosure

The definition of *material disclosure* is a nettlesome issue to investor
relations people primarily because it's never happened. The Securities and Exchange Commission hasn't drawn any firm lines

around what is and isn't material disclosure, leaving the courts to shape the legal parameters based on experience. This has hurt some companies and punished some offenders. The best we can get gives us a general definition, a basis for proceeding, and one guideline:

1. Material information is anything that causes investors to buy or sell the stock;
2. When not sure whether specific information is material, take the conservative course and say nothing; and
3. Proper disclosure of material information means getting it to a sufficient number of media sources to insure adequate coverage that will reach the attention of the investor body.

As a result of common sense, ethical boundaries, court decisions, proper legal reasoning, and experience, some rules and wise practices have emerged as the basis of a safe and sound disclosure policy and practice.

1. A company can avoid trouble by saying nothing when asked about a possible material development. "No comment" is the standard response.
2. A company is not obligated to comment on possible material developments that aren't finalized, such as a pending acquisition or an earnings decline.
3. Should a company choose to comment, what it says must be impeccably accurate and complete.
4. Once a company comments, it has an obligation to continue commenting as the potential material development progresses.

All of these courses of communication suggest non-communication, which bothers many investor relations people interested in being proactive and forthright. Thus, the value of investor relations in such a situation takes on a special significance. The ideal world is one in which the company is communicating its efforts to accomplish material things right along as they are happening. Trouble is, deals fall through, leaving aggressive investors holding the bag as the stock price tumbles. Legal suits are sure to follow. Companies can't take the risk, so they clam up, usually on the advice of their attorney.

Thus, the true role of investor relations people is to say nothing in public, nothing specific in private, but continue to be helpful to analysts and investors by accurately portraying at all times the mission and objectives of the company and specific kinds of activities likely to be undertaken to accomplish them. At that point, it's up to the investment community to draw the conclusions.

The Impact of the Higher Levels of Debt

The impact of debt on corporate capitalization, the future fortunes of the company, and investor attitudes toward the company and its stock as an investment has created a whole new communications situation for investor relations professionals. Debt as a financing instrument, debt as a basis for improved performance, and debt as the cause of a company's downfall are now all part of the investment analysis process that influences decisions to buy or sell equity.

And, debt as the basis of a leveraged buyout or recapitalization can change the investor relations job altogether, perhaps eliminating it, but more likely, shifting the emphasis of contact from equity analysts and shareholders to debt analysts and debtholders.

Investor relations people aren't likely to have much influence on corporate decisions to lever up, but they can point to increasing evidence of the dangers of overleveraging, leaving companies unable to meet interest/principal payments, being forced to sell subsidiaries at bargain basement prices, and, worse of all, finding bankruptcy to be the only alternative left.

That, of course, is the dramatic downside of debt, and not the common occurrence. Most companies use debt judiciously, running healthy debt/equity ratios, although the traditional balance has sloshed over to the debt side in recent years.

Wise investor relations people are preparing themselves to deal effectively with the debt challenges of companies. That can take any or a combination of several turns that essentially involve advising management on a range of debt/equity courses of action, and communicating corporate strategies insightfully to equity and/or debt investors.

MEASURING THE INVESTOR RELATIONS PROGRAM

Measurement of investor relations activity has traditional and noveau elements. The traditional measures deal with such things as counting the number of new analysts following and recommending the company, tracking a rise in institutional holdings and broadening of the institutional base.

The new measures get at quantifying success in communicating the intrinsic worth of the company to targeted institutional investors in the belief that their buying, because the company is undervalued, will elevate share price. The second important basis of measurement is found in the ability of companies to exercise more control in determining which institutions hold their shares, opting for those with investing philosophies that are compatible with the fundamental management strategies for running the company.

4

A Capital Market Profile

Reaching the top of the mountain in the practice of investor relations is impossible without a fundamental understanding of the capital markets. Practitioners continue to stumble and fall by various missteps. Some of those missteps are:

targeting potential investors with minimal to no interest in the company;

sending out incomplete information or missing the point altogether on what's important;

and misinterpreting the actions and attitudes of leading institutional investors.

The foremost role of the capital market is, as the name implies, to serve as a source of capital for companies by financing their working needs and expansion plans. For businesses, the goal is to obtain funds at the lowest cost, which typically involves using both debt (issuing bonds, commercial paper, and arranging credit lines) and equity, tapping markets domestically and elsewhere in the world, in the search for lower cost capital.

The secondary role is to provide a mechanism for investors to make money. Some people believe the emphasis is now reversed as the global asset pie grows to gargantuan proportions (well over $20 trillion) and the penchant of investors to maximize their returns intensifies. Some institutions have exhibited a desire to achieve highest returns in the shortest time through speculation, aggressive trading or by taking takeover premiums, noteworthy among them being brokerage firms investing in their own accounts and investment managers seeking to demonstrate superior competitive performance.

The two roles of the capital markets come together as investors exercise their authority as arbiters of corporate management effectiveness, stepping beyond the purview of the Board of Directors to bring about changes in the control of the company's assets. This can be thought of as a third functioning of the capital marketplace. In a sense, investors are endorsing the work of management by investing in the company's securities, or disapproving management's efforts by initiating or supporting a takeover.

As institutions have become the movers and shakers of the stock market on a daily basis, with the size of their holdings running in the billions of dollars, the wisdom of making smart investments each time takes on increasing importance. Thus, the investment process gets more sophisticated every day. That process rises from foundations steeped in sound economic and investment theory, tested, modified, and proven reliable in practice, continuously being refined, yielding improved or new approaches and methods that also are tested and documented. The brainpower that has been at work over the last half-century in elevating the investing process is amazing to ponder, and the momentum of the last two decades is borne out in the results. Wealth accumulation through smart investing is evidenced everywhere. With the stakes so high and opportunities to make fortunes at hand, it isn't hard to understand why the investment "industry" has been able to attract so many bright and motivated people.

Even the speculative and most aggressive trading practices spin from the same solid framework that underpins the basic investing styles.

ECONOMICS BASIC TO PROCESS

While investment for the benefit of investors may appear to have grabbed center stage from investment for overall economic gain, the evidence is clear that the former flows from the latter. Investors' decisions to put up their capital is contingent upon careful analysis of the risk involved and reward that can be expected. Forecasts of the risk and reward incorporate numerous macroeconomic (systematic) and industry/company-specific (unsystematic) factors. The process brings these expectational analyses down to each asset class and collects and combines them again in portfolio management. These assets include stocks, bonds, and real estate (domestic and international).

Investment and economics are closely aligned. The bottom line for investors is the real return (not nominal) and it stems essentially from real economic growth. Ultimately, the economy has a major impact on the price and value of each security. Investors analyze the ability of a security to produce an acceptable return by evaluating the quality of the company's earnings and forecasting what they'll be in the future, utilizing proven investing methods. Figuring into the evaluation are macroeconomic factors, such as interest rate and inflation changes and stock market movement; and industry/company factors. By constructing diversified portfolios, investors have gotten very good at selecting strong performers and minimizing the downside of industry and company risk.

Inherent in the sophisticated process of forecasting the real growth of companies and thus, returns on investment, are specific analyses of the potential impact of many variables, influencing the outcome of the productive use of corporate assets. They include:

such company-specific considerations as labor costs and quality;

levels of productive use of business capital for R&D, product development, and manufacturing efficiency;

domestic and foreign competition;

regulatory impact; and

tax implications.

The process also includes studying the stability (and potential instability) of each macroeconomic variable, in both short- and long-term investing scenarios. The 1990 crisis in the Mideast is dramatic evidence of how macro factors, in this case, political, can impact stock prices.

The risk/reward formula is crucial in the investing process and the focus of intense ongoing study. Investors seek to balance reward and risk, gaining highest returns for the degree of risk taken. Much of their study and analysis of data is based on calculating the risk involved in certain investments, trying to minimize it. They're also interested in keeping costs down. Risk and cost, for example, explain the popularity of two investing strategies at opposite ends of the investing spectrum. One is the historical starting point of most institutional investing, the other, newer and growing fast:

1. long-term value investing with its joys of compounded returns and the ability to ride out the bumps of down markets; and

2. indexing, with returns guaranteed to match the averages, administered through computer models at costs lower than active management.

The former epitomizes "active" investing (portfolio managers actively make the investment calls); the latter is the essence of "passive" investing (computers make the decisions). Both, at least by definition, also are slower at turning over their portfolios, thus keeping a lid on transaction costs.

While both strategies offer the advantages to companies of longer-term investment, they represent the extremes in terms of investor relations' ability to influence the investment decision. Value investors are investor relations favorites. As active portfolio managers, institutions following the value style tend to welcome contact with companies, and as long-term investors, their return goals are usually compatible with corporate strategies to appreciate assets over time. The passive managers bet with the returns of broad-based indexes, such as the Standard & Poor's 500, and require virtually no direct input from companies. Indexing's growth among public pension funds is consistent with their claim to be owners of patient capital, interested in forging longer-term, cooperative relationships with companies. Chapter 7 deals with the question of institutional activism in matters involving corporate governance.

CALCULATING RETURN AND RISK

Priorities to calculate and measure return and risk get equal weight in portfolio management. Expected returns and risk premiums are integrated into investing models.

The return side of the model factors in:

length of the time for holding the asset (conventional investing wisdom saying the longer, the better);

assumptions on the efficiency of the market;

total return targets (income/appreciation);

net returns after subtracting fees, taxes, transaction costs, and the effects of inflation; and

the impact of historical returns on projected returns.

It attempts to price each security scientifically in constructing a portfolio of investments, using one of the accepted methods, such as the *capital asset pricing model* (CAPM) or the *arbitrage pricing theory* (APT).

CAPM seeks to find and plot that fine line of a combination of risky (stocks) and risk-free (Treasury bills) assets constituting an efficient investment package of assets, incorporating various risk factors. Those above the line are priced correctly, those below are priced incorrectly. Investors select accordingly, depending on their portfolio strategy. APT relies on arbitrage transactions to take advantage of mispricing. Modern portfolio theory plays a part in the process by establishing the validity of comparing risky and unrisky assets within a market portfolio. It helps lead investors to building portfolios that are diversified in order to minimize the risk while maximizing the return.

The risk premium side of the model identifies the risks and then quantifies their impact on returns. The risks are systematic (macro) and unsystematic (micro). *Macro risks* include interest rate, inflation, unexpected moves in the market (the crashes of 1987 and 1989 are dramatic examples), political uncertainty such as the crisis in the Mideast involving Iraq, and changes in currency exchange. The many factors that determine how well or poorly industries and companies perform are unsystematic risks.

Investors have developed a number of systems to measure these risks. The basic is the *standard deviation*. It sets up a series of reasonable returns, figures the probabilities of each, then weighs and totals them. The variances for each return are measured statistically.

Another involves *beta*, popularly called a stock's *measure of volatility,* compared against the market as a whole. But its usefulness goes further. Its significance is in showing the relative risk of each stock or other asset in a portfolio. Beta and modern portfolio theory play together in assessing and reducing risk. The theory, put into practice, shows investors how to reduce risk by combining assets that don't correlate in terms of their anticipated returns. This enables investors to make sure they don't overweight stocks or bonds with the same correlations thus producing the same risk effect. The theory is the foundation of diversifying portfolios which has proven to be an important factors in maximizing returns.

Global investing also can be used to cut risk and improve returns by spreading portfolios to include a broader selection of securities and by factoring political and currency risk.

With risk and return under some degree of control, the last actionable step for investors is to assemble and manage their portfolios. Actually, this step in many computer-driven programs almost becomes part of the risk/return analysis; the best candidates among companies show up on the computer screens. But the models vary, distinguishing the range of investor preferences:

asset allocation;

whether they are fundamentalists, top-down, bottom-up, or technical analysis disciples;

whether they are active, passive, or hybrid investors;

if active, their particular investing styles, namely value, growth, and so on; and

the kinds of investing calculation techniques they use (dividend discount, asset valuation, or discounted cash flow).

ROLE OF ANALYSTS

An important ingredient in the investment process is understanding market and individual asset behavior. Here, securities analysis plays a crucial role, answering the basic investor relations question involving what analysts do with all that information gleaned from companies by scrutinizing annual reports, 10-Ks, or asking detailed, numbers-oriented, highly technical questions about financial statements.

The respective roles of brokerage and institutional analysts come together in producing the buy, hold, or sell decision. Sell-side (brokerage) analysts are charged with the responsibility of being experts on the companies they follow—they must be able to give investors reliable analysis while adhering to the widely accepted analytical practices that are based on in-depth information and understanding of the company. The economic benefits of equity commissions from institutional transactions in return for qualitative research have enabled major brokerage firms to divide the corporate universe into sectors so that their analysts can focus on one industry. This enables the analyst to understand how the performance of that industry will impact the earnings power of each company within it. These analysts are chiefly concerned with the numbers that drive their industries and companies. Comparisons are made within the industry. Sell-side analysts are compensated for the quality of their research, which is reflected in the accuracy of their analyses as measured by their forecasts of future performance of the companies they follow. They are paid on the basis of commission volume generated from the buy/sell orders that are given to the brokerage firm by institutions that rely on the quality of their analysis. The transactions go to the firms of the analysts providing the recommendations.

Buy-side analysts take a broader perspective. They work with the sell-side analysts and their research, and track several industries and dozens of companies within them, or dozens of companies that fit their institution's investment matrix. These analysts study macro factors that affect the economy as a whole. When they determine how good an investment certain stocks are likely to be as an asset class, and which industries can be expected to do well, before they forecast the performance of individual companies. The sell-side input helps these institutional analysts compare industries and companies. Institutional analysts are compensated for their ability to select the top brokerage analysts as critical team members, and make the best recommendations covering asset allocation, and industry and stock selection.

Big institutions narrow the process by having industry analysts, who are judged ultimately by the accuracy of their industry analysis and specific stock recommendations. And some institutions have their analysts function in the more traditional sell-side mode of fundamental analysis. The latter role appears to be returning among institutions that are deciding to rely more directly on themselves.

One of the big analyst jobs is to help investors dissect the anatomy of the market (stocks or bonds) and specific investments under consideration. The purpose is to determine reasonable expectations for returns on investment based on careful analysis of the risks and opportunities. Again, it is a study that involves weighing risks and return.

Analysts provide a lot of this input. Key for the equity market and individual stocks (the process applies to bonds as well) is determining value. Essentially, *value* is the combination of dividends and appreciation discounted by the risk factors to arrive at an expected return. Volatility also must be considered since it can cause the market and individual stocks to move rapidly, the concern being precipitously downward.

Studies indicate that the value of the stock market is determined largely by several factors:

corporate earnings;

return on equity;

book value (tied closely to the vagaries of the economy as a whole);

the growth rate (measured both in GNP and, for investors, corporate dividends); and

the discount rate (measuring the collective risk of the market); and

the tax implications that drive each investor's decisions.

Analysts will compute these factors differently when looking at the market on a longer- or shorter-term basis. For example, the effect of uncertainty tends to diminish in longer-term forecasting. Emotionalism softens as well, as patience takes over. Earnings and dividends take on more meaning. In short-term scenarios, the possible impact of macro factors grows.

The work of analysts is more useful in active investment management, but does have some value on the passive side. Their collective knowledge forms the data in many databases used by quantitative investors. Consensus earnings forecasts frequently find their way into the computer input base of a quantitative model, for example.

In doing their research, the analysts and their portfolio management brethren have come up with ways to divide the vast universe of stocks into categories. This, in turn, has led to sector rotation as a major investing approach, and has set the basis for a number of others.

For analytical purposes, most stocks are classified in one or more of these groups:

- by industry sectors (there are anywhere from about 50 to over 90 depending on how finely or broadly they are defined);
- by size (measured mainly by total market value of the stock [market capitalization]);
- by similarities in their corporate performance (the major ones being cyclical, growth, and stable);
- by using dividend discount or discounted cash flow measures to calculate expected returns;
- by stock price or earnings momentum; and
- by certain measurements of valuation (namely price/earnings ratio, dividend yield, price-to-book value ratio, Q ratio [market to replacement book value], or price to cash flow).

The last level of study (or first for bottoms-up stock pickers) is the company, itself. Essentially, analysts are trying to assess present value and quantify future earnings and cash flows. These are translated into total return projections by using the investment model of choice. The intent is to calculate return and risk, taking into account the macro and sector factors. Analysts are looking for distinguishing characteristics, strengths and concerns, to judge a company fundamentally and in comparison with investment alternatives. Investment decisions are made by predicting returns and assessing risk on a relative basis, which can be global in scope— selecting the best choices by country, by industry, and by company.

A company's financial statements are likely to be the focus of analysis, leading to further research and questions of corporate management. Historical information is important as a basis of predicting future performance. The spreadsheet approach helps track sales, earnings, costs, equity capital, cash flow in gaining a picture of returns, margins, and other relevant measures in relation to stock price movement and dividend yield. Analysts pour over the income and funds statements and balance sheet in understanding the relationships between operating results, costs, cash flow, and financial position.

Then, the information is put to use in making investment decisions and constructing portfolios.

MAKING THE ASSET ALLOCATION DECISION

In following the investing process logically, a decision on how to apportion the total amount of funds available across the various asset classes precedes implementing the specific investing styles to use in the equity portion. The meaning of asset allocation varies widely, commensurate with its role in investing, ranging from light and informal to serious and quantitative. The trend is toward the latter. Many investors consider asset allocation to be the most important decision in the investing process. The desire to use it in maximizing returns is evident in the many studies done in the 1980s and the emergence of new asset allocation strategies.

How best to allocate funds among asset classes has become a bigger decision with the growth of assets under management and the number of investment management firms specializing in stocks or bonds operating their proprietary models. Large pension funds are the leading users of these money managers, with consultants helping the funds select the firms. Fund sponsors make the basic asset allocation decision, by apportioning the assets to various stock, bond, and balanced account investment managers, and deciding how much money will be given to each firm to manage. (A sponsor may have a dozen investment managers, divided among stock, bond and balanced investment specialists.)

In the process, setting a goal—the highest return, widest spread between assets and liabilities, or funding payments to beneficiaries in the case of a pension plan—is the critical first step in asset allocation. In many cases, the goal will depend on the type of institution—fiduciary obligations of pension funds make them more risk averse, for example. The opportunity to achieve highest returns within an asset class is important as well. Studies show which assets perform most favorably under various economic conditions, in certain time frames. The information is presented quite scientifically in these studies. The success records of the selected managers in each asset class also need to be considered.

In deciding how to divide the asset pie into stock, bond, cash, real estate, and other investment choices, investors focus on controlling the exposure to risk in order to enable the assets to perform at their peak, especially when instituting an asset mix change. In so accomplishing, it is desirable to limit the number of variables. Asset allocators have developed a number of return models, which calculate the impact of key factors. These cover the major exposures. The integration of asset allocation into portfolio management involves achieving an optimal result when melding market conditions, by targeted returns and the risk premium on the one hand with the investor's assets and risk tolerance on the other.

As it grows, asset allocation is branching into a number of strategies. A basic strategy is *asset allocation* (just described). It is called *integrated asset allocation* by investors. *Strategic asset allocation* takes the process another step by projecting results from various asset mix change scenarios as the basis of picking one. *Tactical* (or *dynamic*) *asset allocation* is trading oriented as it seeks to capitalize on the inefficiencies between stocks and bonds.

EQUITY INVESTMENT STRATEGIES AND STYLES

Stocks are shown to outperform bonds and cash over longer periods of time. Studies covering 60 years, for example, give stocks virtually twice the return of long bonds. Stocks also tend to be more volatile, but sophisticated investors have learned to diffuse that volatility through asset mix, diversification within equities and well-developed return/risk models. The rewards given by stocks for patience also sit well with longer-term investors (a group which includes pension funds, many other types of institutions pursuing greater returns, and individuals). Institutions in the United States are major holders of stock and now hold about 45 percent of the assets managed by the biggest pension funds, for example.

With total equity investments at over $5 trillion in the United States and some $9.5 trillion worldwide, it's easy to see why there is so much interest in research on how to invest in stocks intelligently. It has led to the development of a plethora of investing strategies, styles, processes, methods, and the use of a host of calculation techniques, so much, in fact, that the terminology gets confusing, even among the investor creators of the various activities. Is top-down investing a *process* or a *method*? Are discounted cash flow and dividend discount models *styles*, *methods*, or *calculation techniques* in figuring out the best investments for *value* buyers? Where do *value* and *growth* fit into the semantics picture?

Institutional investors (buy side) are the principal users of the strategies and disciplines (they make the investment buy and sell decisions) with brokerage analysts (sell side) serving as significant sources of information for the models. But those delineations are hardly simple and not always accurate. Certainly, brokerage firms are major investors and sell-side analysts have contributed mightily to the most popular investing practices now at work.

It's also been demonstrated that investment practices move in and out of favor, sometimes because they are right and then wrong for the macroeconomic conditions and sometimes because their efficacy wears down from overuse.

Institutions are taking more control of the various steps in the investing process, aided by their momentum in model development, the size of computer power, and market changes involving fundamental economics. The vast, growing, and detailed body of literature on virtually every aspect of investing has been extremely helpful to institutions in refining their strategies and programs.

Computers are miracle workers in putting the universe of information at portfolio managers' fingertips. Managers can retrieve information on the economy, the fiscal state, trends, industries, companies, sheafs of statistics on how the markets are behaving and why for both domestic and worldwide markets. Data is electronically received and resultant changes in models that underpin investment decisions are programmed. Computers as a resource have been a penetrating spur in the explosion in number of investment management firms started by portfolio managers and analysts from sizable institutions and brokerage houses. They have the experience, have been forming their own philosophical and pragmatic investment nuances for years, and have developed investing models with unique touches. With their proprietary investing models supported by data pouring from the computerized horn of plenty, they don't have to depend on specialized research, either inside or on the sell side, but may hire the former and buy the latter, if affordable and desirable.

Companies, of course, are information sources, at least for active managers. The flow of information directly to the buy side is expanding the contact target base of investor relations people. Economic factors also influence the rollout of change in how investing is done. Computers have put many money management firms into business—a PC, modem, software, data retrieval subscriptions, and, importantly, the manager's expertise. It can be a high-margin business. Buy-side firms aren't spending as much with sell-side firms in hard or soft dollars. Brokerage commission dollars have been trending downward, the result of lower commission fees on transactions and reduced trading by institutions through brokers. But while the investing models are on the buy side, the real expertise on specific industries and companies still resides on the sell side, despite the reduction in brokerage revenue from stock transactions. The buy/sell-side relationship and its effect on investor relations is covered in Chapter 10.

In the particular investing strategies and styles, history is giving way to modern finance and technique. But there always will be a place for history, especially when what it has spawned is still proving itself to be fruitful. Thus, the tried and true investing strategies continue to be refined, with the help of computers, as new ideas proliferate. They work side by side among the universe of institutions, even while one side talks down the other and vice-versa.

The Growing Use of Passive Investing

Emerging as the central division in basic investing strategy are *active* and *passive investing*. Even these distinctions aren't definitive as hybrid methods, combining active and passive strategies, take hold. The productive imagination of investors is limitless.

These ways of investing can be thought of as *strategies*. An active strategy is traditional, relying on managers to make the asset allocation and the buy/sell decisions based on their research, styles, methods, and models. Passive strategies involve building portfolios of generic groups of stocks and bonds keyed to certain benchmarks, thus matching the averages or performing slightly above average by adding some proprietary twist to the model.

The passive approach has matured since its birth in the mid-1970s with indexing being the most popular offspring. Indexers establish computer models that select certain stocks for investment in equal proportion to the relative weightings of the companies that constitute the index. For the S&P 500, the weightings are based on the industries that make up the U.S. economy. The number and size of chemical companies in the index, for example, approximate the industry's impact on the economy. Another index might aggregate stocks of certain size, determined by equity capitalization. The Wilshire 5000 is the broadest index, collecting virtually all the public companies in the country.

By holding stocks representative of the index, indexers are assured of achieving returns that match the performance of the market. The S&P 500 continues to be the most popular market measurement index. Indexers can hold the entire "basket" of stocks, say the entire 500 in the S&P index, but they also can hold far fewer as long as their selection produces the proper weightings. Investors are quite conscious of minimizing trading costs. They also believe that indexing reduces costs overall, by cutting down on the amount of trading that needs to be done in order to maintain respectable returns.

Index funds mirror such broad benchmarks as the *S&P 500 index*, the *Wilshire 5000*, the *Russell 1000, 2000, and 3000*, the *Trust*

Universe Comparison Service (TUCS) fund indexes, and the *Morgan Stanley Capital International Europe, Australia, and Far East (EAFE) index* for global investors.

Passive management grows, commanding an estimated 20 to 25 percent of institutionally held assets at the end of 1989, and is expected to continue rising. This management form is popular for a number of reasons. It is steeped in the *efficient market theory* which contends that current prices reflect the true value of an issue, making it wise to buy the "market." The efficient market hypothesis, believed at its extreme, says that stocks at any time reflect their full value because all the information affecting stock price has been absorbed into the marketplace and is discounted in the stock price. Active investors are betting on market inefficiency.

Another factor influencing the popularity of passive management is its emphasis on performance (which came to life with a vengeance in the 1980s) motivated by pension fund sponsors wanting superior returns and investment management firms competing hard for that pension fund business. Giving a big boost to passive investing are the statistics indicating that active managers as a group consistently fail to outperform the market as measured by such wide barometers as the S&P 500 index. The debate isn't simple. A percentage of active managers outperforms the indexes every year but that percentage tends to be well under half. There have been years, though, when the active contingent, as a group, has bested the averages.

While indexing provides predictably good returns at low cost, no investor is going to look askance at opportunity to beat the market. For this reason, many funds construct portfolios to include elements of both passive and active strategies. They rely on diversification, while spreading the risk. In most cases, the passive part forms the core which is tied to an index, such as the S&P 500 or Wilshire 5000, with active specialists working to bring additional value. Sometimes the emphasis is reversed with the indexed portion covering groups of stocks not captured by the active managers.

Many investment firms with active management strategies have strung together years of accomplishment. The problem is that no one knows how they're going to do this year, or next, or the year after that. And, sometimes the records are misleading, based more on the style succeeding because of economic conditions rather than the particular expertise of the manager. Pension funds typically use consultants to help select a team of investment managers who will cover both passive and active strategies. In steering the evaluation and selection process, the consultants prefer that their money managers identify their investment philosophies and practices (covering strategy, process, style, method and technique). However, some investment firms resist the typecasting. It is difficult to be precise due to the different definitions often given to the same word descriptions such as "growth," "value," or how "discounted cash flow" is figured.

Costs count heavily in the passive/active management decision. The edge clearly goes to the passive strategies. Indexing's savings of 25 basis points or more, combined with predictable returns that also are likely to be higher than the results of the bulk of active managers, are a powerful inducement for pension funds, banks, insurance companies, and mutual funds as well as investment managers seeking a competitive advantage.

Index funds take several forms. The basic type replicates the benchmark such as the S&P 500 Index. The key is to either hold all the companies by buying shares that represent the relative weightings of each or by buying fewer companies, using statistical techniques to arrive at the proper proportions. One variation of the standard is to sample the index while maintaining its integrity. An example would be to concentrate on large cap stocks and then sample smaller companies consistent with their industry weightings. This enables investors to keep a lid on costs by buying fewer stocks. Another variation would be to optimize the index by buying even fewer stocks while retaining the proportions of the index. An important reminder: The decisions in both of these versions are made quantitatively, not judgmentally.

Index funds also can be customized several ways, for example, to cover small cap, dividend-paying or high-yield companies, certain sectors, or to round out portfolios partially managed actively.

From the variations of the theme, it is clear that indexing strategies can be aggressive, pursuing returns greater than the index itself. Another way is to employ *index arbitrage* by benefitting from the spreads between stocks and futures by pinpoint timing.

A continuing question of interest to investor relations people is whether indexing contributes to the short-term investing tendency. Indexers say no, by definition, because they're not trading to exploit opportunity as active managers do. There is no trading for higher returns, since they basically are matching the market. Indexers trade when the fundamentals of the index change, when there are dividends to invest, or a necessity to add or subtract cash from the market. Many index trades actually are "crosses" within the funds of the firm or among other passive investors executed directly or through Instinet or Posit, independent electronic trading systems established for institutions. There is one big advantage to indexing: Transaction costs are low.

While passive management grows, most of the nearly $2 trillion in stock held by institutions still is managed actively. Some observers see passive and passive/active strategies dominating investing practice by the turn of the next century. Others believe that the use of indexing and pure quantitative modeling is peaking and won't go much beyond its current quarter of the asset pie in institutional hands. The benefits of lower management fees, lower transaction costs, and the trend toward more internal management by pension fund sponsors build the case for passive strategies. On the side of active management is the reality that the appeal of outperforming the benchmarks is embedded in human nature.

One of the major trends that has opened the door for passive investing is the drive toward quarterly return improvements in measuring the performance of investment management firms. Debate continues on how much of the short-term pressure stems from sponsors or money managers competing for business. The problem it causes is a continuing tendency by active managers to tinker with their models and trade more frequently than they want, consistent with their investing styles, in efforts to improve returns right away. The effect, in either case, can be negative: Departing from a style that may produce superior returns over time if left alone or adding costs through transactions that end up lowering returns.

Benchmarks are the basis of measuring returns whether the strategies are passive or active and regardless of the styles and methods. Following their particular style, active managers build in their risk formula, then manage their portfolios in pursuit of maximum or optimum returns.

Styles and Methods of Active Investors

The fundamental tenet of active management is a market containing some inefficiency. This also is a fundamental tenet of investor relations. It suggests that there are stocks available that are currently priced below their true value, based on some combination of qualities within the company not fully understood by the market that foretells a successful future. These can include management, technology and product strengths, commanding market position, low-cost manufacturing, or a clear advantage over competition (or "franchise," as analysts call it). Active investors seek to identify those companies while stock prices are low. Investor relations people seek to help those investors by providing useful information. On the other side of the proposition are the efficient market proponents who say that the important information already is discounted in the current price. Investment strategies are structured basically from evidential assumptions as to the degree of the market's efficiency or inefficiency. Active managers see inefficiency in the market; indexers view the market as virtually efficient.

Active managers tend to follow either the *top-down* or *bottom-up process* or rely mostly on *technical analysis*. The top-down process starts with analyzing critical macro factors, such as the international and domestic economies, which leads to determining the industries to benefit from the conditions and then the specific companies of favor within those industries. A global portfolio in this context would start with international themes analyzed by country and relative currencies and then weighted by industry and individual companies.

Underpriced stocks are the target of bottom-up investors. The research steps are conducted in reverse. Screens are set up to find candidates meeting criteria determined by the specific investing method—low price/earnings ratio (a value buyer) or achieving certain earnings gains each year (a growth investor). The investor monitors industry and general economic conditions and trends, but will still invest in companies that meet the criteria even though the industry may not be in favor.

Patterns of pricing and volume are the foundations of *technical analysis. Momentum* is another name for the process. Prices and volumes are studied to determine trends and turning points in predicting how the prices will behave in the future as the basis of buying and selling stocks. Relative strength or price momentum are approaches for ranking the performance of all the stocks being followed. Those in the top quartile of positive momentum may be recommended for purchase while those in the bottom quartile of negative momentum would be candidates for sale or to be bought by contrarian investors.

Active investors are disciples of a host of different *styles*. The starting point is really the *core manager* whose return objectives are likely to be the most conservative in trying to earn modestly and consistently above the benchmark (such as the S&P 500 index). These stock portfolios tend to be highly diversified.

A second style, known as quantitative, also is broad in approach. It often is described as institutions using computer screens to identify candidates for investment. Most investors see quantitative investing as a combination of active and passive strategies. The models for these screens vary, based on establishing return/risk criteria and certain minimums of performance to qualify companies. The computer is used to develop sophisticated models that explicitly forecast returns, utilizing such criteria as P/E ratio, price to book ratio, earnings momentum, and cash flow forecasts, weighing the effect of each one chosen, quantitatively. The top-down approach is popular, with the index benchmark (S&P 500, for example) serving to weight industries. Models abound.

The active element is added by selective modification, linked with the particular investment manager's expertise. That may be in sector/industry rotation, small capitalization companies, certain value or growth criteria, or country weightings in a global scheme.

In practice, many of these models also use technical analysis as an important input. The basis of a currently popular approach, for example, is to use a quantitative framework in creating a computer screen of candidate stocks. The framework is the weighting of a benchmark, in most cases the S&P 500 index. The screen is built to rate the companies on a scale of 1 to 10 on the basis of predetermined value, growth, and technical analysis criteria, with value and growth each worth 40 percent and technical analysis 20 percent. These weightings vary by model. The ratings are updated weekly, or more rapidly if market conditions are changing fast. A company scoring a 9 on value, 6 on growth and 8 on technical analysis ends up with an overall score of 7.6. Companies scoring 8 to 10 in the model are "buys," under 4 are "sells," and those in between are watched. Buy/sell/hold decisions are based on portfolio weightings. A 9 may be bypassed for an 8 to keep the weightings even within the quantitative benchmark measuring system.

Third are the various specialized styles. This is where the growth, value, cyclical, stable, small capitalization, and sector rotation managers are found on the breakout of the universe. Growth stock investors are looking for consistent above-average earnings growth, probably exceeding 15 percent year after year, even quarter after quarter. The key is *earnings momentum*. A standard measure is the price/earnings ratio. The make-up of the growth stock probably also includes a high P/E ratio and a low dividend yield. Variations include established growth companies (namely better-known, large capitalization companies) and the emerging growth category of smaller, lesser-known companies.

Value buyers are betting on higher total returns by holding stocks longer, pursuing undervalued stocks, shown by having low price/book and price/earnings ratios, while offering higher dividend yields. A stream of predictable income gain also is important.

Sector rotators use their top-down analysis to identify industries benefitting most from the economy and then predict and pick the specific companies that should lead the charge in those industries. Sector and company selections rotate as the economics change. The curves of industrial expansion will have positive or negative impact on machinery, metals, chemical and other manufacturing-based industries. Interest-rate changes especially affect interest-sensitive insurance and financial services companies.

Another dimension of the investing process is the *valuation methods* or calculation techniques used by institutions in implementing their portfolio strategies. Among the most popular are *asset value, dividend discount models*, and *discounted cash flow*. One approach to asset value is used by longer-term value-based investors searching for companies with stock prices below the intrinsic worth of their assets. It was first described in research published in 1961 by Merton Miller and Franco Modigliani, in an article in *The Journal of Business*, entitled "Dividend Policy, Growth and the Valuation of Shares." The work followed one by the authors three years earlier in *The American Economic Review* on "The Cost of Capital, Corporation Finance and the Theory of Investment." In these writings, the professors lay out investment approaches to stock buying on the basis of valuation. Specifically, the asset value model looks at the total worth of the business, based on the value of its securities in the marketplace compared against investment alternatives, the earnings ability of the current assets, and potential for new investments in the company to earn above the return rate of the market.

One version of the model places a value on the company by calculating cash availability after discounting for taxes, inflation, and investor risk. A second version computes the company's *Q ratio* (current share price compared against the inflation-adjusted asset value of the enterprise).

Dividend discount models calculate whether a company's stock price is over or under what should be its market value by applying a discount rate to the stream of dividends per share to perpetuity. Dividend discount models are useful to tax-exempt pension funds. The model attempts to lower risk by providing a larger proportion of the overall return in the form of income instead of price appreciation.

Investors most often use the P/E ratio in estimating the expected return. In fact, the P/E ratio continues to be a fundamental tool in basic models used to project investor value. The P/E ratio capitalizes current earnings. A stock priced at $10 with earnings per share (EPS) of $1 has a P/E ratio of 10. That means an investor is paying 10 times current earnings. The return is 10 percent, paid in dividends and reinvested to raise the stock price. If EPS doubles in five years, with everything else being equal, return on the initial investment will rise to 20 percent.

In addition to current and expected earnings, the P/E ratio is influenced by market conditions. The market compares stocks with other investments that typically are interest-rate driven. Thus, the expected growth rate of earnings rises with lower interest rates and vice-versa. The P/E multiple of the market as a whole is higher when interest rates are lower, and the multiple is lower when interest rates are higher.

The P/E multiple also is used in investing models that compare an individual stock with the market. This relative valuation method compares the stock's present and past P/E ratio to that of the market, as measured by a standard, such as the S&P 500 index. The buy/sell decision is then based on relative under or over valuation, calculated by comparing the company's current, previous, and forecasted next year's EPS, dividend yield, price, ROE and P/E to those of the market.

Discounted cash flow is gaining popularity in valuing companies, especially on the buy side. It defines intrinsic value as the present value of a company's future cash flows. Definitions of cash flow and the discount rate vary among investors. The components of each need to be understood. Fundamentally, "free" cash is what is left to pay dividends, buy back shares and fund growth after all expenses related to replacing current capacity are tabulated. However, the calculation tends to be more complex than that. The cash flow computation includes adjustments to operating earnings, tax reduction adjustments to pre-tax earnings, and even adjustments to cost of goods sold.

In the discount rate are:

the "pure" cost of capital (market interest rates for money);

premiums for the variability of cash flow; and

the rate of return on investments of comparable risk.

Companies with substantial amounts of free cash flow usually are accorded a higher P/E multiple because of the good things that can be done with the money—hiking the dividend, repurchasing shares, investing productively to increase the assets and their value.

USING FUTURES AND OPTIONS

Futures and options are investing strategies broadly used by institutions (and individuals) to improve portfolio returns, control risk, reduce costs, and specifically, to deal with the liquidity, volatility, and return issues that come into play when making substantial cash additions or withdrawals.

Options and futures contracts are called *derivatives* or *synthetics* because their trading practices are related to underlying stocks and bonds. *Options* are a right to accept or deliver an individual stock at a certain price (the exercise or strike price) before the option expires. Options also can be written against U.S. Treasury bonds and notes, Eurodollar offerings, stock market indexes, stock market futures contracts. *Futures contracts* are an obligation to accept or deliver the underlying bond, currency, or cash equaling the value of the stock index. Contracts are written against Treasury bills, notes, and bonds, Eurodollar obligations, S&P 500 and Value Line indexes, the Major Market Index, and the New York Stock Exchange Composite Index.

The key uses of options and futures in portfolio management are to contain risk beneficially by managing changes in weightings between and among asset classes, by enhancing returns by well-timed shifts in investments, and by assimilating transactions involving cash without disturbing market prices. In working these opportunities, investors need to understand the cost comparisons/advantages in playing futures and options against the underlying assets; and they must be experts on the range of instruments available, volume and pricing at any moment, and how prices move in relation to their underlying assets.

Options and futures are used extensively to modify risk, for example. Options can ease the risk of uncertainty about a company's earnings prospects. Futures help hedge against risk from such macroeconomic factors as interest rates and inflation by investing in bonds and market indexes.

The aim of using options or futures to hedge large cash deposits or withdrawals is to eliminate the concern for lower returns caused by market movement. It can be difficult, for example, to absorb a big cash contribution quickly in a rising market. Thus, the deposits are spread over several days, running the risk of producing a lower return.

Investors are finding a *stock index future* to be a better choice. S&P 500 index future contracts are purchased in the total amount of the cash deposit, for example, and then sold as the actual stocks are bought. In so doing, the investor is controlling industry/company specific risk while reducing exposure to broad market and economic risk. The timing of contract sales and stock buys plays an important role in the process. The game can be played successfully with options as well, by buying, for example, a raft of call options totaling the amount of the intended investment and then selling them as the underlying stocks are purchased at times when attractive returns can be made.

When cash is taken from the portfolio, the hedging strategy works in reverse. It requires anticipating the timing of the withdrawal with the basic purpose being to avoid any drop in returns from bad timing because the market is declining or by triggering a negative market reaction from selling the shares. In this process, the investor is buying contracts daily while selling an equivalent amount of stock, starting with the least desirable. By the last day, the designated amount of cash to be withdrawn has been collected and the futures contracts are sold.

Passive investors have learned how to use stock index futures to improve returns. Multiple benefits are offered. The *enhanced index fund* involves buying a quantity of futures contracts totaling the amount of the investment and at the same time improving the worth of the stocks making up the index (the S&P 500, for example). Thus, the risk level matches the index while the investor saves on transaction and commission costs since commissions on futures are lower versus stocks. The investor also gains the advantage of buying exposure to all the stocks in the index, properly balanced at all times even if the composition of the index changes. And, because dividends are pre-priced in the futures contract, there is no need to be constantly re-balancing the index fund.

The ability to refine strategies for gain appears endless. Another is to arbitrage under or over valuation of futures contracts through a *stock index fund*. Cash and futures make up the fund when futures contracts are undervalued; the cash and futures contracts are traded into the stock index fund (S&P 500) when futures contracts are overvalued. The result is a risk level akin to the index, with returns above the index over time. Options also are used; overpriced call options are sold against individual stocks.

Continuing with the legion of investing schemes, there is the use of futures and options in active management (again mainly to hedge risk when constructing portfolios) by adding or subtracting money from a portfolio. The thrust of the models is to deal with the various kinds of risk involved in carrying out specific investment strategies. Dealing with volatility in an up stock market is illustrative. The process can be very scientific, for example, using futures to reach a higher beta, instead of the riskier, more costly process of buying higher-beta stocks while selling lower-beta ones—riskier because of unpredictable market movement and more costly because of the number of transactions.

Investors have figured out how to virtually eliminate risk from such macro factors in the economy and market as a whole by using stock index futures. The process involves eliminating the *beta factor* (volatility) by selling futures contracts that precisely duplicate the pricing of the stock portfolio. The opportunity to earn highest returns comes in picking the stocks well and thus reducing the risk inherent in that uncertainty.

Options also help investors minimize risk by using group index and individual company options as a hedging device.

Even *synthetic instruments* have been created. One is to produce cash synthetically by building a diversified stock portfolio hedged against macro risk by stock index futures. The returns are without risk as long as the futures can be sold at full value. After-tax returns are superior to cash because of the deductibility of dividends. Another is *dynamic hedging*. It involves adding the advantages of put options to a stock portfolio without buying the contracts. The objective is the same as it would be with put options (namely, to ensure a minimum return while leaving the maximum potential open). In operation, the put option becomes more in-the-money as the total stock portfolio price declines. Eventually, the stock-with-put-option portfolio is immune to stock price movement, earning cash without risk.

It is important to point out that the high level of investor sophistication at work today—involving active and passive management, various return/risk models, and a wide range of practices and techniques—applies to fixed income investing as well as equities and, for that matter, to running balanced portfolios that combine stocks and bonds.

SHORT SELLING AS A TECHNIQUE

No discussion of the capital markets is complete without mentioning *short selling*. "Selling short" occurs when an investor believes that the price of a certain stock is going to fall. The shares are borrowed from a broker, then sold quickly in the open market by the investor, who hopes subsequently to repurchase the same number of shares later at a lower cost, repay the broker in kind and make a profit on the price differential. Of course, if the stock price rises instead of falling, the investor loses money. The exchanges publish the short positions in each listed stock about mid-month. These indicate the amount of shares needed to be repurchased and can be interpreted as investor bearishness or it can be seen optimistically as a buying power tool. It has been estimated that the short-selling market among institutions is close to $500 million.

Sometimes, companies complain about *bear raids* a substantial short-selling action in one company involving a large quantity of shares and probably a relatively high number of players). They happen more often with smaller, newer companies where a piece of negative information becomes the basis of the short-selling transactions. Short sellers expect the bad news to bring down the stock price. Frequently, the business press reports on the company's troubles thus increasing the likelihood of a stock price drop.

Suspicion is running strong that these bear raids are initiated by one or a group of known short sellers including institutions and individuals. They are likely to be the ones that leak the information to the press; business reporters acknowledge having noted short sellers as sources.

Under intense debate is whether the information about the company that triggers the short selling is true or accurate. Claiming the news is real, short sellers say they function to reduce the price of unjustifiably overvalued companies. Managements of young companies with bright prospects say they fear the danger of being destroyed before they have a chance to grow.

Over the years, numerous complaints have been filed by companies with the *National Association of Securities Dealers* (NASD), for over-the-counter companies, or their *exchange* (either the New York or the American), and the *Securities and Exchange Commission* (SEC). The complaints have been investigated, but with little result to date. Companies also have gone to the courts and there now is precedent for a favorable ruling.

To protect against deliberate misrepresentation, companies have several legal avenues. They can file complaints based on violations of Securities Acts Rule 10b-5, which prohibits fraudulent, deceptive activity or material misrepresentations. They can mobilize the RICO federal racketeering statutes, which guard against interference with prospective business/economic advantages and contractual relationships. They also can file libel or slander suits, or tort of interference actions, alleging damage to the company's relationships with customers, lenders, shareholders and other constituencies. Winning any of these actions isn't easy.

In heading off problems from short selling, companies are advised to be prepared with an aggressive strategy that involves communication and possible legal action and to be proactive. That process starts by watching the market very closely and picking up early on excessive short selling or the possibility of a bear raid. The company should be in contact with the analysts who follow its movements and any major institutional holders in order to knock down false rumors and also be ready to counter any media exposure by correcting any false stories. Legally, companies can always try to use the threat of a suit to quiet activity.

TRENDS IN INSTITUTIONAL BEHAVIOR

Institutional investment sophistication is leading to a number of trends with interesting implications for investor relations people. Among three of the biggest trends are the *growth of international investing*, more *use of indexing*, and a rise in the *amount of assets being managed internally* by pension funds. Better analysis of probable results has led to "best scenario" investing; that, in combination with portfolio management devices such as futures, options, arbitrage, and hedging, has produced a record of successes, measured in improved returns and controlled risk. The net result is bolstered investor confidence and a willingness to globalize, internalize, and try new strategies.

Institutions clearly are in step with the advantages of global investing, even though the non-domestic portion of the portfolio moves up and down from year to year, riding with comparative opportunity, determined largely by market, and economic conditions. The basic advantages are higher returns and risk reduction through greater diversification. Returns also tend to be enhanced by pursuing longer-term strategies. The quantitative minds among investors continue to produce new ways of making the assets safer and more rewarding; for example, using currency futures contracts to control currency exposure in international stock portfolios.

Institutions chase investments around the world to take advantage of price differences in stocks as well. Those differences are caused by the relative costs of capital and price/earnings multiples. The same company may be selling at 14 times earnings in London and eight times earnings in New York. Investors would pay an unncessary premium for buying the stock on the London exchange.

Cost of capital also varies across the world. The required rate of return on investment historically has been lower in Japan, for example, compared with the United States and Europe. This has enabled the Japanese to pay higher prices for investments—stocks in Tokyo or real estate in America.

Statistics support the move toward international portfolio buildup. *Pensions & Investments* reports a 43 percent increase in the amount of foreign holdings by the 200 largest U.S. defined-benefit plan sponors in the year ending September 30, 1989. The total holdings topped $39 billion with some $32.7 billion of the figure representing stocks. The trend is likely to continue because of the confidence of investors in their strategies and the increase in the number of major institutions entering the foreign investor markets. Numerous U.S. public and corporate pension plan sponsors have begun investing in non-domestic equities for the first time. These decisions were made with care and forethought.

Public pension plans are leading the twin, closely related trends toward more indexing and more in-house pension asset management. The rationale is simple. Indexing pays off because it matches market performance at a minimum and costs less thanks to fewer transactions and less administration. Managing the process inside increases the cost saving. While staff expertise (or outside help) is needed to establish the passive programs, once they're set up, they can be run inexpensively and minus management fees.

Internally managed indexing reduces costs by about a third versus outside active management, according to studies. The trend toward internal pension plan management is evident in both the public and corporate sectors.

Of special note to investor relations professionals is the fact that portions of many, if not most, corporate pension plans also are indexed although in smaller total amounts and percentages of portfolios. A number of corporate pension fund managers are strong believers in the value and future of indexing as a reliable, low-cost investment strategy. It should be added, however, that the amount of corporate pension assets (stocks and bonds) that went into indexing in 1989 decreased slightly from the previous 12 months, according to *Pensions & Investments*.

The biggest portion of indexed equity assets were among the 200 largest defined-benefit sponsors (more than $155 billion, according to the publication). Of this amount, over $69 billion was being managed internally. Some $32 billion worth of equities among defined-contribution plans is said to be indexed, with $27 billion of that total managed internally. And, while the numbers will be changing continuously, the trends toward more indexing and internal management are well established.

Indexing has a strong base beyond pension plan sponsors. Its major advocates are banks and insurance companies. Banks pioneered the strategy for the benefit of their own businesses and their investment customers (trust and institutional). It's more than coincidence that the largest indexers in the United States also are among the leading investment managers of public and corporate pension funds (Wells Fargo, State Street Bank, Mellon Capital Management, and Bankers Trust, among others).

Indexing also is gaining popularity among institutions outside the United States especially in Japan, the United Kingdom, and other parts of Europe. Estimates of the amount of domestic equity funds indexed in the United Kingdom and Japan range as high as one-fifth (close to the U.S. figure) and growing.

If the trend toward more internal management of assets continues, indexing is sure to follow suit. The investor relations role could be lessened, since indexing requires virtually no company contact.

It does, however, rely on information, some of it coming from companies. Annual reports, 10-K, 10-Q, and interim reports are valuable sources. Analyst earnings estimates are built from company information.

Two factors stand to reduce the percentage of new money available for investment; this could heat up even more the already intense competition among investment managers that has contributed to the short-term performance pressures. One is a reduction in the amount of pension funding that needs to be provided by companies and governments (largely stemming from the number of fully funded plans and good returns on investment). New investment money, however, is flowing into the public pension funds. *California Public Employees' Retirement System* (CalPERS) says it has $14 million of new money to invest each day. It's also true that the public funds are among the leading indexers and that they are managing more and more of their money internally.

The second factor is the growth of defined-contribution versus defined-benefit plans. Investing strategies of defined-contribution managers tend to be more conservative with lesser percentages of the funds finding their way into stocks.

IS INDEXING REDUCING THE AMOUNT OF FUNDAMENTAL ANALYSIS?

Indexing's success in the second half of the 1980s and its continued momentum going into the new decade have raised concerns among investor relations professionals and, certainly, in some investing circles as well. One concern is the future of *fundamental analysis*. Will it weaken from neglect, or experience a slowdown in the momentum of discoveries that have brought meaningful new insights? As a result, will the markets become less efficient? Will the number of companies that are not being followed or valued accurately rise? That, of course, opens opportunity for effective investor communications and for active managers to improve their investment returns by finding the undervalued companies.

Indexing, itself, can be affected adversely by a decline in fundamental analysis. Indexing and various forms of quantitative methods are aided by efficient markets and by qualitative databases assembled by good analysts (both sell and buy side) and by good corporate information. Some critics believe indexing is a "parasite" of fundamental analysis.

As the new decade begins, there are clear signs of a growing restlessness over the average results of indexing and signs of a renewed yearning for better fundamental analysis and, thus, better investment returns.

Concerns about the effects of indexing on investor relations may be overstated. Some three-quarters of the equity assets in the United States are managed actively, an even higher percentage in the rest of the world. Most of the investment managers pursue active strategies, especially among private firms, mutual funds, and bank personal trust departments. Corporate pension plan sponsors typically apportion the bigger piece of their asset base to active managers.

Indexing is not without its flaws as an investment technique. Its logical focus on the larger capitalization companies comprising the S&P 500 could lead to an overvaluation of these stocks, at the same time inattention is causing smaller cap stocks to be undervalued. That condition is sure to inspire investors back to fundamental analysis and active selection techniques.

Indexing also may lose favor in down markets, like the one being experienced in 1990. How pension fund managers and battle-tough, index-heavy money managers react to the lower returns of 1990 remains to be seen. A run of low returns could certainly put a damper on the appeal of indexing. It also should make the performance of active managers look better, comparatively.

Meanwhile, investor relations people can be opportunistic. Their proactive communications efforts, working with valuable information, can help overcome the knowledge gap on individual companies that can cause stocks to stay undervalued (or overvalued) longer. The actions can lead to a bonafide share price management program, able to accomplish something concrete, because of the growing inefficiency of the markets resulting from less fundamental analysis and more indexing.

The situation can be positive for both large and small companies, in their own way. Large corporations can capitalize on higher institutional interest, to target the most desirable ones in matching their investment goals with the companies' business strategies. Small companies can take advantage of the greater market inefficiency caused by less fundamental analysis, by taking over part of the process themselves. The investor relations people will have to prove their value as reliable, accurate, "independent" sources of valued information, but in so doing, they'll be able to really make a difference.

5

Why Individuals Should Be Emphasized

Where have all the individuals gone? Or, more precisely, where is all their investable income? Into money market accounts, Treasury bills, IRAs, Keoghs, bond and stock mutual funds, and real estate is the quick answer. And stocks too.

Individuals no longer are the movers and shakers of the U.S. stock market, but they're still the rock. While institutions account for about two-thirds of daily trading, American households still hold some 55 percent of the common stock of U.S. companies, as last counted by the Securities Industry Association. For a fair figure, added to that should be all the assets invested in stocks of pension and mutual funds where individuals are either the customers or beneficiaries, even though the money is being institutionally managed.

Despite their clout, individuals have become something of an enigma to both corporations and the investment community. With Wall Street, it's strictly a matter of economics. Commission revenue from stock transactions is down—both in the retail and institutional segments. Reduced revenue means fewer brokers and analysts; the circle is turning.

With companies, it is the institutionalization of the market that has chased individuals down the priority ladder. Institutionalization facilitates capital formation in many ways. Some of those are:

more stock can be placed more quickly by institutions;

waves of institutional buying push up the price faster;

the institutional market is more efficient, more easily defined, and more readily reached in the contact process, with more measurable results.

INDIVIDUALS HOLD MORE SHARES, BUT IMPACT IS DECLINING

Individuals saw the value of their stock holdings skyrocket in the 1980s, but stocks were less important as an investing device to individuals, and thus, so was their impact on the U.S. equity marketplace. Stocks represented 36 percent of household financial wealth in 1970, but only 20 percent at the end of 1989, according to the Securities Industry Association, the trade group of the brokerage industry. Yet, the total value of stocks held by households during this same time period increased from under $700 billion to over $2 trillion. The explanation: Investors put even more money into other instruments, especially Treasury bills and money markets. Indeed, while the market value of stocks was rising, individuals are reported to have actually sold some $500 billion in stocks from 1982 through 1989.

Individuals not only have $2 trillion in stocks directly, but another $250 billion is estimated to be invested indirectly in mutual funds, plus about $25 billion more in bank trust accounts.

The real competition for direct investment of stocks by individuals comes from two places: 1) money market accounts and government securities and 2) the trend toward professional management of individuals' assets. Bank trust officers are the traditional professional money managers, concentrating on wealthy and higher-income individuals. They're now getting stiff competition from certified financial planners and "stock" brokers who are making the transition into portfolio managers. Of course, stocks are part of the investment package, but it's also true that the entire range of financial instruments is fair game for these portfolios.

In fact, brokerage firms have added a plethora of "new products" to their brokers' arsenal in recent years. The brokerage industry has been on a campaign to encourage professional management of individual accounts, putting less and less emphasis on separate stock holdings.

The big winners in the 1980s for securing the management of individual investor income have been the mutual funds. The mutual fund industry celebrated the start of the new decade by topping the $1 trillion mark in total assets under management, according to its trade group, the Investment Company Institute. The growth of mutual funds in the 1980s is remarkable—from 564 funds managing $94 million to over 3,000 funds with $1 trillion in tow.

A sizable portion of those funds is being invested in stocks. The total has gone from just $24 billion at the end of 1980 to $246.5 billion at the end of 1989. Fixed income investment has done even better—rising from $16.8 billion to $304 billion in the same time frame, according to ICI statistics. But, not all of that money is owned by individuals. Of the $550 billion in stocks and bonds, approximately $125 billion is held by institutions utilizing mutual funds as investors.

But the 1980s will be seen as the decade of the money market and government securities. It is clear that they are stocks' chief competition for liquid assets from the growing number of Americans looking to maximize returns on their discretionary income. The 1980s began with 76 money market and short-term municipal bond funds managing about $45 billion and closed with some 657 funds managing $436 billion. To get a true picture of the strength of money markets add the $45 billion in banks and savings banks.

One in every four households has a mutual fund account and the average amount of money being invested is $4,000 for each person in the country (including children), according to the ICI.

Individuals have invested $1.9 trillion in Federal government debt: Treasury bills, notes and bonds.

BROKERAGE INDUSTRY AMBIVALENT

The brokerage industry has divided attitudes toward stock investing by individuals and toward the whole retail/institutional mix in producing revenues. The loss of brokerage commissions combined with the decline of investment banking activity (mergers, acquisitions, and takeovers) literally had Wall Street in the doldrums as one decade was ending and another beginning. But commissions continue to be the lifeblood of regional firms.

Momentum is a big factor. As brokerage commission revenues grew, rollbacks to levels that once brought joy to the bookkeepers now are seen as unsatisfactory, and for very good reasons. The equity function has become so large that the current commission revenue base no longer supports it.

The other big factor is institutional momentum. It switched the emphasis away from the retail stock segment in most of the major brokerage firms decades ago. The economics speak for themselves in comparing the revenue-generating opportunity of handling multi-million share institutional transactions with the typical 50- to 1,000-share buy and sell orders of individuals. In most national firms, research serves the institutions; retail brokers should use it, too. Only a handful of national firms have continued to stress the importance of stock investing by individuals, promoting it with their registered representatives.

It can be argued that the brokerage industry has been forced by the mutual fund/banking competition to emphasize an array of financial products and portfolio management. It also is true that the brokerage industry has been aggressive about marketing its many products and portfolio management skills. It does bear some responsibility for the revenue-base decline in retail stock commissions.

The decline in equity commissions as a source of revenue to brokerage houses has been steep. While institutions are the big ticket source, the gradual deterioration of the retail market has been significant. In 1961, commissions were 61 percent of industry revenues. As a benchmark, it's a telling number. That was before institutions became big players. By 1975, equity commissions were half of industry revenues; by 1980, they were just 35 percent. Now, they're down to about 17 percent.

The importance of commissions and the impact of their decline with brokerage firms vary widely. Among the big investment banking firms, equity commissions were only 7 percent of total revenue in 1989, just 20 percent for national full-line firms, and 13 percent for firms based in New York City. By contrast, stock commissions contributed 34 percent to the revenues of regional firms and 45 percent to discount brokerage revenues. These numbers come from the Securities Industry Association.

Another piece of research that's helpful in planning an investor relations program deals with the investing recommendations and practices of brokers. From a study conducted by *Registered Representative* magazine, it would appear that brokers still push stocks more than the trends and conventional wisdom indicate. The study not only shows a high preference by brokers for stocks as a recommendation, but also a high success rate in convincing customers to invest in stocks. Of all the investment instruments available, stocks were recommended the most at 83 percent, followed by mutual funds at 82.6 percent, IRAs at 82.5 percent, municipal bonds at 79.5 percent, money markets at 77 percent, and certificates of deposit at 72 percent.

On the basis of products actually invested in, stocks led at 87 percent, followed by mutual funds at 86 percent, IRAs at 82 percent, municipal bonds at 79 percent, money markets at 78 percent, and CDs at 75 percent.

The list of investments for brokers to push is extensive. In a descending order of investment, it also includes other bonds, unit investment trusts, U.S. Treasury bills/notes, fixed annuities, mortgage-backed securities, options, cash management accounts, profit sharing plans, Keogh plans, real estate, variable annuities, 401(k) plans, and life insurance. At the bottom of the list, in ascending order, were 403(b) plans, farm land, collectibles, thrift plans, exotics (artwork, books, and so on), variable life insurance, precious metals, and futures/commodities contracts. In general, the latter appears to be the province of institutional investors.

COMPANIES CAN LEAD INDIVIDUALS BACK

For their part, companies have focused their energies on institutions. At least, the investor relations people have, apparently with the blessing (and guidance?) of senior management. Companies clearly are caught up in that institutional world, easily justifiying it, because that's where the market is and is going, where stock prices are set, and relationships can be built, with measurable results. That's reality.

But the question becomes how much emphasis should individual investors receive in corporate communications programs. Individuals are "the market" for small companies because the amount of shares available tends to not be enough to attract a lot of large institutions. But individuals are good for large companies, as well. They are inclined to be longer-term investors, with goals that involve building a "nestegg" and saving for specific future needs, and they are very bullish about reaping the returns of letting investments mature. They tend to stay focused on the fundamental strengths of the company that are so essential to higher valuation. Chapter 11 delves into the investing motivations of individuals and investor relations strategies geared toward the retail market.

The conviction is almost universal that individuals are important to the economy, stock market, ability of business to raise money, and even to the successful investing by institutions. Concern over the "loss" of individuals to the market is being expressed across the investment community—from brokerage industry leaders to the heads of the stock exchanges and by the biggest institutional investors.

The Securities Industry Association calls the loss of individual investors "a loss to all. Retail investors are a key buffer to the markets. They buy and hold for real quality and for the long run.

This is important to everyone," SIA believes. An executive with a leading institutional firm suggests that the markets wouldn't have crashed in 1987 and 1989 if there had been a strong, well-informed individual investor segment buying stocks at discount with the intent of holding them as long-term investments.

Before he left office in 1990 as president of the New York Stock Exchange, John Phelan urged companies to not allow individuals to be driven from the market. Institutionalization with its use of modern technology and portfolio management techniques is making individuals "less significant," Phelan said, and investment managers are trying to force professional money management on individuals. Calling that notion "nonsense," Phelan said the investing record of individuals is as good as that of the institutions. The success of individuals, he added, is based on their "sticking to the fundamentals of companies" and investing for the long term.

Is it the proper role of business to encourage stock investment by individuals? Yes. Business has a strong record of responding to threats to survival, while capitalizing on opportunities to grow— from taking actions against erosion of markets, to refining technologies and marketing techniques to yield seemingly endless flows of products. The loss of individuals as a source of capital and force of support for corporate policies is good reason for working to re-establish concrete initiatives for individual investment and to mobilize a serious communications campaign aimed at the retail segment.

Corporate America has a tendency to be tongue-tied when it comes to speaking for themselves, despite the abundance of lobbying offices in Washington and state capitals. Companies tend to respond with legal maneuvers while staying out of the mainstream of communication and persuasion. They waited a long time before entering the fray on governance issues, presenting arguments for the unique skills and experience of business managers in running competively strong companies for the economic good.

One way for business to help is to lobby for tax relief for individual investors. The 1986 tax reform act "exacerbated the exit" of individuals, the SIA says, at the same time it was encouraging more corporate debt financing. "By eliminating targeted tax incentives for savings and investment, that act eliminated distinctions on income from risk and riskless investments." The SIA also points out the various ways other industrialized countries support individual investment in stocks. Of 10 countries studied, four have no long-term capital gains tax and four others have rates lower than the United States. Eight of the 10 minimize the effect of double taxation by providing offsetting investment incentives in their tax codes.

Companies also can use their communications programs to encourage stock investment by individuals. They have both the opportunity and need. No one else seems to want to promote stocks aggressively any more. The brokerage industry is targeting individuals, but is pushing portfolio management services ahead of stocks. Mutual funds are promoting the mix of their products, which include stocks, but seldom feature them. Banks are promoting money markets and certificates of deposit in the ongoing "rate wars." Banks aren't allowed to advertise personal trust.

The picture, however, may become more positive in the 1990s. There is good indication that a number of the major national wire houses are starting to market equities aggressively to individuals. Dean Witter Reynolds, Merrill Lynch and Shearson Lehman Hutton seem to be leading the charge. Account executives, trained for years to sell from a package of investment products, are being taught once more how to sell stocks. Securities analysts are going into the field, visiting various branch offices in helping the brokers. This decade could very well witness a return to emphasis of equities by the brokerage industry as it seeks to restore profitability by returning to some past glories.

In marketing the wisdom of stock investing, the evidence is favorable. Over time, stocks are shown to produce the highest returns. The charts and tables are ready for presentation as part of communications efforts. Can senior managements, investor relations, and corporate communications officers be convinced that it's good strategy to spend money in restoring confidence in stock investing broadly among individual investors? Probably not, if companies are striving for maximium efficiency in their securities marketing efforts and measurable results in a fairly short time period. But the considerations should be far more basic and much broader.

6

Takeovers Become the Catalyst for Investor Relations to Cook

Investor relations took more strides in becoming an important corporate function in the 1980s than in any previous decade in the short history of the practice. Ironically, it was the threat to corporate independence caused by unwanted efforts to wrest control of the company's assets from present management that put investor relations into a position of showing what it can do. While one investor relations person after another faced the loss of his or her job in a hostile takeover, the profession found opportunity. Indeed, as the takeover threat now stands somewhat diminished, the investor relations opportunity it created grows.

The reason: managements recognized the value of a higher share price in discouraging unsolicited bids for control. The higher the stock price, the costlier the takeover. The phrase, "the best takeover defense is a high stock price" was probably heard in every corporate boardroom of every public company in America during the 1980s. Or, at least it should have been.

Investor relations people were in the middle of the fray as companies responded to the rash of takeover assaults, putting up defenses, and taking the offensive to discourage, prevent or deflect a bid, or fight its arrival vigorously. Or, at least they should have been. Even though the lawyers were creating most of the defensive moves—the poison pills, staggered boards, and the like—investor relations people were in the trenches, talking every day with analysts and institutions, and gauging whether they favored or opposed a takeover. It was the investor relations person who could report to management the prevailing attitude on whether the company was in danger of being put in play or how it would fare should hostility begin. It was the investor relations people who were in the best position to persuade analysts and investors that incumbent management should continue to be entrusted with control of the corporate assets.

At the same time, corporate managements were building offensives. Their major weapon came to be called *restructuring*. Any number of programs is possible in a restructuring package. Restructuring programs were designed to improve shareholder returns or show investors that the current management was capable of developing strategies that eventually would increase the value of their holdings. The goal was to make the corporate assets more productive by selling the unprofitable pieces and pumping up the profitable parts through products, greater production efficiency, better management, synergistic acquisition, and other steps.

Restructuring also included attempts by companies to establish a stronger financial base through recapitalization, or jump off the takeover path by going private through a buyout (usually debt-leveraged and involving management as principals, which gave them the personal stake and debt payback burden incentives to run the enterprise well.)

Even though investment bankers and specialist consulting firms were creating the various moves and evaluating their effects, investor relations people were in the trenches with analysts and investors testing the waters on each idea, feeding their reactions to management, and providing the critical communications that would determine whether the corporate programs would succeed, first, in gaining credibility, then, in raising shareholder value, and, finally, in accomplishing the ultimate purpose of keeping the company independent.

Not every company escaped the battle. In fact, many were forced to fight. Most who waged, lost. A few survived, even came out stronger; and they certainly gained valuable experience. Win or lose, managements saw first-hand what investor relations can do in the trenches:

give accurate daily reports from the field on how the battle is going;

assess who are the allies and enemies;

identify and facilitate direct contact with those shareholders who are hidden behind brokerage or bank accounts;

do quality research on the bidder;

lead or conduct media contact or provide the information that goes to reporters;

determine the strategic content of information that will sway investors and analysts; and

prepare and disseminate the actual communications materials.

Today, the takeover battleground is a little quieter, and the future pace of takeovers or proxy contests for corporate control is uncertain. However, takeovers haven't gone away. They never will. The inventiveness of investors looking for extraordinary returns isn't about to disappear. Money pools are bursting; they certainly could be engineered to finance takeovers (or acquisitions or buyouts) with every participant profiting potentially. Plus, formidable companies in strong economies in other parts of the world are looking to the United States for acquisitions, either friendly or hostile.

But managements have learned their lessons. History shouts and the future suggests that it isn't wise to be undervalued any more. A higher stock price is desirable, for that fundamental reason of deterring unwanted solicitations for control of the company, for raising capital economically, attracting investors, and enhancing the equity returns that will be enjoyed by employees and management through ESOPs and options.

Managements not only are more conscious of the merits of enhancing shareholder value, many are incorporating it into their strategic priorities. (See Chapter 9 on valuation.) Restructuring is evolving into share price management. In this process, senior corporate executives are becoming very aware of the role of investor relations in monitoring investor attitudes and actions and in communicating corporate valuation programs and results. Or, at least they should be.

TAKEOVER WAVE COVERS 1980s

The takeover wave that swept across corporate America in the 1980s was fascinating and frightening to behold. For sure, it washed away some managements that weren't keeping their companies buoyant. But the tides also took out some admirable managements who were running tight ships, floating impressive results, and navigating programs that augured well for the future.

Battles for corporate control were almost inevitable, given the dynamics of the decade. The forces came together to stir waters colored by fierce competition, excessive money supplies, opportunism, impatience, and greed. U.S. companies were seen as managing their assets inefficiently or failing to fully utilize their capital (freshly funded or retained from earnings). It's hard to argue away the rationale, considering the declining competitive position of U.S. companies in the 1980s.

Still, many strong companies fell victim to the knife of the carve-up artists who were able to make more money for themselves by selling the company in pieces. As corporate managements, strategic buyers and their respected advisors, and institutional investors struggled to place a fair value on a company's collective assets, it was abundantly clear to the raiders and the surgeons of profit that the parts were worth more than the whole.

Raiders and acquisition-minded corporations alike were aided in their pursuit of undervalued or otherwise-qualified corporate prey by the eagerness of fee-hungry investment bankers and easy availability of financing from commercial bankers, brokerage firms, S&Ls and hastily assembled groups of lenders/investors. Takeover money pools proliferated, filled by investors with visions of high returns dancing in their heads. Junk bonds became one of the more popular corporate financing mechanisms of forced acquisitions.

Investment bankers were lining companies up for the auction block, even providing "bridge loans" to the buyers. An investor relations person couldn't be sure what was behind a brokerage analyst's new or intensified interest: bonafide investment research or evaluating the company as an acquisition/takeover prospect.

Institutional investors were aiding and abetting the process. Stock price premiums were the attraction. Few could walk away from the temptations of higher portfolio returns that come with taking the premiums, even if their investment strategies do lean toward patience and low portfolio turnover. Pension funds read the ERISA rules as mandating maximum portfolio returns for beneficiaries. Investment managers need to demonstrate superior portfolio returns in order to keep existing clients and continue to win new ones. The money management business boomed during the 1980s, most started by investment managers and analysts who learned the ropes in the big investing and brokerage houses. Many had developed successful investing formulas, often quant-based, and were anxious to reap the benefits of being entrepreneurs.

That drive toward competitive performance has been a heavy influence in the short-term emphasis of institutional investors. The biggest clients of most of these money management firms are pension fund sponsors—both corporate and public. They've been partners in pushing for the superior results. So it certainly can be said that companies are contributors to their own complaints about being forced to manage for the short term. Because of institutional pressures for immediate superior corporate performance to boost demand for the stock and thus create higher prices they neglected longer-term growth strategies that are good for the economy as well as the company. However, there can be no denying the momentum for superior investment returns that has overtaken investment managers of all stripes. The money that has been made in the investment business in the last decade and promises to be made is a tasty and powerful nectar.

A substantial portion of the high-equity portfolio returns racked up in the 1980s, as measured in such broad market indices as the Standard & Poor's 500 index, was the result of the premiums paid over the current market price in the many takeovers that took place. The reduction in number of acquisitions and takeovers in 1990 was reflected in lower equity returns overall, as shown by market measures.

Some of the buyers had (and continue to have) strategic reasons for forcing the acquisition on the target company. They saw opportunities to increase profits and margins by the strategic fit that would occur in technologies, products and markets. Junk bonds helped finance many of these deals. But, the takeover frenzy also created, and for the most part was led by, a new breed of "investor"—individuals and partnerships intent on putting companies in play for one or a combination of reasons:

> gaining the premium created by the market as other would-be buyers bid up the offering price;
>
> cashing in on "greenmail" payments as companies bought back the stock at a higher price to be rid of the raider;
>
> taking over the company, then profiting from selling the parts for more than the purchase price; and
>
> buying the company with confidence that they could manage the assets more productively than the current management.

A number of the so-called raiders of the 1980s have become the CEOs of the large companies they acquired. Another sign of the times: one of the best-known partnerships (Coniston Partners) has moved its investment focus away from pursuing control of companies.

COMPANIES DUG IN TO PRESERVE THEIR INDEPENDENCE

The fur was really flying in the 1980s as company after company found itself under siege. Volumes of rhetoric flowed on the merits of uprooting entrenched managements for the good of shareholders and the economy on the one side, against claims of upheaval that was being left in the wake of takeovers, acted out in closed plants and lost jobs, distracted executives who didn't have time to manage, millions of dollars wasted in defensive and offensive tactics, and the impending downfall of the U.S. economy that was being promulgated by the necessity to discard long-term programs involving technology and production.

Everyone got into the act in supporting or condemning hostile takeovers, and doing or trying to do something about them—lawyers, investment and commercial bankers, federal and state lawmakers, the courts, regulators, investors and analysts, and corporate executives and communicators.

Corporations got very serious about takeover defenses. Lawyers collected substantial fees creating them. Boards were empowered to establish most of them, although some required shareholder approval. Most basic is the *staggered board*. It calls for having the shareholders elect one-third of the directors each year, preventing an interloper from taking control of the board quickly. Not surprisingly, most of the initial response to anti-takeover devices provided little protection and many raised the ire of investors.

The latter generation of shareholder rights plans, *poison pills* as they were labelled by activists in corporate governance, have been shown to have more impact in deflecting a takeover. These plans can make it more difficult to complete a takeover by putting obstacles in its path. They seek to prevent a bidder from treating shareholders unfairly by offering two different prices in tender offer, for example. Another requires two-thirds of the shareholder votes to approve a merger—the *super majority* provision. Still another enables shareholders to buy into a new series of preferred stock whose issuance would be triggered by the bid. The pill would hike the price of the takeover deal and also extend the voting rights of current shareholders.

Lawyers, expert on corporate control contests, tend to feel that protections won't stop a takeover that is heavily financed with a sizable premium involving cash as the principal currency. Investors will succumb—arbitragers who acquired the shares in the last few weeks to grab the premium, institutions who can't say no to it, and even individuals whose loyalty goes only so far. The job of the anti-takeover pill is to slow the death process, indeed, create the time to put the prey on display, so that others can see its virtues and submit higher bids. This rationale came to life dozens of times in the 1980s. Few companies were auctioned off at their original bid. Many had multiple suitors, bidding up the price to sometimes double the original offer. No wonder investor relations professionals are puzzled and deeply distressed over what constitutes the difference between fair value in the normal investment process and alternate (as in takeover) value.

The biggest help to companies has come from the states and from the courts, somewhat as a one-two punch. But that help has evolved after error and trial. First generation state anti-takeover statutes were struck down by the courts. Now in their third or fourth generations, these statutes are sticking and gaining some court strength. Fundamentally, the states support corporate independence; it's good for their economies. When a company's future is up for grabs, so is its economic participation in that state. The record is clear: new owners move things around. State statutes make it very costly for suitors, in dollars or in waiting. And waiting is expensive. Current laws provide a number of basic deterrents. The "control shares" provision, for example, prevents a would-be buyer already holding a certain percentage of the shares (say 20 percent) from acquiring the rest without approval from the majority of "disinterested" shareholders. Provisions also impose waiting periods on bidders to complete acquisitions, which can chill the deal because of the uncertainty of the outcome or impracticality of putting the financing on hold.

In 1990, Pennsylvania and Massachusetts went even further. Massachusetts endorsed staggered boards as a takeover defense by requiring companies to have them. Pennsylvania stiffened an already tough anti-takeover package by incorporating the control shares provision and also by allowing state-chartered companies that were the targets of a takeover to seize the profits made in the sale of its stock by any would-be acquiror within 18 months of the takeover attempt. The Pennsylvania law also reinforces the intent of the business judgment rule giving managements authority in acting in the best interests of the company's range of stakeholders.

Thus far, the courts have been inclined to uphold the latter-day state statutes. However, constitutional challenges to the Pennsylvania and Massachusetts laws were filed immediately after they passed. In addition, a number of Pennsylvania-chartered companies chose to opt out of the takeover protection, apparently because of the criticism the law spawned among institutional investors.

The courts also have set a precedent that allows corporate boards to "say no" to a takeover bid when the rejection is seen as best serving the various corporate constituencies. That ruling came in the celebrated Time–Warner merger. In his opinion, Delaware Chancery Court Judge William Allen wrote:

> "The corporation law does not operate on the theory that directors are obligated to follow the wishes of a majority of shares. In fact, directors, not shareholders, are charged with the duty to manage the firm."

In analyzing the ruling and thinking about the future, lawyers have suggested that boards deciding to say no must be prepared to present strong evidence supporting their position.

Active in the debate has been the federal government, with little legislative result thus far. The issues are complex. The fear is that new laws involving takeovers might produce more problems than solutions. Consensus seems to be to go slow and be very careful in writing new laws. Definitive Congressional actions taken early in the debate focused on correcting abuses in implementing the *Williams Act*, which essentially encourages the markets to operate freely. The Act is seen as accepting the intent of takeovers: providing for shareholders and advancing the economy by removing entrenched management. The laws covered the length of time a tender offer must be made available, for example, and dealt with reporting procedures once a would-be acquiror held 5 percent of the target's shares. Since then, numerous bills have been introduced, but few have been enacted. The Securities and Exchange Commission always has been an advocate of giving the markets room to pace and correct themselves.

Congress certainly is mindful of the states' aggressiveness. The argument is over state authority versus the free exercise of interstate commerce. Thus far, the courts have sided with the states. The U.S. Supreme Court in 1987 reaffirmed the position in *CTS v. Dynamics*. Wrote Justice Powell in expressing the majority view: "No principle of corporation law and practice is more firmly established than a state's authority to regulate domestic corporations."

Insider trading scandals of 1987 brought swift federal response. Penalties for conviction of insider trading violations were stiffened— disgorgement of profits, fines, trebling the amounts paid, imprisonment, and the ability to make the cases criminal as well as civil. Sweeping investigations were conducted in front of the watchful eye of the media. Celebrated convictions, repayments, and penalties in the millions of dollars were meted out. Jail terms followed.

The other capital market concern of Congress and the regulators is the danger of market volatility, witnessed in the stock crashes of October 1987 and 1989. The government and market experts continue to try to understand the causes of such violence so that they can come up with the proper controls and actions to prevent economic disaster from erupting due to severe capital imbalances. Such computer-based tactics as *portfolio insurance* and *program trading* are seen as causes because they can facilitate massive sell offs in short periods of time, driving market prices down dramatically. Legislative and regulatory controls are being studied. They are geared toward market stabilization, banning "manipulative, abusive or disruptive practices" and giving the exchanges the authority to halt trading if the markets appear to be heading out of control.

HOW CORPORATIONS DEFENDED AGAINST TAKEOVERS

Corporate defenses piled up after the wave of hostile takeovers swept across America in the 1980s. Companies found themselves engaged in the heat of battle. As the number of hostilities grew, so did the number of companies installing anti-takeover measures. It is estimated that more than 900 public companies now have such provisions.

However, for many companies, the deterrents were too late or they failed to discourage a bid. It became evident that poison pills and other devices weren't stopping the momentum. They became useful in delaying the takeover, giving target companies time to pursue defensive actions (often legal), find a friendly suitor ("white knight"), or allow others to enter the auction. Corporate directors began to talk about their fiduciary responsibilities to secure the highest offer for shareholders. Offering prices rose, often beyond the perceived fair value of the company. Once a company was in play, its likelihood of remaining independent was slim, especially if cash was being offered and the premium afforded a profit for the majority of shareholders. By then, many of those shareholders were arbitragers waiting to cash in on the bidding war.

Not all the deals were sweet cash, of course. Early on, two-tier offers were popular; they gave shareholders a financial incentive for tendering fast. Poison pills were a corporate response in guarding against the two-tier offer and in trying to show shareholders its basic unfairness. Frequently, the deals provided complex payoffs that had to be analyzed carefully to understand their true value. Junk bonds became a part of many of the payoffs.

Despite the odds, companies fought against unwanted takeovers. Some succeeded, but few by comparison. The bid could be expected to come from one of four types of aggressors, or a combination if a contest ensued:

individuals, such as T. Boone Pickens, Ivan Boesky, Carl Icahn, and others;

groups of investing partners, such as Coniston or Centaur;

domestic companies interested in forging a strategic acquisition; or

foreign companies wanting a strategic combination and/or a strong American foothold/expansion base.

As takeover momentum mounted, facilitated by the prospects of big investment banking fees, easy financing, and aggressive investors wanting to maximize returns, no company could feel secure. Strong companies with respected managements and consistently good earnings performance also became objects of affection. The alarm bell warning of the danger of being perceived as having an undervalued stock rang through the corporate executive suites of America. Restructuring and proactive investor relations received the calls, and were activated in response.

Restructuring grew, as much as a takeover defense as a corporate value enhancer. Early restructuring moves were direct defenses against a takeover, started after the company was in play, designed to show shareholders specifically how management was going to increase value. Many of the plans were assembled, somewhat hastily, with the aid of investment bankers.

Investment bankers were riding both sides of the fences:

identifying companies as takeover candidates;

conducting extensive due diligence to qualifying companies creating offensive tactics;

helping arrange financing or providing part of it through bridge loans; and on the other side

taking part in takeover defense strategies and programs, setting up restructuring programs by working on recapitalizations or management buyouts.

Huge fees were being collected at every turn, on both the offensive and defensive.

Two other takeover escape hatches came off in the 1980s—*recapitalizations* and *leveraged management buyouts.* Another new breed of consultancy burst into prominence—the *recap* and *leveraged buyout (LBO) specialists* who put the deals together and, perhaps, lent some of the money, but primarily secured the financing. Fees, investment, and interest-rate returns were their incentives. Most LBOs involved management taking the company private, keeping control without the specter of a takeover. The heavy indebtedness (some of it junk bonds) incurred in financing the privatization is seen as an incentive to manage the company effectively and thus the money provided by investors in making the deal is viewed as a solid investment.

However, the debt burden is proving to be too much for a few of the companies that are collapsing under its weight. These companies are being forced to sell assets, restructure or recapitalize again, or, in a worse case situation, declare bankruptcy. (Chapter 17 covers the emerging debt relations role.)

The picture isn't nearly that bleak, universally. Companies in trouble following an LBO, recapitalization, or restructuring are in the minority. And debt hasn't fallen out of favor as a capital-raising instrument. Its cost and tax advantages continue to be attractive. Its role in serving as a management incentive is ever present, especially when executives have significant personal stakes as investors.

Corporate America turned more to debt in the 1980s, taking advantage of its lower cost of capital and tax deductibility. Carrying more debt became a popular financial strategy. The extent of debt leveraging has created some concern. Soft economies can make healthy companies ill. The payback burden of debt interest and principal can drain cash from such long-term growth programs as research and technology. The 1990s began with a small push by companies to reduce their debt load by buying up and retiring some bond issues. The trend could grow, along with an increase in equity offerings to raise capital as the decade unfolds.

Despite the raft of takeovers, the record of the 1980s shows that numerous companies survived the threats intact. They were seen as being well managed, providing value to shareholders and expected to continue offering it in the future. Investors favored incumbent management.

Restructuring became a way for companies to seize the initiative. Many were able to do so before a takeover threat loomed. Successful restructurings were reflected in higher share valuation. Valuation programs were described in investor meetings and reports. Companies progressive in maximizing shareholder value also tend to be aggressive in communicating their efforts.

INVESTOR RELATIONS GAINS RESPECT

Investor relations and public relations professionals got more involved in takeover defense in the 1980s. They became more accepted as members of the team because of what they were able to bring to the table. While victories were hard to come by, the realization that inside communications professionals had something to contribute grew among corporate executives and their outside advisors.

The fraternity of respected warriors with communications expertise in the takeover defense arena consisted of only a handful of consultants before 1980. Their reputations had been forged in the tender offer and proxy contest battlegrounds of the 1960s and 1970s. They became part of the team, often recommended or brought in by the law firms, investment bankers or proxy solicitors.

But, by the end of the decade, a dozen firms were on the select list, including a number of proxy solicitors whose investor relations expertise was growing. And, numerous inside investor relations and corporate communications professionals had demonstrated their mettle in battle. They shined, because they were thrust into grave situations that presented opportunities to show their worth.

In ideal situations, inside and outside investor relations and public relations professionals work together to fashion the most productive result, combining their capabilities in research, contact and communication, while utilizing their Wall Street and media relationships to the fullest, and managing their resources efficiently. There were some noteworthy examples of close, results-generating working relationships in the 1980s. The inside/outside communications team effort should be even more refined and productive in the 1990s to the extent it's needed. Many lessons in using communications to help prevent or stop a takeover are there to be applied.

INVESTOR RELATIONS ROLE IN A TAKEOVER

Investor relations people can be on either side of a takeover; there are communications strategies to be applied whether working on the offensive team or fighting for the company's independent survival. Because jobs stay with survival—including investor relations jobs—defending against unwanted takeovers has grown up as the "honorable" side. (my terminology). But effective communications planning and execution can be a leading factor in swinging the victory to the offense.

Investor relations people bring three essential capabilities to the takeover defense programs:

1. research, to identify the players among the shareholders, institutions, analysts, brokers, arbitragers, reporters, and editors who would ultimately determine the outcome;
2. relationships, to help influence these influential players; and
3. communications, to convince these pivotal players to support the company.

Whether a company defends itself successfully against an unwanted takeover might be decided before any battle begins. The key to thwarting the pursuit can be in the quality of the company's relationships with investors, analysts, and the press. The evidence from studies of the results of takeover bids and their media coverage shows that companies will fare better with investors, analysts, and the press by having strong relationships based on serving their needs. That's not self-effacing, it's good strategy; companies best serve their needs by best serving the needs of their stakeholders.

Perhaps nothing builds the case for proactive investor relations more persuasively than its benefit as a takeover defense. Relationships can make or break success. The influence of brokerage analysts is widespread and can be critical. They are calculating the company's value in a takeover, making sell/hold recommendations to institutions, and commenting to the media on the fairness of the bid, quality of the company, credentials of the suitor, whether other bidders are likely to surface, and the possible outcome.

Ultimately, investors decide the outcome in tender offers and proxy contests. Debate is brisk among investor relations practitioners on the power of institutional investors versus individuals to make the difference. The argument really comes down to how you look at it. Since institutions hold the biggest chunks of stock, their decisions will have more impact. And, since institutions can be reached more readily, and, hopefully, can be persuaded to hold the shares as an endorsement to management, the opportunity to influence institutions is greater. However, those shares in individual hands may turn out to be the deciding force. And, since individuals are inclined to be more loyal and supportive of the company, the opportunity to communicate with them should not be neglected.

The other factor is how much stock each group holds. Companies should have a good fix on the institutional/individual holdings breakout before deciding the focus of their communication and specific methods to use, weighing the relative merits of direct contact, letters, brief background papers, ads in the financial press, and other vehicles.

Institutional relations are seen as prime, especially for companies with half or more of their shares being held institutionally, or looking at the strong possibility of institutions and arbitragers acquiring shares in a takeover situation. The definition of good relations involves being able to talk comfortably with decision-makers at the institution—an analyst, portfolio manager, or chief investment officer. As relationships refine and as we move further into the 1990s, the range of contacts is expanding to include those who vote the proxies. Increasing the network inside an institution can only help. They're talking to each other continuously.

The goal in developing close working relationships is to build the confidence of investors in the company's management. It is the only way some degree of institutional loyalty can occur. "We'll keep the shares as long as we believe in the company's future" is the way one prominent portfolio manager described his attitude as an investor. There had to be a certain confidence in management that led the investor to the company in the first place (except for indexers). Nourishing the relationship is information.

Investor relations people with close analyst and institutional contacts win their way onto the takeover defense team. Membership comes with management confidence in the investor relations function, which is won through the Wall Street relationships that produce valuable feedback and the ability to analyze right along the attitudes and likely actions of analysts and institutional shareholders.

Then, there is the impact of the media. This is so important that takeover attorneys have become media relations specialists in recent years—both in aggressor and defense modes. The issue can be decided by the press coverage. And, the first few days of coverage can go a long way in determining how the last story will be written. The aggressor has the advantage, especially if the raid is a surprise, and can put the target company on the defensive immediately. The bidder has time to plan its attack and its communications strategies, right down to the messages, well-chosen words, and strategic selection of the most desired media outlets to break the news. Even the responses of the target can be predicted in advance and rebuffed with creative wordsmithing.

Companies need to be prepared to make sure a communications gap never happens. That initial story should include some kind of statement from the target that produces a positive reaction among shareholders, analysts, other institutions and arbitragers. That may be all you want to accomplish on the first day—saying something that goes over well. The second-day story becomes the opportunity to seize the day. The press will be looking for comment from the defender and will be inclined to cover it fully. After that, the battle is on.

Companies don't need to be caught short. The ability to respond quickly and effectively comes in part from an aggressive attitude, in part from having a good sense of what the company will say in a crisis, and in part from having pre-established qualitative relationships with the right reporters and editors. The three work in unison. Fundamentally, the company knows how it wants to handle a crisis. It knows the kinds of things it wants to say, has thought them out. It probably has put some words to various scenarios—a takeover attempt under various circumstances, emergencies involving products or plants. The company's aggressive attitude will facilitate a conviction to move ahead with a statement, make it easier to reach consensus among executives on what to say. The media relationships will make it easier to get the statement across: the conversation (or press conference) will go better, reporters will be more interested and receptive, and there will be a greater ability to talk through the ideas in putting them into words.

None of this suggests anything other than extreme care in what is said. Companies certainly can be proactive and relaxed about communications without being careless. In fact, they can be more careful when they're relaxed and proactive, rather than being on the defensive. Lawyers should take part in the process that arrives at what is said. When companies are pros at communicating, the messages that are intended can be sent without raising fears that the litigation interests of the bidder or shareholders have been fostered.

Studies prove that companies with active media relations programs fare better in takeover coverage. Consensus is that the coverage is more balanced and fair. Common sense says it's so. A company is more likely to gain favorable coverage from a reporter who knows it and its management well and who can understand its strategies for increasing value or is inclined to be favorably disposed to its arguments for remaining independent. The most difficult thing in the world to do is educate two dozen reporters on a company overnight.

Traditionally, companies have been slow to build up their media relations and force themselves into adopting an aggressive attitude. In takeovers, they have tended to rely on the outsiders: specialists in media strategies, tactics, and implementation. These consultants bring established media relationships and proven experience in gaining full and fair exposure for their clients, or even carving an advantage by successfully taking the initiative. More and more, corporate communicators and investor relations professionals are taking part in these programs or taking charge of them, using consultants as idea resources and contact specialists. In vesting the role internally, companies are taking better advantage of the deeper corporate knowledge and daily management contact of investor and public relations people.

The outside consultants are more likely to have first-hand experience with the "down and dirty" actions that sometimes are utilized—"scorched earth" tactics, for example, aimed at discrediting the suitor by getting the media to cover questionable behavior in the past. Tough-minded advertising has been used, seeking to cast doubt on the bidder's integrity and credentials to manage the company. No doubt, the broader range of experience by consultants in coming up with hard-hitting, attacking-type campaigns will continue to serve companies well.

Takeover defense preparedness is enhanced by a comprehensive market intelligence system and network. Its chief product is information, and it can be as wide ranging as the company requires or desires—institutional shareholder listings and profiles, their voting records on takeovers and takeover defenses, known arbitragers, company or industry data, critical market performance statistics, and background on the bidding company or raider.

The center of the system is a *shareholder identification program*. Its purpose is to produce a current list of institutional shareholders, including those keeping the stock in "Street name." The list is the basis for contact should a takeover contest ensue. At that point, maintaining the list becomes paramount, and tricky, as arbitragers and institutions jump in and out of the stock as they assess opportunity and risk. Whatever selling individuals are doing is probably for profits. The investor relations role takes on more meaning in sorting through the rolls to identify current investors for follow-up contact, as well as those who still have voting authority if the issue involves a proxy contest.

Some companies have learned how to work through the complexities and maze of lists, uncovering the names of their beneficial shareholders and keeping their shareholder rosters up to date. But the process requires nearly full-time attention and excellent personal networking talents with the insiders among brokerage and institutional traders. For this reason, the bulk of the shareholder identification and tracking is being done by consultants. Most of these are firms that also conduct proxy solicitation. The research base and contact network involved in the two activities overlap.

The last important needed piece in being ready to execute a takeover defensive strategy is a well-defined and structured communications process. It includes specific and appropriate communications vehicles, and a system and methods for making contact and disseminating information that can be guaranteed to work swiftly and efficiently. There is an advantage when the communications vehicles are familiar and acceptable to audiences—releases, facsimiles, phone conversations, regular reports, and regular meetings. There also is an advantage when the vehicle distinguishes itself to create impact—a letter from the CEO, group of special meetings, statements, and series of background reports.

Technology drives an effective information distribution system. The ability to mobilize the machinery in a hurry and use it often is critical. The investor relations department's electronic database should be loaded with pre-written material on the company, its corporate mission, strategies and programs, how share value is derived, descriptions of value drivers, profiles of management. Available at the touch of a computer key should be:

> text from speeches given previously by senior officers and other useful background;
>
> letters covering various scenarios that can be edited quickly to suit the current situation;
>
> names, addresses, and phone numbers of every contact divided into constituency categories that can be turned into printouts and mailing labels; and
>
> facsimile numbers at the ready for fast, simultaneous dissemination.

Some companies have profiles of known raiders, investor groups, even companies in their industry who might turn aggressive.

ONCE THE BATTLE BEGINS

In the takeover drama, investor relations people play three essential roles:

1. participate in strategy development;

2. provide highly useful information and analysis on investor attitudes, actions, and anticipated actions; and

3. help plan and implement communications programs.

That latter role is likely to be a joint effort with the public relations or corporate communications department. It also can include serving as spokesperson with anywhere from one to several key outside groups—analysts and institutions, arbitragers, individual shareholders, and the press.

How well the company is prepared will become abundantly clear in a takeover contest. The quality of analyst, institutional, media, community, governmental, even employee relations will be tested and evaluated in the levels of support given. Strong relationships will show in numerous ways:

easy access and an open mind among institutional holders;

ability of the company to gather enough feedback to assess the outcome of a proxy vote or tender offer;

analysts making comments favorable to the company in press stories; and

reporters giving the company fair treatment as well as pursuing follow-up coverage.

Absence of good relationships will become obvious as well:

difficulties in reaching analysts and institutions;

conversations that are uncomfortable with little basis for common ground;

inability to draw any reliable predictions of the outcome from talking with institutions;

analyst comments in press stories that favor the bidder by suggesting that the offering price is fair and criticizing current management; and

reporters showing impatience with spokespersons, giving

more credence to the bidder's arguments and writing thinly
or inaccurately about corporate strategies.

In "war room" sessions, the investment bankers and lawyers
will take charge of every aspect of the battle including communications to various stakeholders. Investor relations consultants
brought in by the bankers or lawyers will have their respect and an
open ear. Investor relations consultants brought in by the company
will be respected on their reputation or previous working relationships or disliked from prior experiences. Companies threatened
before or concerned about being put in play probably have hired a
specialist firm already, perhaps at the recommendation of their investment banker or legal counsel.

Similar situations will exist with proxy solicitors. Virtually every company has its proxy solicitation team in place, with relationships well established through years of gathering the votes
routinely, or recently in the heat of investor proposals and institutional activism. The bankers or lawyers may have a favorite proxy
solicitor as well. Or, the investor relations/proxy solicitation assignments may be handled by the same firm; many have combined
the activities, since they come together in a takeover or proxy contest as shareholder identification becomes the basis of contact and
communication. The point is: It is important for management and
its advisors to agree on the selection of outside investor relations
and proxy solicitation resources.

The role of inside investor relations and communications
people and amount of authority they're given will be decided by
the senior corporate officer in charge of the fray. Ideally, that is the
chief executive officer, and ideally the CEO will take charge of the
entire battle, utilizing all the resources as advisors and
implementors, but not as decision makers. If the CEO respects the
internal investor relations and public relations people, they'll have
an important role to play. If the respect isn't there, the lawyers,
bankers and their appointed outside investor relations consultants/
proxy solicitors will orchestrate the communications strategy and
probably implement most of it.

As the battle unfolds, the need for sustained mental and physical toughness becomes evident. The takeover siege can last a long time. The pace is furious and seemingly never-ending. The players have to be calm under a myriad of pressures. For communications people, that pressure can take numerous forms:

continually being aggressive in strategy meetings;

handling hundreds of phone calls, where reasonable and unreasonable demands are being made for information;

directing or taking part in creative sessions to come up with new ideas or approaches for saying things; and

writing releases on tight deadlines or new backgrounders in the middle of the night.

Companies have to guard against exhaustion that leads to bad decisions. Participants are advised to try to take the process in stride (easily said) and rest whenever possible.

Here are some practices in defending against a hostile takeover through a tender offer or proxy battle that have proven valuable:

1. Don't be bashful about taking a strong communications position. Articulate the company's fundamental strengths and strategies to continue increasing shareholder value. Lay out its record of performance over recent years. Describe productive assets that may not be fully appreciated by investors.

2. Try to assess the outcome in advance as the basis for measuring what needs to be done to succeed. The evaluation will help quantify the strategy and specific programs. Investor relations people and proxy solicitors will provide valuable input in making the assessment from their investor and analyst contacts.

3. Think through all the possible defenses in advance and do it from the point of view of benefitting shareholders. Gear communications to the shareholder benefits of each company action throughout the battle.

4. Keep the lines of communication with institutional investors and analysts open at all times. Focus on understanding the interests of institutions, learn if possible their investing objectives to help project how they will vote or whether and at what price they will sell their shares. Feed the assessments and projections to the takeover defense team daily.

5. Be talkative with investors and analysts. Learn everything you can from them, about Street perceptions of the deal, likely outcome, what they know about the bidder.

6. Keep tabs on the company's changing shareholder base to know who among the current holders is in a position to vote or tender and who isn't. Many of the new holders will be arbitragers; many of those who have sold may still be on the registration records. Concentrate communications on those who count.

7. Prepare to deal with the arbitragers. Have a list of known "arbs," so you'll recognize names of callers. Be wary, and make sure they don't weasel information from you that isn't part of the communications process. Their entire mission is to gain information that will give them an edge in predicting the result.

8. Communicate aggressively with the individual investors. Proactive media exposure is one way. Special letters from the CEO is another. Call the largest shareholders, giving them status reports and explaining the company's position. Be enthusiastic when taking their phone calls.

9. Anticipate the various actions of the bidder. In preparing to deal with each, emphasize the communications component, covering media, Wall Street, employee and other important constituencies.

10. Dig deep for information on the bidder. Consider using it in CEO letters, media placements, advertising, conversations with analysts and investors.

11. Obtain a list of the bidder's institutional holders and communicate with them. The bidder's valuation frequently falls

in a hostile engagement, or shareholders become nervous about future value as costs rise, debt increases, new risks are faced, and executives are challenged to integrate and manage the combined companies.

12. Consider meeting with the bidder early to descibe the company's own value-enhancement programs. It could discourage further action.

13. Designate spokespersons, to make sure the flow of information is controlled. Small companies may have one or two, talking with the press and investment community. Bigger companies may divide the responsibilities, consistent with regular job responsibilities.

14. Use the media opportunity effectively. Above all, don't be afraid of it. Fear brings stonewalling, ineptness, loss of control of coverage, damaging coverage, missed opportunity to balance or gain an advantage, even possibly win the war. Understand what drives the media and figure out how to shape your information to fit those motivations. Certainly, the press will want to cover the situation as it unfolds; they look for ways to write daily stories. Companies can describe their valuation programs, detail their growth strategies, show how support is building in the community or state, cover the economic risks in the takeover, put reporters on the trail of past activities of the bidder. (Chapter 16 covers media relations.)

15. Elicit the support of influential constitutencies, including employees, business leaders, the community, legislators and regulators. Public opinion can be aroused against an unwanted raid. Federal and state legislative proposals are showing concern over the potential economic downside of hostile takeovers. Citizens, legislators and mayors have written letters protesting specific unsolicited attempts. Koppers Corporation helped engineer a high-noon public demonstration on the steps of Pittsburgh's city hall against the parent company of a brokerage firm that was helping finance a

takeover of the company. Citizens burned or tore apart their credit cards issued by the parent. Pennsylvania installed the toughest anti-takeover statute in the country in response to the attempted takeover of state-chartered Armstrong World Industries.

Investor relations people on the offensive in a takeover are employing essentially the same communications strategies and tactics. They have the advantage of time in preparing plans, researching the target's shareholders, developing background information on the target, deciding the important media to involve and building contacts, writing materials, formulating likely questions and their response, and anticipating the various phases of action. Bidders have two principal messages: establishing their credibility while showing the weaknesses of the target company's management. The acquiror's credibility is secured by documenting the availabilility of financial resources and by demonstrating that the bidder is basically a viable business enterprise whose successful completion of the deal will serve shareholders well. Target managements are attacked by showing that they failed to get the most out of the assets, that they're more concerned about their jobs than shareholder value, and that their attitude toward shareholders leaves a lot to be desired.

DIRECTOR RESPONSIBILITY IN A TAKEOVER

Hostile takeovers and leveraged buyouts have fueled drives to make corporate boards of directors more accountable to shareholders. Fiduciary duties to shareholders have put directors on legal notice that their decisions involving control of a company's assets need to be made with the greatest of care. Federal and state legislators, regulators, and the courts have gotten into the issue.

Debate over the proper role and responsibility of corporate boards has been hot and heavy the past few years, enflamed by contests for control and shareholder activism. Investors claim that directors should represent shareholder interests, but board bias has tilted toward management when interests conflicted. The problem, investor activists argue, is that too many corporate directors are hand-picked by chief executive officers and are beholden to them. The solution, activists say, is to have the majority of boards made up of outside directors, who are truly independent. That way, the interests of shareholders will be represented fairly.

Institutional and individual investors have been backing their complaints with proxy proposals aimed at giving shareholders more authority in corporate governance. To some extent, the push for more authority shows shareholder lack of confidence in the board, but it also seeks to redirect the board to the shareholders' interests.

A closer look at the proposals indicates they are geared mainly to lifting barriers to maximizing stock investing returns on a short-term basis. That includes capturing takeover premiums. The two most popular proposals over the past few proxy seasons have involved minimizing the effect of poison pills and allowing shareholders to cast their votes confidentially. The institutional activists want to take away board authority to approve poison pills, instead putting the decision in the hands of shareholders. Or, they want poisons pills rescinded altogether, or reapproved by the shareholders every few years. The secret ballot would free investors to vote against corporate management. Activists reason that investment firms and banks managing pension funds or doing business in other ways with companies jeopardize the relationships if they go against the company and are found out.

Other governance actions seek to give shareholders more say in the selection of directors. (Chapter 7 covers investor activism involving corporate governance more fully.)

The effect of these various moves has been to create a tension between institutional shareholders and corporations that is changing the basic structure of the board. With the institutional focus on short-term results, time will tell whether the changes will add to long-term corporate strength and be good for the economy. Board makeup is shifting more to outside directors, independent of past relationships with management, whose selection is based on specialized credentials in helping run the company. Companies are nominating and shareholders are electing directors whose backgrounds are likely to put them more in synch with the special interests of the vocal shareholders—persons with academic, environmental, and social experience in their careers. The long-awaited trend toward having directors serve on only a couple of boards, devote more time to their responsibilities, and be paid higher compensation is occurring.

In the last few years, directors have been given the confidence to reject offers for the company that they don't believe are in the best interests of shareholders and other stakeholders. The relief has arrived of late and it has come from both the courts and state laws. In the 1980s, the business judgment rule that tends to assume good decision-making by directors underwent new scrutiny. Courts were showing more inclination to second-guess board decisions and make directors prove their conclusions. Then, the states began to broaden the definition of stakeholders, giving directors more room to turn aside an offer that was evaluated to be narrow in its benefits to stakeholder groups. The Ohio statute says companies can look at the interest of employees, management, the community, and the nation, judge the offer on its long- and short-term merits, and consider whether keeping the company independent would be better for all concerned. Connecticut law says companies can weigh the impact of a takeover on various constituencies against the bid price. Pennsylvania's 1990 law encourages directors to take all stakeholders into account. And, as previously described, in the Time–Warner case, the Delaware Chancery Court ruled that companies can say no to a takeover, with justification.

WHAT CAN BE EXPECTED IN THE FUTURE

Will all of this investor relations experience in takeovers find little use in the future? Investor relations practitioners looking to retire in their current corporate posts can take little solace from the quiet time currently being observed in the takeover wars. Junk bonds may be out of favor and investment bankers may be dismantling their war machines, but enormous capital pools are ready to arm invasions that can come from aggressive companies in Europe or Asia or elsewhere as their economies boil, from North American companies amassing strength in global competition or from a new breed of "raiders" known by whatever definition that fits.

Investors determined to gain control of corporate assets in the 1990s can be expected to turn more to the proxy system. Using shareholder support to win a majority of board seats is the basic strategy, but challenging the current board to be independent in its decision-making is sure to emerge as a technique in the 1990s. Proposals to gain a say or control are a virtual certainty and they're likely to be innovative and tough to defense. They'll be focused on forcing the board to act in the best interests of shareholders or face criticism or the possibility of legal reprisal.

A piece of advice to investor relations professionals who have worn the uniforms of battle: keep your memoirs handy.

7

Institutions Involving Themselves in Corporate Governance

Institutionalization of the equity markets has made institutions much more interested in how managements run their companies. As their stock stake in companies grows (now about $2 trillion), so does institutional concern for protecting their investment and maximizing their returns.

Activism is playing out in an almost evolving manner, with events driving the emphasis at any time. It also is creating an intriguing irony in the institutional investor/corporate relationship: companies are wooing institutions to be investors as the sense of confrontation over governance grows; institutions are taking on larger holdings and worrying more about the safety of their investments.

One such worry, for example, is ample liquidity to sell shares without a drop in market price—the problem stemming from the tremendous growth of the pool of assets available to invest, with a large portion going into stocks. State and big city retirement funds have raised the issue; the money pouring into their plans is outstripping private funds. Soon, the public funds will have more assets to manage than the private plans. And, because of the public funds' penchant to index, a selloff of bundles of stocks can have even more market impact.

The worry also describes one of the major rationales for institutional activism. With institutions feeling locked into stock holdings
that are destined only to grow, it makes eminent sense to them to
gain a bigger voice in corporate decisions that affect the value of
their investments.

Judging from the issues institutions have chosen to advance,
protecting and enhancing the value of their investments are the
major goals. Indeed, institutions see it as a fiduciary obligation
stated clearly for pension funds and their investment managers
covered under the 1974 *Employee Retirement Income Security Act*
(ERISA), and equally clear to firms not managing pension funds
but having responsibilities to clients.

In evolving their current level of activism, institutions have
taken their cue from individual investors. For years, institutions
watched individuals pioneer activism, using the mechanics of the
proxy process to present proposals for voting in conjunction with
the annual meeting. Most of the issues were social in nature, but a
number of the perennial activists raised what became popular
governance questions—giving shareholders the right to approve
the appointment of auditors, establishing board audit and compensation committees, allowing cumulative voting of directors, and
eliminating staggered boards (one-third of the total board elected
each year for multi-year terms).

More than anything else, disapproval of U.S. companies doing
business in South Africa, with its apartheid policy, mobilized and
coalesced investors. Church groups and a number of individual
investors organized proposals and groups of target companies.
Soon, a few institutional investors were supporting or submitting
resolutions to companies to discontinue their South African business practices. Several social-investing funds were begun and are
successful with competitive performance returns.

TAKEOVERS TRIGGER INSTITUTIONAL ACTIVISM

It was the takeover boom of the 1980s that triggered substantial
institutional involvement in corporate governance. It also set the

stage for mutual mistrust that continues today and explains at least part of the fundamental reason the activism appears to be intensifying. Takeover efforts by raiders and companies (domestic and foreign) produced anti-takeover devices by corporations to serve as defenses. Businesses were being urged by lawyers to put the takeover deterrents in place, even where no threat to independence currently existed. At last count, some 900 companies have one or more takeover protection devices.

Mistrust has grown out of the entanglement. Institutions see the anti-takeover measures as additional risks to portfolio returns. They believe that securities values can be deflated by the very existence of the takeover defenses, or by negative investor attitudes toward managements successfully entrenching themselves. Perhaps more important, investors may be denied the substantial stock price premium that typically goes with a takeover. In some takeovers, that premium was 50 percent or more of the current price.

On the flip side, companies saw institutions supporting takeover attempts to capture the premium. The fear was especially aggravating when the suitor was a known raider with a reputation for being interested only in the financial gain that came from putting the company in play or negotiating a *greenmail settlement* (where the raider's stock is repurchased by the company above the market or initial price).

Leading the activism push are the public pension funds. They became especially concerned in the mid-1980s over efforts by managements to prevent hostile takeovers by such deterrents as *poison pills* (measures triggered by an ownership contest which gives companies a favored voting position), and by some greenmail payments that were made to keep the companies independent. For added muscle, the Council of Institutional Investors was formed (currently with some 300 public and union fund members, managing over $300 billion in assets at last count). Emphasis points of the Council continue to evolve as well.

Rolling back the effects of the poison pill and stopping greenmail payments have been two of the leading activist issues. Three variations of poison pill proposals are being presented:

1. rescind the pill altogether;
2. require it to be approved by shareholders; and
3. give it an expiration date (such as three years).

Interestingly, concern about the pill resurfaced in 1990 (as judged by the number of proposals), after a decline in the previous year. Takeover fever has been somewhat arrested by the decline of junk bond financing—a powerful engine for takeovers.

However, the abatement of takeover activity is seen as temporary. Financing should continue to be available from a variety of sources including commercial banks, investment banking firms, and through high-yield loans. The trained experts in junk bond financing are fanning across the brokerage/deal making industry, so junk bond capabilities have not dried up. In addition, the investment community established its inventiveness a long time ago.

The interest in making deals also is readily apparent. Raiders aren't going away. Old ones will return. New ones will appear. Some former raiders now are corporate executives running companies and seeking to add to their empires. Some corporate executives can be called raiders. There always will be a market for strategic acquisitions—friendly or unfriendly. And, the interest of foreign buyers in U.S. companies, shown to be very strong in the late 1980s, is expected to continue well into the new decade.

Proxy contests for control also have undergone a revival, even though the ticket can be costly. The first step is to use the proxy process to obtain board control. Behind at least some of the heightened governance activity is the proxy fighter, seeking all the advantages possible—eliminating the takeover defenses, gaining access to shareholder lists, putting allies on the board with the help of cumulative voting, and seeking to increase voting support by giving investment managers the comfort of confidential voting.

As the proxy mechanism replaces the hostile raid, proposals can be expected to be much more creative. A good example is the Harold Simmons proposal in the summer of 1990 that the Lockheed Corp. board allow Simmons-controlled NL Industries to acquire the unallocated shares in the Lockheed ESOP or amend its poison pill so that NL can buy more common shares in the open market. Rationale for the ESOP proposal is to help Lockheed lower its debt, incurred when the company set up the ESOP. The pill amendment would enable Simmons to get beyond the Lockheed anti-takeover device that permits Lockheed to issue more shares in the face of a dissident holding of 20 percent or more of the outstanding shares. The Simmons stake through NL Industries was over 19 percent at the time of the filings. Simmons' proposals challenge the Lockheed board to function independent of management. The Simmons action represents his continuing effort to wrestle control of Lockheed. He had lost a proxy battle with Lockheed during the 1990 proxy season.

POISON PILLS CAN RAISE TAKEOVER PREMIUM

A Securities and Exchange Commission study on poison pills in 1986 attracted activist interest. It showed a negative effect on stock price of companies passing the measures. A subsequent study by Georgeson & Company, Inc. showed an opposite result, while also documenting the positives of poison pills: enhancing share value ultimately by giving companies more time to find a suiter willing to pay a higher value. Bidding contests, driving up the price finally paid in a takeover or forced acquisition, became common. They also have contributed to the difficulty companies have in determining the differences between their warranted and "takeover" value. In some cases, more was paid for companies than should have been. (See Chapter 9 for discussion of Valuation.)

The evidence on poison pills has prompted many institutional investors to modify their positions by judging the merits on a company-by-company basis. Preventing management from "entrenching" itself becomes a reason to do away with a poison pill; supporting good managements to keep control or find a higher bid become reasons to retain the poison pill. The record of the past decade of takeover fervor shows that most companies put in play inevitably are acquired, especially if the financial deal is judged to be secure and strong to shareholders (as in cash or high-quality securities).

OTHER KEY GOVERNANCE ISSUES

Banning greenmail payments isn't seen as particularly controversial. Corporate managements abhor it as much as institutional and individual investors. It has been used only as a weapon of last resort to keep the company free to pursue its long-term strategies. Many companies voluntarily are agreeing to not pay greenmail.

A number of the other prominent or emerging issues reflect institutional interest in shareholder rights to decide the fate of corporate managements in power or prevent them from interfering with processes that should improve securities values. Most popular currently is to grant shareholder voting confidentiality. Activists on this issue believe managements can coerce shareholders into supporting the company on key voting issues. The ability to do so starts with knowing how the investors are voting on the issue. Especially vulnerable, say the activists, are investment management firms and banks who may have, or are pursuing, business relationships with the company.

In rebuttal, companies deny coercion and further claim that it's impossible, practically, as can be seen in analyzing each investor group. Public funds aren't going to be coerced, and they are required by law to make their voting record public to beneficiaries. Investment managers are not of the personality or temperament to accept coercion, regardless of the business relationship. Banks worried about commercial relationships take on the burden of creating the possible conflict of interest by becoming investors. However, one investor group—employees—should have rights of confidentiality, to avoid any question of retribution for their vote on any matter. More companies now are giving employees this right.

What "incited" institutional investors to dig in on the poison pill issue was a 1988 letter-writing campaign by CEOs to other CEOs urging their pension fund support against the proposals.

Some companies voluntarily are agreeing to permit confidential voting. The agreement typically comes after a resolution is filed, then meetings are held with the sponsor. The resolution is withdrawn following the agreement. These agreements, however, are largely unenforceable, and at this time, the institutions have very little, if any, monitoring system. Under Rule 14(a)8 of the Securities Acts, resolutions proposed by shareholders are not binding, even when they receive a majority vote. That vote, however, does suggest that serious board attention be given to the matter.

Several other issues are on the table. Shareholders are still seeking cumulative voting and recision of staggered boards. New is a proposal to prevent companies from placing blocks of stock in "friendly" hands as a takeover prevention device. To improve opportunities to win a proxy vote, a resolution has been advanced that would disallow counting absentions among the total votes cast. That would change the percentages, possibly creating the needed majority.

Institutional activists also have become very concerned about the strength of state anti-takeover statutes. They say the most stringent of these laws render hostile takeovers virtually impossible. A Massachusetts law mandates classified boards. A Pennsylvania statute forces investors to give over to companies any profits that would be made from selling shares within 18 months after a takeover bid. It also says directors can consider the interests of all stakeholders in a control contest, not just shareholders. Takeover protection laws in Delaware, Indiana, Pennsylvania, and other states also prevent a bidder holding 20 percent or more shares from voting those shares without majority approval of shares held by "disinterested" shareholders. Some of the laws are being challenged on constitutional grounds.

The year 1990 brought a number of proposals for companies to "opt out" of the Delaware protection laws. None passed, but support grew. Opting out proposals to companies incorporated in Delaware and other states are sure to be on ballots in the future. If passed, a proposal to opt out of the Delaware law would be binding to the company, since the law itself builds in the obligation.

Further, the Delaware courts have supported, through a specific ruling, the business judgment code that says a company's board of directors can say no to a takeover bid with just cause. Lawyers expect the ruling to be challenged eventually, suggesting that boards saying "no" better have strong evidence showing the benefits to shareholders and stakeholders of keeping incumbent management in charge of the enterprise.

Stepping deeper into corporate governance, the 1990 proxy season brought a dozen proposals to ban companies from establishing *golden parachutes* (compensation packages for executives on the losing side in an ownership contest). Another proposal sought to require shareholder approval of golden parachutes. Activists consider the ability to submit these proposals as somewhat of a breakthrough that could be extended to similar types of resolutions heretofore thought to be part of regular corporate business, and not subject to shareholder authority. The Securities and Exchange Commission gave the proposals the green light to move forward by responding to the initial filing with a "no action" letter.

ACTIVIST CIRCLE WIDENING

All of the golden parachute proposals were submitted by individual shareholders who received technical and legal help in preparing them by the United Shareholders Association (USA), a group of investors founded by T. Boone Pickens and said to number over 40 million members. USA set a target of 50 companies to receive proposals by its members in 1990. The 50 were judged to be among the most serious underperformers in terms of shareholder value and shareholder rights on the basis of a rating system set up by USA that covers 1,000 major companies. Resolutions submitted in 1990 by USA members also covered confidential voting, classified boards, and opting out of the Delaware anti-takeover statutes. USA has announced its intention to continue compiling the ratings system and helping its members file resolutions. Companies also can expect a pickup in proposals to ban golden parachutes or require their endorsement by shareholders.

In governance issues, the 1990 proxy season was the busiest ever. Some 280 proposals came to a vote at 230 companies—both new records. Several passed; it was the first time any passed. Voting support overall was the highest in history. Any success activists have in the future in removing the inclusion of abstentions in total vote counts is likely to have the effect of creating more approvals by lowering the total dissident votes needed to win a majority.

The year 1990 also turned out to be a time of vigorous renewal in social activism. A record 290 proposals came forward with 170 coming to a vote at 140 companies. The others were either misfiled or withdrawn following discussions with managements. While the South African issue and a couple of other traditional concerns still are prominently on the agenda, what brought the record turnout is the heightened worry in America about the condition and future of the environment and the health and safety of man and nature, both domestically and worldwide. Some 45 environmentally related resolutions were filed including adoption of what have come to be called the "Valdez Principles," named for the oil-bearing ship that went aground off Alaska. Resolutions for adopting the principles were presented to some five companies in 1990. The principles cover such promises as protecting the biosphere, reducing and properly disposing of wastes, using energy smartly, conserving use of nonrenewable resources, minimizing risk to employees and the community involving the environment, safety, and health, making and marketing only safe products, paying compensation for environmental or personal damage, maintaining open communication with employees, customers and the community on health and safety hazards, and establishing environmental accountability at the board of directors' level.

Other social issues surfacing involve banning tobacco products manufacturing (also allowed by the SEC for the first time), forbidding advertising of manufactured infant formula, and banning the use of certain plastic-containing packages.

Lines of distinction between social and governance issues and between individual and institutional investor sponsorship also are blurring, if not crossing. Three of the largest public pension funds joined in sponsoring the Valdez Principles, for example.

Resolutions concerning staggered boards and cumulative voting are just as likely to come from either group.

Current Climate and Trends

Institutional activists are advancing their agenda on three fronts simultaneously:

1. lobbying for changes in the proxy system that would facilitate their ability to gain greater participation in corporate decisions and possibly some control over the governance process itself;
2. steadily refining their approach that might be leading to some type of definitive course of action, the most likely possibility at present being a more influential voice in the selection and role of the corporate members; and
3. increasing the amount of support coming from other investors.

Activists—mainly the public funds—believe a reconstructed proxy system is the foundation for making gains in involvement. The proxy process, they argue, favors companies by limiting eligibility to submit proposals and the number that can be submitted; placing the cost burden of using the system on dissidents while allowing companies to use corporate funds in either presenting or defending against changes; giving companies the basic controls in the proxy mechanics—tabulation, list maintenance, preparation of materials, and so on.

Companies counter that the system is doing fundamentally what it should, and changes that would bring improvements are minor in nature, dealing more with inconsistencies, technicalities, and practices outmoded by modern investing times. The system requires companies to supply information that enables shareholders to make an informed vote, gives shareholders the opportunity to express their views, exercise their vote, and cause change by making management and the board accountable through proxy contests. The corporate view is that the system will be abused if made too easy to use.

One of the more aggressive public funds, the California Public Employees Retirement System (CalPERS), took a step aimed at moving the debate beyond the discussion stage late in 1989 by sending a lengthy letter to the SEC that laid out some 48 recommendations dealing with the structure, procedures, SEC filing, and review process of the proxy system, and called for more disclosure and communications. The SEC is expected to get involved. Proponents for change also are encouraging Congressional review.

The CalPERS proposals capture the chief interests of institutional activists in repairing the proxy system. Among proposed changes:

limit and disclose a company's discretionary counting of shares of beneficial owners that don't include voting instruction as abstentions;

require confidential voting and independent vote tabulation;

allow large shareholders ($1 million or more worth of shares) to submit more than one proposal;

prohibit bundling of unrelated proxy proposals into one voting procedure;

provide shareholder lists to shareholders requesting them;

eliminate abstentions in deciding the outcome of proposals;

disclose in advance how votes are counted, whether abstentions are included and who tabulates them;

eliminate the right of beneficial owners to withhold their identity;

reform the proxy disclosure process to make the materials easier to understand, clearly state rules and deadlines for submitting proposals, and provide more information about directors, including whether any shareholder nominees have been selected.

Activist Momentum Growing

The year 1990 could be marked as a watershed time in the momentum of activist-led efforts to have more say in the running of U.S. public companies. It clearly is taking hold and gaining investor support. The statistics show sizable progress in number of proposals, number of companies targeted, rise in voting support across the board, breakthroughs in winning resolutions, and what, as a result, can almost be called a dramatic turn in the institutional agenda.

A firm agenda appears to be taking shape that consists of positive actions to accomplish change, rather than what has been a series of somewhat organized annual attempts to strip away deterrents to successful bids for company control. The agenda is being built on three linked platforms simultaneously:

1. Forcing or gaining agreement to change by mobilizing shareholders to express their views, chiefly in disapproval of corporate actions;
2. Influencing the selection of board directors; and
3. Creating discussion with management and boards on governance and control issues that leads to agreement on certain changes or concessions in return for institutional support in proxy contests.

While companies aren't bound by shareholder approval of such governance issues as confidential voting and doing away with poison pills, the influence of the vote has to affect management willingness to discuss issues and its decision making. The number of resolutions being withdrawn each year continues to increase, following discussion or exchanges of letters leading to company decisions to change their policy or voluntarily agree to the action sought in the proposal. Companies are watching the cost and amount of management time needed to deal with shareholder activism rise appreciably along with votes favoring the resolutions.

In pursuing corporate governance initiatives, the activist institutions say their objective is to have more contact with management as the base point in being more involved in the decisions that affect the value of their investments. Closer participation goes hand in hand with making major investments in the long-term growth of the company. The institutions say they are interested in being long-term investors, in gaining the rewards of higher returns through use of "patient capital," and by not having to worry about the liquidity situation as their stakes reach the 10 percent and more level. They claim that managements have been inaccessible.

Management/institutional investor dialogue is definitely on the increase with the subjects focused almost exclusively on governance and control issues. Institutions are making headway on several fronts. Their clout has been used to gain concessions from companies in return for institutional voting support in proxy battles for corporate control. Of course, they also have supported dissidents. Institutions have been recommending candidates for board nomination and, as the occasion occurs, are seeking to influence the choice of new chief executive officers.

Participation in the board selection process is a major goal of activist institutions, not so much with the intent of electing themselves to boards (that probably would constitute a conflict of interest), but with the desire to nominate directors who would represent the interests of shareholders. CalPERS has suggested formation of shareholder advisory committees, made up of the company's leading institutional holders. They would meet periodically, make recommendations to the board, with costs of the process borne by the companies.

THE PROGRESS AND ARGUMENTS ON BOTH SIDES

As dialogue picks up, companies remain skeptical of investor intentions. Companies see the goal of activists primarily concentrated in insuring the flexibility to maximize investment by preserving the opportunity for highest returns in hostile take-overs. Institutions believe their agenda is broader: maximizing returns is a process that is facilitated by making sure that managements aren't entrenched, that obstacles to encouraging investment don't exist (such as anti-takeover provisions), and that a well-qualified board/management team to run the company is in place.

It would seem that shareholder activism is an unfolding process with the next step determined while the current one is being taken. To the extent this is true, the next steps are likely to involve intensifying efforts to do away with takeover impediments and gain increasing influence on management decisions, through direct contact and board representation. Beyond that is uncertain.

The other unanswered questions are how far will investor involvement in corporate governance go and what will be its ultimate result, in terms of the fundamental strength of each company, the economy as a whole, and securities valuation in particular?

Institutions believe they are being encouraged to pursue their goals while companies worry about their real motivations. First, on the institutional side. As the 1990 proxy season was about to get underway, the U.S. Department of Labor reaffirmed its ERISA guidelines and put some teeth into the notion that corporate governance to achieve highest returns is not only acceptable, it is almost required, consistent with fiduciary responsibility.

A speech before the Financial Executives Institute by David Ball, assistant secretary of labor, set the tone. His remarks were reported in the newsletter of the Investor Responsibility Research Center. These quotes and attributions are from the newsletter. "If one accepts the premise that management of corporations have a duty to maximize the value of the corporation over time for the benefit of their shareholders, and that management of corporations have to be accountable to their shareholders, the duties of fiduciaries of pensions funds . . . are clear," Ball said.

And, in the same speech, Ball said: "I believe that, as institutional shareholders own an ever greater portion of corporate America, it is inevitable that those responsible for the management of plan assets . . . will have to become more activist as shareholders.

If you are unhappy with the way management of a major corporation is performing, you have three choices: Either persuade management to change those things it is doing that are leading the company to underperform, or attempt to change management, or sell the stock." Ball added that selling the stock in large blocks can produce a price drop.

The ERISA guidelines put investment managers on notice to fulfill their fiduciary obligation by voting their shares and by concentrating their voting decisions on the best economic interests of the plan participants. The ERISA guidelines carry a strong voice of authority. Let's listen. Investment managers are excused from voting only if the plan trustee reserves voting authority to itself or other named fiduciary. Fiduciaries/investment managers should establish written proxy policies and practices, make sure proxies are received, keep records of their voting on each proposal, and if they delegate voting authority, monitor the performance of managers assigned to cast the votes. That last provision applies particularly to corporate pension plan sponsors assigning voting authority to their investment managers.

From all indications, investment management firms now are taking their voting responsibilities more seriously. Most now have written policies, proxy voting committees, and appear to not be intimidated in their voting practices, even though they may have corporate pension plan clients. Money managers profess to have policies similar to the more visible public funds, opposing poison pills, for example. The steady gains being made in support of dissident shareholder resolutions can be attributed to a combination of growing public fund and private investment management support.

However, some grumbling is being heard among investment managers who are questioning the value of all the activism and governance fuss. It can be costly to investors and companies, when management spends dollars on defenses and in wasted executive time. Investment returns can be the victim.

Big investors also have begun to put their money where their mouth is in terms of their stated desire to be supportive long-term holders. A number of private investment funds have been started, with large stakes taken in the companies (as much as 25 percent) and promises to keep the money there for a while. In return for the capital support, the investors are given board seats and some say in running the company. Public funds are looking at committing funds for similar purposes. In fact, monies are being raised and deals are cooking.

On a related front, how pension funds use their assets in making investments for the overall economic benefit of society is becoming something more than an idealistic idea. One argument is that pension funds should "optimize" their returns, not necessarily "maximize" them, with assets being directed at investments that would have a meaningful economic benefit. A proposal has been made to reword the ERISA rules to allow optimization instead of maximization. Institutions aren't expected to embrace the notion universally.

In further action, a group of public funds from several states have pledged to support each other's economic growth through investments within the states.

THE CORPORATE SIDE OF THE QUESTION

Companies aren't sure whether they should welcome institutions as high stakes "partners" or fear them. Investor relations people have been programmed to pursue new institutional investment but also to spread it around so that a handful of investors aren't deciding the fate of the company, for instance, in a takeover. Fear of a precipitous stock price decline also is real, coming on the heels of a massive institutional sell off should the company fall out of favor, but the institutions seem to be equally protective against such a valuation-shattering event. Liquidity and broadened institutional ownership are two leading investor relations priorities.

"Too much concentration in too few institutional hands" is the way the concern is expressed by John C. Wilcox, managing director of Georgeson & Company, Inc., a proxy solicitation and investor relations consulting firm. Wilcox points out one of the recommendations in the CalPERS proposal that, he says, would enable a few institutions to exercise control over companies. The proposal would grant an exemption from the proxy process for institutions qualifying on the basis of the size of their holdings. "We don't want state funds running the companies," Wilcox says. The reason, he adds, is that they are financial intermediaries and not stockowners, and their fudiciary goals of maximizing investment may not be consistent with companies' strategies to build long-term health.

Another concern is the growing power of advisory firms to institutions. They are paid by the institutions (including pension funds and investment management firms) to prepare analyses of the proxy proposals that are before a company. The analyses are designed to help fiduciaries come to grips with the sheer numbers of proposals they receive and need to vote on each proxy season. The advisory firms prepare the analysis, the institutional shareholders cast the votes.

Some companies, and even some private investment managers, wonder whether personal political aspirations are influencing any of the public fund administrators. Their actions can be highly visible as well as favorably influence beneficiaries who also are voters.

Companies are wary about whether too much institutional say in governance could impair corporate competitiveness and be detrimental to the economy of the United States. CEOs belonging to The Business Roundtable endorsed a position paper stressing the need for innovation, risk-taking, and quick response to the marketplace as essential in serving society, steadfastly bolstering the economy, and keeping American business competitive. The focus on long-term growth must remain clear, and the responsibility for keeping that concentration intact rests with the board of directors, according to The Business Roundtable paper.

The paper advises that corporate and political governance not be considered similarly. "Our political system is designed to create compromises between competing interests, to seek the broad middle ground. It is a slow and deliberative process that discourages bold moves or right angle turns. This system of governance would be fatal for an economic enterprise."

Further: "Excessive corporate governance by referendum in the proxy statement can also chill innovation and risk taking.

Shareholders voting on such things as acquisitions and divestitures can put immediate shareholder financial return ahead of sound longer-term growth which may have the potential of being even more rewarding to the corporation, its shareholders and its other stakeholders. Corporate governance by referendum instead of by the board of directors has all the same drawbacks as federal governance by referendum instead of by Congress."

A position paper by the National Investor Relations Institute, a professional society of investor relations practitioners, calls for greater awareness of investor concerns by corporate boards and also recommends that boards encourage closer communication between shareholders and the company. NIRI also endorses board authority in governance matters and the role of directors in supporting long-term management of the business.

In the debate between companies and investors, the piece of common ground seems to be the board of directors. The Roundtable says the board plays the central role in governance, with its first responsibility being "the long-term successful performance of their corporation." The organization of CEOs believes that boards should made up predominantly of independent directors and those directors should make it clear to shareholders that "selecting director nominees is the board's responsibility."

The governance debate appears to be moving to the board table. It could be the place for the issue to settle: independent boards, whose members are chosen with some input from investors. Add more direct contact with senior executives to discuss the hot topics on investors' minds and two of the top items on the stated institutional priority list are accomplished.

As they gather more influence in board selection, institutions' investment behavior will be watched closely by companies. Will the patient capital remain patient if returns are slow to improve? Will investors try to make more decisions in areas that always have been seen as management prerogative? How will performance be measured, especially as institutions follow through with their promise to support long-term strategies and programs? For institutions, until now, the measurement has been the price of the stock.

Then, there is the issue of indexed investing. Active institutional investors have long records of contact with corporate managements. Fund managers and institutional analysts aren't reticent about jawboning with CEOs on how results can be improved. Funds largely indexed aren't doing the kind of fundamental analysis that makes for meaningful discussion. Perhaps, it will come with larger holdings.

As the governance issue moves forward, the investor relations role will be critical. Investor relations' understanding of the capital markets and inside, insightful knowledge on how investors think and operate should be the basis of corporate planning, action, and communication.

PART TWO

How the Essential Parts Fit Together in an Investor Relations Program

8

Marketing Becomes the Operative Investor Relations Approach

Investor relations is classic marketing. It has all the ingredients: research to determine target audiences and to understand what makes them buy your stock; designing operational improvements to make the company more attractive; honing and testing communications messages and vehicles; measuring results and fine tuning the process to vanquish weaknesses and increase the use of what works best.

Practitioners need to apply the marketing tools carefully in making sure investor relations is operated at that classic marketing level. Investor relations has only been thought of as essentially a marketing function in the past decade. During this time, numerous marketing tools have become available. They range from databases to help identify and target institutional investors, analysts, and brokers, to various direct mail venues that send messages directly to these audiences.

It is important to work these tools into a comprehensive marketing plan that includes a predetermined basis for measuring the results. Otherwise, some of these programs will prove to be costly with little value. Buying lists of institutional investors or retail brokers is an example. Many companies are buying these lists then doing nothing with them. The lists should be part of a plan to target a certain investor segment. In the marketing sequence, the lists are an important early step in the research phase of a carefully laid out contact program. Another example is a mailing to brokers. Again, results will be more quantifiable when the mailing is part of a planned program that probably is concentrated on a specific location and includes meetings and follow-up activities.

By using the marketing process effectively, investor relations people can overcome objections to the idea that marketing should be the essence of the function. The doubters include senior corporate management and a host of investor relations veterans who grew a practice that was much "purer." They (including top management) are looking mainly at the popularized negative connotations of marketing—superficial, self-serving, promotional.

Indeed, these must be avoided in the execution of an investor relations program. They are deadly traps and easy to fall into. Sometimes, managements are too aggressive, too anxious to see the stock price rise quickly. This typically occurs with smaller, younger companies, or new managements feeling a pressure to perform. (However, at most companies, investor relations people have a tough time getting management comfortable with communicating enough information to enable investors to make an informed decision.) Sometimes, the communications professionals are too aggressive, especially when the program is being conducted by people with strong promotional backgrounds—advertising and public relations, particularly. A mistake newly public companies often make, for example, is to have their advertising agencies prepare the annual report and lead the investor relations effort. The reports tend to be overdesigned and overwritten, coming off as slick, and containing little real substance.

Marketing as the second dimension of investor relations has evolved. Investor relations "pioneers" created a function that was information-based and proactive, to a degree. Information is and always will be the first dimension and basis of investor relations. Marketing makes sure the potential value of the information is realized by concentrating it on audiences that will use it and by shaping the content to be sure it's useful. Marketing enables the information to find the audience and the audience to find the information.

Marketing takes a big step beyond the pioneering stage of investor relations. It refines the information base and proactive effort down to the most important information and most important audiences for that information.

Investor relations is an opportunity to practice marketing at a lofty level, for two reasons: the impact of the activity on the fortunes of the company, and quality of the information process. The stakes are serious for a company and the opportunities are significant: the ability to raise capital, and at the lowest possible cost; the enhanced reputation that goes with a higher securities value, which translates favorably in daily business operations in numerous ways; the advantage of a higher stock price in making an acquisition or discouraging a hostile takeover.

There's a richness to the information set not always found in other marketing situations. Marketing stocks is a whole lot more intellectual and challenging to master than marketing a commodity consumer product. Reaching a quality plateau that makes information valuable to analysts, investors and brokers is a complex, somewhat undefined and constantly changing process that challenges communicators every day. The first challenge is internal—convincing senior officers of the benefits of being forthcoming. In the marketplace, the challenges are multiple. Information needs among analysts and investors are as varied as their analytical approaches and investing strategies. And, the information parts plugged into their models change with every fine tuning.

In carrying out the marketing process, the communications vehicles need to be appropriate for the message and the information flow. The principal vehicles utilize the print, verbal, audiovisual and electronic formats—chief among them being annual and interim reports, fact books and sheets, newsletters, news releases, fascimile distribution, mailings of various types of information pieces, media exposure (editorial and advertising), video and slide presentations, face-to-face meetings and ear-to-ear telephone conversations.

What is appropriate in all these channels of communication is an information-supply approach. What counts is content. It has two main components—the information wanted by investors and analysts and the information management knows is vital in accurately understanding the company's intrinsic value. In satisfying the information needs of analysts and investors, the company creates for itself an acceptable environment for communicating its side of the valuation equation. It also creates a positive atmosphere for debate. Attitudes and perceptions are a big part of active investment. With a comfortable and open climate for communication, companies can change perceptions and overlay a new level of strategic and operational information aimed at motivating analysts and investors to raise their estimates of performance and intrinsic value.

Style, tone, and language are important as well, whether the conveyance is written or spoken. The speakers and communications materials are the sources of good information. In this phase too, the opportunity is for classic marketing. There is seldom value in overstatement, promotional or self-serving language. In fact, these tactics could turn negative. Even pushing or dramatizing ideas in word choice should be done with great care. The danger is that the content is right on the mark, but the method of presentation produces a skeptical psychological response. The writing and graphics in printed and audio-visual presentations should illuminate the information, invite readership, suggest an openness, and project the professionalism and personality of the company and its people.

THE PURPOSE OF INVESTOR RELATIONS

The fundamental purpose of investor relations is to create an investment marketplace that is fully informed about the company and a company that is fully informed about its options in the investment marketplace. Obviously, it's a purpose that can never be achieved, virtually by definition. The recipients dictate what should come out of the information pipeline, and they are an incredibly diverse group, with needs that are changing continuously. Reaching and edifying all of them to the moment is impossible.

But companies can build the knowledge base quantitatively and qualitatively step by step with a good information program. In so doing, the focus must be on the information that enables analysts and brokers to recommend the stock and investors to buy it. Naturally, companies are looking for "buys," but being informed about the company is even more important. The informed analyst, broker and investor provide a basis for communication that can lead to a recommendation and decision to buy when the investing criteria are met.

The ability of investor relations professionals to function as information sources who are so effective that the gap between warranted value and current stock price actually closes is a fascinating proposition. Information has tremendous value in the investing process. In the most efficient of the three efficient market hypotheses, information essentially is the basis of valuation. In the least efficient of the three, information becomes the weapon to gain an advantage by capitalizing on the inefficiency of the market .

How important is the investor relations function as a source of valulable, investable information? The question really begins with the importance of the company as an information source. It is critical in making the entire investment process whole. Companies collectively are a leading data source in understanding and evaluating the industry. Companies individually supply the numbers and offer their interpretation. Many companies share their strategic thrust and view of the future on both macro and micro bases. And, what company hasn't quietly sniped at the competition in private conversation with an analyst or two? Or, at least, added some worthwhile industry data?

Analysts and portfolio managers following active investment styles rely heavily on direct company contact and relationships as a viable source of information. Most brokerage analysts covering a specific industry base their recommendations on information learned through management/investor relations relationships, especially with those companies that lead that industry. Company contacts are vital to institutional analysts and portfolio managers, especially if they are following the industry closely and/or are heavily invested in it. And brokers can get very close to managements. They tend to develop an expertise on certain industies and make a lot of money in commissions by sticking with one or several successful companies within that industry.

Even professionals in the investment community utilizing computer-generated data are relying on information that has come from the companies, either directly through their 10Ks, annual and interim reports, and other communications sources or through the research reports and conversations with the analysts who are talking to the companies regularly. There is little doubt that companies are a useful information resource.

How much of that information conduit is being filled by investor relations becomes the next question. Here, investor relations people have to earn their spurs. The natural first choice of analysts and institutional investment managers is the chief executive officer, followed by the chief financial officer, and then the chief operating officer or treasurer. For specialized knowledge, the picks will be various operating and functional experts. Many investment professionals see investor relations people as obstacles in the way of the valuable resources.

Everything about the information process has the potential to contribute to an unevenness in the quantity and quality from company to company that analysts and investors somehow must make up or exploit if they are to consider a company for investment. In fact, that's another factor from an investor relations perspective. Unless the company is an instrumental player in the industry, it probably won't be followed by brokerage analysts if it isn't a consistent and candid information resource.

As a result of the unevenness, there is gaping leeway between highest efficiency and inefficiency in the information base from company to company. Contributors to the unevenness within a company are multiple. It occurs in the level of senior managers' appreciation of the value of investor communication, which drives their degree of participation in the process. No matter how effective the investor relations person is, the CEO is the highest word. The unevenness or opportunity to excel occur also in the talents, skills, experience, intelligence, knowledge, and energies of investor relations practitioners. And, it occurs in the supporting cast that includes related inside functions and external resources.

The range between fulfilling the communications process effectively and not fufilling it very well at all is what makes the investor relations job fascinating and challenging. There is more room to succeed, fail or, more likely, fall somewhere in between than in any other corporate job, except possibly public relations, which is even more intangible. That high degree of uncertainty provides a strong rationale for structuring investor relations as a marketing function, rather than simply information response, which is likely to be seen on the top floor as passive and of minimal value—a necessary evil rather than a critical component in the financial strategies of the company. The discipline of proper marketing applies research, message development and testing, audience targeting and testing, execution and testing, and measurement.

THE VALUE OF INVESTOR RELATIONS

An informed marketplace is the means to achieving the real value of investor relations. The opportunity for investor relations to earn its keep is realized in four essential values that it brings to the company. Investor relations can help a company:

1. minimize its cost of capital;
2. maximize equity valuation;
3. provide liquidity for the stock; and
4. help avoid hostile takeover attempts at an inadequate price that disrupt the company.

Investor relations can have more influence on valuation and liquidity than the cost of capital, which is determined more by the impact on equity and debt of interest, inflation, taxes, and other macro factors. However, investor relations contributes to a lower cost of capital to the extent that its role in creating information efficiency brings stock price close to the intrinsic value of the company. High valuation also is a positive factor in debt ratings. And higher stock price and debt ratings lead to a lower cost of capital.

Information flow helps produce a liquid stock flow. The goal is to have buyers for sellers and sellers for buyers, providing the liquidity and avoiding volatility that can cause dramatic moves in stock price. Waves of transactions that aren't balanced can trigger volatility, especially on the downside. Too often, investors sell first, then ask why. An informed investment decision process tends to better balance buyers and sellers of shares. Trading patterns are more even. Selling waves end quickly, because investors know the fundamental strengths of the company and are ready to buy shares when they believe the stock is undervalued. Buying waves diminish as the price approaches the company's fair value, unless there is merger or takeover speculation. Then, the alternate value game begins.

Investor relations' best opportunity to use information effectively comes in the complex process of understanding the critical components that constitute the essence of the company's valuation. Valuation is what the price of the stock should be, based on the most productive use of the company's assets. Investors try to estimate and project that full value then use the number as a benchmark in making an investment decision by comparing current price with intrinsic value. Investors are looking for undervalued stocks. Often, stocks are sold by institutional investors because the price reaches the projected fair value, not because the investors are disenchanted with the company. New calculations later may show higher valuation potential and prompt the same institutions to buy the shares again. Models are used in measuring the value, chief among them being projections of the amount of cash that will flow into the business after all the financial obligations are met. Chapter 9 covers valuation fully.

Information ascends to its highest range of value in the valuation process. Its use can be quantified. Investor relations' role as an information source and conveyor is two-sided:

1. to utilize its investment contacts to help management appreciate the importance of valuation and understand the criteria being used by the key investors; and
2. to communicate the company's "value drivers" to investors.

While investors set the parameters and build the models, companies seem to be taking on a greater role in determining their valuation. The whole notion of maximizing shareholder value has taken on a life of its own in the executive suite. Companies are instituting share price improvement programs. Hopefully, these programs also are good strategic courses in the long-term successful run of the company. Time will tell for each company, but the moves appear to be muscle-building. They are:

deconglomerizing to concentrate on core businesses where management skills reside, then adding strength through strategic acquisitions;

investing retained earnings in technology or lower-cost manufacturing;

taking divisions public to motivate employees and gain investor recognition; and

buying back shares as the best present use of excess cash.

The two keys in maximizing value are earning returns above the cost of capital and pumping highest productivity from the company's assets.

The valuation approach also gets investor relations people out of that confinement created by the charge that their function's usefulness can't be quantified. Valuation provides the freedom. Valuation is determined by corporate performance and prospects and measured in investing models. The investor relations role is to provide information on the value drivers and their impact on valuation as a whole. That role can be educational. It can be persuasive, when company and investors disagree on the value drivers or their specific effect at the moment. It can be quantitative, based on investor relations expertise in knowing precisely what investors need for their models in filling out the valuation properties that gives them the valuation number.

Thus, the notion of valuation provides at least some of the answer to the ancient debate on whether the investor relations function influences share price. The answer can become yes, but in its proper context. The market sets the stock price. Information helps the market value the company and its stock fairly. Investor relations' role is helping provide the market with the information that enables the market to price the company's stock efficiently. Investor relations can do no more than that, if the market is efficient and reflecting full value in the current stock price. If management believes the stock is undervalued, management has to conclude that the information process is lacking, and more emphasis should be put on "investor relations." The other answer is for management to recognize that the market is pricing the stock fairly, and if that price is unsatisfactory, there is strategic work to be done in raising valuation.

BASIC INVESTOR RELATIONS DUTIES

The underlying investor relations responsibility is to create and maintain the most informed investor marketplace possible: broadly, in terms of providing a level of general knowledge; and specifically, with shareholders and prospective shareholders in providing detailed information that supports or generates investment decisions.

The principal duties of the investor relations person come down to a five-part package:

1. set goals and objectives that aren't general but are specific to the company's capital needs and business strategies;

2. plan and establish the thrust and content of the information process and direct the development and use of all the communications vehicles that make up that process;

3. build meaningful relationships with key investment participants including, as appropriate, present shareholders, brokerage analysts, institutional analysts and investment managers, retail and institutional brokers, traders, exchange/NASDAQ officials, and the business/financial media;

4. serve as spokesperson for the company with the financial community; and

5. appraise results continuously, adjusting the program to meet stated goals and objectives.

THE BASIC STRUCTURE OF AN INVESTOR RELATIONS PROGRAM

Structurally, the marketing-oriented investor relations program divides into four equal parts:

1. The *information base:* Determining the content, which is built from an analysis of the fundamental capabilities (value drivers) of the company translated into investment characteristics and strengths.

2. The *audience base:* Determining the investor groups (including current shareholders) and specific investors within them whose investment strategies and methods match the company's characteristics and strengths.

3. The *execution stage:* Determining and using the best methods of reaching these target groups with targeted information.

4. The *ongoing measurement process.*

One extension: The information flow should be enveloping the marketplace at the same time it is seeping into its targets. It should not be so concentrated that it fails to create broad awareness, or what is known as "conditioning" the marketplace. This suggests a two-dimensional communications program: using media visibility, direct mail, and large meetings for increasing awareness in general while focusing on the targets.

There is a fifth part to the basic structure—research. Research underpins the entire investor relations process. It should be forged into each of the four parts. Research helps companies connect their message to interested investors. It fuses the two; logic suggests they must be inseparable. The message has to appeal to the investor's method or model. The company has to search out investors whose methods or models find the company's value drivers appetizing.

First comes the introspection to fashion an investable corporate profile. It involves defining the company's basic strengths and any unique advantages that give it a competitive hammerlock in its markets (the value drivers, in "valuation" language). A company with a unique advantage should recognize it and exploit it. It's amazing to see the number of companies who fail to do this, either because they don't recognize it as important to investors or because they believe it constitutes a secret competitive weapon. That's probably naive: how many companies can really keep their unique advantage a secret from their competitors? Analysts and investors call the coveted edge a "franchise"—something no one else has. It can be an unduplicable technology, patent or license protection, an invincible marketshare lead.

In outline form, there are three vital subsets to the information base—strategic, operational, and financial.

Strategic information. Strategic information helps analysts and investors understand the direction of the company. Growth will come through arming a powerful marketshare position with a new product stream built from superior technology. Acquisitions will round out the product line or fill in the markets geographically. A global presence is a goal that will be achieved through joint ventures and possible acquisition.

Operating information. Some of it may be inherent in the strategic decisions. There may be other pieces in the picture. In cash flow generation or earnings momentum, the value driver for a consumer company is likely to be the acceptance of its brand names. Plans and programs to capitalize on those reputations become critical. For an industrial company, the keys may involve proprietary technology, low-cost manufacturing, and a broadened product line.

Financial information. The value drivers will be closely tied to the investment models, centered on projecting the company's rate of earnings on existing and planned assets, with a bottom line of predicting its ability to earn returns on investment above the cost of capital. Details on capital spending are important—amounts, purposes, and expected returns. So is an understanding of operating costs today and into the future. Depending on their models, investors will be estimating earnings, cash flow, and dividend payouts. Chapter 9 on valuation and Chapter 10, which covers the analytical process, detail further the information desired by analysts and investing model makers in each of these subsets.

WORKING WITH RESEARCH AS PROGRAM BASIS

Companies commit their investment rationale to paper as the basis for seeking out investors of like mind. The match-ups can be found in various ways:

- investors who favor the characteristics of the company (the "peer" group, as it is called);
- those investing in the same industry, and thus already having evaluated the industry; and
- investors with specific criteria (dividend payouts, P/E ratio levels, or earnings momentum) that are realized in the company.

A number of sources are available to identify specific institutions that are candidates to be investors in the company by virtue of their interests. The required SEC 13(f) filing serves as a base reference. It requires U.S. institutions with $100 million or more in equities to break out those holdings company-by-company, also giving the number of shares. Suppliers are programming the

computer to produce institutional shareholder lists from this base
13(f) data, refined by their own value-added input to suit virtually
any match-up set of parameters. Companies can buy lists showing
their own institutional holdings, those of industry competitors, or
those of a pre-defined peer group.

The data can be used to track buy/sell patterns of any company thus identifying new holders, build-ups, or those selling portions or all the shares. That's just a broad description of how the
data is being "massaged" today as useful marketing research.
Companies buying these lists usually also receive some guidance
in making contact with the institutions, for example, the name of
the analyst following their industry if there is one, the director of
research, or possibly names of portfolio managers. Phone numbers
are included. The data also indicates the size of the institution, in
amount of assets under management and percentage invested in
equities.

In advancing the state of the list-producing science, suppliers
have been adding to the data from the 13(f) filings. Their goals
have been to make the information more accurate and timely since
not all institutions are faithful to the SEC rule and some investment
managers have been able to opt out of the requirement by claiming
customer confidentiality. Also noteworthy: The investor relations
vendor corps has developed retail broker lists. More on list services
is found in Chapter 10 on institutional relations and Chapter 11 on
making headway in the retail segment.

Companies can do a lot of the research themselves, working
from directories that profile institutions, especially investment
management firms, banks, and insurance companies. The directories typically show the amount of equity being managed, describe
the investing style, and provide some names and phone numbers
for contact guidance. Also available are profiles of private and
public pension funds, including the names of investment managers, and often indicating the extent of passive (indexing) management. Most useful of these directories are the annual issues of
Pensions & Investments and *Institutional Investor* and the annual
"Directory of Pension Funds and Their Investment Managers."

Applying the principles of good marketing, investor relations professionals are well advised to use their lists of shareholders and prospects as the basis of attitude and perception research before beginning an actual contact/relationship building program. The broader the interview base, the more productive will be the research. It is advisable to interview brokerage analysts who follow and don't follow the company, brokers who have and haven't researched and put clients into the stock, current individual shareholders, institutions holding and not holding shares. It is advisable to interview analysts and brokers of regional and national firms, to cover institutions of various type and size—banks, insurance companies, pension fund sponsors, and investment management firms that are large and small, local and national.

The interviews together are designed to gain the views of professionals following and not following, investing and not investing in the company.

The research serves four valuable purposes.

1. It helps the company understand the attitudes, perceptions and misperceptions of current shareholders, institutional prospects, analysts, and brokers. The research gives the company a true picture of the extent to which it is understood accurately, the degree of misconception and negative bias, the degree of positive attitude and perception.

2. What is learned from the research becomes part of the communications. Information missing in making an accurate valuation of the company is provided. The job of overcoming misperception and negative attitude has a better chance of succeeding because it will be tackled with a true understanding of the underlying sources of the problem.

3. The research becomes a feedback tool in gaining management support. It helps quantify the investor relations program. The real purpose is to help management see the value of the program and commit to it, based on knowing first-hand how the investment community views the company. It also provides a fact-based foundation for getting management's

agreement on the specific information that's needed (and missing) to do the job.

4. It starts to warm up the audience, by sending a message that the company is planning to be more proactive in its relationships. Hopefully, it starts to create some interest and enthusiam. At minimum, it establishes some early dialogue.

USING THE COMMUNICATIONS VEHICLES

A four-step process gets a company to the point of rolling out its investor relations program.

1. The basis of the company's equity valuation is defined and understood internally, committed to paper, and keyed to the value drivers. Management understands its components of value and develops a sense of the gap between its intrinsic and current market value.

2. Through research, the investment universe is dissected into palatable pieces—the logical targets of a communication/ contact program, based on their existing stake in the company and on being able to define good reasons for them to develop an investing interest. They include brokerage research analysts, current individual and institutional investors, prospective institutional investors and brokers.

3. Benchmark research ferrets out present attitudes and knowledge levels of the targeted investors, analysts and brokers, serving as documentation for gathering management support and determining the message theme and specific contents of the information base.

4. The valuation story and specific information points are prepared for presentation, utilizing the best communications vehicles available to reach the targeted audiences. No doubt the investment community interviews will influence the valuation story and help determine the most important information points. The interview likely revealed some

meeting of the minds on the value drivers and their present/ potential impact. From the interviews, some changes may occur in the content of the information stream. Certainly, the company will learn a great deal about how to cast and detail the information.

The trend in investor relations is to focus communications vehicles on certain audiences. This is consistent with a marketing thrust. Fact books are written for detail-hungry analysts. Fact sheets are investable-summary quick takes for busy brokers. More and more, direct response mailings are being designed and written to appeal narrowly within a segment. Audiences for financial meetings are being organized more tightly; the ideal is to get down to one-to-one sessions with the leading brokerage analysts or serious institutional holders or prospects.

Investor relations can be called a winnowing down process. In fact, it can be considered a two-dimensional communications strategy, with companies well advised to be conducting both broad market educational and specific targeted communications simultaneously and continuously. For a public company, there is no end to the desire to attract new investors, whether they be individuals or institutions. Buying and selling shares is ongoing.

Often, the potential for broad and narrow exposure exists within the same category of communications vehicle. Plus, the definition of broad and narrow is contained within each. Contrast advertising in *The Wall Street Journal* with the *Institutional Investor* magazine or *Pensions & Investments*. There is a significant narrowing process, but even at the narrowest point, the exposure is broad. But first comes the evaluation of advertising as a communications vehicle compared with such other exposure opportunities as media coverage, direct mail, and face-to-face meetings.

Similarly, a story that sheds favorable light on a company in *The Wall Street Journal* or the *New York Times* will reach a bigger, more diverse audience than a story in *Pension World*. However, if the contents of each story can be influenced, both the general awareness and specific information objectives can be accomplished.

The effect is obvious from mailings of fact sheets or article reprints to all 65,000 retail brokers in the country, versus those in metro Philadelphia or at a brokerage firm that just published a favorable report on the company. A large capitalization company (or even a smaller one) may believe the cost in a national mailing is justified in building up broker awareness, creating a mailing list of brokers "qualified" by their responses, or in preparing invitation lists for upcoming meetings across the country. The option to a national program is to build the following market by market, probably starting at home and expanding in concentric circles.

Financial meetings can be used to winnow contacts from the missionary to the one-to-one levels. One option for companies in building contacts and relationships is to address sell/buy side analyst/portfolio manager professional society and broker group meetings or host their own. Attendance may be from 10 to 110. These sessions start relationships that often grow to the point where the analyst or fund manager wants to be alone with corporate senior executives, gaining information exclusively by asking exclusive questions. Analysts and investors alike are seeking to distinguish themselves from the pack in their search to be first to discover a new investment idea or favorable new aspect to an important value driver.

Annual reports are opportunities to be broad or narrow in scope. Or both. A well-conceived, information-laden, designed-to-read-and-impress annual report can satisfy simultaneously current and potential investors, analysts and brokers. The many components of the report give a company room to appeal to the divergence of audiences by using:

corporate strategy in the letter for the benefit of all readers;

a quantitative operational review of the company that includes the breakout of vital financial detail by business units; and

quantification in the management discussion and analysis that provides the information base for analysts and investors in making good projections of performance.

Companies are tending to include the essence of the required SEC 10-K report in their shareholder annual reports.

Electronic information dissemination has emerged as one of the leading investor relations tools. It too can have a wide reach or be aimed precisely. The public relations newswires cover the media and numerous sell and buy side houses. However, companies can concentrate the distribution to brokerage firms and institutions by subscribing to *First Call* (a brokerage-started information service that includes both broker and corporate originated information). *Telescan* offers a targeted institutional/analyst opportunity. Facsimile service makes the distribution totally selective. The combination of these tools is causing companies to rethink their method of supplying quarterly earnings information to important analysts and investors. Multi-page releases that include balance sheet and segment data are being sent via facsimile, First Call, and the wires for fast arrival. They are virtually rendering the traditional quarterly report obsolete, at least for the professional investment portion of the corporate audience that wants complete information quickly.

On-line data retrieval is a vital information source of investors. Thus, it is becoming critical for companies to check the accuracy of these electronic databases. With investors relying so much on computer data for computer models, a company can fail to make the pre-screened candidate list because of inaccurate financial numbers in the database.

The carefully planned, goal-oriented marketing approach built around valuation helps investor relations directors sort through the exploding number of outside services available, all able to add something useful, but not necessarily representing the most productive ways of spending money or achieving the desired results. Companies can more readily evaluate the benefits of direct mail, information dessimination, target list development, and other services. There is a tendency by companies to try these activities, without a game plan, then not follow up on them. They should be part of a program, not the program itself. Or, companies buy the service, then don't use it or maximize its use, because they're not sure how to do that. Tailored mailing lists are an example.

TWO HYPOTHETICAL CASE HISTORIES

The application of activities can be seen in two hypothetical case histories that illustrate how to run productive investor relations programs at a large and small market capitalization company.

Base profile of the large capitalization company: Market cap of $4 billion, with over 100 million shares outstanding and 37,000 shareholders, most of them individuals, who collectively hold less than a quarter of the common stock. The stock is in the Standard & Poor's 500 index and is seen mainly as a value play by institutional investors using active management strategies. The company is followed closely by better than half of the industry analysts, with the stock viewed as a hold or buy/hold for long-term appreciation and dividend income. The divided payout is satisfactory.

Primary investor relations objectives:

1. keep those brokerage analysts close and fundamentally positive by giving them opportunities to bring something of value to the buy side;
2. continue to add sell-side coverage one-by-one, targeting the analysts individually;
3. establish direct contact with all the leading institutional holders;
4. broaden the institutional base by reaching out to specific institutions in a pre-determined targeted group;
5. maintain contact and encourage access with existing shareholders through a consistent communications flow; and
6. increase individual ownership by concentrating on segments that can be reached intelligently and efficiently.

These objectives call for a program that is focused on information quality and selective contact on the analyst/institutional side.

Building and maintaining relationships are the key, expanding the number as the program ensues. The most important qualification for the investor relations people is to be highly knowledgeable across the board. That means being part of the inner information circle internally and knowing how to use information effectively on the outside, with analysts and investors—the latter resulting from understanding their needs and wants, based on their analytical techniques and investing methods.

The research base includes the various tools to identify current institutional holders, including those with their shares beneficially held by a brokerage firm or bank; and institutions that are logical prospects by virtue of their investment strategies or present industry/peer group following. The company has decided to go after the institutional market at two tiers: the biggest, most respected active managers with methods matching the company's investment characteristics; and small firms, managing between $100 and $200 million in equities, approaching this segment city by city, working from research that shows some base familiarity with the company.

The investment story is being built around the company's valuation and programs to improve it. The company has worked with a valuation management consulting firm and is slanting the information base toward the value drivers—the components of cash flow and earnings.

Prime communications vehicles are in-person and telephone contacts. Meetings tend to be individual, or in regular forums, such as quarterly discussions of earnings right after they are announced. The company has identified corps of smaller investment management firms in 10 cities and is visiting them, hosting small group luncheons and setting up individual appointments. Major institutional holders in the cities are being seen during the same trips.

The company also plans to address the Financial Analysts Federation chapters in a half-dozen markets where peer group holdings are evident, also arranging one-to-one meetings with a number of current shareholders in each city.

Facsimile, First Call, the public relations wires, and on-line databases become important sources of the complete set of financials.

The company is following a line of reasoning with the retail segment that is consistent with the attitudes of many large capitalization businesses. It goes like this. An institutional majority is seen as inevitable and desired, since the institutions make the trades and set the stock price. Institutional domination, however, can be frightening, because it suggests control—expressed potentially in a number of ways: deciding the outcome of a takeover quest, causing downside stock price volatility, proposing, and passing certain governance measures.

These and other concerns are motivating larger companies to test and conduct selective investor relations programs aimed at retaining/encouraging individual ownership of stock. Their goals and programs seek to be realistic: stop the erosion of the ratio of individuals to institutions or improve it modestly by concentrating on groups that can be reached and are inclined to listen. The rationale in most cases is a special reason to invest in the company: employees, suppliers, customers, residents of the community, professionals in the same industry as the product line (doctors, in the case of a health care company), wealthy individuals with substantial stock portfolios.

The tools for reaching and influencing them involve:

1. devices to facilitate or encourage ownership such as employee and customer stock-purchase incentive plans and automatic dividend reinvestment programs;

2. targeted contact with the channels of influence that include retail brokers, bank trust officers, and certified financial planners; and

3. persuasive communications through such vehicles as high media visibility, advertising, mailings, and effective use of company-originated publications and audio/video materials. A list of communications paths also must include participation in investor forums and clubs such as the National Association of Investors Corporation (NAIC).

In our hypothetical case history, the company has chosen an ESOP (Employee Stock Ownership Plan); is a corporate member of NAIC, takes part in the fairs and takes advantage of the club's stock selection guide in helping members evaluate the company as an investment; has a dividend reinvestment plan, set up to also encourage new ownership; conducts an active media relations program; and works selectively at maintaining/building broker relationships through efforts aimed at identifying the top producers in terms of equity commissions.

Case history number two is a small company with a market capitalization of about $125 million, 7 million shares outstanding, and some 16,000 shareholders. Around 10 percent of the stock is held by institutions. There are four market makers, with varying degrees of enthusiasm. The company is seen as a possible growth stock, but with a short track record.

The company's investment story can be attractive to institutions. A leading technology position in a product line with excellent growth potential suggests bounding gains in revenues in the future. Management has won high regard. Additional capital needs are apparent, to support continuing research, plant capacity, and an expanding marketing/sales group.

Principal investor relations goals are:

1. increase sell-side coverage, targeting retail and institutional firms;
2. add market makers and make the present ones more active;
3. increase institutional holdings broadly, while finding those that like emerging growth small cap stocks; and
4. widen broker awareness and coverage.

The company begins by concentrating on regional brokerage coverage—analytically and in terms of building broker interest. Because it is a regional company, regional brokerage coverage is the logical starting point. It serves as entrée to the local retail broker community. Saturated regional coverage also will seep into the institutional side. A wide regional following tends to attract one or two industry analysts with national firms. Companies can help that process by mailing regional reports and recommendations to the national wire houses. As the program rolls out, regional expansion of the brokerage community occurs contiguously.

Institutional contact also begins locally and fans from there. The company uses research to help identify banks, insurance and money management firms, get a handle on their investing styles and learn the names of key contacts—analysts, portfolio managers, and the chief investment officer. Smaller investment firms may not have analysts, some of the firms may not identify their fund managers, but every listing contains at least one name as a starter in the contact process. As suppliers and investor relations consultants fine tune their methods of gaining information, the lists are getting increasingly better. Of special interest are names of institutions with special small cap company funds.

Three avenues of contact are taken:

1. mailings of pertinent information only (annual and interim reports, earnings releases, financial material, and operational news) to carefully developed brokerage analyst, institutional, and broker target lists as an awareness-building step;

2. one-by-one phone calls to selected targets in efforts to set up appointments; and

3. hosting meetings with analysts and brokers and making appearances at their societies. The effort is fairly aggressive. Because they're not as well known or aren't seen as strong players in their industries, small companies have to be much more aggressive in doing the missionary work—creating awareness, drumming up interest, and establishing contacts.

Mailings also can include those prepared by professional direct mail firms. These can be national, but that can be expensive for a small company and may also be inefficient, since there is little pre-established recognition. They also can be regionalized or even centered on a single brokerage firm; these fit better into a regional approach to communication and contact. The company has chosen to develop its own fact sheet, mailing it to brokers and investment firms regionally in support of its contact program as it expands.

It also is conducting a proactive media visibility program, concentrating on the regional business press and trade publications in its industry. National business story opportunities are a goal; the storylines are in place and the contact process is underway.

Valuation is not so much the foundation of the investment story of smaller companies. More likely to be the basis of communication is the company's inherent strengths, distinguishing capabilities, and, if there is one, its franchise. Many of the new "glamour" companies have come forth with a marketing breakthrough—a product that captures the consumer fancy. Technology innovation and smart management are the keys for the company in our case history.

Senior management is leading the communications charge. While investor relations skills are important, the chief executive, financial, and/or operating officers must be active participants in the communications. With many small companies, the CFO or CEO takes on the principal spokesperson role, aided by investor relations expertise. The analysts and investors must see senior management in action.

MEASURING THE PROGRAM

Management, of course, wants and usually demands some method of measuring any program. Investor relations is measurable, and the yardsticks certainly have a chance of being seen as valid by management. It is important to measure investor relations progress and results for a second reason: as a gauge to determine what works, what doesn't work, and why. Because investor relations deals with attitude, perception, information flow and receptivity, personalties and so many other less-quantified, often downright intangible factors, the measurement process should be ongoing.

The fundamental measure is stock price. The investor relations role is in closing the information gap that causes present stock price to be less than intrinsic value. There's a certain boldness in suggesting that the investor relations process can help close that gap. The ability to do so is linked with the efficiency of the market for the company. If the market is efficient, the current price is the full value. The value is based on the ability of incumbent management to maximize the productivity of the assets. Thus, management has control over stock price, but since the market sets the price, it becomes critical for the company to communicate effectively. At least part of the efficiency of the market in pricing the stock fairly must be the result of the effectiveness of the corporate communications process.

Managements and their investor relations people become true partners in telling the valuation story: management by its deeds and investor relations by its words.

There is a caveat to this whole notion. It has to do with how much influence a company has over its stock price. Usually, the number given is about 20 percent. The remaining 80 percent or so influence comes in economic and market factors out of management control. The entire market may be rising or falling, because of inflation levels or interest rates, recovery/recession news, global competitive advantages/disadvantages and the like. Industries may be in or out of favor for similar reasons. Market conditions may override: Companies learned in October of 1987 and 1989 how hard it is to buck a falling market.

Valuation also is relative. Professionals are making decisions on how to invest their pools of money on a comparative basis—from a debt/equity mix based on macro economic conditions to the relative strengths of industries and relative strengths of companies within an industry. Investor relations professionals should be measuring their companies against the market, their industry and peer group: relative price to market, price to the S&P 500; and company by company, price to book value, and price to earnings. If the company is comparing favorably, investor relations is helping measurably.

Measurements also can be found in results of direct contact: an analyst who becomes familar with the company or decides to follow it after the contact was made; increase in the number of institutions holding shares, with their interest traced to the initial investor contacts; more brokers putting their clients into the stock, or more stock being purchased by individuals from brokers. Increased analyst following and institutional holding can be tracked and recorded. It probably will be difficult to quantify broker response, short of follow-up phone contact. Investor relations consultants, however, are doing just that, in justifying the expenditures for an aggressive broker contact program.

Investor relations influence can be seen in an even information flow that creates an even level of investor knowledge about the company. The reflections of this are consistent volume, low volatility, steady stock prices.

Investor feedback is a valuable measurement tool. It should provide both attitudinal and fact-based enlightenment. The benchmark survey (taken before the program starts) is useful in measuring change as a result of better communication. The ongoing investment community research seeks to check attitudes, perception and knowledge about the company. Hopefully, attitudes are becoming more positive and perceptions more accurate as information grows. If things aren't changing or if they're turning sour, the research is providing an important basis for finding out why. Management credibility might be low. The communications effort might be failing. Or, the company may be unrealistic in its sense of value.

From planning and research to execution and measurement, information is the common ground. Investor relations is the marketing of information.

Two Basic Concepts That Shouldn't Get Away

There are a couple of tenets that investor relations people should have in their minds at all time, no matter how sophisticated the investing and communications processes may become. One is the simple concept that investors want to buy low and sell high. Hopefully, they'll be motivated or content to hold, satisfied with total return as stock price appreciates and dividends are paid, in the case of dividend-paying companies. The other is that buying interest pushes up stock price and selling pressure drives it down.

The notions are always at work in valuation. While closing the gap between fair and under valuation has become the investor relations charge, some room to raise value is always desirable. Long-term "value" investors are looking for undervalued stocks. If a company is truly fairly valued, the near term probably holds more sellers than buyers. Of course, most companies believe they're undervalued, which seems to be the case if the evidence from price run-ups in takeovers is accurate.

The real investor relations charge is to help build a nucleus of investors who understand the company's fundamental strengths and have confidence in management's capabilities so that they'll hold the stock, recognizing that its intrinsic worth will be reflected in rising stock prices when economic and market factors are driving up the market, and its price will weather storms caused by economic, market and political upheaval, recovering and advancing in price as conditions once again improve. Stocks have passed the test of time in showing their superiority as an investment.

The buy low, sell high and supply/demand equation principles apply in the short-term investing reality that has come with increased institutional holdings. Corporations and their investor relations practitioners can react opportunistically to this reality. Institutions that sell quickly when quarterly results dip or the market declines or is poised to drop create buy-low opportunities for investors who are inclined to hold shares longer, supporting management's strategies. Companies replace their quick-draw investors with patient ones. The investor relations job is to make sure the marketplace is fully informed, especially those investors fond of buying low and holding on for the ride.

9

Valuation as Basis of the Investor Relations Practice

Corporations began to embrace the concept of *valuation* in the pricing of their equities in the 1980s. Variations of the phrase "maximizing shareholder value" started appearing in annual reports and became the focus of presentations before analyst and investor groups. The "shareholder value" theme took off so fast, in fact, that it drew criticism from investors, judging the actual valuation efforts and communications of some companies to be more a case of jumping on the bandwagon than formulating strategies that really will result in higher returns.

However, the concept clearly is established. Valuation is sure to be a corporate priority of the 1990s. Managements are learning how investors calculate value and are pursuing specific activities shown in research studies to elevate value by virtue of winning investor favor. Valuation strategies and *share price management* are being taught by a number of consulting firms who have gained prominence through their work.

The mission of these firms is to show managements how sophisticated investors arrive at a company's intrinsic value in making investment decisions. Valuation has two definitions, or dimensions, which are closely related. In its broadest context, valuation is the fundamental process investors use in determining a company's worth in deciding whether it is a good investment at its present price. The investors' objective is to find companies with stock prices currently under their *intrinsic value* (full worth, based on the company's assets being managed to perform at their maximum productivity). Undervalued stocks are bought, while overvalued stocks are sold. In practice, there are many valuation models. They deal with projecting returns from the investment (dividend income and appreciation).

In the second dimension, valuation involves value enhancement—the corporate actions that produce superior returns as measured by investor models dealing with growth in earnings, cash flows, and book value. Value enhancement is acheived by productive use of the existing assets and new investments that earn returns above their cost.

The primary role of the consultant is to help companies direct their principal actions toward heightened share value. No two consultants have the same exact philosophy or approach to teaching valuation. Some come at it from academic evidence, some from years of investing practice, and some from the major consideration of the company's fundamental need for capital and desire to acquire it at the lowest possible cost. Most valuation strategies combine all of these elements.

Consulting advice also covers the investor relations aspects of valuation. Here, the work of investor relations consulting firms picks up the process, although valuation and investor relations consultants overlap, in both directions. Generally, the role of valuation consultants is to put the investor relations function into the big picture, which can be of help to investor relations people who may be laboring to convince senior executives of the potential of a proactive communications program. A number of investor relations consultants have taken the lead in the last decade in helping companies get across their "valuation story" to institutional investors.

The investor relations component of the valuation process has four interrelated, major responsibilities:

1. To understand how the investment community determines the company's valuation;

2. To communicate what the company believes should be the basis of its valuation;

3. To correct any investor misperceptions about the company and its important primay valuation parts; and

4. To communicate all major news that will affect valuation.

NEGATIVE VIEWS ON VALUATION

Valuation, as an emphasis point of corporate strategy, is not free of criticism. Chief concern among business observers is that management can become myopic, namely, running the company for investor satisfaction through higher securities' values. The question becomes: "Are these actions going to make the company stronger and more successful over time or will the activities end up being mistakes because they weren't properly thought through or directed in some kind of rush to enhance value?" Critics say that companies should be managed for the long-term benefit of a group of constitutencies, not mainly or exclusively for the investors.

Time, of course, reveals the answers. Those answers come in the form financial results: of earnings that satisfy investor expectations and continue to reward shareholders with dividends; and cash flow levels that enable the company to continue reinvesting in programs that will maintain positive momentum—programs like new technology and product development or other operational-enhancing activities or quality acquisitions.

Companies reward investors through management strategies and practices that maintain a stream of higher earnings year after year and increased cash flows in order to run and expand the business. That reward comes in the form of dividends and incentives to buy the stock, which results in a higher stock price. Investors reward companies with a higher value for their securities, which results in a lower cost of capital.

Two other concerns emerge in corporate concentration on valuation. Not all institutional investors appreciate being "instructed" on how to value the company. These institutions say that only they know the market, investment strategies, and their particular models well enough to set the valuation parameters, plug in the data and set the fair price. These investors are saying: "You give us the facts, we'll calculate the value."

The investor relations response to that should be "fine." By understanding more about valuation from both the investment and corporate sides, investor relations people can do a better job of providing the most useful information and interpretation.

Controversy about valuation also swirls within the investor relations field. Valuation seems to be an idea being embraced by the newer breed of investor relations practitioner who is coming at the proposition with a financial logic. Among the more veteran practitioners, there is still some belief that the investor relations function is broader—serving the shareholders well and encouraging investment throughout the investing universe by being a reliable information resource. They argue that the role is best fulfilled by expanding the information base and information flow, not by quantifying value and concentrating on it.

ARGUMENTS FOR A VALUATION APPROACH

Still, investors, in general, are happy to see companies focusing on their intrinsic worth. Investors are pushing the notion so companies will concentrate more of their energies and resources on improving their value.

While investors can encourage valuation-building strategies, economics ultimately determine their real success. The acquisitions either add or subtract from earnings. The technology expenditures do or don't increase market share. New plant capacity does or doesn't earn a return above the cost of capital. Dividend increases continue, stop, or the payout declines based on operations and the need for cash.

Proponents of following the valuation process see everyone and every aspect of the economy benefitting ultimately. The valuation proposition is based on achieving long-term growth. The thinking goes this way. By concentrating on valuation, executives make better decisions about investment and management of their companies. Improving the company's worth for the benefit of investors has a very interesting side benefit—it produces a better business.

Evidence is available to show that the valuation emphasis of the last few years is improving corporate performance. Decisions are being based on more quantitative and qualitative data. Accountability for results is being demanded and received. Results are quantified and rewarded. Rewarding performance that produces shareholder gain with raises, cash, stock bonuses and other forms of compensation serves as a healthy incentive for managers. A company's competitive position improves. The economy strengthens. As a result, all the constituencies of the corporation benefit, not only the shareholders.

HOW VALUE IS DETERMINED

Valuation methods recommended by consultants and used by investors tend to have long-term horizons. The methods are prescribed by and for active portfolio managers, although indexers freely take advantage of the valuation-based stock prices that are represented by the companies in the index (such as the S&P 500). The value creation approach of The Alcar Group, for example, uses discounted cash flow principles, just as the asset-value investing model of Stein Roe & Farnham uses discounted cash flow techniques to measure a company's return on investment. Advisors and investment managers in both firms describe the components of cash flow and the components that constitute the essential ingredients of the return on investment as "value drivers." The term was first used by Alfred Rappaport, the Leonard Spacek Professor of Accounting and Information Systems at Northwestern University, in his book, *Creating Shareholder Value.*

The basis of a company's valuation is its *return on investment* (ROI) or its ability to earn returns above its cost of capital. The higher the return above the hurdle rate for managing the capital, the higher the valuation. ROI is the chief measure of valuation, focused on the amount of new investment projected returns, and returns on existing assets. It is a combination of returns earned on underlying assets and returns projected to be earned from new investments.

The return on investment is measured in the discounted cash flow number. In the *Stein Roe asset-value investing model*, the value of the asset is the amount of cash flow net of corporate taxes and discounted for risk, inflation, and investor taxes. In the *Alcar value-creation model*, the expected cash flows cover the forecasted period (the life span of the investment) plus a "residual" value for productive life after the investment has been paid off. Thus, the investment should earn returns greater than the cost of capital.

Cost of capital is important to both companies and investors. For companies, the cost of capital includes the risks of the economy that influence the growth rate of the investment and the premiums to be paid for investor taxes and inflation (including interest). Thus, the cost of capital includes both the cost of equity and debt. Investors make decisions, comparing the risk/return equations of various instruments. The standard measuring stick seems to be the earnings rate of a risk-free security, most often identified as a long-term government bond. Investors also discount the cash flow on the basis of risk, inflation, and taxes.

Cost of capital changes continuously and companies are limited in their ability to control it. In their pursuit of low-cost capital, however, companies have become more active in the global financial markets, believing that the cost of capital varies across continents and countries—in North America, Europe, or Asia. The analysis applies also to differences in the cost of debt and equity, giving companies opportunities to develop strategies and find choices in meeting their capital funding needs in the most cost-economic basis.

Companies do have some control in improving their return on investment and shaping their long-term growth through technological breakthroughs, marketshare gains, low-cost manufacturing, smart marketing practices, and investments in the future that end up garnering returns above capital costs. They also can dispose of poorly performing assets as a way of increasing value.

These various operational improvement activities produce some of the key value drivers that make up the Alcar cash flow model. The five main ones are *sales growth, operating profit margin, incremental fixed capital investment, incremental working capital investment* (to generate future sales), and *cash income for taxes.* These factors result in a definition of cash flow: cash from sales and operating profit margins minus outflows for capital investments and taxes.

Value drivers also are defined as the strengths that make a company tick. These include highly successful brand name products, the company's revered reputation, and a "franchise" position resulting from an exclusive patented technology or license. Certain consumer companies lead markets because of the power of their brands, for example. PepsiCo and Coca Cola dominate the soft-drink industry, for example. Quaker Oats identifies its brand name products as key drivers in its valuation.

Dividends are seen as a major component of value by many investors. But there are two schools of thought on the value on dividends. In one, dividend income wins a high rating in the total return picture that also includes price appreciation. Dividends are a source of income. In the other school, dividends are not so desirable because they penalize the ability to appreciate the stock price. The theory says the money paid in dividends could be put to more productive use through wise investment. Companies also incur a tax penalty by paying dividends, which could have an overall negative effect on total investor return.

Dividend income always will be a part of the valuation process because dividend income always will be liked by certain investors—both individual and institutional. Income is an objective of many investors; the ability to reinvest dividends to increase the size of the holding and gain the returns of compounding is favored by many other investors. Studies indicate that dividends have accounted for one third of total investment return in recent years, and further, that "dividend" stocks have outperformed "capital gain" stocks since the 1986 tax law change, which equated the tax rates on dividends and capitalization by reducing the rate on dividends while hiking it on capital gains. Of course, the capital gains tax doesn't apply until the stock is sold, another good reason for being a long-term investor. Unfortunately, the tax applies both to the real and inflationary gains during the holding period. In periods of high inflation, this "inflation tax" can seriously erode capital.

WAYS OF MEASURING VALUATION

Institutions and sell-side analysts have been moving to discounted cash flow (DCF) analysis as the basic method of measuring the value of a company's securities—equity and debt. It is taking its place alongside earnings as the two leading methods; earnings per share (EPS) has been the standard for decades. DCF proponents argue that cash flow is a true number and the real measure of a company's worth. It forms a realistic basis for projecting future performance. They also argue that EPS is essentially a historical number that can be manipulated in accounting models.

As discounted cash flow grows as a way of measuring value, earnings remain an important tool of models of active investors searching for growth and value stocks. The consensus estimates of future earnings per share continues to be a critical piece of information in the investment analysis and decision. The price/earnings ratio is not about to disappear in measuring expected return in a dividend discount model or comparing return expectations against the market.

On the debt side, cash is fundamentally what matters—cash to cover the interest and principal, pay the operating bills, and invest in the future.

VALUATION AS A BASIS OF STRATEGIC CORPORATE ACTION

Valuation as a process is useful in managing the company as well as putting a price tag on its securities. In fact, the two can be made inseparable. Internally, managing individual business units to maximize cash flow defines executive accountability and also ties it to shareholder value. Decisions to allocate capital to fund expansion programs within each business unit depend on accurate calculations of the cash flow projections made by the managers. Executives are compensated on their ability to deliver those cash flow projections. The cash flow orientation tends to rekindle an entrepreneurial spirit throughout the company. Real targets can be set at each functional level—sales, marketing, manufacturing, as well as the business unit itself. Many companies have divided into smaller business units as a way of extending the entrepreneurial accountability to more managers.

KEY VALUE DRIVERS SHOWN IN INVESTMENT BEHAVIOR

Even though investors are shown to reward companies for strategic actions undertaken to improve their intrinsic value as a business enterprise, research conducted in 1989 by Mitchell & Company indicates that what constitutes the basic valuation of each company is more complex and deeply seeded than we might believe. The firm's study concentrated on 75 large capitalization companies (over $5 billion in revenues) and calculated the results company by company rather than ganging them into generalized conclusions. It also covered 10- to 15-year periods for each company to establish definitive patterns of corporate and investor behavior. Primary reason for the research was to shed more light on what truly determines stock price, not so much what conventional wisdom suggests or what appear to be the leading factors in the value equation based on the use of the most popular models.

   In taking valuation to another level, the research was designed to give companies more information in conducting value-enhancing programs and moving further into "share price management." The research indicates that investor perceptions of a company's value are strongly rooted and well understood. For this reason, even though companies are in a position to change fundamental perceptions that can lead to higher valuation, actually doing so takes substantial action. One program, in isolation, usually has little effect, according to the study. Where valuation change did occur, the company had carried out from two to four significant programs.

Considered to be the key corporate activities that can have a positive impact on valuatio in a share price management endeavor are:

acquisitions of businesses with strategic linkage to the company's strengths;

divestitures of operations dragging down profitability and key ratios;

share repurchases of sufficient quantity to signal shareholders of management's confidence in growth prospects;

partial public offerings of highly performing subsidiaries;

dividend increases above the trend of the market or industry;

cost reduction programs that produce massive savings; and

recapitalizations, typically occurring in troubled situations and bolstering investor optimism as a step in the right direction.

In addition, the Mitchell study revealed an absence of patterns within industries and among a list of leading stock price determinants. One major intent was to find correlations among valuation-building components in industries or certain types of companies. Analyzed in the study were 11 widely accepted valuation factors:

earnings per share (EPS);

free cash flow;

return on equity (ROE);

book value;

revenues;

dividends;

costs;

selling prices;

contracts;

backlogs; and

interest rates.

Two conclusions: The leading variables differ among industries and no two companies in the same industry have the same primary factor.

The primary factor in 46 of the 75 companies was their book value. Well down the list were cash flow (for seven companies), then revenues, ROE, EPS, and dividends. The number one secondary factor for most companies was interest-rate sensitivity, but for very few companies were investor decisions based on the combination of book value and interest-rate sensitivity.

What does a study like this say about discounted cash flow and earnings per share? It gives them another dimension showing how they are used in the investment decision process. Earnings per share is an important variable to book value, cash flow, dividends, or return on equity in addition to being a basic measure in popular investing methods. It shows that, for many investors, only the earnings that are retained, and not written off, matter in estimating future results. Discounted cash flow is a bottom-line reality that is driving more and more investment models.

SHARE PRICE MANAGEMENT AS INVESTOR RELATIONS PRIORITY

As corporations concentrate capital resources and management energies on efforts to enhance value for investors, the role and opportunity for investor relations comes into sharper focus. Investor relations practitioners are in an excellent position to advise their companies and clients wisely by virtue of their relationships with the principal players in the investing process—institutional and individual investors, equity and debt analysts, institutional and retail brokers, traders, specialists, or market makers.

Two criteria are critical: That investor relations people really have quality relationships with investors and analysts based on mutual respect that results from being a reliable source of accurate and meaningful information, and that, if managements are committed to valuation strategies, they recognize the unique contribution that an effective investor relations function can make.

The second leads to the first, and the first makes the second possible. That's not just an idle play on words. The most talented and experienced investor relations practitioners will find it difficult to build mutually respectful rapport with analysts and institutional investors without the green light from management to share vital strategies and useful investment information. But, many managements need to be persuaded to be forthcoming by investor relations people who can demonstrate the benefits. In most cases, the best opportunities to do that are quantified situations, such as forecasting how influential investors will respond to a possible acquisition, share repurchase, change in dividend policy, or other planned valuation move.

Investor relations people bear the responsibility of making their jobs valuable to companies. There really isn't any debate on whether management or investor relations takes the lead in making that happen. While it certainly helps to have managements enlightened about the benefits of maintaining an informed investing universe, it is up to the investor relations professionals to show the way.

Executive attention to valuation offers a concrete path for investor relations to do exactly that. Valuation as a corporate priority is providing the investor relations function its best opportunity yet to demonstrate and elevate its own worth. In a heightened valuation environment, the investor relations role is two dimensional. Through its good capital markets contacts, the investor relations person can advise management on how investors are likely to react to specific valuation plans (that is, favorably or unfavorably), and to what degree, and he or she can communicate corporate strategies and programs that will have an effect on equity and debt values.

Investor relations people must bring extensive knowledge to these responsibilities. They must be able to dissect the investment community organizationally as the basis of knowing who to contact. They should have working relationships with these key players or be experienced enough to know how to develop these relationships expeditiously in becoming reliable sources of investor feedback to management and persuasive communicators of valuation programs. In fulfilling this dual role as analyzer of investor attitudes and perceptions, and information conduit between company and investment community, investor relations professionals must understand the company, capital markets, and investor needs as well as have a command of all the information—from the most technical to the broadest interpretative levels—and be facile and persuasive communicators.

Investor relations' opportunity is helping in closing the *value gap*—the difference between a company's current stock price and its intrinsic value. The gap presumes that the current stock price does not reflect the full value of the company—something most managements believe. Most investing models measure full value in the discounted cash flow projection, namely, the value of future cash flows. The value gap also suggests an inefficient market. The responsibility of filling the gap belongs with the company. It knows more than the market about its fundamental strengths and its next moves.

This brings us to the crux of the matter. There are a number of working scenarios. The first is that the company is valued fairly (it also can be overvalued), with pertinent corporate information fully absorbed into the marketplace and accurately reflected in the stock price. Second, the stock is valued fairly, as shown in the predominance of investor models, but the company doesn't agree. In this situation, the problem is not one of communication; investor expectation is below that of the company based on historical performance and an analysis of prospects. Or, third, the stock is under valued because:

1. the information hasn't been communicated effectively;
2. the information is only partially absorbed into the marketplace; or
3. the information carries an undeservedly low level of credibility.

In calculating their value, most companies conclude that their present stock price is less than the warranted value.

In the first and second scenarios, the investor relations function is probably doing the best job it can. In the various turns of the third scenario, some fault may lie with both investor relations and senior management. Undervaluation caused by undercommunication or lack of credibility can be laid at the doorstep of investor relations, whether investor relations, management, or both groups are at fault. It is incumbent on investor relations people to execute the communications process professionally: the right information to the right people, using the right channels. Getting these right is the toughest part of the investor relations job and the focus of much of this book. In general, the investor relations profession continues the tendency to not fully appreciate or comprehend the real information needs, or to create the proper communications vehicles. Management contributes to the problem by insisting on holding back important information, usually because it is competitively proprietary, or because the company's lawyers are concerned about possible disclosure inequities leading to suits.

Insufficient information can keep analysts and institutional investors away from small companies. It can raise credibility problems with small and large companies alike. Analysts and investors are forced to make their assumptions and buy or sell decisions with less information. When this leads to a negative surprise, or a development occurs that isn't anticipated, credibility is shattered. It isn't the investors' fault for poor analysis; it is the company's fault for being a poor information resource. The surprise can be either bad or good news. Institutions are just as unhappy about selling stock before the price rises on good news as watching the price decline on bad news.

But more important are the opportunities for companies and their investor relations people to influence analytical and investment views in a positive way. Fundamental analysis contains elements of science, judgment, intuition, and personality. Investment models depend on many pieces of information to help analysts and portfolio managers develop projections of future performance.

Companies can influence all the steps in the process: the science through good raw data, and the rest by a host of actions—knowing exactly what information to provide and how to explain it, responding quickly, recognizing and respecting an individual's request, demonstrating a desire to be candid, being seen as dependable. The benefits can be even greater for smaller, lesser-known companies where market inefficiency is higher.

Investor relations people can help their managements make good decisions that affect valuation by taking advantage of the research available or by adding to the science through their own research endeavors. Indeed, consultants are urging their corporate clients to conduct comprehensive research before taking any valuation action. It can be the difference in raising valuation, lowering it, or having no impact. Millions of dollars can be spent on valuation-improvement efforts with no pay off. The research doesn't necessarily guarantee the result, but it does bring forth historical evidence on how similar activities have fared at other companies, and reveals investor experience with such moves as shown in their reactions to buy or sell the stock or not buy the stock.

SCIENTIFIC PROCESS FOR SELECTING VALUE-ENHANCING ACTIVITIES

The Mitchell consulting group has channeled the science of pre-evaluating valuation strategies into a five-step process. All are mathematically constructed and quantitatively analyzed, based on behavioral science techniques. The first is to bring the long list of potential actions down to a working list of real options. Interestingly, the number of "permutations" of share-enhancing ideas that may or may not work can be in the billions when scrutinized microscopically against the variables and combinations of variables that can influence the outcome, according to the consulting firm. This first step is a simulated market test, with institutional investors and sell-side analysts reacting to various options; this simulation uses fundamental analysis techniques in working with the body of available "literature."

Next, the consulting firm recommends researching the historical impact of key value factors on the company's stock price. This is the research mentioned earlier in this chapter. A 10- to 15-year study should quantify the effect of such value factors as discounted cash flow, earnings per share, book value, revenues, and so forth on the company as the basis of projecting their relationship and impact in each of the proposed valuation-enhancing activities. For example, a company revealed as being book value sensitive is more likely to elevate value through a partial public offering of a successful subsidiary than a share repurchase. A buyback at prices above book value usually produces a price drop in the intermediate term.

Third, companies are encouraged to conduct extensive case history studies to document the results of the valuation programs being considered. Companies studied should be similar in performance, value correlations, and financial structure. The studies can help verify the odds for success or failure, define the patterns of successful companies, indicate the degree of impact that can be expected, and give managements confidence to proceed.

Fourth, companies should test the combined ideas with sell-side analysts, institutional portfolio managers, and substantial individual holders. Institutions not holding shares currently also should be covered, especially the leading institutions whose decisions tend to be emulated (the "lead steers" as they are called by consultant Joel Stern), and institutions with shares in peer (or industry) group companies. It is highly useful to gauge the reaction of potential investors. Mitchell's method is to calibrate current responses with past responses and their price change results in similar market conditions. The firm also tests the strength of responses compared with those for similar companies and the respondents' general preferences.

Last step is constructing a company-specific model that uses a mathematical formula in estimating stock price response to the various value-creation ideas, combining the fundamental analysis, case histories, investor attitudes, and historical stock sensitivities.

EXPERIENCE RATES INVESTOR REACTION TO VARIOUS VALUE-RAISING MOVES

Evidential information also is available on the results of various types of valuation programs. It has been shown that share repurchases must constitute a substantial percentage of the outstanding amount available (around 15 percent or more) to send a strong enough signal to investors of management's confidence in the company's future. The positive impact on earnings per share also is more meaningful.

Partial public offerings of successful divisions, subsidiaries or business units have been well received by investors. In many instances, these spinoffs reveal "hidden assets" that are outperforming the parent or have the potential to do so soon. Investors also recognize the improved performance that can result from the high incentive to succeed given the management group of the newly formed public company.

Spin offs also can boost the stock of the parent company. The division may have been seen by analysts and investors as dragging down valuation. Both operations are likely to perform better as a result of the separation. Or, the parent is seen as stronger by returning to a concentration on its core business. It is a "pure play."

Acquisitions have met with mixed investor reaction, chiefly because many have failed to produce targeted results or taken too long to do so. Thus, acquisitions tend to arouse investor skepticism, putting the onus on companies to prove their value. The best way to do that is to make better acquisition selections in the first place, then do a more effective job of integrating the new operations into the company. Managements are being seen now as doing a better job of both. The trend is away from acquisitions that diversify the company and toward those that strengthen the core businesses. Investors are much more tolerant of acquisitions that can be integrated economically into the existing operation. Conglomerization is out of favor; managements have been criticized for bad acquisitions that represented a poor use of reinvested earnings or worse yet, dangereous debt leveraging.

Now the idea is to make strategic acquisitions that strengthen the core business by adding technology, winning products, market share, low-cost production, management talent, in addition to boosting revenues immediately and brightening the profit picture, if not right away, certainly a short trek down the road. Companies seem to have learned the lessons of conglomerization, or making even one or two nonproductive acquisitions, and are doing their homework more carefully and quantitatively in selecting mostly synergistic candidates. The emphasis also is on integrating the acquired business into the corporation quickly and efficiently, avoiding earnings dilution, while reaping the operational rewards of synergism and financial benefits in the shortest time possible.

Divestitures and cost-reduction programs also can raise corporate securities' values, according to studies. But investor reactions to these efforts aren't likely to be as buoyant as some of the other activities, unless the moves themselves produce measurable financial gain—a divestiture that lops off a serious money loser or cutbacks that save millions of dollars without injuring growth prospects.

VALUE CREATION AS AN ONGOING PROCESS

Restructuring is evolving into valuation. Or, at least, the two are coming together. Many of the restructuring moves of companies in the 1980s are today's share price improvement actions—acquisitions, spin-offs, repurchases. Companies striving to improve their valuation by such deliberate acts are advised to study the evidence suggesting that more is better; strings of programs are greeted with more applause by investors than one-time performances. Thus, valuation improvement becomes a continuous process.

The evolution of restructuring into valuation improvement appears to be completing itself. Restructuring moves of the 1980s that were motivated as defenses against unwanted takeovers, are being replaced by carefully-planned activities designed to elevate valuation in the 1990s.

Many of the restructurings of the 1980s were aimed at breaking up conglomerates which were being assigned low valuation numbers and becoming targets of raiders or acquisition-minded companies. For many companies, the move was defensive and often hastily assembled, with the aid of investment bankers—and failed to prevent the takeover. For many other companies, the restructurings proved to be the start of a valuation process that continues today. Some of that higher valuation is the result of buying the pieces of those conglomerates that fit strategically into the core businesses, or even buying the entire company, then selling off the unwanted parts (at a profit) to corporations that can make strategic fits of their own.

The wave of takeovers and strategic acquisitions (some forced, some friendly) forged a second description of value—*alternate* or *bust-up value* (defining the total worth of a company divided into pieces for resale). *Intrinsic value* was coined by consultants to describe a fully valued company in investors' language and to separate it from the alternate or bust-up value. Investment banking firms made a lot of money in the 1980s by identifying companies that were candidates for acquisition and calculating their break up value, on the one hand, and advising companies on restructuring/valuation strategies that enabled them to grow independently and avoid being acquired, on the other hand. The mergers and acquisitions business began the 1990s in a state of decline, with a shakeout as investment banking firms cut back on the size of their operations. However, mergers and acquisitions are still a viable way for companies to grow and enhance their value. M & A activity will continue, albeit not at the pace of the 1980s, and not with the same hostile intensity.

Companies and their investor relations people struggle with the reality that bust-up values are higher than warranted values. The premium for a strategic acquisition or raid with intent to break up the company has run as much as 50 percent above the current stock price, in many instances, and can be 20 to 25 percent higher than the best calculations of instrinic value at the time of the proposed transaction. One explanation is that companies tend to undervalue themselves, at least to strategic buyers. That would also suggest that the parts are worth more than the whole, which supports the arguments against diversification and suggests the need for careful pending acquisition analysis.

Another explanation gives rise to a possible communications gap and opens opportunity for companies to do a more effective job of telling their valuation story. Does the research analyst at a brokerage firm assign one value to a company as a takeover/acquisition candidate and another value as an investment choice? Does a portfolio manager support a takeover premium at a certain price, while believing the company is worth less as an investment? Does this mean the analyst and investor believe the company's assets can be managed more productively by another management team or group of management teams, in a breakup? Many surveys indicate the answer is "yes" to all three questions.

There is a third explanation—that the price in certain takeovers, acquisitions, and leveraged buyouts was simply too high. The assets weren't worth the prices being paid for them, in terms of their present and future performance abilities. That would explain why analysts won't recommend fully or overvalued stocks for purchase and why investors won't pay more than intrinsic value. It would also explain why certain acquisitions—friendly, hostile, or part of a breakup of assets—proved disappointing to both managements and investors. In this third scenario, the game got out of control. Takeovers and some of the "friendly" acquisitions were strictly financial transactions; they were being made for the premiums, transactional costs, and high fees instead of being made to strengthen the operations of a company or benefit the economy as a whole. Greed was running well ahead of overall economic gain.

Theory would suggest that intrinsic and breakup value be the same. Perhaps they never will, but companies and their investor relations people can contribute to closing the gap. Certainly, the primary objective must be to convince investors that the present management is qualified above all others to maximize the value of the assets on a long-term basis. Investor relations people must have management's cooperation in that process in two ways: abiding by their investor relations people's best judgment on the specifics of the information flow; and respecting and using the feedback in making valuation decisions that result from close relationships with investors and analysts.

Most of all, investor relations professionals must demonstrate the value of what they bring to the management table.

Building Buy- and Sell-side Relationships

Technology and economics are changing the emphasis within the working structure of the investing process. Investors, especially institutions, but also including individuals, are becoming more involved with gathering the information they need in making buy/sell decisions or feeding data to their computer models. Brokerage research is still vital, but the institutions are cranking up their own in-house research capabilities once more and taking advantage of the many good electronic data services available.

In response to the institutional initiative and out of a desire to have more influence on who holds their shares, corporate investor relations people are giving equal emphasis to the sell and buy sides—establishing contacts and building relationships with brokerage analysts and brokers (the sell side) and institutional analysts and portfolio managers (the buy side). The investor relations charge is to influence the stock buy decision and to influence those key participants who influence the decision. Thus, it's logical to be in contact with all the players.

Institutions are gradually taking on more of the steps in the investing process—research/analysis, decision making, and order execution. This trend is being spurred by the institutions' ability to gather, assimilate, and actionize more information internally to continue to refine their computerized models as the basis of investment decision making, and to execute trades without brokerage involvement. Many institutions now have computerized trading capabilities superior to brokers. Many are using such third-party services as *Instinet* or *Bernard L. Madoff Investment Securities.*

Institutions see the steps toward independence as cost saving. Variously constructed, depending on the particular investment strategies of the institution, they're reading the brokerage research, buying computer-dispensed information and research, doing some or a significant amount of internal analysis, and making investment judgments or paying for the brain power of their computer modelers. The alternative has been the historical way of getting good information and executing trades, namely relying on brokerage firms, paying for the research directly in "hard" dollars or in "soft" dollars through the buy/sell transaction commissions.

Economics also impact the brokerage side. With commission income tumbling, the industry has been forced into reviewing its research/trading services. Meanwhile, institutions are complaining about the quality of both. The brokerage industry entered the 1990s in a tailspin as the fall-off in investment banking activity, resulting from slowdowns in mergers, acquisitions and takeovers, got together with the steady decline in securities commissions to throw the industry into financial crisis. In executing their own trades, institutions also are showing their distain for supporting investment banking activities of brokerage firms.

While the trends are real, they hardly constitute the whole story. In day-to-day operations among investment managers across America, the process is far more complex and mixed. Analysts continue to write research reports and make recommendations that are highly respected by institutions and serve as the basis of their decisions. The dramatic rise or fall of a company's stock price in reaction to an analyst's buy or sell recommendation provides ample proof. Brokers continue to push successfully the ideas of their leading industry analysts with institutional clients. Analysts are on the phone every day, discussing with institutional analysts and fund managers the strengths, weaknesses, and new developments within an industry or those concerning a company. And, they're not just sources of information; frequently, they're trying hard to be persuasive in convincing the institution to accept the investment recommendation, for example.

Obviously, sell-side research continues as a crucial component to the investing process and qualitative research and trading are critical to many institutions that have come to rely on the brokerage industry for both services. Some institutions now are willing to pay more in commissions to receive better stock trading execution from brokers. Unbundling the services may provide the economic answer. Institutions buy the services they need for real ("hard") dollars—research, order execution, or trading with capital—or they continue to acquire research for "soft" dollars by giving the brokerage firm the transaction business as well. Brokers still have a profit-producing revenue source.

HOW THE RELATIONSHIP IS EVOLVING

Despite the revenue slide, most of the fundamental research is still being done on the brokerage side. It is being used in making basic judgments and is contributing to the base data for the work being done by institutional analysts and portfolio managers who are utilizing their computerized investing models to make decisions. The sell side still has scores of analysts concentrating on one industry, following the every thought and move of a half-dozen or so companies.

In fact, as economics threaten to contract the sell-side research product, the role of the brokerage research/analysis takes on more value, even as it gets used less in day-to-day action. The real expertise on certain industries and companies resides on the sell side of the Street. Leading industry analysts will be counted on more for their specialized and in-depth knowledge of companies and their ability to interpret trends and developments accurately in assessing their effect on industries and the economy.

The brokerage research feeds into institutional research and investment modeling. One institutional analyst may cover three industries and 50 companies. These analysts certainly are doing less fundamental research and analysis than their brokerage counterparts. They're also doing less than they did 10 years ago. Cutbacks in research staffs among institutions occurred in the mid-1980s, as part of a restructuring and change of philosophy.

Again, technology and economics were at work. The picture that started to be formed then is the same picture that is enjoying the broad brush strokes of refinement today. Investment models took shape. Research and analysis were separating. The research was coming from the brokerage product and electronic databases. Institutional analysts were adding to it. The analysis was being done by the institutional analysts, investment committees, fund and portfolio managers, and the computer.

It's important to note, however, that as the 1990s were getting underway, there were definite indications of an increase in interest on the buy side to conduct more fundamental analysis. Driving the move may be institutional concerns about the depth and quality of brokerage research. Another motivator is the desire of individual investment managers, including banks and independent firms, to outperform their counterparts for competitive reasons. Evidence of the trend is being seen in the rise of direct contact with companies on the part of institutional analysts, and to some extent, portfolio managers. It's certainly a trend worth developing.

SELL-SIDE RESEARCH CONTRIBUTION DEPENDS ON INSTITUTIONAL NEED

Brokerage analysts are contributing to institutions' research and investment decision making in various degrees depending on the investment firm. The range is from total dependence on research—generated internally, externally, or in combination—to total dependence on the computer with indexing as the basis or with investment decisions being made quantitatively. Here is a quick study of how sell-side analysis is affecting the various institutional investing approaches.

There are numerous investment management firms that still believe firmly in the value of research; they practice active investing styles, searching mainly for value and growth stocks, or following the sector rotation or another investing method. Some of these firms have large internal research staffs who do virtually all of the research/analysis. Some supplement their effort with outside research.

Some firms equalize internal/external research; their analysts are doing fundamental research and gathering information and ideas from trusted brokers and analysts.

Some investment firms have one, two, or a handful of analysts. They collect data and investment ideas as the basis of their own research/recommendations and for direct use by portfolio managers.

Some firms have no analysts. The investment managers subscribe to electronic data services, study the research from brokerage houses, take calls from institutional brokers and analysts, and construct their portfolos, either mainly manually or mainly through the computer.

Some firms have learned how to combine quantitative investing methods with active investing styles. They establish quant databases to fit their investing strategies and methods—price/earnings ratio, dividend yield, or earnings momentum screens. The computer is programmed to rank companies based on the parameters. Active managers use their research/analysis capabilities in further evaluating the candidates.

Other firms virtually let the computer make the decisions. In their models, those stocks ranked above a certain line are "buys" while those below a certain line are "sells." Those in the middle continue to be tracked and may move up or down in the time ahead. Whether buys or sells are made depends on the portfolio construction and other factors that influence the decisions. These may involve industry over or under weightings, or even stock/bond/cash asset breakouts. These firms are buying electronic data such as the *Compustat* information package and *Zacks' consensus analyst earnings forecasts*. They're not talking with outside analysts much, if at all.

The last group consists of the indexers setting up their models, holding portfolios that replicate the performance of the chosen index, making buy and sell decisions, and hedging their portfolios with options and futures all in a timely manner to move cash/dividends or capture certain premiums. They're not in contact with brokerage analysts.

No matter what the investing style may be, performance is the goal. Indexing matches the most popular measurements of performance—the S&P 500 index being the domestic standard bearer. Indexing is being used primarily by public pension funds and banks and insurance companies in investing for their large pension fund clients and for their own accounts. The indexers' group also includes a handful of private investment managers.

Investment firms and banks utilizing quantitative and active styles are seeking an advantage in securing management contracts from pension funds, foundations, endowments, and other investors. An effective proprietary quant-based hybrid model is likely to have an edge; it will probably beat the S&P 500 performance most of the time. The active managers stand a better chance of putting more positive distance between their returns and those of the index, but only about 25 percent of them actually do outperform the index on average each year.

Economics ultimately will determine how viable the sell side can remain. The economics question is tied closely to how the sell/buy-side relationship unfolds.

The institutional perspective focuses on the quality of information and its sources. Institutions are relying more on outside data to feed their computer models by typically using a combination of services—brokerage reports, electronic data retrieval, for-purchase packages, corporate information, and such vital services as *First Call* and *Telescan*. How important the traditional brokerage information product will be in the future will depend on its quality and the quality of these other sources.

Clearly, there is an opportunity for companies to function as reliable sources of critical information and, thus, assume some of the information flow that has been coming from brokerage analysts; fill part of what is now seen as a brokerage information gap.

INSTITUTIONS EVALUATING COMPANIES AS INFORMATION RESOURCES

Companies are concentrating more of their investor relations effort directly on institutions as investors look more to companies for information. The true test of time is now underway. In the next few years, companies will determine whether they can establish themselves as reliable sources of needed investment information to institutions. To do so, managements must be forthcoming, companies must understand what information to provide and how to provide it. Investor relations practitioners must learn how to be effective information disseminators. Many are now, but the profession as a whole has a lot of work to do.

For that latter reason, institutions are complaining about the role of investor relations. They have two complaints:

1. investor relations people don't know what investors (and analysts) want and don't know how to present it; and
2. they stand in the way of reaching the right sources, namely top management.

The chief executive (CEO) and chief financial officers (CFO) are most often identified as the best sources for this information. The investors say they would rather have a shot at a somewhat-reluctant CFO or CEO than be stuck with an uninformed, indecisive investor relations person.

Investors also are concerned about objectivity as companies become a more important information source.

Sell/Buy Side Relationships Being Redefined

By and large, analysts provide the objectivity, although institutional complaints about analyst objectivity are on the rise. The pressure for revenues has made analysts and institutional brokers more aggressive in pushing companies as investments, the institutions say. They're also questioning the strength of the "Chinese wall" between brokerage investment recommendations, stock underwriting, and merger/acquisition deal making. Institutions fear that some companies are being touted for these latter reasons rather than their fundamental investment worthiness.

Indeed, there is a growing restlessness about the overall quality of brokerage research among institutional analysts and portfolio managers. The depth of research and accuracy of analysis are being challenged.

Can institutional investors maintain or improve their investment performance without a solid brokerage research foundation? Can brokerage firms continue to provide research, at some level, based on some acceptable renumeration system?

Some industry observers see the unbundling of research and trading as the answer. Each would be provided for a price, apart from the other. Moves in this direction are started. A number of benefits result, in addition to giving institutions the research and brokerage firms the income, as long as the cost-benefit structure can be made to work. It would enable brokerage houses to continue to afford to do research for their own investing, retail business and investment banking activities. It also would enable brokerage firms to retain the top analysts by paying them enough. Undoubtedly, a number of them would begin their own boutique research firms. Income potential or brokerage profitability problems have motivated many to launch money management firms or join large, successful investment advisors in recent years. Most of all, it would continue to provide that critical layer of fundamental analysis seen as desirable by companies and investors alike.

BUILDING BROKERAGE ANALYST RELATIONSHIPS

Brokerage analyst coverage of a company is desired, beneficial, and necessary. It remains the starting point in an investor communications contact program no matter how much direct effort is made to attract institutions.

Sell-side analyst relationships have two components: getting the analysts interested and being an ongoing source of quality information. The interest of analysts often varies with the company. Large, leading companies in an industry almost have to be covered even if they're not particularly cooperative. Companies have found it pays to cooperate. Analysts won't be talked into anything, but knowledge creates wisdom, and wisdom about valuation can translate into a higher stock price. The "market" for information is never totally efficient. Companies are dynamic by definition: developments don't always go according to plan and strategies are being refined continuously.

These dynamics give analysts individual opportunity to add value, even with a widely followed, industry-leading company. They also give big companies opportunity to maintain and increase analyst coverage. For example, eight analysts following the company may seem to be the limit. No one else wants to join ranks because they can't justify the time commitment since the coverage already is comprehensive. The investor relations charge is to keep the information flowing to those eight analysts and also figure out how to help an additional analyst, or two or three, make a unique contribution to the body of knowledge available from the sell side. Investor relations people call the program the "commissionable idea," because they are leading analysts to information that produces the kind of value-add research that generates transaction business for the brokerage firm.

There is a caveat to that strategy, however, that could end up benefitting companies. It is being voiced by complaining institutions and certainly being heard by cost-conscious brokerage firms. Institutions are showing an increasing impatience with redundant coverage of industries or companies. They're not interested in reading the same research and clearly not interested in giving copycat brokerage firms any transaction business. The monkey is on the back of each analyst to bring something new of substance to the research table. Smart investor relations people should be able to take advantage of that. One critical precaution: in their zeal to help an analyst, investor relations people must be sure to stay away from providing selective material nonpublic information. Chapter 18 covers that subject.

Smaller companies, in general, have to work harder to attract analyst following. They also can have an advantage. The market is more inefficient, since the company isn't as well known. Thus, the impact of the coverage can be greater as "discovery" of the new investment idea reaches institutions (and individuals). Increasing the number of analysts following the company becomes an important investor relations goal. Not only does it expand positive awareness, it also raises the company's investment credibility. In getting serious institutional attention, it helps to have coverage from one or more of the most respected analysts following the industry. They probably are with national brokerage firms, but also may work with a noted regional house with a reputation for expertise in that industry. Narrow coverage by regional firms and/or market makers tends to be viewed by institutions with some skepticism.

Investor relations practitioners are advised to do their homework in beginning and running an analyst relations program. The work involves thorough research of the analysts covering the industry, peer group, and company. Most companies fit into an industry group. The Association for Investment Management and Research lists some 52 industry categories, not including special situation analysts, generalists, and those covering diversified companies. Companies that aren't pure industry "plays" may be able to make a good case for being considered a special situation or bonafide diversified business. If one or two leading analysts pick up on the notion, others probably will follow suit. The special situation is usually a company important enough to follow that defies easy classification in one industry. Or, it is likely to become involved in some special situation, such as a merger, takeover, liquidation, restructuring, or buyout. To be legitimately diversified, the impact of each business within the company has to be sufficient to balance the impact of the other businesses. If the lion's share of revenues and profits come from one business, that company is likely to be analyzed within that industry.

Companies can attract followings in more than one industry. In fact, there is room to evoke an investor relations strategy. Some companies are followed in one industry by certain brokerage firms and in another industry by others. Some companies have managed to elicit coverage from two different industry analysts in the same firm. Some companies have convinced brokerage firms to shift coverage from one industry to another, arguing successfully that the emphasis in their business mix warrants the change. The investor relations strategy involves putting the coverage on the industry being awarded the highest valuation and price/earnings multiple.

With some special study, investor relations people also can identify a group of analysts who are following a peer group of companies; these analysts are ripe for contact. They're not necessarily the same analysts following the industry group. The peer group will consist of companies with similar investing characteristics— within the market capitalization range, with low price/earnings multiple, and those racking up year-to-year earnings gains at certain levels. The next section of this chapter covers this in more detail.

Several sources are available to investor relations detectives gathering analyst intelligence. The *Association for Investment Management and Research* (which combines the *Financial Analysts Federation* and the *Institute of Chartered Financial Analysts*) publishes an annual directory of analysts and the industries they follow. The directory also breaks out members who are quantitative analysts, research directors, analysts specializing in foreign securities, bond analysts, market technicians, investment managers, pension managers, and others. Analysts are listed by industry in the *Directory of Pension Funds and Their Investment Managers*. *Technimetrics*, *CDA Investment Technologies*, *CORTRAC*, and *Vickers* also produce analyst lists by industry and other specializations, plus the names of research directors, as well as institutional and broker identification data. Research directors serve as a useful substitute in brokerage firms without a specialist in the company's industry. Most of the services are available on-line at the touch of a computer key for companies with a modem.

The *Nelson's Publications* group provides analyst information in several formats. Its annual research directories profile the various brokerage firms, describing their investment philosophies and listing each analyst and specialty. The directory also lines up the analysts by industry and other specializations. In addition, Nelson's tracks the research reports of analysts by publishing an annual

directory and monthly updates. The information is divided by brokerage firm, analyst, and by company.

Study Before Starting the Contacts

This information not only provides contact candidate lists, but the
basis of some good old-fashioned pre-contact research. Before a
word is spoken, investor relations people should gather up all the
reports written by the various analysts—reports on the industry,
your company, competitors, as well as industry and peer group
companies. Studying these items will be revealing and will end up
influencing the formation of a contact priority skein. It will enable
you to determine and compare the depth of each analyst's
knowlege and particular attitudes on the industry, the company,
and the industry/peer companies. It also will help you understand
quantitatively how each analyst constructs the valuation matrix for
the industry and each company. Before approaching any analyst, it
helps tremendously to know about the person's style, attitudes,
biases, knowledge levels, and approaches to research and analysis.

An analyst priority plan is recommended. In the real world,
you may not be able to attract the analysts you want, in the order
you want, but this roadmap provides strategic direction. The most
influential analysts in the industry should be included as well as
those following specific industry or peer companies whose institutional investors will be on your contact target list. Certain institutions may like the research of a certain analyst. Also included in
your list should be the regional brokerage firms in your company's
home base and any regional houses around the country with expertise in your industry. If the home-based firms haven't assigned
an analyst to your industry, some persuasion may be needed to get
one interested. The favored home status, accessibility to information and management, and good performance prospects are the
main ingredients of interest.

The current level of analyst activity will guide your judgment
to the best approaches for making contact. The range of familiarity

with your company among perspective analyst targets will be from "following the company" to "never heard of the company." In between will be "high knowledge, but no interest" for whatever reason, "some knowlege, but little interest," "some or little knowledge and no opinion," "little knowledge" and "an open attitude, little or no knowledge, but interest" because the analyst is new, aggressive, curious, or opportunistic.

Studying each analyst's writings will yield good clues on their knowledge and attitude regarding the industry and company. In an analyst-by-analyst survey, the company is likely to find itself sometimes well covered, sometimes treated only in industry reports and sometimes missing from the action. First stage contact will uncover more.

With the target list in hand, begin the process. Some choices exist, likely dictated by the desired pace, budget, and enthusiasm/ availability of senior management. The first choice is tactical: to pursue one-to-one contact, sponsor group presentations, or mobilize management to appear before analyst societies. The practical course suggests a combination; the objective is to meet and get to know as many of the analysts on the target list as possible.

Personal meetings with influential analysts are the ultimate goal. This is when the opportunity is best to build the quality of the relationship. As their interest grows, powerful analysts will want personal meetings. They're not going to write a research report or recommend the company for stock purchase without getting to know management and be assured that their information needs will be met. In doing their own value-add research, these analysts also don't want other analysts eavesdropping. Some may agree to an early meeting, say, after an initial contact, but it isn't likely. Convenience may play a part; it's easier to see in-town analysts or arrange appointments when you or your management is in their town. Industry analysts and generalists in home-town regional firms will be more receptive than the leading industry analysts at national wire houses.

That's why working the Street is useful. The avenues include hosting your own meeting, addressing analyst societies, and industry conferences. Geography also comes into play in making these decisions. In laying out the contact program, the preliminary research will spot up the key locations for the company. Undoubtedly, New York will be prime. It holds most of the brokerage analysts because most of the firms are headquartered there. Corporations in or near New York have an accessibility advantage. It's easier for analysts and investor relations officers and senior executives to be in contact with each other. Investor relations trips are not a big budget item, at least not in seeing the sell side.

The analyst societies represent an excellent way of reaching brokerage analysts, with the largest contingent being in New York (which also has some 25 separate industry analyst "splinter" groups). In addressing the analyst societies, companies are talking to both the sell and buy sides; throughout the country as counted by AIMR membership, the ratio runs about two to one, favoring the institutions, mostly analysts and portfolio managers.

Only a handful of national brokerage firms are outside of metro New York. In addition, there are significant regional firms, who typically are important participants in certain industries. The upfront research into the analysts following industry and peer companies should turn up these names.

When you do the brokerage analyst research, a pattern takes shape; most of the contact will be in the company's own region and in New York. When you go elsewhere, the sell and buy sides will mesh. Indeed, that will be true with the New York analyst society as well. Companies keeping the two sides apart are either sponsoring the meetings, and thus, controlling the invitation list, or focusing on the one-to-one approach.

The logistical puzzle and dynamics of the investment community suggest that it is good investor relations strategy to meet with both sell- and buy-side players on trips to various cities, including New York. It certainly is a good idea in maximizing management time and costs. The sides already will come together in society meetings; they're used to it. Companies have the option when sponsoring a meeting or holding one-to-one sessions. In most cities, the decisions are dictated by the size of the investment group. Here's an operative agenda, for example:

breakfast meeting with the handful of brokerage analysts;

institutional luncheon;

reception with retail brokers at the close of market; and

one-to-one visits with current institutional shareholders.

That easily could expand into a two-day format. Additions may include one or two media interviews. The options involve combining brokerage analysts and institutions in a breakfast or luncheon presentation and seeing more analysts, institutional holders, or prospects in one-to-one meetings.

In starting the program, make initial contact with the target group of analysts by letter or telephone. The letter indicates that the person is being put on a mailing list and includes a suggestion to make contact or expect a follow-up phone call. The letter is accompanied by an information packet. Starting with a telephone call expedites the approach. It also seeks to establish some rapport, gain permission to put the person on the mailing list, and determine interest in attending a presentation or meeting with the investor relations person. The letter or phone call also can precede a visit to the analyst's city by the investor relations person and perhaps the CEO or CFO, with the intent of making an appointment.

And, there is a timetable for the program based on budget and executive availability. Investor relations people are smarter to coax the timing along, letting the interest rise as more analysts and investors learn about the company. Much of the word is being spread by the analysts and investors themselves: one analyst reading the report of another or an institutional portfolio manager asking an analyst about the company. Momentum has value.

Working with Analysts

As resources, companies help analysts by providing and enriching the information. Providing what's essential to fundamental analysis should be basic, but isn't always. Enriching the information by knowing the refinements analysts make distinguishes the effective investor relations professionals from the crowd. To be a trusted resource, investor relations people have to show analysts they understand the analytical process and have the authority, information and communications skills needed to contribute beyond the basics, giving some meaningful amplification and interpretation, consistent with the rules of disclosure.

Fundamental analysis combines science as well as application and concludes with judgment. How analysts apply the techniques vary and so do the conclusions they reach about a company's future performance. Analysts compute ratios as the basis of their work. The analysts' abilities, experience, and judgment are challenged every day as they decide the information and ratios that are driving the company, and then interpret, track, and reinterpret them in the dynamic world of change. Plus all these measurements of value have to be compared company by company within an industry before making the buy and sell recommendations on a relative scale.

The two basic components of fundamental analysis are the *macroeconomic factors* (taken down to the industry level) and the *economic indicators of performance* within a company—key among them being earnings, sales, cash flow, assets/liabilities, and returns on equity. The analyst gathers and channels all this information into forecasts, first of business conditions and changes, then of a company's performance, in determining the best timing for recommending when to buy, hold, and sell its stock.

Most fundamental analysis is done this way—top-down, macro to micro. But, there also are stock pickers, who, more than less, are reversing the process—first applying the analysis to companies, then verifying their prospects by assessing industry and economic strengths. They may decide the company under scrutiny will do well, despite a soft industry or economy.

The analytical picture isn't complete without piecing in the technocrats who are making buy/sell calls on the basis of the effects of supply and demand, rather than the causes of price movements, which is the basis of fundamental analysis. The chartists are tracking price, volume, timing, and trends in predicting how a given stock will behave; they're not concerned about price to earnings, book value, or cash flow ratios. They believe they can interpret past stock price movement accurately in projecting future patterns.

Fundamental analysis starts with a study of the business cycle and its effect on stock prices. The objective is to be able to see the turns in the cycle months before they arrive in order to make stock sell/buy decisions in front of the price changes. The stock market tends to peak two to eight months ahead of an economic drop. It also rises in anticipation of an upturn. Analysts have developed three theories on the business cycle/stock impact relationship:

1. stock prices lead up and down turns;
2. aggressive investors act on current prices, bid up prices and sell just in front of the downturn; and
3. a stock price decline produces an economic downturn as consumer confidence falls.

Analysts also are evaluating the effect of the industrial life cycle in pricing a company's stock. Generally, the cycle has four stages: initial high growth, rapid expansion, mature growth, and a last phase that either involves continuing mature growth, slowing growth or decline. Stock prices correlate with the life cycle since analysts are trying to forecast future performance. Strategic acquisitions, diversification, and restructuring are corporate efforts to enhance valuation, often in the face of thinning prospects in their historic business.

Market-wide stock price movements also need to be factored into analysis of individual companies. Investors believe prices of individual companies move with the markets as a whole. The conviction guides portfolio construction, replete with diversification strategies. It has led to the adoption of market indices to provide composite readings on market performance and to the ultimate computer-based investing method—*market indexation*. Among the leading market indicators are the Dow Jones Industrial Averages, Standard & Poor's 500, the New York Stock Exchange industrial, utility, transportation and composite indexes, the American Stock Exchange, and the National Association of Securities Dealers value-weighted indices.

In taking apart companies to understand their basis of financial performance and project their ability to sustain or improve those results, analysts rely principally on the balance sheet and income statement. The numbers in these financial statements are translated into key ratios, giving analysts standards and benchmarks for measuring the company's growth against itself and comparing its assets and performance against other companies.

Balance sheet analysis is critical to asset-based value investors and analysts looking for undervalued companies. They are evaluating the earnings ability of the assets. The balance sheet compares assets and liabilities. The assets listing starts with the liquid assets which typically include cash, marketable securities, accounts receivable, and inventory; and then contains such illiquid assets as property, plant and equipment, prepayments, and intangibles. Liabilities typically include accounts payable, accrued expenses, and taxes. They are listed in the order they come due. The net worth of the company, or shareholders' equity, is the surplus between assets and liabilities. It likely includes preferred and common stock, capital surplus and retained earnings. Shareholders' equity appears on the liabilities side in order to balance the balance sheet.

The income statement is the basis of analysis for growth investors and analysts. The focus is on sales and earnings growth, with the numbers produced quarterly and annually. Key income statement numbers are revenues; operating income, which is cash left after cost of goods sold, depreciation, and selling, general and administrative (SG&A) expenses; and net after-tax income, which follows deduction of interest, taxes, and unusual income or expenses. The remaining money pays dividends or becomes retained earnings (capital) for funding growth. In the income statement scheme, depreciation is an important number. Usually a large expense, it can affect cash flow. Accounting-wise, cash flow equals net income plus depreciation, which means that depreciation is expensed against money taken in, not out.

As they create balance sheet and income statement ratios, analysts are setting up a method to track trends and compare them among companies. For investment purposes, it is the comparative trends that are meaningful, not as much the absolute numbers.

Ratios divide into three groups:

1. liquidity, which helps analyze cash to meet obligations and provide working capital and finance capital expenditures;
2. capital structure, which analyzes the relative use of debt and equity; and
3. payout, which looks at money spent on dividends and retained in the business.

The current ratio measures a company's liquidity. The ratio is current assets divided by current liabilities. A year is the normal calculation time frame for assets that can be converted to cash and liabilities that must be met. A 2:1 ratio is considered to be normal. If it's higher or rising, analysts get either skittish or opportunistic. Too much liquidity can indicate management inefficiency or under-utilization of assets—conditions that can lead to a takeover attempt.

Analysts use financial leverage ratios to measure the demands on cash flow being taken by debt. A low ratio of stock to total capitalization can create share volatility and indicate some risk in the company's ability to repay its debt. For example, a combined bond and preferred stock ratio above the 33 percent norm raises the specter of bankruptcy. The issue has ascended dramatically with the rabid growth of debt leveraging in the late 1980s.

The capital structure, or debt/equity ratio, shows the relationship between common/preferred stock and bonds: capitalization equals funded debt (bonds) plus shareholders' equity.

Analysts use the price/earnings ratio to measure market risk; it shows investor support of the stock based on earnings per share. The P/E ratio equals current market price divided by annual earnings per share. It continues to be the most common analytical tool in making stock buy/hold/sell decisions, although price/book value, and price-to-cash flow also are very popular. In analyzing the company, the P/E ratio has two general uses: it helps identify a stock as a growth investment when earnings are predicted to fly along above the industry/peer group and/or market; and it helps analysts and investors gauge whether the market is behaving confidently or pessimistically. Investor buying that drives P/E ratios up signals a bull market. Of course, patient value investors are looking for undervalued stocks, indicated by their low P/E ratios.

Dividends are important to many investors including individuals and institutions. Many investment strategies are built around calculating dividend yield. Total return is the combination of dividend yield and stock price appreciation. The dividend yield ratio is equal to dividends divided by stock price. It shows the proportion of the rate of return on the stock provided by dividends. The dividend payout ratio measures the percentage of net earnings after interest and taxes paid to shareholders. If earnings after taxes were $2 a share, with an annual dividend of $1, the payout would be 50 percent. The average is about 45 percent, using the S&P 500 stocks as a base measure. Utilities have attracted individual investors with higher payouts, as much as 80 percent.

Dividend payout ratios help analysts separate growth from income companies. Growth companies tend to plow the earnings back into expansion programs designed to boost stock price appreciation. Income companies believe in the value of dividends for retaining shareholders, by keeping stock turnover and volatility down. There seems to be enough short-term trading, especially with larger cap companies, to keep the stock flow liquid.

Analysts also study closely a company's source and quality of earnings. They want to be able to break out the sources of revenues and earnings, as well as understand the relative contributions of various units and the dynamics of what makes those businesses tick. The numbers give detail, analysis, and evaluation become the basis of projecting earnings growth. The process is both quantitative and qualitative. The business "segment" data, providing sales, earnings and other key balance sheet/income-oriented information, is key, and analysts have been strenuously asking for it for years. Many companies now provide it, and more are joining ranks each year. Investor relations people are vital resources in both the quantitative and qualitative aspects, providing needed financial data, offering explanations, answering questions that get behind the numbers, amplifying, and perhaps helping interpret the information.

Earnings sources also are brought down to numbers. EPS measures the company's dollar return on shareholders' equity. In figuring out the rate of return on shareholders' equity, the dollar return is divided by the per-share value of shareholders' equity. Dividend policy and return on equity determine the amount of earnings and dividend growth.

Many analysts also put considerable weight on the price/book value ratio. As a reflection of the use of retained earnings, book value is a major source of growth in earnings per share.

In helping analysts build quality of information, investor relations practitioners focus on the strategy, financial and operating detail of the business. The discussions center on the corporate mission, its essence and most important elements, programs to accomplish them, and where each stands. The financial detail can include the philosophy and dynamics of the capital structure; intended issuance and use of debt and equity; capital spending plans, purposes and progress; cash flow value drivers and plans for them; dividend policy and plans; programs to improve returns; acquisition/divestiture strategies; any restructuring considerations, such as mergers and acquisitions, share repurchase, spin off activities; financial impact of international operations, global goals and plans. Operating detail can include importance and future of technology; plans and impact of new products; marketshare and programs to improve it, product by product; manufacturing capacity utilization, expansion, cost-reduction programs; inventories; product pricing trends; organizational changes.

Analysts and investors rate the quality of management as a crucial determinant in recommending or buying the company's stock. The process can be somewhat subjective, with personalities and management's willingness to be open affecting judgment, but analysts attempt to evalute managements quantitatively. In bringing the role of management to the bottom line, analysts are measuring sales growth, rate of return on assets and equity, and the strength of the balance sheet. Since today's decisions affect these numerical measures in the future, analysts also track closely the results of decisions.

The process includes watching for problems as well as assessing the ability to capitalize on opportunities. Analysts assess managers on their ability to understand the dynamics of their industry, capitalize on opportunities, and deal effectively with the problems. Each analyst has his or her own set of "red flags" that are waved individually at each company. Banners include product lines going stale without fresh bursts of innovation, declining marketshare, insufficient investment in new technology, competitors taking charge of the incumbent's markets, failure to enter new or related markets, unawareness of the major trends in the industry, weak middle management as seen in the number of outside hirings to fill senior positions, environmental or other socially related problems that could lead to legal liability.

THERE ARE GOOD REASONS TO INFLUENCE INVESTORS DIRECTLY

Companies have been in touch with institutional investors all through the greening of the investor relations function. Institutional analysts have been initiating contact with companies, attending their meetings and corporate presentations before the New York and other society chapters for years. Corporate managements have been invited to address the institutional clients of specific brokerage firms, with the meetings frequently attended by portfolio managers as well as analysts.

Companies are finding there are a number of good reasons to pursue direct influence over the stock-buying decisions of institutional investors. For one thing, the dynamics of the investment process are encouraging it. As they build their own information bases and models, institutions are more receptive to corporate input and more inclined to seek it, as long as it's useful. Companies are in a position to pick up the flow as broker analyst research ebbs.

Contact, and even some relationship-building, is extending beyond analysts to include fund and portfolio managers. Investment firms with few or no analysts are seizing the opportunity. Many portfolio managers spend part of their time doing research and seem to be more willing to meet with managements and carry on running dialogue with investor relations people they respect. Increasingly, investment firms with large analytical staffs are including portfolio managers in meetings with investor relations and corporate officers.

Indeed, investors taking or considering big equity positions in companies want direct contact. They're no longer relying on the sell-side as an exclusive information source. The institutions may initiate the contact or respond to it, when made by the company. That's reason enough for investor relations people to be aware at all times of their major shareholders. Some degree of shareholder identification and tracking, that also covers beneficial owners, should be ongoing. It serves as the basis of a proactive contact/communications program and also is part of preparedness should the company ever be threatened by a hostile takeover bid.

With institutions relying on their computers and analyst recommendations, investment decisions often are made without any contact with the company. Indexers, of course, aren't always aware of the companies they're holding. But active institutions sure are. Some of them expect to be contacted once they make the investment. They intend to know management better and are prospects for additional buying. They're also likely to be longer-term holders, running their portfolios with less turnover. Others aren't interested in company hand-holding. Their computers essentially make the decision, following their quantitative formula. The initial stock purchase, any additional stock purchases, or stock sales, will be based on the company's ranking on the computer screen, plus whatever weightings are included in the model.

Using Research to Target Institutions

It's up to the investor relations people to sort out the various types of investors on their shareholder rolls. It takes a combination of analysis and phone contact to do that job well. The analysis involves studying the transfer sheets, depository trust, 13(f), and any value-add listings from suppliers and consultants in getting a good understanding of the shareholder base. Research also can give clues on the types of investing they do. *Nelson's Directory of Investment Managers, The Directory of Pension Funds and Their Investment Managers,* and the directory issues of *Pensions & Investments* and *Institutional Investor* profile institutions' investment styles, for example. Phone calls determine their interest in maintaining contact with the company as a continuing source of information.

Companies are seizing the moment, in reaching out to institutions. That's consistent with the whole notion of proactive marketing. It also offers the opportunity for companies to have more influence in the institutional makeup of their shareholder base. That has pretty much been under the influence of brokerage analysts and the institutions themselves. Brokerage command is waning, as described. Just how much influence companies can have probably can't be known. Institutions are looking for certain types of corporate stock investments. Companies are looking for certain types of institutional investors. Institutions find the companies by applying their investment strategies, methods, and models. Companies find the institutions by understanding how their investment characteristics fit those styles, methods, and models and then making contact with those institutions that represent potential fits.

It may be wishful thinking, but the process of making investment marriages might also help ease some of the governance strain, eventually. It does begin with communication. If investors want certain companies, and companies want certain investors, there ought to be a basis of communication. The common ground should be strong enough to stand on, while the discussions take place. The investors want to protect and maximize their investment. The companies want to raise capital. If the investors can be patient and reasonable about returns, and if the companies can manage the assets well enough to accrue reasonable returns over reasonable time periods, the marriage should be mutually productive and cause both partners to be pleased.

Finding "Desirable" Shareholders

As companies take some initiative in carving an institutional shareholder base, their first aim is in attracting those that are "desirable." For most companies, desirable means institutions who utilize fundamental analysis in selecting companies consistent with their investing philosophies. For starters, that means the companies are being judged on their strengths. Hopefully, the investors also are inclined to be patient, pursuing strategies that reward them over time. Value investors tend to be the most patient. Dividend income counts and the earnings gains should be consistent. Growth investors are patient as long as the earnings momentum is maintained. Sector rotators are patient as long as the industry stays in favor and the company's performance runs above par.

Investor relations people can learn about the turnover rates of various institutions by checking the research directories, tracking holdings among their industry and peer group companies, working with consultants who make a living knowing about these things, and by talking up investment philosophies and turnover rates in their institutional conversations.

The first place to test the desirable shareholder group is with the company's current investor base. It makes a good test case for applying the principles of valuation and understanding what it is about the company's fundamentals, prospects, and investing characteristics that attracted these particular institutions. The company needs to understand how it is being valued, prospected, and what investing characteristics are important. These are analyzed and weighed against the company's own understanding of its valuation, value drivers, investing characteristics, and prospects. The analysis produces the basis of communication: providing information investors want and information the company believes is vital in fully understanding its valuation, as a way of closing whatever information gap may exist.

Thus, the focus of "the story" is valuation and its value drivers—cash flow, brand names, dominant marketshare, sales or earnings momentum, strong global presence, exclusive technology, and others.

The self-analysis also should delve into the company's particular investing characteristics. These need to be known because they help set the communications tone and become part of the information base, and because they help identify part of the target institutional group, namely those investing in companies with like characteristics. Among the characteristictics, or themes, that draw investors are stable performance, participating in cyclical markets, fitting into market capitalization ranges, consistent earnings momentum, being in a turnaround mode, not paying a dividend, or having a certain dividend payout ratio, exhibiting similar market or investment analysis traits, such as price/earnings, book value, or cash flow ratios. Investor relations people can understand how to match a company's investing characteristics with institutions by studying their investment methods.

Start with Current Holders

Current institutional holders are the first target group. The analysis helps the company understand its shareholder profile as well as sort out the desirable and "undesirable" institutions within the group. For companies wanting shareholders supporting longer-term objectives, the undesirables include short-term speculators, such as tactical asset allocators, arbitragers, hedge fund managers, and to a degree, indexers. The desirable institutions are the active investors—those following asset-value, dividend discount, top-down, sector rotation, and discounted cash flow methods.

Skeptics may doubt the ability of companies to change their institutional shareholder mix by deliberate targeting and focused communication. They shouldn't. It is being done. Of course, if the company "is in play" for a possible hostile takeover, all bets are off. At that point, the arbs will move en masse into the stock. But, evidence supports increased holdings among desirable current institutional shareholders and new investment from targeted institutions as a result of a concerted contact/relationship-building effort. Follow-up shareholder analysis is being used to document increased holdings by current investors, new investment by targeted institutions, and reduced holdings by undesirable investors, as the shares change hands favorably. Sending out the right message in this process is critical. That's why accuracy is so important in understanding the company's valuation basis, investable characteristics, and the institutions' investing methods. It's true that the investments might have been made anyway, but the timing has to be more than coincidental.

In searching for compatible institutions, companies are turning to their directories that profile institutions' investing methods, ordering up tailored computerized lists from suppliers, and working with consultants who specialize in helping develop the corporate valuation story and target investor groups. The vendors and consultants start with the SEC-required 13(f) filings that break out holdings of institutions managing $100 million or more in equities. These lists are dated and incomplete, but provide the basis for further research and analysis in assembling actionable targets.

The quality of these lists continues to improve. Lists are being constructed with numerous tailored variations, essentially in identifying institutions holding shares in pre-designated groups of competitors, industry, and other types of peer companies. These institutions are logical targets, because they are known to be following and investing in companies with similar characteristics. Companies construct their competitive, industry and peer groups as the basis of programming the computer to spill out the institutional names.

Selecting Communications Vehicles

As part of a targeting program, companies have various communications vehicles at their disposal. All the targets should be on the
prime mailing list. Material announcements and earnings releases
can be "faxed" to key institutions (and brokerage analysts), with
tailored cover notes positioning the information to the investing
interest. Advertising becomes potentially useful, since the message
can be honed in on the audience.

Predicting Institutional Response

In selecting their targets, investor relations practitioners also are
analyzing how the relative sizes of institutions and their current
investing patterns should translate into holdings in their company.
Here's a typical rundown:

> big institutions with large positions in the company should
> maintain them;
>
> big institutions with small positions should increase them;
>
> big institutions with good research coverage and substantial
> holdings in the industry should start or increase their stake
> in the company;
>
> big institutions that sold should be encouraged to rebuy;
>
> middle-sized institutions with small positions in the company
> or seeing their assets under management grow rapidly
> should be encouraged to buy more shares.

Today marketing to institutions that should have a built-in interest on the basis of a matched corporate profile/investing
method; it is the trend and is fast becoming the technique of choice.
However, there also are tighter and broader approaches, both
popular with companies.

Concentrating on Leading Institutional Market Influentials

The narrower approach is the "lead steer" theory, with the term popularized by the respected consultant Joel Stern, and endorsed in practice by the equally respected consultant, researchist, and investor, Charles D. Ellis. They believe that a relative handful of highly influential investors determine at the margin the market price and institutional equity ownership patterns of virtually all large capitalization companies. The investing actions of somewhere around 100 lead steer investors are followed by the investing herd, according to Stern. Ellis says the statistics show that a small number of institutions manage the lion's share of equity assets in the country. These investors are principally located in New York and Boston, but are showing up elsewhere in isolation or clusters as public pension funds and certain investment firms grow. Stern and Ellis suggest that companies can best impact the market for their stock by concentrating their contact and communications on these lead steers and major institutions.

Taking a Broad Approach

The broad approach is the traditional one. Proponents suggest that the investing motives and practices of institutions are too diverse, dynamic, elusive and complex for targeting. As a result, companies restrict themselves by not giving the market a broad communications brush. Critics of the narrow approach also worry about the accuracy of the conventional wisdom that says institutional investing methods can be pinned down. Certainly, many investment management firms don't like to be pinned down. They claim they write the investment style descriptions to satisfy the consultants who are helping pension, foundation, and endowment sponsors select asset managers.

Many firms also resent having their investing styles described for them by investor relations people. Only they know the depth and daily subtleties of the market and refinements of their models. Then, there are institutions who react positively to an investor relations person showing knowledge of the investing style and being able to get right to the essence of the matter. The lesson for investor relations professionals is to be careful with the words they use in talking with analysts and portfolio managers. Impress them with your knowledge of how to describe your company. Don't tell them you know all about how they invest.

It's a good idea to continue reaching broadly in stirring up institutional interest. The wide-reach will be there for many companies without any investor relations effort. The inquiries and buys will come from institutions influenced by brokerage analysts following the company. The company will appear on investment screens by virtue of its performance. Companies can benefit immensely from addressing the various AIMR societies around the country where membership is bigger on the buy than on the sell side.

Society meetings also are a good vehicle for rolling out the targeted program. Once identified, the company can let the institutions in the particular city know that they will be addressing the society. More assurance of gathering the right audience is given by hosting the meeting and inviting institutions on the list. Small group meetings are best; they provide a better forum for quality discussion. Better yet are one-to-one meetings.

11

Marketing to Individuals and Retail Brokers

There is this modern maxim about investor relations: big companies concentrate on institutional investors, while trying to stop the erosion of individuals; medium-sized companies have an individual-investor base, giving way to institutions; and small companies pursue their "natural" individual investor segment while trying to attract institutions. It's all true, but it isn't that simple.

Companies are of a mixed mind. They like the stable, patient, supportive role of individuals, but that can produce minimal stock movement in a company dominated by individuals. They like the active buying of institutions that produces volume and sets the stock price, but they're not pleased with the short-term trading habits of institutions that can create volatility and downward pricing in companies dominated by institutions.

Institutions are moved by corporate actions. Valuation-enhancement programs should improve stock price for companies dominated by institutions. The effect is likely to be less in companies dominated by individuals.

It can be more satisfying to market to institutions. Companies can see more progress in efforts to communicate with institutions.

They can be readily identified and contacted. Communications materials can be put in their hands and meetings can be held. At that point, they'll probably tell you when they buy the stock, but even if they don't, you can still track their actions by watching the transfer sheets and 13(f) reports.

It can be tough to market to individuals. They're hard to find and reach. Many avenues are available, and few are straight—from both results and cost standpoints. Very few direct methods of contact exist. Those that do are with current shareholders and such targeted groups as employees, customers, and suppliers. The indirect methods of contact are dispersed and elusive—the media, brokers. Results are near impossible to quantify and, since individuals trade less frequently, the impact on stock price is marginal unless they dominate the company's shareholder ranks.

Thus, logic says companies are being much more cost-efficient in marketing to institutions and stand very little chance of being cost-efficient in marketing to individuals. But logic also says individuals should be in the market: the returns are superior to most other investment choices. And, indeed, individuals are.

They have some $2 trillion worth of stocks, but it represents just 20 percent of their investable income, compared with over a third two decades ago. That would indicate individuals are more confident about other investments, such as money markets, mutual funds, Treasury bills and bonds. They're shying away from the stock market, concerned that, because it is dominated by the big players, they're not getting a fair shake in terms of information and trading timing. It has been estimated that individuals actually sold about $500 billion in stock from 1982 through 1989. Instead, individuals are letting the big players invest their money, through mutual funds, and even more indirectly, through pension funds. So, a portion of the individual market is institutionalized.

But, it isn't that much, comparatively. About $250 billion is in stock mutual funds, with $2 trillion still being invested directly.

Perhaps, companies should think more seriously about marketing stock to individuals. It offers the advantage of producing a more stable, loyal group of shareholders, supportive of management's long-term strategies to improve operating and financial results, in return for dividends that are compounding and price appreciation.

The marketing ammunition is there: the evidence shows stocks reward patient investors—an historic standard deviation return of around 18 percent. And, unless tempted by the takeover lure, individuals still are inclined to be patient investors.

Companies are marketing to individuals, with varying intents and degrees of intensity. Let's take a closer look at why and how.

MARKETING APPROACHES DEPEND ON MOTIVATIONS AND REALITY

Companies with relatively few shares available and small market capitalization that are aggressive about investor relations must focus the bulk of their energy on individual investors and retail brokers, almost by definition. The small float makes them a marginal play for institutions because of the lack of liquidity in the stock. The float just isn't there for institutions that buy shares in larger quantities and then like to see other institutions do the same, to boost stock price. They can't justify the time in concentrating extensive research and evaluation on small companies.

However, that's a generality and it doesn't apply across the institutional sweep. Part of the institutional asset base is dedicated to small cap stocks. Some institutions have small cap funds, others send a portion of their equity assets in search of smaller, newer, emerging companies. Small cap stocks are shown to outperform their bigger brethren, especially under certain economic conditions or as new technologies or marketing concepts burst on the scene. Often, small and medium-sized investment firms—managing about $50 million to $200 million in assets—lean toward smaller companies in efforts to gain a competitive advantage over the larger money managers. Brokerage analysts are sleuthing for new investment "ideas." Institutions want to be the first to discover an opportunity so they can ride the price up from its bottom. The inefficiency of the market for new and small companies always will intrigue investors.

The investor relations job is to capitalize on that inefficiency, persuade analysts and brokers of the company's soundness and bright future, and find and contact the institutions looking for, and investing in, small companies. And, as the prime program, the investor relations person should meticulously pursue individuals and brokers.

Large companies are caught up in the growing holdings of institutions. The investor relations audience is institutional, as its percentage of shares in big cap companies rises, inevitably, because of market institutionalization. Companies are concentrating on institutions, questioning whether efforts aimed at individuals are worthwhile, and wondering what kinds of activities can have a payoff.

Interestingly, a trend is showing up in large companies—a renewed concern for having individuals hold more of their shares. It's being motivated by a combination of forces—rising institutional activism in matters of corporate governance; sense of greater support in hostile takeover contests; putting more shares in the hands of investors who are patient, trade less and are inclined to support longer-term corporate goals; fundamental belief in the economic value of encouraging individual stock ownership; and a general fear of institutional dominance.

Since appealing to individuals is the lesser piece in the overall program, investor relations practitioners at large companies are being more selective in their activities. Companies seem to be taking one of two directions: either conduct national programs to attract brokers and individuals in the broadest sense; or concentrate on affinity groups, such as employees and existing shareholders, trying to control contact and communications flow very tightly.

Medium-sized companies can make the investor relations run right down the middle. As secondary stock offers or splits increase their float, the ability to appeal to institutions grows. The shift to an institutional emphasis almost becomes a natural evolution of the communications program. Management is looking for the impact on stock price and investor relations people are justifying their efforts through live contact and measurable progress. Shareholder mix changes.

In this scenario, medium-sized companies shouldn't start over-looking their individual investors, broker network and the activities that won favor with both groups. Medium-sized companies are in somewhat of a unique investor relations position. Their program is expanding successfully from a retail base.

For purposes of definition, in its broadest sense, large capitalizaton companies have a total stock worth of $1 billion or more, and small cap companies are equity capitalized at around $200 million or less.

In the back of every corporate officer's mind is the worry over an unwanted takeover attempt. The concern casts an interesting light on the institutional/individual investor mix question. Despite all the anti-takeover devices, a high stock price is still the best defense. Individuals may be more loyal (emphasis on *may be*, in the face of an attractive cash offer), but institutions determine the stock price. Individuals tend to hold shares, institutions tend to trade. It is the upward trading, working the laws of supply and demand, that boosts stock prices. Thus, a predominantly loyal shareholder group could hold prices down. Then, there is the other theory that scarcity raises value. Some stocks have risen dramatically, with very little trading, because the shares were hard to find and buy, as perceptions of the company's strengths continued to grow. Warren Buffett's Berkshire Hathaway is the classic example. Its common stock price rose to over $8,000 a share, with a "float" of only about a million shares.

PSYCHOLOGY AND DEMOGRAPHICS: VALUABLE TO UNDERSTAND

Brokers, bank trust officers, and financial planners study the psychology and demographics in winning individuals as clients and managing their portfolios. Investor relations practitioners are advised to take a page from their book in gaining insights into how individuals invest.

Unlike institutions who measure risk as the standard deviation of return and calculate it carefully, individuals see risk as losing money or venturing beyond their comfort index. Options and futures can be risky for a stock investor; stocks can be risky for a money market investor. Convincing an individual to invest in something that previously resulted in a loss also is a hard sell. And so is showing them the benefits of going against the investment grain and being a contrarian. The most potentially persuasive example hits at the essence of being a succesful individual investor— namely functioning as a patient value buyer by purchasing shares when their price is declining.

Thus, education becomes an important part of managing portfolios for individuals. It involves dealing with the individual's perception of risk, being a good listener and questioner, to make sure the client isn't surprised by results. The good portfolio strategist takes into account the fears and tries to modify the risk perception within reason.

Individuals tend to be active or passive investors. Passive investors are more risk averse. They may have inherited wealth. Or they may be professionals or businesspeople who have not managed to become accustomed to risking money that isn't theirs. Corporate executives, lawyers and accountants in major firms, and certain business owners are examples. Active investors are comfortable with taking greater risk. They include people who have made their money themselves—business owners, lawyers, accountants working on their own, high-income physicians, dentists, and entrepreneurs of all types. That latter group claims the highest number of members joining the millionaires' "club" each year. Active investors get very involved in their investments and must feel in control of them. They do a lot of their own research, and for investment counselors, aren't easy to work with.

Personality influences how an individual will invest. Portfolio managers divide them into two classes: those who deal with their lives confidently; and those who are more conservative and analytical. Indeed, five personalities of individual investors have been identified and described in the Bailard, Biehl & Kaiser model, which has proven to be useful to portfolio managers. *Adventurers* are the most confident. They also can be intuitive or impetuous. They'll take the biggest risk. *Celebrities* like to be on the inside, tuned into the latest hot investment idea. They include sports, entertainment, and professional people. *Individualists* are inclined to be independent, making their own decisions. They include entrepreneurs, lawyers, and doctors. *Guardians* are more careful, perhaps a little concerned about preserving their wealth accumulation pace. They're older, approaching retirement. *Straight arrows* are well-balanced, meticulous, deliberate, and rational.

Demographics are weighed heavily in managing portfolios of individuals. The "wealth" demographics can easily be overly encouraging. Further research in tailoring the communications effort is advisable. For cost-efficiency, wealth demographics suggest concentrating communication on those individuals with the largest portfolios and those who can be reached directly in some controlled manner that allows measurement of results. The list includes high tax-bracket individuals (the doctors, lawyers, dentists, business executives, entertainers, and so on), those managing their portfolios professionally through investment clubs, and such "affinity" groups as existing shareholders, employees, customers, suppliers, and people who are in a position to know and like the company.

While a 1985 New York Stock Exchange survey showed 47 million Americans with investments in stocks, the average portfolio was just $6,200. However, the average stock portfolio of the 100,000-plus members of the National Association of Investors Corporation is nearly $110,000 at last count. More than 3.3 million people have a net worth topping $1 million. Some 2.7 million people in the United States hold $1.3 trillion in stock. Their average is $408,300. These numbers come from the Internal Revenue Service. The number of millionaires now surpasses $1.5 million.

The other important demographic consideration is where the person is in the life cycle. It affects their risk/return profile. The life cycle, for stock investing purposes, has four phases:

1. accumulation;
2. consolidation;
3. spending; and
4. gifting.

In the earlier, accumulation phase, income is being channeled into such expenditures as the home, saving for children's education, and the like. Investments for security and retirement are made with whatever discretionary income exists and often carry higher risk/return equations since time to make money is on their side.

Income is greater than costs in the consolidation phase, enabling portfolios to grow. Risk is balanced since there is less time to make money. Portfolios typically blend higher and lower risk/return investments.

Investment and retirement assets cover living expenses in the spending phase, rather than income from working. The emphasis in asset management shifts to dividends, appreciation, and interest. Gifting occurs when excess assets are shifted to heirs or charities for personal and tax reasons.

Investment goals, liquidity, and taxes also are important considerations in an individual's portfolio management. Essentially, goals are near and long term and of low and high priorities. Near-term goals set up the need to have access to the money at a certain time. The long-term, high-priority goal, such as financial security, allows for accumulation and is ideal for stock investing.

Liquidity is necessary for emergency cash and advisable to take advantage of investing opportunities. Taxes are part of investment strategy, with choices available providing varying tax consequences. Timing is tied to capital gains taxes. Yield, liquidity, and quality are factors in making the tax-free versus taxable interest decision. Tax planning often dictates certain year-end buy/sell decisions in taking capital gains or losses. A big piece of the process can be estate tax planning for wealthier individuals.

By understanding the motivations and requirements of smart investing by individuals, investor relations practitioners can focus on their audiences and enrich their communications.

THE AFFINITY GROUP CONCEPT

Efficiency, in results and spending, suggests that companies concentrate on individuals who are more likely to be influenced by the effort. They often are referred to as "affinity" groups, because they're composed of people who should have a reason for liking the company and investing in the stock. They include current shareholders, employees, suppliers, customers, and on a wider scale, residents of communities in which there are significant corporate operations and professionals in markets where the company's products are prominent. A golf-equipment maker appealing to doctors is an example.

Participation in investor club programs also is a viable way to reach individuals, because the contacts are organized and direct, and because the members utilize professional analysis methods and thus can be influenced by the company's fundamentals and prospects. The most popular club for companies is the National Association of Investors Corporation.

Large companies whose focus is on institutions consider affinity group programs to be the best way to reach individuals. They're efficient and measurable. Smaller companies whose primary market consists of individuals must do more than appeal to affinity group investors.

Approaches to affinity groups take two directions: providing incentives to invest; and open and active "friendly" communications. Two important incentive programs are *dividend reinvestment plans* (DRPs) and *employee stock ownership plans* (ESOPs).

These programs fit into the underlying objective in an investor relations program designed to reach individuals: They answer the question of how to make the stock appealing.

Dividend reinvestment plans have shown their value in building holdings among existing shareowners and attracting new ones. In the typical plan, the incentives can be multiple: reinvesting the dividends and adding cash without having to shell out for brokerage fees and commissions; and even receiving discounts from the current market price. Companies have used DRPs to attract new holders; the cost savings (and discounts) are a powerful motivator. The concept is popular with companies that have readily definable customers such as utilities and financial institutions. Citicorp runs a highly successful program appealing to its credit card customers. The program has added many millions of dollars in new investment. Citicorp also has broken ground across the country in obtaining state-by-state approvals; they are required since the program is considered to be a stock offering. Companies in other industries with credit card customers are considering the concept.

The advantages of the DRP escape many small companies that aren't in a position to pay dividends because it is wiser for them to reinvest retained earnings in capitalizing on their technological, product or marketing edges in keeping the business growing.

ESOPs also are aimed at putting more shares in loyal, individual investor control, in this case, employees. Employees stand to gain financially, through transaction cost savings and matching funds, and they have a convenient way of investing at their own affordable pace. Employees and companies both benefit from the heightened incentive to be more productive that comes with being "owners" of the company.

ESOPs that are leveraged through borrowing were the rage as a takeover defense in 1989 after the Delaware Chancery Court upheld Polaroid's establishment of an ESOP that could hold 14 percent of the company's shares. The notion of putting 14 percent of the shares in friendly hands in a state that requires a would-be buyer of the company to acquire 85 percent to complete a takeover, or wait three years, seems to serve as a strong deterrent. The possibility that Congress might take away the deductibility of dividends paid in ESOPs and the 50 percent deductibility on interest income for lenders helping finance ESOPs sent companies scrambling to set up the plans in 1989.

Active, friendly communications is the other fundamental way that companies are appealing to affinity type investors. In fact, the concept of friendly communications applies universally in retail-driven investor relations. The psychology of communications is a vital ingredient. It extends from the amount of information supplied to the ease accorded in understanding it and tone in expressing it. Companies can make their communications very appealing to individuals—in taking advantage of such regular channels as the annual and interim reports, and creating such vehicles as special letters, dividend stuffers, a shareholders' manual and other publications. It comes close to catering to individuals; a lot of money has been made on catering.

Shareholder mailings and company publications are excellent opportunities to promote share ownership—through the DRP or ESOP, as examples. Companies have found their percentage of DRP participants and new money invested in stock rise dramatically as a result of aggressive coverage in annual and interim reports, mentions in special letters from the president. In recent years, companies have begun marketing their DRP: increasing the maximum amount of the optional cash payment; documenting the return benefits against other types of investments.

Friendly, reputation-enhancing contact is the purpose in establishing some sense of a regular flow of communication with current shareholders. It starts with a letter of welcome from the CEO, and can even start again with a letter when the person sells the stock. It includes a booklet for new shareholders, helping them through the administrative detail, fleshing out the year's calendar, and encouraging their contact. It includes occasional special state-of-business reports from the CEO, arriving in between the interims. It includes an 800 telephone number, which, for efficiency purposes, can be available on certain days or certain hours.

Some companies are expanding their quarterly reports, making them into magazines, instead of news dispatches on results. The philosophy runs this way: The quarterly numbers are flashed to the analysts and institutions via facsimile or computer services; the quarterly magazine comes out later, emphasizing educational articles on markets, products, shareholder services, in addition to the CEO giving a strategic progress report. Well done, these reports are proving themselves to be useful to professional investors as well. Check the quarterlies of Quaker Oats, McKesson Corp., and AT&T, as examples.

The special opportunity of consumer companies to attract individuals is being exploited by many investor relations professionals. Consumer companies are thought to have an advantage: higher consumer visibility leading to being well-liked, and carving a good reputation. Their products are seen and used every day, enabling these companies to build brand loyalty. Consumer companies are marketing this advantage more aggressively, with articles in their shareholder reports and by offering product incentives, such as coupons.

Shareholder meetings are communications opportunities, even the annual meeting. Shareholder activism focused on the annual meeting is a fact that companies should deal with positively. The situation may call for strong communication and the result can be favorable—appealing to the audience in attendance, reaching others through the resultant media coverage, and reaching the entire shareholder body through the presentation reprint or post-meeting report. Disruptive meetings often win increased shareholder support, triggering a sympathetic response.

Companies have conducted successful shareholder information meetings, apart from the annual meeting, typically in areas where they have plants or other operations, strong product market coverage areas, and other communities with large individual investor followings. These meetings can be packaged as part of a group of presentations in the same city that cover separate institutional, analyst and broker forums, with a media interview or two added for good measure. The visibility and enthusiasm generated have a momentum-building effect. It's surprising that more companies aren't conducting these types of package programs more frequently.

Surveys help bring the company and its shareholders together. The surveys have double value: creating warm feelings in shareholders, by showing interest and respect; and in learning more about them and their reasons for buying the shares. Surveys can be done at minimal cost by incorporating them into annual and quarterly reports or other shareholder mailings. Some companies survey shareholders every year by including the questionnaire in the annual report.

Surveys also are an excellent way to learn more about beneficial owners. Companies are encouraged to purchase their lists of "Street name" shareholders whose accounts are kept with brokerage firms and banks, rather than recorded directly with the company. Shareholders decide whether to allow their names to be provided. Most individuals don't object to being identified. Brokerage firms hold most of the individual investor accounts. Banks hold most of the shares of institutional investors, who tend to retain the mystery of their identity.

The NOBO lists (*non-objecting beneficial owners*) of individual investors are useful in investor relations programs for many reasons. The surveys of NOBOs help companies understand their individual investor base more fully. As a result, the research enriches the information process. Companies also have direct access to this important group of investors—for regular mailings and contact, should it be desired. No one has ever been quite sure about the percentage of communications materials that actually reaches beneficial owners, forwarded to them from companies through the brokers and banks holding the accounts. NOBO (brokerage) and COBO (*consenting beneficial owners*, through banks) lists are available through intermediaries that have contracts with the brokerage firms and banks to process proxy materials and thus, supply the names to requesting companies. At present, two intermediary firms provide the bulk of names; *Independent Election Corporation of America* (IECA) is the biggest, and *Automated Data Processing* (ADP) recently entered the market. Most of the banks and brokerage houses use the intermediaries, but a few of the big firms still have "back room" operations, handling the proxy processing.

Companies are complementing employee stock ownership plans by elevating awareness of efforts to improve performance and make the stock more valuable. They're running stories in company publications about corporate strategies, the reasons behind certain operating programs and the results being forged. The articles are designed to get employees thinking more about performance, their contribution toward it, and the benefits of being an investor. In addition, financial strategies and results are being explained more fully. Daily stock prices are posted. Senior executives are reporting on progress in speeches and in the company publications. Audio and video tapes reviewing results are available.

Investor relations practitioners consider the members of investor clubs as a controlled audience. National Association of Investors Corporation (NAIC) sponsors a host of activities that help companies make direct contact with these serious investors who are managing substantial portfolios using professional methods. The basic NAIC program is a series of investor fairs held across the country, culminating in a national fair each year in a sizable financial market like Philadelphia, Dallas, Detroit, or Los Angeles. Companies give presentations and operate booths, where they can talk with investors, show videos or slides, provide printed information.

Corporate members also are subjects of the stock investment analysis methods taught members by the NAIC. The investors follow a proscribed analytical process in evaluating the company. Essentially, they ascribe to the "value" school, seeking to double total return (dividends and price appreciation) every five years. That patient philosophy is hand-in-glove with the intents of companies to have shareholder support in their use of capital for expansion over time.

Direct mail is a popular NAIC activity. The association produces profiles that capture the key strategies, operations and financial returns that are critical in making investment decisions. Similar in content and style to the S&P and Moody's reports, these *"green sheets"* are mailed to members, and also can be sent to brokers. Companies gain regular visibility in the NAIC magazine, *Better Investing*, through profile stories and reports of investor holdings in corporate members. Many companies also advertise in the magazine, reaching the controlled NAIC member audience. And, companies can choose to take part in the dividend reinvestment program offered by NAIC as a low-cost way for investors to build the size of their holdings. Investors can participate with very little investment, chosing from among the companies enrolled in the program. The concept epitomizes the value of accumulation.

"Stability" describes the reason companies take part in NAIC programs. Big and small companies endorse its benefits. For large companies, the total holdings among NAIC members may only be a percent or two of the float, but that can add up to a million shares or more in stable, professional individual investor hands. What's more, for most companies, that total number shows steady growth, almost immune from market vagaries. Cost of participation depends on the degree of activity—number of fairs, elaborateness of the booth, and the use of the other programs. The annual corporate membership fee is modest ($15,000 as this is being written).

REACHING INDIVIDUALS THROUGH BROKERS

The next best thing to reaching investors directly in convincing them to buy a certain stock is reaching them through their primary sources of influence. Brokers and financial planners top a list that also includes self-conducted research/analysis, ideas from media stories, and the suggestions of relatives, friends, and business associates. Stocks are still financially rewarding to brokers, and brokers still like to push stocks, even though they have many other products to sell and are making less money now on stock commissions. The New York Stock Exchange survey of individuals done in 1985 showed that 42 percent of the investors acquired stock for the first time through a broker. A 1989 *Registered Representative* magazine survey of brokers indicated that 83 percent of them recommended stocks to their customers and 87 percent made stock investments on behalf of their customers.

The question for companies is how to score any worthwhile results, staying within a reasonable budget, in trying to arouse broker enthusiasm for the company. The broker universe is big, even though it appears to be declining somewhat. Technimetrics says the 1990s began with about 57,000 retail brokers in the United States and 5,500 in Canada. However, the closing or consolidating of some firms is sure to lower the population. There were around 64,000 brokers in North America right before the October 1987 market crash. Some 65 percent of the current count of U.S. brokers is in the eight largest national firms, with 23 percent in 63 major regional houses and 8 percent working for 133 small, exclusively retail firms. Incidentally, the other 4 percent (1,500) are brokers specializing in institutional sales.

In constructing broker contact programs, having some analyst coverage serves as a strong foundation. Besides attracting other analysts to the company, the recommendations give brokers a basis of confidence in the stock. At the same time, it's better to not be overcovered. Leaving a measure of inefficiency enables brokers to "discover" the stock for their customers. Analyst coverage also should include the company's investment bankers—regional and national—although their recommendations frequently don't carry as much weight with institutions who are looking closely at the cracks in the Chinese wall.

In approaching their programs, companies seem to be traveling the two opposite avenues. One draws a national circle around the broker universe, pursuing prospects everywhere at the same time; the other divides the nation into small groups and is selective, whether by community or brokerage firm. Size of the company doesn't seem to dictate the direction; big and small companies are taking both avenues.

Nationally, direct mail is the main tool for reaching brokers. Primary purposes behind a national program are to radiate exposure broadly, build up mailing lists for continuous communication, and establish contact targets. The latter is used in inviting brokers to meetings; companies then sort through their invitation responses to identify cities with the largest concentrations of apparently interested brokers. Some companies are creating the mailings and buying broker lists, but more are relying on the direct response specialization firms for turnkey projects. *Research* is an "advertorial" magazine, distributed to brokers throughout North America. Companies pay for the articles which are written as investment profiles. Brokers order reprints of the articles to use in convincing their retail customers to invest in the stock. Technimetrics offers a similar program, utilizing a different format. It prepares and distributes four-page investment profiles to its North American list of brokers, who order copies.

However, most of the broker contact is being done selectively and progressively—locally, regionally, and nationally on a city-by-city basis. Companies are working the market in various ways, and logically, beginning at home. Smaller companies are well advised to start at home, tapping their own regional brokerage firms for coverage as a base for expanding into other regions and to national wire houses.

There should be a measure of "affinity" between a company and its local brokers. Call it loyalty or the local advantage. The brokerage firms can capitalize on their convenient access to information and management for their own investing analysis and in using their research to garner institutional trades nationally. Over-the-counter companies should be looking locally for active market makers; again, the appeal to the brokerage firm is the inside track on gaining expertise.

Regionally and nationally, research and affinity can point companies in the right directions. Here are some courses of action to uncover:

1. Expand regionally from home. Firms and brokers nearest the company should be more familar with it. Brokers in Baltimore should know companies in Philadelphia.

2. Go to cities where the company has plants and other business operations. Familarity breeds support.

3. Go to cities where the records show strong shareholder bases. It indicates active broker interest and selling.

4. Cover cities that are beehives of retail activity as evidenced by the size of the broker population and the amount of individual investor dollars chasing stock returns. Research can lead the way. For example, Technimetrics tracks broker populations and selling strengths. The biggest and strongest are, predictably, California, New York, Florida, Texas, Pennsylvania, Illinois, New Jersey, and Michigan. But, there are sleepers; smaller cities loaded with brokers and interested individual investors. The Technimetrics list reveals Bridgeport, CT, Richmond and Norfolk, VA, Sarasota and Boca Raton, FL, Little Rock, AK, Omaha, NE, Harrisburg and York, PA and Louisville, KY. And, don't neglect "the Big

Apple." Brokers in New York tend to be ignored as companies emphasize analysts and institutions. Many of the brokers are managing huge portfolios; there are lots of wealthy people in New York.

5. Use the "conditioning" accomplished through the national direct mail programs that brought the brokers out of the woodwork. Check the responses from *Research* magazine, Technimetrics, or your own mailings to identify pockets of broker activity.

Now for the methods of establishing contact and building important relationships.

1. Address the stockbroker clubs. This is the least selective and cost-efficient vehicle. It can be categorized as a missionary step, because there is little that can be done to qualify the audience. At most clubs, companies pay for the lunch or dinner. Attendance may be large, but interest in the company, small. The value to a company should not be minimized, however. The decision to talk to the group is one of corporate choice. One in three, four, or five brokers in the audience may turn on to the company, recommend the stock and place customers in it. The impact can be substantial. Stockbroker clubs are nationwide. Some are individually organized, but the bulk, about 35, are part of The Stockbrokers' Society covering major cities—in Los Angeles, San Francisco, New York, Boston, Hartford, Washington, Baltimore, Pittsburgh, Miami, Dallas, Cincinnati, and others.

2. Host meetings. They can be breakfast or luncheon meetings, or take place after the market closes, typically with a format that includes a presentation, questions, and refreshments. The advantage of this type of forum hinges on the ability of companies to do their homework qualitatively in selecting analysts who either are top producers, have an interest in the company, or can be shown that they should have an interest

in the company. Typically, these meetings bring together brokers from various firms within the community.

3. Talk to brokers at a particular firm. The atmosphere in the room will be more charged if the firm's industry analyst has a buy recommendation on the stock. It isn't a requirement, however. Regionals have shown a ready willingness to welcome managements seeking an audience with the firm's broker contingent. The meetings usually take place late in the day at the firm's main office or biggest local branch of national houses. In the pursuit of commission income, national firms are relaxing the tradition of requiring brokers to promote only stocks on the official buy list.

   With the pickup of local broker interest in local companies, branch managers have grown in importance to investor relations practitioners. More and more, it is the branch manager who is deciding whether to let managements talk to the brokers in that particular office. This is especially the case among national firms away from their headquarters city.

   In talking with brokers, companies are encouraged to send their CEO or CFO, but it isn't mandatory. Often, the situation suggests judgment. A powerful group probably warrants the top officer. However, the spokesperson at many of these sessions is the investor relations director.

4. For American Stock Exchange companies, address the Amex Clubs. Members are mostly brokers, with clubs operating in Atlanta, Boston, Chicago, Dallas, Houston, Jacksonville, Los Angeles, downtown and midtown New York, Philadelphia, St. Louis, San Diego, San Francisco, Seattle, and Washington, D.C. in the United States, as well as other key financial markets around the world, namely London, Edinburgh/Glasgow, Hong Kong, Montreal, Toronto, Singapore, Zurich, and Geneva.

The National Investor Relations Institute publishes an annual directory that provides details on the various presentation forums available to companies, covering not just broker, but also analyst and institutional groups. The directory describes meeting formats and gives the names of contacts for the Amex and Stockbrokers clubs, analyst societies and splinter groups.

There is a current state-of-the-art in broker communications. It involves aggressive pursuit of the top producers in strong retail markets. The concept has been developed and is being refined by a number of consulting firms that specialize in identifying, tracking and building relationships with these brokers on behalf of their clients. The concept is seen as the most efficient and potentially productive method of conducting broker contact. The consultants literally "work" the markets, getting to know the brokers, networking, ferreting out the "heavy hitters," adding/subtracting names, and presenting their client companies for investment consideration. The agencies arrange meetings between corporate management and interested brokers, in small groups and one-to-one. The chief executive or chief financial officer is encouraged to participate, but meetings also are held with the investor relations officer.

Consultants have developed a profile of the top-producing brokers. They're older, have been selling stocks all their lives and still believe fervently in the value of equities. They're powerful, operate as investment managers, with a client roster that includes wealthy individuals and some small institutions. While employed by regional or national firms, these brokers have a high degree of autonomy. Most rely on themselves for the bulk of their investment ideas, absorbing research from diverse sources. Over time, they have become experts on certain industries or types of companies. They prefer having close contact with senior corporate executives.

In any given market, there probably are 15 to 25 top producers; across the country between 2,000 and 2,500, according to the consultants.

The basic corporate communications tool for brokers is the *fact sheet*. Typically, it is four pages, covers the company's strategic priorities, summarizes investing strengths, provides key financial and stock data, gives financial returns, describes the essence of operations, lists analysts recommending the company, and includes the names of chief contacts. These fact sheets perform two jobs: they help sell the broker on the company and help the broker sell clients on the company.

Fact sheets become mailers to create broker awareness, accompany invitations to meetings, and serve as handouts at presentations. Information packets, used in mailings or meetings, also can include latest annual and interim reports, 10-K and 10-Q reports, reprints of recent speeches or favorable articles. At meetings, brokers (and analysts/investors) should be given hard copies of slides or overheads used in the presentation, especially charts.

COMMUNICATIONS PROGRAMS TO SUPPORT RETAIL MARKET EFFORTS

Companies valuing individuals as investors have tried many other ideas, with varying degrees of success. Here is a somewhat random list of additional ideas.

1. Be aggressive in obtaining visibility in media outlets respected by individual investors. These include business/financial publications, business shows on television, business sections of local papers, and the trade press, which is widely read by analysts. Media visibility can make a difference in attracting investors and is treated as a separate subject in Chapter 16.

2. Consider media advertising. Several approaches are available. The most dramatic are ads in business/financial publications suggesting investment by detailing financial strengths and performance. Companies also are advertising in publications reaching targeted audiences—*Registered Representative, Pensions & Investments, Institutional Investor, Pension World*, the *Standard & Poor's 500 Index Directory*, and *Better Investing* (NAIC magazine). Ads are being placed in professional and hobbyist magazines read by wealthy investors.

   Also popular are the ads enabling readers to request the company's annual report. Because they are sources of revenue, numerous media outlets now run the special annual report sections each year including the highly respected business publications and dailies, metro dailies, investing and hobby magazines, and trades. While the ads can draw from hundreds to thousands of requests for annual reports, it's virtually impossible to quantify share purchases resulting from the apparent interest in the company. Companies tend to justify the ad expenditures in the context of building market awareness.

That can be said for the other kinds of advertising as well, including running advertorial releases on earnings or major corporate developments. While taking the form of releases, they are marked as advertising in the publications running the sections.

3. Produce a mini or employee annual report. The mini reports condense operations and highlight financial data. They can be used as mailers to brokers, with employees, at meetings, or in response to requests for annual reports. The reports tailor information to the audience and save on production costs. The same benefits apply to employee versions of the annual report.

4. Have an 800 telephone number available to both individual investors and brokers. Times for calling can be designated.

5. Identify brokerage firms recommending the stock and new research reports in annual and interim reports. Report on appearances at investor fairs in the interims.

6. Encourage odd-lot holders to round up rather than out, by offering to handle the transactions and cover costs.

7. Pay higher dividends for longevity in holding the shares.

8. Send reprints of favorable articles to brokers and investors.

9. Use product packaging to invite customers to contact the company for investment information.

10. Produce a video that tells the company's investment story for use at broker, shareholder information and investor club meetings. Promote the availability of the video to investor clubs in interim reports.

As Markets Globalize, So Does Investor Relations

U.S. and Canadian institutions are investing in the industries and companies of Europe, Japan, in Latin America, and other countries in the Pacific Rim. They're studying closely the developments occurring in Eastern Europe. They're constructing international portfolios to diversify and thus lower their risk while improving returns by investing in strong and growing enterprises, trading around the clock through various exchanges and electronic transaction systems, and tracking their performance by using reliable global equity indices.

British, Scottish, Swiss, German, Italian, Dutch, Swedish, Norwegian, Spanish, Japanese, Korean, Chinese, Australian, Middle Eastern, and Latin American institutions are investing in the industries and companies of the United States and Canada, trading mostly through the American exchanges and NASDAQ, but also using their local exchanges, and tracking performance by following the Standard & Poor's and other reliable equity indices.

U.S. and Canadian corporations are raising capital around the world, utilizing debt and equity instruments, and seeking deals that afford low cost. European and Asian companies as well as many in other countries of the world are raising capital in North America and elsewhere through the use of both debt and equity instruments and are gaining an enthusiastic response from American investors who are showing an eagerness to buy the issues as they diversify portfolios and seek superior returns.

The capital markets are truly global. The implications for investor relations are enormous. Investor relations people will need to prepare themselves to know a great deal about the global market as a whole and each part their company chooses to take part in. Indeed, investor relations people should be doing their homework, in advance, so they can advise their companies on the markets to participate in, whether the decision involves hunting for new capital or for investors for the current shares. Many investor relations people are working at both jobs now—conducting investor relations programs abroad and counseling management on the best markets at the moment for debt or equity offerings.

Opportunity and technology are coming together in creating an integrated worldwide capital formation/investment market. First, opportunity. Economies around the world are growing, using capital and creating a need for more of it. But those same booming economies, in the countries of Europe and Asia, for example, also are producing huge money pools available for investment. Companies can tap these capital sources where the deals appear to be best; staying home or leaving home, with many choices.

At the same time, investors, looking for the best returns, are placing assets worldwide. U.S. institutions invest in the strong economies, industries, and companies of Europe, as Japanese and European investors increase their holdings in the "blue chips" of America.

The increase in capital needs and the increase in capital funds are generating more sophistication in the methods of searching for the best deals and the best investments, creating competition everywhere the searches are taking place.

Technology is driving and facilitating these sophisticated pursuits. Information flows internationally, communications is ongoing, and transactions are accomplished in seconds. Deals to raise funds are done as quickly as the windows of opportunity rise. Research moves around the world, giving investors information for their decisions or input for their models. Transactions take place

24 hours a day, completed electronically or through the exchanges and bourses of the world. Underlying securities are bought and sold, actively, in programs, or through indexation; risks are hedged with options and futures.

The United States is no longer the dominant source of stock. At the end of 1988, U.S. equities were 13.7 percent of a $22.2 trillion investable capital market, according to numbers from First Chicago Investment Advisors. Non-U.S. equity was 28.4 percent of the total. Thus, 42 percent of the wealth was in stocks. Bonds accounted for over 44 percent: 20.2 percent in dollar bonds and 24.2 percent in non-dollar bonds. Real estate was just over 7 percent and cash equivalents just over 6 percent.

Share of the equity market held in the United States as measured in capitalization has declined from 54.9 percent in 1980 to 29 percent at the end of 1988, reports the Securities Industry Association (SIA). However, the actual value during that time virtually doubled in the United States, rising from $1.2 trillion to $2.4 trillion. Japan shot ahead, moving from having under 17 percent to over 45 percent of the total in a mere eight years. Share in the United Kingdom has slipped from 9 percent to 8.5 percent, while equity value in the rest of the world combined has dropped from 19 percent to 17.4 percent. Worldwide, SIA reports that total equity capitalization went from $2.3 trillion to $8.4 trillion in the eight years. These numbers of course, are changing continuously, and sometimes can move rapidly, especially when dramatic economic or political events grab hold of capitalization.

The fundamental changes reflect economic reality. Money is leading and following the economic gains being made around the world—supporting them and resulting from them. Japan's economic might is legend. A half-dozen additional Pacific Rim nations are building impressive economies. Countries of Western Europe are forging head; whatever success comes from a unified Europe will only add to its strength. And now, Eastern Europe appears about to embrace capitalism. Meanwhile, the economies of the United States and Canada sustain their patterns of growth, even though they may be losing ground comparatively by some measures.

INSTITUTIONS DIVERSIFYING GLOBALLY

Institutions are leading the movement toward international investing—American funds being invested elsewhere, foreign funds coming to America. At any point, foreign investors in any domestic market may be net buyers or net sellers of stock, depending on whether the investing conditions are bright or stormy. The October 1987 crash, for example, drove foreign investors from the U.S. market, but they returned as undervaluation opportunities became evident.

That institutional investment wandering is a reality and it is revealed by the numbers. U.S. pension funds were estimated to have about $80 billion invested outside the country in 1990, most of it in Europe, Japan and Singapore. In its annual report on activities of the 200 largest pension funds, *Pensions & Investments* reported a 43 percent increase in assets invested internationally, with some $32 billion held in stocks. About half of the 200 biggest pension sponsors have equity investments outside the United States, with more jumping in all along.

Foreign investors are just as busy in the United States. A European portfolio manager estimated that something between 25 and 30 percent of typical European institutional equity portfolio is in U.S. stocks. Recent numbers also show the Japanese to be net buyers of American equities.

International investment essentially is a portfolio strategy for institutions. Fundamentally, it seeks to reduce risk by increasing the universe of assets included in the portfolio. Sticking with the domestic segment is limiting, because it is smaller, leaving out a passel of stocks that work to diminish the risk. Risk reduction rises with a greater number of assets possessing lower return correlations than the domestic group alone. The strategy also works to improve returns by expanding the number of high-performance companies that can be included in the portfolio.

That global diversification pays off is shown in comparing performance of the *Morgan Stanley Capital International Europe, Australia and Far East Index* (EAFE) with the returns of the composite

Standard & Poor's 500 Index. The EAFE scored an 18.8 percent compounded annual return over 15 years, compared with 12.2 percent for the S&P 500. In recent years, the differences have been even wider, and higher. Volatility of the two measures of performance is shown to be about even.

To get the returns, the diversification must be truly international, studies indicate. Investing in domestic companies with overseas operations doesn't move the needle. The studies conclude that national risk dominates in multi-national companies.

Institutions have learned how to compensate for one of the two major risks peculiar to international investing—the vagaries of currency fluctuation. The other, political risk, remains a judgment call. Investors are dealing with the currency fluctuation by buying currency futures. Several are traded in the United States, through the *International Monetary Market* on the Chicago Mercantile Exchange. Since currency gains or losses are adjusted in the local currency, the fluctuations can impact portfolio returns for better or worse. The hedging through currency futures is used instead of selling the stocks to avoid the currency risk. The technique eliminates the need to do any selling or buying of the underlying stocks that could upset the return calculation, saves on transaction costs, and enables the portfolio manager to stay invested in the attractive stocks.

Foreign investing in the United States is growing measurably, and incentives to pick up the pace are being facilitated by some rule changes. Americans are showing a preference for *American Depositary Receipts* (ADR) in investing in non-U.S. companies. With most of the trading in foreign companies executed through the U.S. exchanges and NASDAQ, the ADR popularity should continue. Making ADRs available also is seen as a confidence booster by American investors; it indicates the foreign company is in the U.S. investment market for the long haul.

Activity in the U.S. private placement market among foreign companies and investors is expected to take off now that rules relaxing the registration and disclosure processes have been waived. Until the new Securities Act Rule 144a went into effect in 1990, the American private placement market had been the nearly exclusive domain of domestic companies. Just in corporate debt, private placement has proven viable, moving from a $16 billion annual market in 1980 to nearly $200 billion by the end of the decade.

Rule 144a is being hailed as a breakthrough in easing capital formation and is expected to create a whole new market of substance, running alongside the public market and consisting of both debt and equity. The rule allows sizable institutions (managing $100 million or more in securities), brokerage and financial institutions to cut private placement deals with companies in either stock or bonds, and then trade those securities among themselves—all without the laborious, time-consuming, costly, legalistic registration/disclosure process. The SEC reasons that big institutions are capable of doing their due diligence well and don't need the protection of registration and massive disclosure.

Foreign companies are overjoyed at not having to disclose information that they are not accustomed to revealing. They also appreciate the cost savings and ability to move quickly in offering securities also is appreciated. Domestic companies also see the benefits of lower cost, negotiated deal making and potential for a net drop in the cost of capital.

One concern of the SEC is making sure privately placed securities never reach the public markets. The commission is convinced the private and public markets can operate side by side. Safeguards against spillage are being built into the system.

The rule can put investor relations professionals into a more powerful position, provided they capitalize on it. There's also a downside if they're caught napping. The challenge and opportunity involve tracking the private placement holdings among institutions in the aftermarket. That's a process involving much closer contact with institutions and brokerage firms, probably extending the contact base beyond analysts and portfolio managers to include traders. Stocks in the private placement market will be sold verbally, not by prospectus. If they haven't until now, investor relations people will need to be inside the investor network, knowing the players and following the action on a daily basis.

Their role as information sources also will expand. On occasion, they'll have to figure out why they're being asked so many

questions. The inquisitor may or may not say that a private placement transaction is being considered.

ASSEMBLING AN INVESTOR RELATIONS PROGRAM

Opportunities abound for North American companies to obtain
capital and broaden their investor base throughout the world. Investors are drowning in the money pools of Europe and Japan;
they have no choice but to invest abroad. Local governments are
making it easier to do so by lifting traditional technical and regulatory barriers to investing away from home. The United States and
Canada continue to be leading choices—government securities,
mutual funds, and corporate bonds and stocks.

Sources of these investment funds bode well for the future. In
Japan, it has been the combination of a booming economy and the
Japanese penchant for saving. Japanese investment in foreign securities is estimated at around $350 billion, with over half in the
United States, covering government and corporate debt with a
growing interest in stock. In Europe, the assets of insurance companies and pension plans are growing dramatically, especially the
latter as a maturing population and declining tax base motivate the
building of what is becoming a massive private pension system.

In Europe, the investment market is largely institutional,
which includes huge holdings of individuals that are managed by
professionals in unit trusts. Wealthy individuals tend to follow
professional practices. In Japan, the market historically has been
made up of individuals with their strong saving bent. But, professional money management has taken hold, as mutual and pension
funds grow. The giant Japanese bank and insurance segments also
are investing more in overseas equities.

The first question for companies seeking to extend their institutional shareholder base internationally is one of practicality: Will a
proactive communications effort produce any meaningful result?
And, at what cost, in terms of money and executive time? There is
no easy answer, since several factors work into the web, not the
least of which is the quality of the program.

But, there are some guidelines. Number one involves assessing the likely interest of overseas investors. Big and well-known companies clearly have an edge, among both European and Asian investors. Main reasons are the ability of investors to conduct meaningful research and trade in the stocks easily. Chief source of information is the research of the company's home country analysts. Thus, substantive brokerage analyst coverage becomes the basis of an international investor relations program. Most of the trading is done through the appropriate American channel, namely the New York Stock Exchange, or to a lesser degree, the NASDAQ National Market System, or American Stock Exchange.

Already having an investment base overseas is valuable. It demonstrates established investor confidence. That foundation may have been set by a previous offering, or the company's presence, carved through local operations, direct contact or some build-up of investment originated entirely by the investors themselves. On that latter point, existing foreign brokerage or institutional support adds a big boost.

In these scenarios, "blue chips" have an advantage, as do consumer companies with popular brands, and giant industrial companies whose names have gained global prominence. Chemical, metals, electronics, and energy companies are included in that latter group.

A presence in the local country can serve as an incentive to investors, emanating from familiarity, a sense of support, or close access to information and contact. That presence can be product participation in the markets of the country or region, a production plant, local subsidiary or joint venture operation.

Companies also can be favorably disposed for foreign investment by virtue of niche leadership that is seen as auguring well for the future. In most cases, the niche is a technology, new product concept or unique and exciting marketing idea. European and Japanese institutional investors like to follow certain themes, that can be as broad as favoring a nation or sector, or as specific as a technology or product group. Smaller companies often are the beneficiaries of these opportunities.

Companies with a built-in advantage can exploit it with an aggressive investor relations program. Foreign institutions aren't reluctant to invest in American companies just on the basis of research and analysis, but their interest and confidence certainly are peaked or confirmed when these investors are able to study the company's management in action first-hand.

Thus, a well-planned and executed international investor relations program has to have a positive effect for companies that meet the qualifications of investors or can be shown to be attractive. However, many companies make the mistake of starting a global program before the markets are ready to consider them. A basis of familiarit, or support evidenced by a strong rationale for investing or meeting fundamental qualifications just isn't there yet. Investors aren't likely to take the time or feel secure enough to do the investigation and buy the shares without the endorsement of respected research or institutional holders. Small companies especially are vulnerable to the temptations of overseas investors.

Nothing says companies must pursue investors outside their own country of operation. In fact, many companies stay home and fare quite well. Observers see a two-tier investment market emerging. One is global, occupied by companies with worldwide markets, benefitting from tapping capital sources here, there and everywhere, drawing research interest from brokerage firms internationally, and attracting institutional investors from far and wide. Most of the companies will boast of large equity capitalizations. The other tier will be operating essentially in their home markets, supported by a domestic shareholder base. Market capitalizations will range the spectrum.

PLOTTING THE COURSE

The next decision is where to go. The focus of American companies has been on Western Europe and Japan. Other markets in Asia such as Singapore and Hong Kong, both substantial money centers, may become targets. Other parts of the world are sure to be considered as economies grow. Part of the decision depends on an investor relations strategy. One approach says go where the money and investors are; another suggests hand-picking smaller markets where the presence of a company's senior executives may have more impact on investors.

However, the odds favor accomplishing more in the bigger markets: prominent brokerage and institutional segments are available for contact; there is a greater likelihood of utilizing contacts for effective networking; and familiarity with the company should breed support. The biggest securities markets of Europe in terms of capitalized value are the United Kingdom, West Germany, France, and Switzerland. The key major money centers covering these countries are London, Frankfurt, Paris, Zurich, Geneva, Basel, and Edinburgh. Leading stock exchanges among these countries are in London, Frankfurt, Paris, and Zurich. But there is a caveat: most of the foreign institutional trading of U.S. equities is accomplished through The New York Stock Exchange. Still, some of the European exchanges are "more friendly" toward non-domestic companies than others. Over half of the companies listed on the Zurich exchange are foreign and more than a third of the equity volume is non-Swiss. The Frankfurt exchange is almost half foreign listed, while foreign trading volume in Paris runs over 40 percent.

About half of the listed members and volume of the Amsterdam exchange also is non-domestic. The Netherlands, Sweden, Italy, Belgium, and Spain are candidates for an extended program. Europe's 10 leading exchanges, measured by equity capitalization, also include Milan, Amsterdam, Stockholm, Madrid, Brussels and Luxembourg.

In Asia, Japan is the clear choice for results-producing, cost and time-conscious American managements. The Tokyo Stock Exchange has vaulted into prominence in the past several years and now takes its place among the big three of international exchanges—second at this writing. For years, the "big four" Japanese brokerage houses were pushing U.S., Canadian, and European companies to list on the exchange. They and the other brokerages of Japan are a link to the vast resources of the country's citizenry, and have contacts with the growing institutional segment.

The rush to get foreign companies on the Tokyo exchange has abated, however, because little of the trading in foreign stocks is done in Japan. Most of it is handled by the exhanges in the company's home market through the local country's own brokers. In conducting the transactions this way, Japanese institutions are relying on foreign broker expertise while saving on taxes and benefitting from not paying the fixed commission rates of their country. Companies wanting to go beyond Japan should at least consider Singapore, Hong Kong, Korea, and Australia.

Before the century ends, U.S. companies are sure to be tapping capital and investors in the Soviet Union and other Eastern European nations.

In selecting locations, the company's presence in the country should be a weighty factor. A strong product acceptance gives consumer companies a head start. PepsiCo and McDonalds come to mind. Market penetration also might exist for industrial companies with certain important investor groups, such as business leaders and institutions. More concrete are business relationships—a sizable production operation or visible subsidiary or joint venture operation. Foreign companies are taking a page from U.S. investor relations strategy and turning the tables in North America, inspired largely by their acquisitions. Many foreign companies have hired U.S. investor relations firms or installed an investor relations director in the States. They're advertising their corporate presence in America in popular and business magazines and on television. Siemens is an example.

Local market research and a basic decision on who to use in arranging investor contacts should precede any foreign foray. The research is aimed at developing an investor profile of the country and determining the key channels of investor influence. It breaks out the institutional/individual investor mix, and quantifies the key investors in each segment. For institutions, it measures the percentages of the equity pie held by banks, pension funds, mutual funds, insurance companies, investment managers and others. The research also is designed to help companies learn the trends in equity investing among institutions. Are certain institutional groups investing more in stocks, and why? Regulations restricting or limiting the amount of foreign investment, for example, are going by the boards in certain countries. The research also gets a better handle on the brokerage role and seeks to quantify the relative importance of each firm. For individuals, wealth and location demographics and trends are desired.

The following sketches are general because the trends are evolving and the numbers constantly changing. The United Kingdom is dominated by institutions, but individuals have returned to the market in droves in recent years, responding to Prime Minister Margaret Thatcher's urging for "popular capitalization." The number of individual investors has risen from about two million to nearly 10 million, representing over a fifth of the adult population, according to the research firm of Banque Paribas Capital Markets. About half the assets are in pension funds, a third in insurance companies and one-seventh in unit and investment trusts.

The Swiss market is marked by wealthy private investors who are active in foreign markets. As indicated, half the listed companies and a third of the trading volume are non-domestic. The domestic market is dominated by 10 huge companies that account for over half of the total capitalization; they include Nestle, Ciba-Geigy, Hoffman-La Roche, Sandoz, and the nation's three biggest banks and three biggest insurance companies.

Foreign investors heavily influence the West German market, mainly institutions. Historically, the market has moved with foreign interest. Individual investment is relatively small—about 3.5 million shareholders. Most of the trading involves leading German companies. Thus, while capitalization is large, the market is seen more as an investment vehicle for outside institutions than as an opportunity for companies to place shares in local hands.

The French market has opened wider to international investors, with Europeans leading the way. Institutions in France pace the internal action, primarily banks, insurance companies and investment firms. The brokerage industry has had lesser impact, characterized by small firms, but it is starting to move. France has about 6 million individual investors. The once-chummy Paris Bourse is giving way to modern times as it competes with the Frankfurt exchange for continental Europe supremacy in rolling toward a unified Europe by 1992.

Mountains of surplus income combined with the high prices of Japanese securities sent Japanese investors around the world in search of good investments. They came to Europe and North America, investing mostly in government instruments (Treasury bills as an example) and corporate debt first, expanding into corporate equity. This picture may change as the Tokyo stock market declines, creating more investment opportunity at home for Japanese investors. Japanese institutions have gotten more comfortable investing in foreign equity, overcoming some original reluctance. Many Japanese banks and brokerage firms have set up operations in metro New York, competing for investment business and doing their own investing homework. Some 70 institutions represent about 70 percent of Japan's holdings of foreign securities, according to IR Japan, Inc., a Tokyo-based consulting firm. Japan has some 20 million individual investors, who remain important to the country's local markets.

In addition to the pre-launch research, companies need to decide carefully on the assistance teams they engage. An inside track to the investment community serves as a powerful engine. The choice of sponsorship comes down to brokerage and banks. Both provide benefits—relationships and contacts the company doesn't have. But the sponsorship cuts out other banks and brokerages, running the risk of limiting the audiences at meetings or failing to gain hearings from some major investors. Brokerage sponsorship also can include U.S. firms, whose style leans to setting up one-to-one or small group meetings with their institutional clients.

The alternative for companies is to arrange the meetings themselves, working with consultants who have strong investment contacts. Europe has a corps of respected investor relations consultants, as does Japan now. A number of leading U.S.-based investor relations firms also have offices in Europe and Japan. Typically, the consultants help identify institutions and research analysts, use their contacts to arrange appointments or gain their attendance at meetings, and handle much of the administrative detail, such as setting up luncheons, distributing materials and drumming up press interest.

Companies seem to be opting for a combination of sponsored and self-managed programs. The decision may come down to the quality of the brokerage or bank relationships and their clout with investors versus the company's own ability to attract the right people with some consulting help. The best course of action also may vary by country.

MAKING A COMMITMENT

European investors have complained about a lack of commitment by American companies, as shown by their proclivity for getting in and out of town fast. The idea that U.S. trips through European money centers should be something of a whirlwind probably took hold out of investor relations people's concerns for executive management's time. In some quarters, at least, it has left an ill feeling.

The visits are the heart of an international investor relations program, but investors need to be assured that the brain is working every day. Formats can be fashioned variously, as long as the information flows evenly, not running for a while, then disappearing. Continuity is what counts, once the information process begins. That suggests communication well before any initial meeting, continuously after that, and in-between visits. The regular communications pattern includes frequent telephone contact, plus assurance that information is only a phone call away, and the steady arrival of mail, with timely material releases and announcements sent by facsimile or telecopy. Companies are using their overseas investor relations consultants in filling the pipeline.

Companies also seem to be expanding and slowing their schedules, taking additional time in each city, seeing more people individually or in small group or meetings. They're not covering as many cities on a trip; before, six to 10 in one or two weeks was not surprising. They're being more selective in the choice of cities as well, not feeling a compulsion to go everywhere, but instead focusing on the centers that make sense because of capital market size or the company's operations in the country.

The traveling contingent can be from one to several persons—chief executive officer, chief financial officer, president, key operating executive, investor relations officer. Debate is unending on whether there is a right person. And, there are schools of thought. One says investors and analysts insist on getting to meet and know senior management. Because the tradition in general still is to be long-term investors, the evaluation of management is the pivotal determinant in whether or not to invest in the company. In addition, these investors have relatively easy access to corporate chief executives in their country or region; American companies demonstrate their commitment by being available. And, competition for investment in Europe has tightened with the growing economies and strong companies there. The second school says the CEO tends to draw institutional and brokerage officials of like title, leaving the chief executive talking with the people who aren't making the investment decisions and deciding which companies to follow.

The consensus seems to be send the top brass the first time, with the CFO or investor relations person becoming the regular spokesperson after that, in follow-up contact and perhaps subsequent visits. However, the CEO should not vanish, but be available for telephone calls and to meet with investors on their trips to America. As the program extends over years, the CEO should return periodically.

Investor relations people need to demonstrate their qualifications as reliable spokespersons, according to a number of surveys of foreign investors and analysts. The investor relations practice is newer in most other countries; apparently, investor relations people are still winning the respect of the investment community overseas.

FORMATS FOR MEETINGS

Cultural and custom considerations are critical in planning meetings and conducting investor relations programs. They provide opportunities for good and bad impressions. Local consultants can be helpful in getting companies to mind their manners properly. Luncheons are the most popular meeting time. Breakfasts are frowned on, dinners are seen more as social events.

Group luncheons are likely to function as introductory situations, especially when the number of people attending is sizable. Small group and individual meetings are essential and necessary to stimulate serious discussion and interest among portfolio managers and industry specialists from brokerage firms. In cases of individual and small group meetings, the participants probably have a built-in interest; they're shareholders, already know the company, or have confidence in the person extending the invitation.

Presentations should be geared for the audience. A basic overview should be given in introductory sessions, but can be boiled down for more knowing audiences, where the emphasis is on relative performance of business units at home and internationally, details of the financial structure, operating and financial strategies for the future, impact of macro scenarios on the company, and plans to deal with problems. The overview should cover the company's fundamental strengths (product, technology, market share, financial position) and describe both home markets and other operations. Local operations in the country or region should be covered thoroughly. Foreign analysts and investors are particularly interested in hearing about the potential impact of macro economic and political issues.

Local officials from the company can add measurably to the success of the endeavor. They can make introductions, offer the welcoming, give the talk on the local or regional operation, and participate in the question session. They should take part in any social events.

It's fine to use the English language. Presenters are advised to speak clearly and deliberately, avoid jargon and slang. The communications process is aided by providing copies of the speech, any charts or graphs, and other printed materials. Providing these in the local language can only help, but isn't considered necessary. It's more of a help, however, in Asian countries.

In planning trips, companies are advised to be extremely thorough, working out every logistical detail before boarding the plane. Checklists should be comprehensive. Executives should be given detailed schedules. If the trip is to be packed with stops, chartering a plane will save hours of time.

Companies have experienced mixed results from listing their shares on local exchanges. Trading volume seldom increases substantially, an indication that whatever share buying is occurring is being done by institutions utilizing the exchanges in the company's home country. Meanwhile, the costs of listing can be hefty. The best rationale for listing seems to be the combination of a product or joint venture presence and desire to be more visible in the country, regardless of whether that helps build revenues or interest in the stock.

Historically, companies venturing around the world with their investor relations programs had to be content with softer measurement results than managements might demand in the United States. Tracking share ownership was difficult at best. There aren't any required filings that identify the holders or give clues. But now, services are available in Europe that work with the minimal basic data and add their own research. The leading U.S. list suppliers are adding substantially to the names of European and Japanese holders. U.S. consultants are identifying institutions with investing styles that match the investing characteristics of individual companies. Sophisticated investor relations is moving abroad. In addition, companies have gotten comfortable with simply asking institutions if they're holding shares once the relationship has been established.

13

Annual Reports Are the Leading Printed Communications Tool

Companies have a powerful array of communications weapons in scoring with targeted audiences. Top guns in the corporate communications arsenal are annual and interim reports, 10-K and 10-Q reports, special letters, fact books and sheets along with a collection of other armaments including newsletters, videos, white papers, article reprints, and dividend mailers.

These various vehicles give companies the opportunity to focus their communications by selecting the best methods for each targeted investor group. The selection process can be two dimensional:

1. using research to understand the communications vehicles preferred by each audience; and
2. maximizing the value of those vehicles by tailoring the content and style to the audiences.

Companies also can build communications packages to cover the information flow efficiently. The combination of a 10-K, an annual report, and a fact book is an ideal package for industry analysts, for example. The 10-K provides the proscribed data in detail; the annual report builds from the 10-K by describing strategies and amplifying on results; and the fact book fills in critical information gaps for fact-hungry analysts.

There is a tendency among companies to hold back the full potential of their communications opportunities. The reason, at least in part, may be psychological, but the result, in terms of missed opportunity, can be real. Financial communications carries that "required disclosure" stigma. It puts managements into a negative thought stream: "We won't reveal any more than we have to, and we would prefer not to give as much information as we do." Chief victim of this kind of thinking has been the annual report; it has had trouble growing up as a viable communications document. It have been glossed over graphically while earning an unsavory reputation among investors. Fortunately, the annual report child is now maturing.

Companies should be aggressive about their communications materials. Billions of dollars are spent on them by corporate America (including Canada) every year. The *cause célèbre* is the annual report. It's senseless to waste that money, replacing action-driven information with pretty pictures. Together, good information presented in a graphic format that enhances readership and accurately portrays the company's personality can be a powerful communications medium.

THE 10-K AND ANNUAL REPORT AS A TEAM

In most surveys, the 10-K report (required to be filed with the Securities and Exchange Commisison each year) wins the vote of securities analysts as the most useful corporate communications document. The report requires companies to provide essential information that is numbers-based but also includes other key descriptions of operations, financial structure, and the conduct of the business.

Typically, the reports are written in the corporate finance department with close legal scrutiny. Investor relations people should have two hands in the process as well—in preparation, hopefully, but certainly in editing and as advisors in making sure the reports fulfill their potential as highly informative investor sources.

Surveys also indicate that analysts and investors alike give low marks to the information quality of annual reports. This skepticism has grown up over the past 20 years and has become a bias that companies are now hard pressed to overcome. Annual reports are the "Rodney Dangerfields" of corporate communications. But, just as Rodney is effective, so are annual reports becoming increasingly so. Yet, analysts and investors are slow to acknowledge that annual reports are getting better.

Professionals in the investment business who rely on information would be happy to see every corporate communiqué become rich in value. Companies can't seem to end the search for the annual report's rightful place in the communications mix. Or, for that matter, decide how the communications mix should come together.

Some companies put the 10-K into the annual report, add a shareholders' letter, a few other annual report standard items, and wrap it all in an attractive cover. Some companies are stingy with information. They rationalize (perhaps unwittingly) that the report is being prepared mainly for individual investors. Some companies cling to the tradition that annual reports are for individuals. A persuasive investor relations person sometimes is successful in convincing the managements of these companies to publish a separate fact book for the analysts. Some companies try to expand the audience, using the clout and the credibility of the report to make it a marketing piece. And, some companies load their reports with data beyond the 10-K, concentrating the content on analysts and institutions.

Ideally, the 10-K and the annual report work in tandem in order to build the investor story. The 10-K gives the essential descriptions and lays out the numbers. The annual report:

sets a strategic framework, reports on the year, and projects the future within that strategic context;

brings the operations to life in numbers, word descriptions, and illustration;

makes the financial structure and philosophy meaningful;

defines and updates the investing value drivers; and

provides additional factual detail and numbers that are vital in understanding the absolute and relative investment strengths of the company.

How far companies are willing to go with these reports determines whether a fact book also should be produced as a data and detail supplement. As annual reports have been beefed up, they have taken on some of the content of traditional fact books. However, fact books are still preferred by many companies, for a number of reasons. They can be updated more readily; some companies produce them in "loose-leaf" form. The format lends itself to tailoring the information for the audience (namely, analysts and portfolio managers doing their own research). Thus, the annual report is kept flexible to appeal to a wider audience. The annual report might contain a six-year selected data summary, for example, while the fact book gives 11 years. Or the annual report may provide 11 years of data while the fact book reports on 20 years. Comparatively, the fact book may show more operating data or industry statistics. It might include detailed biographical information on directors and senior management or in-depth, numbers-driven profiles of each business unit. These are, of course, candidates for coverage in annual or quarterly reports as well.

POSITIONING THE ANNUAL REPORT

Companies get sidetracked in producing their annual report because they worry about overdisclosure, get too promotional, let the project grow larger than life, or take it all too personally. Sometimes, a combination of these factors is at work. The tendency to be more promotional and less forthcoming is potentially the deadliest. In these cases, self-serving language and graphics take the spotlight from the information or message. Analysts see the report as "slick" and shareholders accuse the company of hiding the truth. Striking photography and innovative design can turn into negatives. The stories of analysts lament over beautiful coverups are legend.

Too much management concern and involvement also can produce an ineffective result. The report takes on a larger-than-life role inside the company. Management appears too serious, too nervous, or striving for perfection. In these instances, there can be an intent to hold back or write around the information as much as there is a desire to express an idea with maximum impact. Everything gets worded so carefully that attempts at effective communication fall short or the copy loses any journalistic quality, frequently coming off as mundane, self-serving or filled with "corporatese." The CEO, CFO, operating heads, chief counsel, and others with authority become more involved than they should. The report becomes a committee project, often fraught with disagreement that leads to a bland, or at best uneven, finished product.

Companies seem to struggle the most with the first question that should be answered in planning an annual report: "Who is it being written for?" The issue gets overworried. The primary audience should be present and potential investors and those who influence the investment decision, namely analysts and perhaps brokers. The annual report is meant to be the report card for investors; it fails when its principal purpose is perceived as falling short of the mark. A report that does its basic job well will satisfy those other important audiences—customers, employees, and future executives. The information that should be contained in the report is exactly what these audiences should know—a good corporate profile, strategic plans and programs, results and prospects, and a thorough financial rundown.

By thinking too much about these other audiences, companies can fall into the trap of being too promotional; they overwrite and overdesign the report. It becomes something closer to the so-called "corporate capabilities" brochure. Capabilities brochures also are difficult to do well. Too many turn out more as "image" than information pieces, thus lacking credibility. Instead, they should rely on fact-based information and an attractive, readership-enhancing design.

Companies have packaged the annual report and capabilities brochure, printing them separately, but mailing them together initially to shareholders, analysts and others. Additional copies of the capabilities brochure are produced. The rationale is that the capabilities brochure has an extended audience and a life after the annual report. The concept challenges companies to make sure the capabilities portion is highly informative and credible; otherwise, the annual report can be tarnished. It also questions corporate thinking. It would seem that the credibility of a well-executed capabilities brochure is elevated by being part of an already credible annual report. After all, the annual report is seen as the "official" corporate document. So why not mail it to customers, suppliers, and other key audiences? They're also prospective investors. The part of the rationale that does make sense is the ability to use the capabilties brochure beyond the natural life of the annual report. However, the concept carries the danger of creating an overly promotional brochure to take the place of what could be a hard-hitting operations review within the report itself.

Next, many companies debate pegging the report to certain audiences within the investor mix—institutions or individuals or the sell or buy side. A qualitative report can satisfy everyone. The report in total, and its various sections, provide ample opportunity to cover everything that anyone would want to know. For it to reach its potential, companies just need to be forthcoming, and effective in the writing and design of the report. Fundamentally, the annual report is a research, reference, and investigative tool for analysts, brokers and prospective investors, and a results-reporting vehicle and confidence retainer for existing shareholders. It serves as a comprehensive introduction and a source of information. It will be used differently by each person; what's crucial is that it be useful to each person.

Some dissection of a report helps illustrate the point. Every reader benefits from an excellent discussion in the shareholders' letter of the company's key strategies, the progress made on each during the year, and the near-term prospects. The information may be edifying to an individual investor or institutional portfolio manager beginning to consider the company as an investment, but familiar territory to an industry analyst who has been following the business for a dozen years. Still, that analyst is very interested in the insight that can be gained from seeing how management describes its priorities and frames the results of the year. The language easily can be universal. A well-written letter isn't above or below the knowledge levels of any investor segment.

Those same analysts may study the income statement, balance sheet, and other financials more closely than the individual investor. They will scrutinize the footnotes and hope for something meaningful in the management discussion and analysis section. The fund manager will appreciate a well-presented review of operations which provides a breakout of revenues and profits among business units and a basis to compare the company against others in the industry. Worthwhile industry data rings up applause.

Whether the report should have a theme becomes a major issue at some companies. The conviction that a theme is needed can be a detriment; it can get in the way of producing a good report. There is a tendency to select themes that distract from what should be the central message of the report. Employees, facilities, products, the emphasis on service, marketing, technology, management, or globalization are all popular annual report themes. The focus of the report should be on what makes the company a sound investment. In recent years, companies have begun concentrating on describing what constitutes the essence of their intrinsic worth. Themes, if you want to call them that, have covered key value drivers, such as cash generation from brand name products, leadership in technology or marketing, or being the industry's low-cost producer.

Progressive companies are using their annual reports more aggressively in carrying forth the notion of shareholder value. The report becomes part of the "share management" process; part of the company's efforts to have a greater influence on how its equity is valued. Companies are describing their principal elements of value. The approach is in tune with corporate interests in appealing directly to institutions. The objective is to attract institutions' by showing how the company's investing characteristics and strengths match the institutions investing strategies.

As a result, the educational value of reports is rising, broadly among all investor audiences, not just institutions. The reports also can widen the understanding of individuals and brokers and can be more useful in expanding sell-side analyst following, as well.

The tack taken by Quaker Oats Company in the last few years serves as an excellent example. In its 1988 annual report, the company described its basic strategy as "turning brands into cash flow" in a statement on the cover. Inside, a special interview with CEO William D. Smithburg described the process, starting with the delivery of value to shareholders by providing "more cash over time—in the form of dividends and capital appreciation—than they invested in our stock when they bought it."

In the interview, the CEO discusses the financial goal of optimizing cash flow from brand names to fund current returns for shareholders and "strategic reinvestment for future profitable growth." The description is worth quoting.

> "We gauge the cash flow generation potential of a project by looking at three key factors:
>
> 1. the brand's prospective sales growth;
> 2. its profit margin; and
> 3. the amount of investment cash needed to support sales growth and our projected profit margin.
>
> We have borrowed the term 'value drivers' to describe these factors because sales growth, margin levels, investment and cost of capital do, indeed, determine a company's 'value.' Our assumptions about these key factors let us assess the relative desirability of future investment and do it in terms of today's dollars. This process is known as *discounted cash flow* (DCF) analysis. After we weigh the strategic business issues, we use the discipline of DCF analysis to choose investments producing a profitable return, equal to or better than our minimum required rate of return, which is also known as our 'cost of capital.' That way we keep improving our profitability for shareholders."

In the shareholders' letter, Quaker laid out its financial objectives which dealt with quantifying returns on equity and earnings, dividend policy, and capital structure; and its operating strategies, which were focused on brand leadership and growth in specific businesses.

The investment story continues to be told in the company's quarterly and annual reports. Quaker publishes an extensive, magazine-style quarterly, which enables the company to produce comprehensive, educationally oriented articles on a range of financial and operating subjects. One issue, for example, had side-by-side pieces on "Why Cash Is Still King" and "Demystifying DCF." The publication is used to profile various branded product value drivers and describe key corporate strengths, such as consumer marketing.

Quaker's 1989 annual report contained a follow-up interview, called "Perspective: Be the Best." In it, CEO Smithburg describes the company's goals of excellence, detailing strategies to achieve them through products. In the interview and the letter that follows, financial and operating objectives again are spelled out. The company clearly is managing its assets consistent with these philosophies, as evidenced in more recent announcements that involve substantial moves, such as spinning off its toy operations.

The Quaker publications also illustrate the concept of continuity. Continuity of communication is both desirable and achievable through the sequence of annual and interim reports. One way of assuring continuity is to view the reports as chapters in telling the investment story. Companies are writing four or five chapters each year, depending on how many interim reports they produce. The number of chapters can be even higher—post annual meeting reports, special letters, and materials mailed with dividend checks all count in the communications flow. Companies should consider the reporting and education processes as ongoing. What is presented to investors as important one year shouldn't be ignored in the next annual report. In fact, it may be important enough to cover in quarterlies. The annual and interim reports are information building blocks.

THE REPORT'S MAIN SECTIONS

The communications value of an annual report rises when its four main sections are unified—the four being the letter, the "narrative" or operations review, the management discussion and analysis, and the financial statement and footnotes. Fighting cohesion is the corporate tradition of having too many cooks creating the meal—accountants, lawyers, financial, public, and investor relations people, as well as perhaps one or two assigned writers. As a result, the report can contain contradiction, inconsistency, and unevenness. It can be written well in one section and poorly in another, give information in depth and then be superficial, or present the same factual information differently. The investor relations officer should be the head chef, with enough authority to blend all the ingredients into a successful communications recipe.

If the shareholders' letter is the main course, the financial statements/footnotes are the *pièce de résistance*. The operations review makes up the side dishes. The management discussion and analysis is the special salad. No meal is complete without it. Not to be overlooked, in this food-for-thought experience, are the corporate profile (the appetizer), financial highlights (the soup), and investor information section (the sorbet or fine assortment of fruits and cheeses, as you wish).

Let's dig in. Please pardon us, if we consume this fine meal somewhat out of order.

The Letter to Shareholders

The letter to shareholders is the most important section. Surveys indicate that the letter is the most widely read part of the report. It also sets attitudes toward the overall quality of the report. The letter is signed by the top executive or group of executive officers. Investors and analysts judge not only the content of the letter, but the CEO or executive team as well. The letter is revealing in many ways. It can reveal:

what the chief executives consider to be important;

what they see as opportunities and issues;

their approaches to management; and

their expression of themselves.

It also gives clues into their personalities—relaxed or tense, flamboyant or conservative, free or tight with information.

Managements tend to not take full advantage of the letter. Those who sign it should spend time contemplating its meaning. The exercise will prove to be a boon to annual report writers who want to get inside the CEO's pysche. Together they can create an outstanding communications effort. Or, the aware CEO will do it alone. It is a letter. It offers tremendous flexibility in terms of content and style. It also offers the opportunity to impact the company's reputation and value as an investment. A number of companies and CEOs have used the annual report letter to build singular investment interest. The annual report letters of Berkshire Hathaway Company's CEO Warren Buffett, for example, are legendary. The letter can be warm, relaxed, and highly informative. It should project a personality. Unfortunately, most managements succumb to the stereotypes by adapting the same formula that has been followed by virtually every company for years and using the same kind of language.

Writing a good letter isn't easy. This advice is offered. The trick is for the CEO to forget that the letter is for the annual report. Pretend that it's being written to a trusted friend or associate. Focus on how you would describe the company's vital strategies, where they stand now and what you expect in the near future. Cover any problems which have occurred and what the company is doing about them. Report on any important recent developments. Describe any industry or other factors that will affect the plans and programs. Show concern for the investment implications of the corporate actions by indicating results expected from them. Write the letter as though you were talking with the other person. People write letters that way.

When all the remaining elements in the report are loaded with information, the letter can be brief. In truth, it shouldn't carry the report. It should serve as the strategic overview, covering financial, operating, organizational and administrative highlights. The detail and amplification follow in the operations review, management analysis, and financials. The letter should state or restate the strategic priorities and report on the progress made with them during the year and plans to continue advancing them in the time ahead. It should review the financial results in the context of previous years and previous goals. It should discuss problems (continuing or new) and the efforts to resolve them.

The corporate information committee of the Financial Analysts Federation, now a part of the Association for Investment Management and Research (AIMR), critiques annual reports and other aspects of investor relations every year. Because the committee is composed of analysts and portfolio managers, its suggestions carry a lot of weight with investor relations people. The committee offers specific suggestions on the content of each section of the annual report. The letter needs to be objective, relevant in reporting results and candid in appraising problems, according to the committee. The letter should:

review the year;

give insights into operating rates, unit production levels, and selling prices;

cover any acquisitions or divestitures, capital expenditures, or start-up expenses;

report on R&D programs;

give employment costs, labor relations, and union contract information;

cover energy, environmental, and OSHA costs;

give backlogs;

describe new products;

discuss any legislative and regulatory developments;

detail unusual income or expenses; and

provide an outlook.

Most companies precede the letter with financial highlights showing net sales, operating and net income, earnings per share, and return on shareholders' equity as compared for two years. Professional investors like to see the percentage differences from year to year, and some prefer three-year comparisons. The top section of the highlights may include such other information as total assets, return on equity, capital expenditures, as well as senior and suborbinated debt. Most companies also provide per common share data by giving net earnings, dividends, shareholders' equity, and book value. The financial highlights also are likely to include a shareholder profile section, giving the number of shareholders of record, average number of shares outstanding, shareholders' equity and market price range for the year. The highlights page might include charts displaying key financial returns.

The Financial Statement/Footnotes

The financial section enables analysts to do their ratios, conduct a detailed study of the company's performance, make comparisons with previous years, and comparisons with other companies being followed. The income statement and balance sheet will get most of the attention, but the other statements and notes will be scrutinized as well.

Here are the major information pieces that should be covered in the financial summary and footnotes, according to the analyst and portfolio manager members of the corporate information committee:

statement of accounting principles (with explanations of any changes and their effects);

adjustments for earnings per share dilution;

operating information on unconsolidated subsidiaries and affiliates;

sources and applications of funds and a cash flow statement;

a complete study of tax accounting that includes investment tax credits, as well as a breakdown of U.S. and non-U.S. current and deferred taxes;

reconciliation of effective and statutory tax rates as well as the impact of changes in tax law;

a clear explanation of currency-exchange-rate accounting including the earnings impact of balance sheet translations and indication of the operating or income account effect of exchange rate fluctuations;

a discussion of property accounts and depreciation policies including methods and asset lives used for tax and financial reporting, and quantification of the effect on reported earnings of the use of different methods and/or asset lives for tax purposes;

valuation of investments;

inventories covering the method of valuation and spelling out each method used for various products or geographic locations;

terms and liability of leases and rentals;

debt repayment schedules;

pension fund information including costs charged to income, interest-rate, and wage inflation assumptions as well as the amount of any unfunded liability and its amortization period;

a discussion of any other postemployment benefits including their liability and impact of the proposed standard for retiree healthcare benefits;

capital expenditure programs and forecasts including costs for environmental improvements;

acquisitions and divestitures covering the activity and its operating impact, type of financing, effect on sales and earnings, and detail on any pooled deals that don't require restating prior years' results;

year-end adjustments;

restatement of quarterly reports to year-end accounting basis;

research and development covering new products and costs;

a discussion of contingent liabilities;

the amount of goodwill being amortized and number of years;

derivation of shares used in calculating primary and fully diluted earnings per share; and

a 10-year statistical summary that includes adequacy of income account and balance sheet detail, useful "non-statement" data such as number of employees, adjusted number of shares, stock price data and capital expenditures, and consolidated data if applicable.

Operations Review

Two sections of the report perceived by investors as not living up to their potential are the operations review along with the management discussion and analysis. Companies have carte blanche with the so-called "narrative" or "editorial" section that typically follows the letter to shareholders. For most companies, this section either reviews operations or tells the theme story. It also takes the biggest hit among critics who see the section as self-serving, without good detail, or graphically glossed up. Companies need to work to change that perception. This is the section of the report offering the best opportunity for sending a strong message that can impact share price. It is the section providing total freedom in describing the company's value drivers or reviewing operations in a fact-based, hard-hitting manner.

The value drivers may involve:

brand-name superiority;

cash-generating products or dominant marketshare;

technological excellence which produces a competitive advantage;

industry-leading production skills;

programs that are bringing results in managing each business
unit on a cash flow basis;

the reasons why consistent earnings and sales growth will be
maintained well into the future; and

new management incentive programs.

In reports which review operations, here is what the pros are
looking for:

complete breakouts of sales, materials, costs, overhead, and
earnings by each division or business segment;

an enlightening discussion of each division's product position,
market size and growth, market penetration, and geographi-
cal coverage relative to the industry;

details of unusual developments and management's response
to them;

a review of foreign operations, covering revenues (including
export sales), consolidated foreign earnings versus equity
interests, and market/regional participation and trends.

The Management Discussion and Analysis

The Securities and Exchange Commission has gone back to the
well a couple of times in seeking to improve the information value
of the Management Discussion and Analysis of Financial Condition and Results of Operations—the MD&A as it is known. In
studies conducted throughout the 1980s, the SEC has found that
the MD&A is falling short of its intended job. Its job is to have
companies describe their operations and financial condition in narrative form, covering material information, and giving the story a
forward thrust. The proposition is tricky; companies are expected
to shed light on the future in a material way. Companies are expected to disclose known trends, known demands, commitments,
events or uncertainties that will result or are likely to result in

material increases or decreases in liquidity, capital resources and their mix or cost, changes in sales, revenues or income from continuing operations. They're also expected to disclose material events/uncertainties that are likely to cause current financial statements to change in the future.

The latest round of interpretive guidelines from the SEC came in 1989 as a result of studying the MD&A reports of some 345 companies. Several companies were cited for inadequate reporting. The SEC does have the power to require compliance. Part of the problem from the beginning has been the original guidelines which suggested a format for the discussion. Companies have followed the form to the letter ever since. The effect has been to turn the MD&A into a routine and not a very revealing report. Instead of using the MD&A creatively and aggressively to provide meaningful information that can help analysts and investors evaluate the company's investment opportunities, managements have taken advantage of the untested initial guidelines to underplay the information requirements.

The new guidelines encourage companies to disclose more by tightly defining the requirements and by giving numerous examples. By issuing them, the SEC also has a basis for its demands as it judges compliance. The SEC defines the difference between "presently known" and "optional forward-looking disclosure." The key, it says, are events or changes that can be "reasonably expected to have material effect," and cites product pricing reductions, lower marketshare, or nonrenewal of a major contract as possibilities of such. Companies are advised to review every known trend, demand, commitment, event, and uncertainty for each operation of the business. In addition, the SEC says companies should be "anticipating a future trend or less predictable impact of an event, trend, or uncertainty."

The SEC guidelines also put companies on notice to evaluate the material effect in the future of each known, or past event or situation affecting operations or financial condition. Again, the commission gives examples. One involves decisions to continue spending capital in maintaining a major market position versus a decision to cut spending back and risk losing that position. Another involves reporting on the uncertainty of renewing a major contract and its material effect.

There even is some help in assessing materiality. If management's best judgment is that the event, demand, or uncertainty won't happen, disclosure isn't necessary. If management is unsure, it must judge whether the event would be material if it occurred. Disclosure isn't required if the effect of the action is immaterial; otherwise, it needs to be aired.

Qualitative discussions of liquidity and cash flow are a strong intent of the SEC, with the MD&A as the vehicle. The company must evaluate the amounts and certainty of cash flows; indicate which balance sheet conditions, income or cash flow items affect assessing liquidity; and discuss future short- and long-term sources and needs of capital. Short-term liquidity and cash sources cover cash needs for the next 12 months. Long term is defined as covering material capital expenditures, major balloon and other payments due on obligations, any off balance sheet or other commitments beyond the next 12 months, and the sources of funding expected to cover these needs. Material deficiencies in short- or long-term liquidity must be disclosed as well as management's present indecision on how to deal with the problem.

The guidelines point out the advantages of recently passed Financial Accounting Standards Board (FASB) Rule 95 in helping investors gain a clearer picture of cash flow by analyzing liquidity and by dissecting cash flowing from operations. Replacing the report of changes in financial condition, the statement breaks out net cash provided or used by each operation and the net effect of those flows on cash and cash equivalents. Items included are discretionary operating expenses (advertising, for example), research and development, equipment maintenance, debt refinancings or redemptions, and financing provided by customers or suppliers.

SEC studies found a number of companies wanting when it came to explaining material year-to-year changes in line items and in quantifying the contribution of two or more factors in these changes. Examples of situations calling for analysis include:

those that are material;

where the changes diverge from changes in related line items;

where the changes create material rise or decline in sales or revenues; and

where explanations are needed to understand the extent of each of two or more factors in the material change itself.

The SEC is careful to say that MD&A disclosure requirements involving mergers or acquisitions are not meant to produce premature disclosure. There isn't any need to disclose preliminary merger negotiations if disclosure isn't otherwise required or hasn't been made partially.

Investor relations people can contribute to the information value of the MD&A. Their sensitivity to what is useful to analysts and investors would be enormously helpful in elevating the quality. Writing and editing skills should be applied as well. Companies will benefit from having the assigned annual report writer take part in the exercise or by editing the draft at minimum. The end result should be a more readable MD&A that flows with the rest of the report.

The Cover, the Corporate Profile, and the Investor Information Page

Three parts of an annual report that often get short-shrift are the cover, corporate profile, and the investor information page. Companies seem to want to make the cover either beautiful or bland, instead of it being a hard-working communications device. The cover is the first opportunity to gain reader attention. It shouldn't be wasted. It should communicate. A striking photograph or other attention-arresting idea is fine as long as it sends a message that is central to the thrust of the report. A line of copy that captures that thrust is even more valuable. Certainly, the photo or illustration and copy can work together. Copy lines these days are concentrating on shareholder value.

The corporate profile is a writing challenge that can be well worth the effort. The SEC officially calls it the Description of the Business. It usually appears on the inside front cover or first page. The profile needs to be brief, but in that brevity it can speak volumes. It should lay out the company's key businesses and products, give its market positions, and articulate its fundamental strengths. Companies frequently use the profile to present their mission statement and vision of the future. Or, they include the statement on the same page. The AIMR corporate information committee asks that a separate statement of corporate goals appear somewhere in the report. This can be the place. The corporate profile is particularly valuable to new shareholders or prospective investors using the annual report as an introduction to the company.

An extended version of the profile is finding its way into an increasing number of reports. It divides the company into its business units or product groups, presenting essential information on each—a tight business description focused on products and markets, competitive analysis, summary of results for the year, segment data or charts showing the returns that drive the company, and the near-term outlook. Its purpose is to give readers on one page or spread the totality of the company and a quick, but still thorough study of its parts. The entire company is dissected in a detailed two-page spread. Companies have taken to calling the spread, "At a Glance."

Companies are promoting their expanded shareholder information services in the annual report. A growing tradition, the investor information page is likely to include the name of the investor relations contact, availability of a toll-free 800 telephone number for calling the company, description of the dividend reinvestment plan, quarterly range of stock prices for the year, names of the transfer agent and registrar, date and place of the annual meeting, identity of the auditors, instructions on how to acquire a copy of the 10-K report, and the names of listed exchanges. Seen lately in a few reports have been the names of brokerage analysts with recent research studies on the company and a list of the largest shareholders.

PREPARATION AND PRODUCTION OF THE REPORT

Corporate tensions about annual reports inevitably spill into the preparation and production phases. An annual report is a project where a cast of 10 is better than a cast of 100. Creative successes are not best accomplished by committees. Putting the report into the professional hands of a few people is desirable. The result will be superior when the work is done by a handful of very professional people. That doesn't mean input should be exclusive. It can come from a diversity of people qualified to provide ideas and information. But not editing and approval. Input and authority need to be separated.

Indeed, authority needs to be established. There is executive authority, probably the CEO, and there is creative authority, probably the top public affairs or investor relations officer. A wise CEO guides the report to make sure it covers and accurately positions the essential information, and nurtures the creative process, curbing any desires to dictate it. The ideal annual report team has two tiers: executive and creative.

The executive team is led by the CEO and probably includes the CFO, president, key operating officer, legal and accounting representatives, and one or two functional officers (R&D, marketing) depending on the focus of the report. Others selectively are given the opportunity to comment on copy because of their inherent involvement.

The creative team consists of the top officer with responsibility for communications, investor relations officer, the writers and designers, and production supervisor, if that job is separated from design. Most of the time the designer assumes responsibility for production.

A production schedule is critical. It gives the company a charted course. The company that stays on course stands a better chance of maintaining creative control and thus retaining the integrity of the original storyline, and of maintaining cost control and thus keeping the report from costing more than was budgeted. The production schedule works back from the date the report must be mailed. From start to finish, the basic production elements are:

determining the central focus and content;

hiring the designer and setting up the complete schedule;

hiring photographers and scheduling photo shoots;

conducting information research and interviews;

approval of a design concept and how it will be implemented throughout the report, obtaining an estimate of the number of pages and the required paper stock so that it can be ordered;

first draft of copy presented for editing and approval;

determination of subjects for charts and their design approach;

selection of photos and page-by-page approval of the design execution;

final copy approvals and typesetting;

final approval of all copy and financial pages;

page mechanicals and approval;

blueline from the printer and approval;

printing, with on-press supervision;

binding; and

delivery.

The design and writing determine the quality of the report. Both must be built on substance. It shows, when one is up to standards and the other isn't. For years, design led the way. Companies encouraged their designers and photographers to be creative while they held back their writers. Or many times, management assumed most of the writing. Some of the finest examples of commercial design and photography over the past three decades are found in corporate annual reports. Unfortunately, a highly designed and beautifully photographed annual report that contains little substantive information leaves analysts and sophisticated investors skeptical.

Times are changing. The message is taking center stage and design/photography is taking its rightful place by enhancing communication and readership, providing information, portraying the company's personality, and projecting its image. Managements are recognizing the importance of information and good writing. The ability to influence investors is based on information and the annual report is a costly communications opportunity that should be maximized.

As the value of information rises, the quality of writing improves. Perhaps, this progress is the result of dealing with more meaningful information and a willingness to describe strategies and developments openly. It is easier to write well when expressing concrete ideas and facts than when trying to avoid them.

Traditionally, writers have had a more difficult time in having their way than designers or photographers. That appears to be changing. It has been a fundamental inconsistency. The writing represents the company just as much as the design and photography. Most managements are conservative by nature. Why would they strive for creativity in design and photography and insist on bland, stilted writing? Until now, the answer would seem to rest in the opportunity for managers to write and edit copy; most are not confident enough to take pictures or lay out pages. However, most managers aren't writers either but it doesn't stop them from writing, editing, and applying their conservative personalities to the company's written communications. If the mindset is truly moving toward being forthcoming, corporate communications will be improved and investors and other constituencies will be better informed. Optimistically, brighter days are ahead for the writing in annual reports.

Annual report writers need to be insiders, whether they are inside or outside the company. They should have access to corporate information and executives. They should spend enough time with the signers of the shareholders' letter to understand their personalities as well as the major points to be communicated in the letter. This same kind of research base and access should be provided by executives and managers giving input into other sections assigned to the writers.

The graphic designer's role in preparing annual reports is multi-dimensional. Not only does the designer create the physical attributes of the report, but he or she also steers the production process. In this capacity, the designer is in a position to take the lead in scheduling and production control. Companies do themselves a favor when selecting a designer who is an expert on production and printing and who will work hard to keep the report on schedule and within budget.

Good designers know how to fit the graphics into the overall communications process. They understand that design is not the end, but one important and potentially exciting means to the end, namely enhanced communications. Be wary of designers who see the graphics as larger than life, who only are interested in the design and show neither an understanding nor desire to understand the basic purpose of the report. Look for designers who are eager to get a sense of the audience, understand the objectives of the report, know the major information points to be made, and who want to help shape the creative direction. Designers create graphic approaches and implementation methods for presenting information. Design does three fundamental jobs:

1. it gives the report its physical stature;
2. it makes the report inviting and easy to read, thus maximizing its informational value; and
3. it uses various graphics tools in presenting the company as a living, breathing entity.

It helps give the company a personality or an image. Designers create graphic concepts, bring them to life in layouts that make use of such elements as type faces and sizes, column structures, space, shapes, lines, color, paper, photography, and illustration. There's something magical about the ability of designers to employ these elements in a myriad of creative ways and combinations to convey information, evoke acceptance of an idea, or get a divergent group of readers to see the same personality traits in a business monolith.

Designers will be dogged in keeping the report on course and schedule. To do so, being in tune with the communications purpose is essential. From their unique perch, designers can spot situations that are sending the message astray. Editing may be the culprit. The designer's uninvolved objectivity comes to the fore. Subjects selected for the charts may not be as relevant as other candidates. Or, the photos picked from among the choices may not carry the impact of others in telling the story.

Because they know how long it takes to complete each production phase, the designers should take charge of the scheduling process. They will insist that approvals come through on the appointed dates, keep reminding the company about the costs and time delays that result from changes. Here is where a company's insecurity that gives too many people approval authority can raise costs, slow production and subtract quality from the report, whether it be in the writing, graphic appearance of charts, or other llth-hour nitpicking that seems so common. What the designer worries about the most is losing press time or encountering overtime at the production or printing stage. The good annual report printing houses run tight schedules since so many reports are being printed at the same time.

Designers will live alongside the presses during the run. They're conducting a continuing quality control monitor. They will scrutinize each press sheet before the run begins, making sure the inks are working in unison for color precision and that there aren't any blemishes on the pages. They will ask that sheets be pulled during the runs to make sure that the integrity is being maintained. Companies like to approve the press sheets as well; it is their last opportunity to catch an error—in the typesetting, a misspelled director's name, or a line of copy that somehow was dropped in the page paste-up.

In recent years, efforts to communicate more forcefully have been growing. Writers and designers are working together to improve the communications power of reports. The emphasis is being motivated by responses to surveys that indicate annual reports have low readership and out of a desire by companies to make their reports more effective. The heightened aggressiveness starts with the cover where companies now are signalling the essence of the report with a brief, punchy copy line. The attitude is that the cover is critical in getting readers into the report.

There is a much greater use of such communications devices as working headlines, subheads, and call-outs. The *headlines* drive an idea, instead of simply identifying the subject. *Bold subheads* both announce and summarize the next major topic within the copy. *Call-outs* are the specific ideas within the text that capture its substance. Typically, they appear in boldface, surrounded by white space, to gain attention. They are chosen carefully to communicate the significant points of the report. A person reading only the call-outs will have the story.

Photo captions are working a lot harder as well. They are being written to provide additional information, not simply repeat what already is in the text. Photos are being selected for their informational value, as well as their visual appeal. Charts, graphs, and illustrations are showing up more in annual reports. Often, they are the best way to convey information, making it easier to understand or punching up its impact on the reader.

SUMMARY REPORTS HAVEN'T CAUGHT ON

The basic annual report, as we have come to know it, has three cousins—the summary report, the mini report, and the employee annual report. Several years ago General Motors cleared the way for a summary report with the Securities and Exchange Commission. Ironically, after getting permission from the SEC to publish a condensed version of the annual report, GM never went ahead with its plans.

Companies are free to publish a summary report as long as they fulfill the basic disclosure requirements which call for providing shareholders with audited financial statements about the same time they are receiving proxy materials. The idea is to make sure shareholders have sufficient information to vote knowingly on proxy matters. The audited financial statements can take any form.

A number of companies have picked up on the summary report concept. They argue that the report is better in communications value than the traditional report because companies are freed up to focus on the message, unencumbered by the dictates of financial disclosure and number of pages that adds to the report. Cost savings also result. Critics counter that the inclusion of financial detail only strengthens the report without detracting from a company's ability to plan the content, as well as write and design the report to maximize its informational contribution.

Only a handful of companies are publishing summary reports regularly. The rest of corporate America may be reacting to negative security analyst response to the idea. Analysts expressed concern that the summary versions would be lacking in information, and further that it would be difficult to gather all the data, dispersed across several publications. Companies producing summaries seem to have answered that concern by providing analysts and investment managers with the report, audited financial statements, and other pertinent materials in one mailing package. These companies seem to have become proponents of the concept, citing surveys they have taken that indicate higher annual report readership and favorable analyst reaction. They also claim to be saving money.

Some companies have seized upon the summary report concept in order to streamline their financial communications. McKesson Corp., for example, has gone to four quarterly publications, each about the same number of pages, with one serving as the summary report. McKesson says the net result is shareholders are receiving more information over the year, meted out more evenly. The magazine-style reports contain financial detail each quarter and include substantial articles on the investable strengths of the company. The reports are distributed to employees and other stakeholders as well as investors.

In its summary report, McKesson has worked hard to condense the financial data without leaving out any of the essential information. The result is a more readable financial section, the company believes.

Mini annual reports are published each year by a number of companies. The idea seems to have been pioneered by Hershey Corp. and picked up by Harsco, two central Pennsylvania-based companies. The mini versions usually contain 8 pages or more and capture the essentials of the company, strategically, operationally, and financially by providing numbers, a review and preview, and a business profile. They are designed to enhance communication with certain audiences, while reducing costs simultaneously. The reports are used in broker communications contact programs, sent in response to inquiries from advertising and in filling requests for information. They also can be used at investor club fairs and provided to such audiences as employees. They serve as a gauge of potential interest in the company as well. Brokers order quantities of the reports for their customers. Some people ask for the full report.

Employee annual reports seem to come in and out of favor. In these times of cost reduction, few companies are preparing employee versions. The reports are seen as highly educational. They tailor financial information and the economic impact on the company to employee interests. The objectives are to encourage employee-share ownership by elevating their critical operating and financial knowledge of the company, and increase their sense of participation in the fortunes of the company.

MARKETING THE ANNUAL REPORT

Aggressive companies are marketing their annual reports by either getting them in the hands of potential investors or by using the reports as a basis of gaining more information.

Companies incorporate questionnaires into the report, for example, using a tear-away insert form to retain the integrity of the rest of the pages. The survey cards are being used for a number of purposes. These include:

1. marketing the dividend reinvestment plan or customer share purchase plan;
2. asking for comments on the report and communications program; and
3. seeking investor profile data.

The questions give the company such information as how long they have held the stock, reasons for investing in the company, size of their holdings, whether additonal purchases have been made, whether they use a broker and his/her firm and name, and something about themselves—age bracket, where they live, male/female, approximate income, profession, and so on. Lowes Corp. has used annual report questionnaires for some 20 years now as a way of keeping a running profile on its shareholders. Other companies give beneficial owners the opportunity to identify themselves and be put on the regular mailing list. An insurance company even sells its products through a return card included in the report.

Companies are promoting the availability of their annual reports through advertising and direct mail. Numerous publications run "annual report advertising" sections each spring. They range from business/financial newspapers and magazines and metro dailies to special interest, hobby, sport, and similar publications. The number and quality of responses in terms of turning up prospective investors vary all over the lot. Companies rationalize the value of the programs as a way of broadly reaching out to the retail investor base. They also believe in the general exposure benefit of appearing each year in these marketing sections. It's virtually impossible to determine how many of the hundreds or even thousands of people requesting the reports become shareholders.

Financial or corporate advertising is a second method of marketing the annual report. The ads promote the company as an investment, suggesting that people write or call for a copy of the latest annual report. Corporate ads also can be designed to market products and/or the reputation of the company. The ads provide companies a choice: the financial message is primary, with product or reputation secondary, or other variation.

Annual reports or their mini version are the basis of mailing campaigns, mainly to brokers. Companies may have an existing list or purchase the national or certain regional lists available from such sources as Technimetrics, CDA Investment Technologies or *Registered Representative* magazine.

POSITIONING QUARTERLY REPORTS IN THE MIX

The traditional quarterly report may be heading for obsolescence. "Traditional," in this case, is defined as a skinny little report, typically measuring about 4 inches by 9 inches, and covering 4 to 8 pages that consist of a shareholders' letter, a couple of news briefs, and minimal financial data. The report is losing out for three interrelated reasons. Analysts and institutional investors want more information and they want it fast. Technology is proving to be the vehicle for providing the information quantitatively, qualitatively, and quickly. Quarterly reports don't arrive in the mail until well into the next quarter.

Quarterly earnings results are the pivotal piece of information driving the change. The institutionalization of the equity markets has heightened the desire of analysts and portfolio managers to receive detailed earnings data swiftly when released by the companies. Investor relations people are beefing up the data provided and turning to faster methods of disseminating it to analysts and institutions. Reading the results in the media or over the Dow Jones/Reuters wires is inadequate because the information is sketchy. A company's numbers appearing on the ticker only serves as the trigger for analysts that the news is out. Until recently, the investor relations person could be assured of a rush of phone calls from analysts and major investors wanting the full text of the release read to them. A host of questions typically followed.

Now companies are sending the complete release with detailed financial backup directly to key analysts and institutions via a number of electronic dissemination methods—facsimile, First Call, Telescan, the PR Newswire, or BusinessWire. First Call and Telescan have extensive analyst and institutional subscriber bases. PR Newswire and BusinessWire reach directly into hundreds of brokerage firms and institutional investment houses. The information also is available online on a host of electronic retrieval databases from minutes to the day after it first runs. Investor relations people report that the number of phone calls from analysts on release day has declined. Those that are coming through are

uide to financial market

concentrated on the quality of earnings or involve specific discussion as analysts look for insights that can help them with their institutional clients.

Accompanying the basic news release are consolidated balance sheets, income statements, financial highlights, cash flow statements, segment data, updated key financial ratios and returns, and other information appropriate to the company.

Some companies also widely mail the comprehensive release packages, covering brokers and shareholders in general as well as the media, analysts, and key institutional holders.

This new emphasis on speedily transmitted thorough quarterly information has left the quarterly report in limbo. A few companies are considering dropping it. Many are leaving it alone, believing it still is useful to individual investors, even arriving 45 days or so after the quarter ends. They're right. Individuals shouldn't be given short-shrift in the communications flow. The trend is toward an expanded quarterly report that does triple duty in appealing primarily to individuals by increasing the educational content, but in the process, also adding information for the benefit of institutions and other constituents. Companies producing expanded quarterlies like to send them to employees, political, business, and community leaders as well. Quaker Oats, McKesson, AT&T, and a number of the regional Bell companies are among a growing group preparing substantive quarterly magazines. The idea isn't new. It actually dates to the 1950s and 1960s, with such pioneers as General Electric and Abbott Laboratories. The heftier quarterlies are seen as creating a closer dialogue with investors through the continuity of fuller communications.

Sell- and buy-side analysts have been urging companies for years to give more information quarterly. They are virtually demanding quarterly segment data; companies not providing it are judged by the AIMR corporate information committee as not having a worthy investor relations program. Here's what members of the committee are asking companies to provide in quarterly reports:

depth commentary on operating results and developments;

discussion of new products, management changes, and problem areas;

detailed profit and loss statement, including divisional or segmental breakdown;

a balance sheet and cash flow statement;

restatement of all prior and current year quarters for major pooling acquisitions and quantification of the effect of purchase acquisitions or divestitures;

breakout of nonrecurring or exceptional income or expense items, including effects from inventory valuation and foreign exchange translation factors; and

explicit statement of accounting principles underlying quarterly statements.

The analysts also are asking that the reports be prepared in a timely manner, and that companies produce a separate fourth quarter report. Much of the information they seek is being provided in the expanded news release packages.

In its guidelines on preparing more useful MD&As, the SEC also deals with the need to describe material changes in 10-Q reports. Changes to be evaluated for their importance include the impact of known trends, demands, commitments, events or uncertainties coming up during the interim period. The SEC cites as examples internal and external sources of liquidity, expected material changes in the mix and relative cost of these resources, and unusual or infrequent events or transactions affecting reported income from continuing operations.

THE VALUE OF OTHER PRINTED COMMUNICATIONS MATERIALS

While the 10-K, 10-Q, annual and interim reports are the big guns in the corporate communications arsenal, other weapons can be highly effective. The AIMR corporate information committee lists a number of materials its members particularly favor:

an annual meeting report that includes coverage of the question/
answer session;

statistical supplements and fact books;

copies of addresses to analysts groups, also including the Q&A
portion; copies of company magazines, newsletters, product
and personnel pamphlets; and

copies of important press releases.

The committee suggests that companies do themselves a favor
by making sure the analysts and institutional portfolio managers
are sent proxy materials, the 10-K and 10-Q reports, and any other
pertinent financial documents.

Fact books or statistical supplements are aimed at analysts and
portfolio managers who do some direct research and thus want to
delve into corporate and industry data. As previously described,
these books fill the information gap between annual and 10-K reports, providing such key numbers as:

inventories, backlog, operating rates, and production levels for
the company and industry;

breakouts of expenses;

financial ratio and return data;

numbers-oriented, detailed business unit profiles;

thorough biographical data on directors and officers;

complete descriptions of each international operation, subsidiary, or joint venture; and

ll-year or more selected financial data charts.

What specifically goes into the fact book is driven by what's essential in understanding the company, its markets and the industries it
fits into based on its products.

Fact sheets are geared to brokers and their retail customers who
are prospective shareholders. These are most often two- or four-
page reports highlighting the company, spelling out its basic investable characteristics, and summarizing key financial data. A

report may contain five value drivers in a headline format; each amplified in single paragraph copy blocks. The typical report will include:

a corporate profile;

quick discussion of current business developments;

a narrative description of fundamental business strengths;

a list of top officers, key financial returns and ratios;

a consolidated balance sheet;

an income and cash flow statement;

possible segment data;

the names of largest shareholders;

current analyst recommendations;

exchange listings;

recent share price highs and lows; and

the name/phone number of the investor relations contact.

Companies either prepare the fact sheets themselves or hire a professional direct mail house to work them up. Technimetrics and Research Services magazine are leading sources. Technimetrics mails a packet of fact sheets on a group of companies each month to its list of brokers in the United States and Canada. Brokers interested in a particular company order additional copies to use in showing their customers the investment merits of the company. *Research* is a monthly magazine, carrying "advertorial" articles about companies paying to be included. Brokers order reprints to help in their customer sales.

The fact sheets also can be used in selective mailings. Companies might want to focus on certain regions, metro areas, states or even a specific brokerage firm. The particular locations may be part of a road show or other direct contact effort. Tailored broker lists can be purchased from Technimetrics, *Registered Representative* magazine, or CDA Investment Technologies, which offers its Bullseye Service. Companies can use their own produced fact sheets or those made up by the professional direct response firms. Fact sheets serve as handouts at broker meetings or accompany invitations to the meeting. These handy, hard-hitting investment profiles also are being used in responding to information requests generally.

A close relative of the fact sheet is the Investor's Information green sheet employed by the National Association of Investors Corporation. Investor relations practitioners are buying quantities of these investment profiles, similar to S&P or Moody's reports, for mailing to investor club members, use at investor fairs and broker meetings, and mailings to brokers. In addition, fact sheets or NAIC fact sheets should have value in direct mailings to individuals— selective mailings to existing shareholders, with dividend checks, in information packages sent to people responding to annual report and regular financial advertising.

Special letters from the chief executive officer have impact with investors. Some share-value consultants believe these state-of-the-business letters are more effective with institutional investors than other forms of communication. They're certainly popular with individuals, who have a sense that the chairman is writing to them. The letters offer the flexibility of being conversational and informal in describing developments in the business or covering the strategies and programs that are determining the company's intrinsic worth. Letters also are used to explain major shifts of emphasis within the company or news that may have been announced recently in the press such as an acquisition, divestiture, restructuring, or significant management moves. A letter can be written to shareholders any time the company deems it appropriate.

Investor newsletters are starting to be published by companies. What's appealing about newsletters is their format; they can be whatever the company wants them to be. In this flexibility, newsletters have a psychological edge over some other printed communications format. A newsletter, for example, may be the ideal way to "talk to" the analysts. More detail or depth analysis of a strategic corporate move is given. But the newsletter also lends itself to tailored communications with the buy side—analysts and portfolio managers. There might be a series of articles on how the company values itself; the first article lays out the elements of valuation, subsequent stories cover each value driver. Equally comfortable is a newsletter that updates brokers on corporate news and carries features on various products, markets or businesses. What distinguishes these newsletters is not so much the subjects, but the amount of information given and approaches used in providing it.

Dividend checks shouldn't go into the mails empty-handed. A check without some kind of printed piece is an opportunity to communicate missed. Appropriate *dividend stuffers* include brief product brochures, cents-off product coupons for consumer companies, reprints of media articles, news updates, that letter from the CEO, survey questionnaire, dividend reinvestment plan brochure, and virtually anything else that serves shareholders and adds to their knowledge of the company.

Companies like to welcome new shareholders with a letter from the president or chairman. The letter may include an *orientation brochure* that helps acquaint new shareholders with such corporate services as registering and transfering shares, recovering lost certificates, contacting the company. Some companies even send letters when shares are sold. Reason for the sale may have nothing to do with disenchantment in the company; the investor may be a prospective buyer in the future.

State of the art in printed communications is the in-depth *white paper* on a subject that is critical in the company's stock price valuation mosaic. Bausch & Lomb, for example, has produced a series of white papers for analysts and institutional investors covering value drivers in greater detail than what is found in the annual report.

EMERGENCE OF ELECTRONIC COMMUNICATION

The emerging world of electronic communication for corporations includes videos, audio-visual presentations, audio or video teleconferencing, appearances on subscriber television, and availability of a toll-free 800 telephone line for direct conversation with analysts, brokers and investors.

Videos get mixed reviews. Main audience seems to be brokers, but broker response runs the gamut from no interest to such a high level of interest that the tapes are being shown to customers. Videos also are shown to individuals at investor fairs, shareholders at annual or other informational meetings, and used in introductory meetings with brokerage analysts and institutional portfolio managers. The veteran sell-side analyst who knows the company inside-out isn't likely to learn anything from a video.

Videos are being produced directly by companies, or through professional distributors, such as Research Video, which links up with brokers. Corporations also end up with videotapes after appearances on subscriber or cable television programs or at meetings that are taped. The opportunities for open or closed television are growing. An appearance before the New York Society of Security Analysts at a cost of $7,950 includes airing the presentation on the Institutional Research Network. About 100 leading institutions and brokerage firms are IRN subscribers. The shows are televised live, and subscribers also receive videos of the meetings, allowing any of the analysts or portfolio managers in the firm to watch the presentation at their convenience.

Incidentally, the New York Society of Security Analysts' meeting affords companies a wide range of communications exposure for their $7,950: the live appearance, IRN video, audio teleconferencing, audio cassette and video coverage, transcripts included in most of the electronic database retrieval "libraries," coverage in *Investors' Daily, The Wall Street Transcript* and more.

IRN, Financial News Network, and Reuters are offering companies opportunities to tell their investment story electronically. Companies pay for the appearances and receive videos of the programs. Reuter TV 2000 is a subscriber service with an audience of institutions and brokerage analysts. Shows are conducted live in Reuters studios in New York, London, or Tokyo, with other locations on the drawing board; investors watch on desktop TVs. The program follows an interactive format, with viewers able to phone in questions and take part in discussion. A built-in VCR also enables them to tape the meetings.

IRN has a number of show formats. A company can appear in the studio, interviewed by an industry analyst, with institutional subscribers asking questions from their offices. Or, IRN produces on-location videos of company events for airing at certain times. Companies also can share the spotlight with two other businesses in the industry insight program. IRN institutional and brokerage subscribers number about 100. For an additional fee, the basic 50-minute corporate presentation shown on the closed-circuit IRN network is edited into a half-hour program that airs three times on the Financial News Network cable station.

Teleconferencing serves as a technique for bringing investors together across the country or even the world in participating in a corporate financial presentation. The meeting takes place at one location; analysts and investors see it live on television at various other locations, are able to ask questions via telephone. Because of its high costs, teleconferencing hasn't been done that often in investor relations situations.

Also popular with companies are toll-free 800 telephone numbers. They usually are set up to encourage broker and individual investor calls. To control their use, investor relations departments are wise to designate certain calling days and hours.

The old standard in audio-visual presentations is the slide show. It is still popular (slides or overhead transparancies) for giving a basic corporate profile to new audiences or making it easier to understand the information, especially when it might be complex.

14

Well-planned Meetings Enhance Program Results

Meetings are a viable medium in the mix of ways companies provide information to analysts, brokers, investors, and prospects. Actually, meetings do double duty: they send information and they help establish and build relationships.

The second use may be more valuable than the first. Meetings bring corporate executives and investor relations people together with analysts, brokers, and investors. They pave the way for follow-up phone conversations, face-to-face sessions, and they help create greater interest in printed and electronic corporate materials.

Meetings become the communications continuum. They can be viewed as the glue that holds the process together. Let's follow the steps. Meetings start relationships. A brokerage analyst attends a society presentation; introductions occur between people and on behalf of the company. Meetings grow relationships. The analyst begins phone dialogue with the investor relations person, occasionally talking with the CEO. Meetings sustain the relationship. The analyst meets with several executives at the corporate offices and regularly attends the company-sponsored quarterly earnings Q/A sessions held in New York. Now the analyst is following the company, reading the quarterly reports, announcements sent by facscimile, media stories, consensus earnings forecasts and research reports of the industry analysts, and other pertinent materials.

Strategically, companies plan meetings into their investor relations mix. In ranking various communications vehicles, meetings are at the top for most companies. Working to improve relationships with analysts, institutions and brokers has never been more important than it is today, because of the changes taking place in the capital markets. The rise in indexed investing gives more impetus to widening exposure of the company's investing characteristics to a greater number of institutions actively managing their portfolios. The economic pressures on analysts makes being among the companies still widely covered even more valuable. Having contact with a network of the most productive retail brokers hikes visibility for the company and generates higher levels of stock recommendations.

ORGANIZING MEETINGS AROUND OBJECTIVES

Using meetings to reach and cover prime audiences is an integral part of investor relations strategy. In this context, it is desirable to lay out a meeting plan that covers the full year. Programming meetings in advance helps ensure an organized effort that will cover the intended targets. It also puts the meetings on the calendars of senior officers well in advance of the dates, and leaves more time to line up the best locations in each city. And, it adds flexibility. Knowing in January that a trip to Richmond, Atlanta, and Washington is planned for September allows for some juggling of dates, or sequence or other mid-course corrections that might favor quality attendance or booking the best restaurant or club.

Meeting planning is a fine art that can be turned into an exact science by an expert. The really good planner puts the people the company wants to see in the room each time, fills each day productively to maximize management's participation, moves executives from city to city efficiently and at minimum cost, leaves time for critiques, briefings, rehearsals and a little relaxation. Keeping executives fresh and enthusiastic for the last round of meetings in a three or more day excursion is no mean trick.

In planning meetings, companies need to piece together three sometimes disparate factors:

1. identify their prime targets among analysts, institutions, and investors;
2. determine where these targets are located, both domestically and internationally; and
3. decide the best kinds of meeting forums for reaching each group, and indeed, each individual within them.

There are no simple guidelines. Nor is there any consistency. An investment management firm in Los Angeles may attend a small-group breakfast meeting with other institutions, while turning down an offer to meet in their offices. A money manager in Kansas City may prefer the personal meeting to the group gathering.

The place to start in putting a meetings program together is to identify the principal targets. Doing it by category is the easy job: just like Rome, the universe divides into three parts: brokerage analysts, institutions, and retail brokers. The harder part is deciding which ones among each group to target. Building those lists answers the question regarding location. You go where the action is.

However, some companies reverse the order: they pick the locations and then research the top prospects in each. That works okay when investment firms and top-producer brokers are the targets, and the cities are large financial centers. There certainly will be money managers and successful brokers in each city. But the better way is to find the players first. Let's see it if we can make some headway in figuring out how best to do that with each of the three investment community segments.

With sell-side analysts, the identification task is fairly easy. The leading sell-side analysts tend to be clustered in and around New York City, because it is the headquarters for the brokerage industry. It's a good bet that the most respected analysts covering your industry will be working for the national wire houses in New York. The next important place to hunt for sell-side analysts is in your own backyard at the well-regarded regional brokerage firms. The regional firms typically have a handful of industry specialists and a number of generalists. The first thing to do is check each regional brokerage in the directory of the Association for Investment Management and Research or Nelson's *Directory of Wall Street Research* to see which firms may be covering your industry. The person to target in firms without an industry specialist is the director of research.

Regional firms have a number of good reasons to take an interest in a local company. They have the advantage of proximity. They can get to know the senior executives and investor relations people well. Information should be flowing to them nonstop. There's an affinity as well. The analysts (and brokers and institutions for that matter) can see the corporate office and plants, probably have neighbors and friends who work for the company. They almost gain information by osmosis; it's all around them. Ideally, a sense of loyalty grows. Regional firms have two good reasons for being interested in a local company:

1. they can make money from commissions in placing stock with individuals and institutions in the area; and
2. they can make even more money by being among the first firms to introduce the company as an investment to institutions nationally.

Regional houses in nearby cities are candidates. Firms in Baltimore, for example, keep an eye on Philadelphia area companies. Milwaukee and Chicago look after each other. The cities are close enough for the investment firms to consider calling on the company convenient.

Somewhere else in the country, there is likely to be at least one regional brokerage firm that has developed an expertise on your industry. The firm may have one or more analysts covering it. Chances are the firm built its knowledge and national stature with institutional investors from researching nearby corporations that were becoming significant participants in the industry. That research created expertise that eventually was noticed by institutions or promoted to them. Hambrecht & Quist in San Francisco qualifies as a high-technology authority.

Next come institutions. Companies can start by doing some research that leads them to strategic decisions. Or, they can make the decisions and then do the research to decide where to concentrate their contact efforts. The "which comes first" question always surfaces in these kinds of decisions. An illustration helps illuminate the decision choice. In targeting institutions, deciding where to hold meetings and who to invite, the basic piece of research is data gathered from 13(f) filings which are the required SEC records of equity holdings by major institutions. From CDA Investment Technologies, Vickers or Technimetrics, companies can order various breakouts of those filings that list their own institutional holders and those of any number of other companies—in their industry or otherwise-constructed peer group.

These lists virtually reveal the identity of every institutional investor in the country. The only time that won't happen is when the company requesting the lists and its industry/peer group have miniscule institutional holdings. The lists serve as an excellent research base for prioritizing institutions and cities to cover. From them, a company can get a reasonably faithful list of its own institutional holders, plus those that are good prospects because of their interest in industry or peer companies. One caveat about these lists: they're not always state of the day since institutions have 45 days to file them after each quarter closes and because some institutions have been able to wiggle out of the requirement to file. A counter to that caveat however is the work being done by investor relations consultants and vendors to keep the lists current. At any rate, they are the basis for decisions on who to target and where to go.

Again, some companies reverse the order. They decide where to go and then figure out who to contact. Or, they target finely within the universe, which can be excellent strategy. For example, they will select investment management firms, banks, mutual funds, insurance companies, or a combination of these institutions that are managing assets invested in equities within certain dollar ranges—over $1 billion, from $500 million to $1 billion, from $100 million to $500 million, and under $100 million. Large market capitalization companies may target only the biggest institutions, managing over $1 billion in stocks. Most vendor lists of 13(f)-based data give the size of institutional equity holdings. There are clear strategies behind these decisions. Smaller money management firms and banks outside of New York are less likely to have analysts on board, are more likely to have their portfolio managers doing some research, working their investment models, and meeting with companies directly. Smaller money managers in medium-sized or smaller financial markets are less likely to be inundated with calls from companies to attend meetings or get together individually.

Meeting with brokers is a trickier proposition. Companies have wasted a lot of time and money in trying to woo brokers. The problem is in qualifying them. They number over 60,000 nationally, by various counts, and they sell numerous investment products. Finding and opening the lines of communication with those who concentrate mainly on stocks or at least derive enough of their income from stock transactions to make it worth contacting them require specialized research. It's being done in several ways. Companies can buy lists of brokers either nationally, regionally, or by brokerage firm. They can buy lists of brokers who seem to be following certain industries as indicated by their interest in ordering reprints of direct mail pieces for their customers. A number of consulting firms are using personal networking to ferret out the names of the top producers as measured by stock commission income.

Companies also need to decide which groups they want to emphasize in meetings to build up contacts. Companies are choosing their targets. Institutions are in favor now as recipients of the corporate rush. Some companies push broker relations because they have a fundamental belief in the value of having a strong individual investor representation in their stock. Or, the company's thrust may be toward brokers because retail interest in the stock is high. Smaller capitalization companies essentially are in this situation. Neglecting the broker channel to individual investors altogether seems short sighted. A solid individual investor base is healthy for companies of all sizes. (Chapter 11 details efforts to emphasize individual investors.)

PLOTTING THE BEST MEETING FORUMS

The grand plan for a meetings rollout takes advantage of the forums most popular with each segment of the investment community. Companies have two choices: serve as the host or be invited to address the regular meetings of the various groups.

Brokerage Analysts

For analysts, that means their professional societies. The key group is the Association for Investment Management and Research, which combines the former Financial Analysts Federation and Institute of Chartered Financial Analysts. AIMR has some 55 chapters across the United States and Canada. The directory also serves as an excellent reference, listing members alphabetically and by chapter, while also identifying their industry and functional specialties—equity analysts and the industries covered, debt analysts, research directors, technical analysts, merger/acquisition specialists, portfolio managers, portfolio strategists, investment bankers, investment counselors, underwriters.

A number of industries and specialties have separate groups, holding their own meetings. Most of these "splinter" groups are in New York and represent a range of industries—airline, auto, bank and finance, building, chemicals, specialty chemicals, computers, construction and building materials, diversified companies, electronics, environmental controls, health care, insurance, machinery, media and entertainment, motor carriers, non-ferrous metals, oil, paper and forest products, real estate, retail, textile and apparel, and utilities. New York also houses a fixed income analysts society, international investment group, separate quantitative (Investment Technology Association) and supply–demand investing (Market

Technicians Association) groups. Boston is home to electronics, petroleum, public utility, and retail analyst splinter societies. Chicago has consumer, financial institutions, technology company (Chicago Science Analysts), transportation, and utility/telecommunications splinter groups. Los Angeles has an energy analysts group.

Companies can pursue invitations to either the full or splinter societies or host their own meetings. The AIMR directory lists officers of each chapter, including the program chairperson. The National Investor Relations Institute publishes an annual directory, profiling each AIMR chapter and splinter group, giving the size of membership; describing specific interests of the group; covering meeting formats, average attendance and any costs involved; listing procedures for distributing company materials; identifying whether the press is invited; and including names, addresses and phone numbers of the program chairperson and/or president. In seeking a date to address the chapter, an inside contact is useful. Find an analyst who covers and recommends the company. Calls to the program chairperson or president can bring positive results, however, especially if the company is a player in the industry or is up and coming and gaining notice, or should be. A persuasive investor relations person can build the case.

In mining for gold among analysts, the must-list chapters are the New York Society of Security Analysts (NYSSA) and industry splinter group. Societies in other cities are a mix of sell and buy sides, leaning in one direction or the other, depending on the location. Most societies have more institutional analysts and portfolio managers than brokerage analysts. That's also true for the New York Society, but it and the relevant splinter group are the place to reach the lion's share of your industry analysts at one time.

Addressing the New York society has become a communications extravaganza. The tab isn't cheap ($7,950) but the message has the potential to reach around the world (occurring as the presentation takes place).

Here is an idea of what a company gets when appearing before the society. Pre-announcements abound—listed in the society's and AIMR's events calendars and carried on Financial News Network, Institutional Research Network (IRN), BusinessWire, Reuters, Dow

Jones Quotron, and *Investor's Daily*. Companies can mail announcements to NYSSA members using lists provided from the Bullseye service and made available by the society. The meeting is televised live on the Institutional Research Network, reaching some 100 institutions via satellite hook-up. These institutions also receive a video of the meeting for their libraries, which is available to any of their analysts and portfolio managers. The presentation also is broadcast to other AIMR societies and stockbrokers' clubs, and reaches some eight countries. It can even be sent to the corporate offices to be watched by employees, invited local brokers, analysts, and investors. Companies can order videotape copies for follow-up distribution. Electronic delivery of the presentation is available to subscribers of First Call, Investext, Corporate and Industry Research Reports (CIRR), BRS, Dialog, DataStar, Pergamon Infoline, Dow Jones News Retrieval, Source and NewsNet. The list grows. An on-line transcript is available through Mead Data Exchange's Lexis/Nexis service. BusinessWire carries a summary of the presentation. Audio tapes are available 10 minutes after the meeting ends. Teleconferencing services stand ready with the equipment in place. Meetings can be scheduled around breakfast or luncheon formats or be held late in the afternoon, followed by a cocktail reception. Smaller companies can hold meetings without the television feature, paying less.

Companies have the option of hosting their own meetings for sell-side analysts. New York is the only place where this makes much sense. The gathering will be relatively small, which can create a climate for a productive discussion. Or the meeting can be expanded to include institutional analysts. The biggest institutions have analysts following specific industries or a number of related industries. Their industry expertise frequently matches that of the brokerage analysts. The meeting value often rises in combining the two analyst sides; the learning quotient goes up as serious, in-depth discussion unfolds. Buy-side analysts covering several industries or less familar with yours benefit from the questions and responses. Brokerage analysts usually don't mind having institutions represented in the room; they are contact opportunities.

As relationships grow, brokerage analysts become more interested in individual meetings with management. They're looking for an edge as they sell their research and trading services to institutions. It is the individual's experience and skill in asking questions, listening insightfully to the answers, prodding for more information, and the ability to piece together what was learned into a deeper understanding and more accurate appraisal of the future that distinguish one analyst from another in the competitive race for institutional business. There is just as much comfort in holding the meetings in the offices of the brokerage firm or company. Analysts are always hitting the road, calling on several companies they follow closely on the same trip. Companies in an industry tend to cluster. They like to interview several of the top executives of the company, meet with the research, marketing, manufacturing, financial or other wizards, tour the R&D facility or new plant. Analysts want to know all they can about the depth of management and strength of internal succession.

Quarterly meetings in New York to discuss current operations and performance are well-attended by both sell- and buy-side analysts and even some fund and portfolio managers. The concept has taken off in the last few years, with more and more companies doing it. Companies starting the program have seen attendance grow, then stabilize at a certain level, unless it is a time when interest is high for a reason. Timing for the meetings is right at the announcement of quarterly financial results. Typically, the corporate officer conducting the meeting talks briefly about current results, then answers questions. With most companies, it's the CEO or CFO handling the cross-fire. Sometimes both are there, and sometimes the company brings along another senior officer to talk about an aspect of the business that's growing or of special interest to Wall Street, or to continue widening the circle of contacts. Quite a few companies entrust their investor relations officer to handle the meetings. The meetings usually are held over breakfast so analysts can be in their offices as the market opens. They take place at the corporate apartment, private club or upscale restaurant that accommodates the meeting format comfortably. They can be in midtown or downtown Manhattan; the investment community divides about equally. If anything, the trend is toward midtown.

Industry conferences are one more way to reach brokerage analysts. They're organized by financial or industry trade groups. In addition to industry associations, the AIMR sponsors several of them, as does the Investment Management Institute. Leading companies in the industry give presentations. Analysts and institutional portfolio managers attend; it's an excellent way for them to hear from and talk with a half-dozen or more companies at the same time. In recent years, several companies in the same industry located near each other have gotten together to co-sponsor conferences. The convenience factor has brought good turnouts.

Institutions

The best ways to reach institutions follow patterns similar to analyst methods, and indeed, overlap. Society presentations attract as many, if not more, institutional analysts and portfolio managers than brokerage analysts. Most of the AIMR chapters across the country have more buy-side than sell-side members. It's a wise investor relations strategy to seek invitations to address these societies, either because research has marked them as target cities or in extending corporate visibility among institutions.

Cities across the heartland and away from the "Big Apple" may fit nicely with investor relations strategies to attract more institutions. Many have sizable numbers of small to mid-sized investment management firms and banks that may not have any analysts or only a few at most. These institutions tend to be receptive to opportunities to hear corporate presentations or accept invitations to a breakfast or luncheon meeting. Some cities are capitals of certain industries. Boston has a big buy-side community—mutual funds, banks, and investment managers. Hartford and Philadelphia are insurance centers. Chicago and the Twin Cities (Minneapolis–St. Paul) are corporate centers with fistfuls of pension funds. Investment management firms have sprung forth in California.

AIMR chapters cover every major city, and some where you might not expect to find them, giving an inside look at where investment assets are growing—Austin, Des Moines, Indianapolis, Chattanooga, Oklahoma City, Tulsa, Toledo, Richmond, Providence, Rochester, Omaha, Lincoln, central Florida (Orlando, Sarasota, Tampa, Clearwater), western Michigan (Grand Rapids, Kalamazoo, Holland), and North Carolina (Charlotte, Winston–Salem, Greensboro, Raleigh, Durham). Canada has seven chapters: Calgary, Edmonton, Montreal, Ottawa, Vancouver, Toronto, and Winnipeg.

In town for a day or two, companies are inclined to combine addressing the society with hosting a handful of meetings. This approach gives companies more control in picking the communities with the highest number of existing institutional shareholders and prospects based on their holdings in industry/peer groups and strong ties between their investment strategies and the company's investing characteristics. Small group meetings over breakfast or lunch are the preferred format where relationships are still in the formative stage. Individual meetings are the desired choice with current holders, large institutions or firms where relationships are budding. Meetings with an institutional analyst can frequently grow into meetings with the firm's portfolio managers as well.

Here's another forum: Brokerage analysts set up institutional meetings. They may sponsor the event—a luncheon presentation for their institutional customers. The analyst may take the top corporate officers and the investor relations director across the country or to the leading money centers of Europe. Industry conferences often are sponsored by a single brokerage firm as a way of being time efficient in enabling dozens to hundreds of institutional investors hear corporate presentations and meet with executives from the various companies.

Brokers

The three ways to take up with retail brokers are to address their clubs, convince one firm to let your company speak before their retail reps as a group, or sponsor the meetings directly. Stockbroker clubs exist across the country and are emerging around the world. The largest organized group is the Stockbrokers' Society with some 50 clubs now nationwide and additional ones outside the United States. They hold luncheons; some clubs also have afternoon (after the market closes) presentations followed by cocktail receptions. Companies pick up the tab in any case.

There are numerous independent clubs. Locations include Phoenix, Oakland, Pasadena, San Diego, Fairfield, Hartford, and New Haven (CT), Jacksonville (FL), Indianapolis, Portland (ME), Boston, Springfield and Worcester (MA), New York, Cincinnati, Allentown (PA), Philadelphia, Providence, Montreal, and Toronto. With virtually every club, the company covers the costs.

As a centerpiece in its efforts to help companies reach brokers, the American Stock Exchange has set up clubs both domestically and outside the country. Currently, there are Amex clubs in Atlanta, Boston, Chicago, Dallas, Denver, Houston, Los Angeles, downtown and midtown New York, Philadelphia, St. Louis, San Francisco, Seattle, Washington, D.C. and internationally in Hong Kong, Singapore, Montreal, Toronto, London, Edinburgh, and Zurich and Geneva, Switzerland. As a guide for investor relations practitioners, the National Investor Relations Institute directory profiles each of the Stockbroker Society, independent and Amex clubs.

Meetings with these many and various clubs produce a mixed result. There is little if any opportunity to hand pick the audience. The degree of sincere interest among attendees has to be suspect, since the company foots the bill. But like the preacher on Sunday, companies may be more interested in winning a few good converts than playing for highest odds. Among the 40 to 100 brokers in the crowd, enough may get interested in "the story" to go after more information or start recommending the stock. It can be assumed that brokers are being more aggressive than ever in looking for new investment ideas to keep their customers active.

Companies also are using direct mail and computer lists to generate broker names and in trying to qualify their interest as the basis for inviting them to meetings. Brokers who respond to direct mail programs by ordering copies of the piece to give their customers can be considered to be prospects for attending meetings. Computer printouts give names of current broker rosters of the various firms, but no advice in qualifying their interests in stocks, a particular industry or company. The real push in coming up with the best list of names is being made by investor relations agencies specializing in retail stock investing programs. They're networking in person and by telephone in various cities to produce and maintain lists and contacts with the "heavy hitter" brokers in stocks.

A tailored approach to broker relations is to work with individual firms. This can be especially productive when the firm has recently published a positive report on the company and/or is recommending the stock. The firm invites its broker corps to hear the corporate presentation, usually after the market closes, but occasionally over lunch. The meeting can be repeated in highly populated retail offices of the firm and in cities across the country. Favorable research reports aren't a prerequisite, however. Companies are enjoying success in convincing branch managers of firms to let them address the broker contingents. It becomes the branch manager's call. Regional houses are predisposed to say yes to local companies, but national firms respond positively to the requests as well. Conditions are ripe; everyone is looking for investment discoveries.

TAKING A PROGRAMMED APPROACH

While companies can easily spend days seeing institutions or brokerge firms in New York, the tendency when making trips to other cities is to set up a schedule that combines meetings with institutions, brokers and analysts.

Bell Atlantic Corporation is an excellent example of a company emphasizing both institutions and individuals in its investor relations program. Bell Atlantic is targeting the top producers in stocks among brokers, while focusing on investment firms managing equity assets ranging between $100 million and $1 billion. Prime as well are institutions in the over $1 billion category who are share-holders or likely prospects based on their investment strategies and current holdings patterns. In 1989, the company covered 22 cities; a similar program was conducted in 1990. The format for most cities: a breakfast meeting with a small group of institutions managing under $1 billion and luncheon meeting with between 50 and 60 brokers on average, interspersed in the morning and afternoon with individual sessions with big institutional holders and prospects.

Variations of this format will surely suit every company's pur-pose and agenda. There may be a meeting alone with a leading sell-side analyst or medium-sized investment firm that likes the industry but hasn't invested yet in the company. Brokerage ana-lysts may be invited to the breakfast meeting with institutions. The broker presentation may be in the afternoon, followed by a recep-tion, creating an opportunity to meet with institutions over lunch and one major shareholder at breakfast. A particular city may have a strong investment management/bank contingent, but only a handful of top brokers, suggesting a broker breakfast and institu-tional luncheon.

In covering every turn on out-of-town trips, companies some-times include a fourth group on their priority lineup—individual shareholders. The invitation lists can be drawn up in several ways. Companies active in investor club programs may invite club mem-bers in the area. Or, the meeting may cover all the shareholders in the area, with invitations based on zip codes culled from the regis-tered and non-objecting beneficial owner (NOBO) lists. Also include employee shareholders. A corporate presentation followed by a reception seems to be the most accommodating and friendliest for-mat. If the gathering is smaller, with the audience more select, the event can be a luncheon. One such group might be holders of 1,000 or more shares; the idea is to encourage additional investment.

Meetings with shareholders usually occur in headquarters or plant cities, where corporate visibility has been rewarded with a substantial shareholder following. Other advantageous locations can be discovered by checking the record and NOBO lists for shareholder concentrations.

Not to be overlooked when on the road is the benefit of media coverage. The odds on gaining a story are good enough to make the effort. A significant local operation should serve as the basis of stirring business press interest. Plans and programs to improve operations, forge additional marketshare gains or other activities that stand to bolster the community's economy command attention. The media can be expected to have investor interest in the company as well. Storylines geared to valuation are appealing. In going after coverage, the company should try to set up interviews with the CEO or top-ranking officer in town to conduct the investor meetings. While the business/financial section of the daily newspapers and city's business journals are the best candidates for seeking coverage, investor relations people also are advised to look into the television possibilities. TV business shows are starting up in market after market. The media visibility can reach individual investors and institutional firms, and it supports broker efforts to market the stock. Chapter 16 covers media relations.

FIELD TRIPS AND ANNUAL MEETINGS

With sell- and buy-side interest established, the field trip presents a source of deeper learning and widened relationships. Those attending will be serious about the company, although the outing may attract a brokerage analyst or two and a couple of institutions early in their research. Companies, of course, can limit their invitations to followers and holders of the stock, but missionary work in extending the message on a continuing basis is a good idea.

Field trips are company-sponsored excursions to the headquarters or other company facility such as the research center, a new plant, or a key production operation. They last at least a day, probably two or three, and cover an agenda that includes presentations by operational, technical and financial people in addition to senior management executives. Research/production tours are included to enhance appreciation and understanding of the attributes that distinguish the company.

Field trips bring the company/investor relationship to a new level. No forum offers more opportunity for close relationships to grow and new ones to begin and blossom. In most of these outings, the atmosphere is informal. Jackets and ties are shed, hard hats are in vogue. Before, between, and after presentations, many one-to-one and small-group conversations take place—on planes and buses, at receptions, over meals, perhaps even in tennis or golf matches if they're on the card. However, most companies keep the schedules tight and focused on business in respect for time.

Companies like the format because it gives them a captive audience for describing capabilities that may not be fully understood or appreciated. While these meetings provide thorough reviews and updates of corporate strategies, financials and operations, the real intent of the company may be to enlighten analysts and key institutional investors on the range and depth of technology, unique market position that will begin paying results in two to five years, or show them how the company has become the cost-efficient producer in the industry. The meetings also enable the company to demonstrate the breadth of its upper management and quality of its research or manufacturing people.

Sell- and buy-side professionals like the format because they gain new insights into the abilities of top management. Watching these executives at work for a day or more is very revealing: how they think and answer questions, interact with other executives, behave in quasi social situations. More of the personalities of the executives come out in these sessions. The analysts and investors learn more about management in these situations than in any other kind of format. And, they get to know the next layer of management, plus that corps of vital technical, manufacturing or marketing specialists with direct linkage to the bottom line.

The field trip must have a strong payoff for the audience. Nothing is worse than wasting the time of this audience. The pressure starts with the decision to hold the trip. There must be good reason: new management, new products or research breakthroughs, modern manufacturing operation, or a significant educational benefit that will result from the totality of the event. Senior management must be completely supportive of the concept and enthusiastic about putting in the time to make sure the project is a success. This means working with the writers on the speeches, rehearsing, being there for most if not all of the meeting. Popping in for your speech and then disappearing is not desirable.

The budget must be sufficient to produce an effective result. For trips outside of New York, companies tend to pay attendee airfare (or offer to pay), charter planes or use company aircraft. Ground transportation to and from airports is provided or costs are covered by the company. Frequently, companies will use their own employees as chauffeurs on trips to research or plant facilities and during tours. It adds a personal warmth and allows for useful conversation. Selected employees are familiar with local operations and the area. In these situations, briefings are essential to cover what should and can be said and what shouldn't and can't be discussed. Budgets also need to allow for presentation graphics, meals, mementos, and other essentials.

Planning must be comprehensive and it must begin well before the event dates. First step is to set dates free of conflict, internally and outside. That means getting on the calendars of all company participants, and it means making sure there aren't any events taking place at the time that would cut into attendance. Companies should check with a couple of analysts and institutional holders for conflicts, as well as such organizations as the New York Society of Security Analysts and Association for Investment Management and Research.

Contact with attendees begins with phone calls to a few people closest to the company to discuss the idea and get feedback on their level of interest and any specific subjects to cover. It's also a time to clear dates. Most meetings will combine the sell and buy sides; some companies have concentrated field trips on institutions. Target lists should include brokerage analysts following the company, analysts nibbling who haven't taken the bait yet, any leading industry analyst who is missing from the ranks, larger institutions holding shares, smaller institutions with large holdings, large institutions with an expressed interest that haven't purchased any shares yet, and large institutions holding shares in industry or peer group companies.

Letters of invitation start the process. They should be sent a month to six weeks before the event. Be sure they contain strong reasons for attending—capture the essence of the agenda, pitch the value drivers. Include a date for responding. After that, the logistics steps are underway. They involve confirming attendance, arranging transportation and coordinating schedules. Follow throughs will be occurring right up to the first day of the meeting. There will be cancellations, substitutions, perhaps even an 11th hour request to attend from someone who heard about the trip or previously had turned down the invitation.

Inside the company, planning includes meetings with senior management to decide on subjects and speakers, as well as range and depth of content. Plenty of time should be provided for script preparation and revision, creation and production of graphics. Rehearsals should be thorough and as frequent as needed for speakers to be fully ready. Speech coaching may be desired.

Consider taping the presentations using both audio and video recorders. They can be very useful in extending the value of the meetings and for reaching other institutions, analysts who couldn't attend, individual investors, and employees. Audio tapings enable companies to produce a transcript which can be given in follow-up to attendees and other investors as well as to those who wish to write a report on the content of the presentations. If the meetings are taped, video training may be desired as well.

Menu selection should be handled carefully. Ask each person planning to attend about any special menu needs. Meals can figure into meeting formats. For example, arrival may be timed for late afternoon, with the opening session being a dinner at a well-known local restaurant or country club. A breakfast meeting at the hotel or lodge may start the program the next morning before attendees are brought to the offices, research center, or plant for subsequent sessions. Some meals may be served inside the company facilities, catered or prepared internally. If guests are to stay overnight twice, the second evening should probably include an event away from the corporate facilities—dinner at a famous local ethnic restaurant, perhaps even a trip to a sporting or cultural event.

Put every assignment on the checklist. Cover every detail. Spell out each person's assignment. Make the schedule complete down to the time of arrival of each attendee, airline and flight number if appropriate, person responsible for making the pickup. Hold progress meetings and walk throughs.

There is a strong opportunity to communicate with the selection of handout materials. A notebook is a good idea. It can include copies of the speeches, charts and graphs, biographies of speakers, the full schedule, background pieces on various operations, and reprints of articles. Annual and quarterly reports, 10-K and 10-Q reports, a recent earnings release, or other major announcements, prospectus, proxy statements, and the like also should be available.

Taking good care of the analysts and investors while they're on the field trip also includes making sure telephones are available during the day and being ready to help them with any needs that may arise unexpectedly. Have someone standing by who knows the local community well.

A field trip should have a memento, a reminder that lasts: paperweights, pens, calculators, and so on. Hard hats are old hat, but they're still useful. Mementos are good especially when localized—the paperweight relating to the product or location of the meeting, for example. A creative tip: look for some way of making the memento useful, while imparting information at the same time. It can be given out at the meeting, if easy to haul home, or sent later with a thank you. That's the last item—a thank you for attending which serves as an invitation for follow-up.

A question to be answered: Should media be invited? The answer is probably no, or selectively, for certain events, as long as attendance can be limited easily. The company won't be as comfortable in discussing some subjects or answering certain questions fully. The analysts and investors may not be as comfortable with what they want to discuss either. An alert to investor relations people: if media aren't present, be listening for material disclosure. It's up to you or any attorney present to point out any material nonpublic disclosure that is made inadvertently during a meeting. The situation may require preparing and issuing a release, or at least discussing whether the information is material.

Most managements see annual meetings as more of a chore than a communications opportunity. Shareholder activism of recent years has only served to lower executive enthusiasm for the event. But the annual meeting can be a vehicle for adding information. It is a ready-made forum for communicating, if a hard-hitting presentation is prepared. The audience value extends beyond the people in the room to include investors reading the post-meeting report or a reprint of the speech, and readers of the business press. The presentation also can be videotaped and then edited for showing to employees, at investor fairs, broker or other types of investor meetings. Availability of the tape can be promoted in quarterly reports. Analysts and portfolio managers can be encouraged to attend the meeting. Some companies meet with professional investors separately.

GETTING THE MOST OUT OF MEETINGS

Careful planning and creative execution of the communications steps along the way will enhance the value of investor meetings. On the communications side, the initial contact with those on the target lists is important. Some companies like to begin with a phone call, followed by an invitation letter; others reverse the procedure, following up the letter with a phone call. What's best shakes out on the basis of the relationship status with each person and verbal versus writing skills of the investor relations people. When the recipients are known, the phone call is probably best. You can talk about the company, what's going to be covered at the meeting, elicit a reaction, and send the details and reply card in a letter.

In "cold" calls, the phone contact is still desired, but the investor relations person needs to be effective in getting conversation started with people who are busy, possibly uninterested and perhaps a little unfriendly at first. Good advice is to know precisely what you're going to say, and focus on a message that the listener will find beneficial. That means getting right into the investment qualities of the company and programs to exploit them. The letter needs to have the same kind of sell in it. Follow-up letters reinforce phone calls. Follow-up phone calls make sure the letter was received, enable you to talk about the company and continue efforts to persuade the person to attend. The phone call also may open the contact, because the letter wasn't read. At that point, you have an established base of reference for the conversation.

Presentation content will vary with the audience. Companies shouldn't give the same speech to every group, but tailor their presentation not only to brokers, analysts and institutions, but on the basis of how much is known by the people in the room at the time. As relationships evolve, knowledge levels dictate more refining of information. Chapters, 10, 11, and 13 go into detail on the approach to take with each investor segment and specific information to provide. Basically, brokers want the investable strengths highlighted and summarized; analysts want to crunch the numbers and compare companies within their industries; and institutions want to see how companies fit into their investing models.

Ongoing is the debate on the usefulness of audio-visual presentations, slides, or overheads in a presentation. A short video or slide presentation for new audiences which covers the basics effectively is a good idea. It should be less than half the presentation, giving the speaker time to update, customize and strengthen the story. A video that clearly explains and brings to life a new technology, product or market strategy will be appreciated even by sophisticated audiences. Charts and graphs add value when they make information easy to understand. They also help organize a presentation. But they can become a crutch that takes away the speaker's personality and expressiveness.

Handout materials should include copies of charts and graphs; they help the audience follow along with the presentation and take notes. It's also a good idea to give out copies of the speech, but not until after it is given. Annual reports, recent quarterlies, and releases should be available; most members of the audience don't bother to bring them along.

Profiles of attendees should be prepared for senior management. The information on analysts should include basic data, and also indicate their attitude on the company, current recommendation and when it was made, the last time a research report was written and what it said, other companies followed and attitude/position on each one, how long with the firm and other firms, whether the person is on the *Institutional Investor* all-American team. With institutions: whether an analyst or portfolio manager, how long with the firm and any other firms, attitude toward the company as reflected in writings or comments, number of shares held and order patterns over recent years, whether the institution sold all the shares and has repurchased or currently isn't a shareholder, reasons for investing in the company, and investing style. With brokers: experience track and other firms, degree of investment interest in the stock and/or industry, age and style of investing, as well as attitude toward stocks as an investment.

While it isn't as exact, some research is possible to help get a handle on who likely will be attending an AIMR society or splinter group meeting. Membership rolls of the chapter can be studied to better understand the analyst/institutional mix, buy side analyst/portfolio mix, specializations of brokerage analysts, type and size of investment management firms and banks, number of corporate pension funds and major industries they represent.

Here are a dozen more ideas designed to improve the quality of presentations and make sure meeting logistics are covered professionally.

1. Obtain follow-up commentary and critique from audiences. Several options are available. Short questionnaires can be left at tables for response before the people leave. These usually work best with brokers; the cards need to be kept short for easy fill-in. Most companies do follow-up phone interviews in an effort to get comprehensive feedback on the presentation and speakers. The investor relations person can conduct the interviews if relationships with analysts, investors, and brokers are comfortable enough for them to be candid. The option is to use investor relations consultants, who are seen

as more independent. The feedback should be used to improve the presentation and speaker skills.

2. Rehearse speeches. Try to overcome the natural tendency of CEOs and CFOs to be uncomfortable about doing this.

3. Anticipate questions from the audience, especially those that are delicate, and discuss how they should be answered. Some companies write out the answers.

4. Be prepared to have the press in attendance at the meetings that are sponsored by societies and clubs. Alert senior management. Have press materials ready. Best attitude is to turn the situation into an opportunity, which can include making the speaker available for separate questions after the meeting.

5. Be prepared to write and distribute a release should nonpublic material information be given out during the meeting.

6. Have an attendance list on hand, check off the names of people as they arrive and add any new names. The list has follow-up value, for further contact and as additions to mailing lists.

7. In out-of-town company-sponsored meetings, do some research before selecting the site. Convenience to the invitees is a factor. Quality is another. They will have their most and less favorite restaurants or clubs. Ask one or two analysts, brokers or institutional investors about desired locations.

8. Make initial contact about three to four weeks before the meeting, whether by phone or mail. Send an advance information packet. As a reminder, call each person who accepts the invitation the morning of or day before the meeting.

9. Select menu items with care. Pick a dessert that can be put on the table ahead of time along with the salad to reduce serving time and help stay on schedule. Sit down to start eating on time, even if stragglers are apparent. A wine bar and soft drinks at lunch are preferable to hard liquor. Send thank you's to attendees.

10. Have the room be a little larger than the expected turnout. Arrive early to make sure everything is being arranged properly, needed audio-visual equipment is there, and to test it. Make sure the tables are arranged the way you want them. Round tables are best; they make for easier luncheon talk. Try to seat corporate executives with the most influential guests.

11. Critique the meeting with management right after it's over. Cover what turned out well in addition to discussing any weaknesses.

12. Watch the stock action to see if you can trace any new buying to the meetings, especially in cities other than New York. In follow-up conversations, ask the brokers, institutions, and analysts about any specific actions they may have taken as a result of the meeting.

15

Technology and Outside Services Playing Beautiful Music In Investor Relations Orchestra

By now, it has become obvious that technology and outside services occupy the first chairs among the leading instruments in the hands of the investor relations director. Not only do they enrich the quality of the performance, they blend their talents in delivering the music to the audiences. No wonder the maestros of investor relations are orchestrating their programs to give technology and outside services starring roles. Imagine not having them today. Just as a symphony can't play Tchaikovsky's *1812 Overture* without violins and cannon, the investor relations orchestra can't hope to please sophisticated investors and analysts with half its instruments missing.

Technology is the real boon in the maturation of investor relations over the past decade. Narrowing the term, *technology* means computers and the electronic dissemination of information. Just as it has enhanced the discipline in the investing process, technology is helping quantify investor relations by producing hard information and revolutionizing the methods of receiving and distributing it. Technology has made many of the vendor services possible. Essentially, they all involve information. Technology does many

323

things to give investor relations people information and to enable them to use it productively. It assembles the information, combines and analyzes it to create new information, puts it into highly usable forms, and transmits and receives it. Companies are working both ends of the transmission lines—receiving information, using it in various ways to increase its worth, and sending it to prime investor audiences.

Interestingly, technology is proving itself to be an investor relations teacher. It has revealed to us the world of institutional investors, helped us learn more about them, and is showing us how they go about the process of investing. It is helping us understand the capital markets better, allowing us to watch how our stock behaves and compare its behavior against other companies and the market as a whole. It is giving us access to more information—on an unlimited range of subjects—than we could ever hope to obtain in other ways.

At the same time, technology is becoming investor relations' best friend in teaching our two main constituents. It is making us more effective in providing information to investors, analysts and brokers. It is opening opportunities for us to enlighten management on the behavior of investors and the markets.

THREE LEADING ROLES OF TECHNOLOGY

The use of technology in the investor relations office has three fundamental roles, which expand into numerous activities:

1. It is serving as an information resource;
2. It is enabling the investor relations department to send information in virtually any amount at nearly the speed of light; and
3. It is remaking the investor relations office, lifting time and manpower efficiency, while cutting away chunks of cost. Spending saves.

REACHING NEW HORIZONS AS AN INFORMATION RESOURCE

Market Intelligence

As an information resource, technology performs a multitude of functions. It is a source of vast market intelligence—from the impact of current macroeconomic factors on investing to consensus earnings forecasts of thousands of companies. In building computer-based resources for obtaining comprehensive and reliable market information, investor relations people are getting in step with investors. The truly sophisticated corporate investor relations functions are seeking to duplicate the data sources of institutional investors and analysts as a way of learning investing methods and tracking the information used most widely.

The best way to ferret out the popular data sources at any time is to ask several sizable institutions holding shares in your company as well as a couple of leading industry analysts. Among the answers will probably be Compustat, Lotus One Source, First Call, Telescan, Quotron, Dow Jones, Bloomberg, Standard & Poor's. The Zacks database has gained widespread acceptance among investors utilizing quantitative methods.

A database that mirrors Wall Street resources elevates investor relations' value. The principal objective is to serve investors better by fully understanding their information needs. The method ultimately involves continually refining the information until it flows right into investor computers. Former analysts, traders, portfolio managers and brokers now practicing investor relations are setting the pace, having successfully transferred their knowledge by creating databases that emulate the information build-up and modeling of investors. Compatibility occurs, not just in software, but also in the information base. Companies and analysts/investors literally can exchange information. An example: In the mid-1980s, Travelers Insurance Corp. began putting quarterly performance data in electronic spreadsheet format and sending it by modem to analysts. Many companies now are following the practice.

The world of investment opens ever wider and deeper to investor relations people as they explore, learn how to gather, organize, store and use the incredible array of information available from electronic data sources. You stand at the threshold of becoming true experts on the capital markets and their participants. Thanks to computers, the future offers exciting opportunity for investor relations professionals to turn what some practitioners call a "craft" into a more quantified discipline. By working hard and intelligently, eventually, investor relations practitioners will understand so much more about the inner workings of Wall Street and the international investment community. Sorting through the complexities of Wall Street is a tough challenge, exacerbated by the pace of change; the players themselves struggle to keep up, and they disagree, sometimes strenuously, on what's driving investments at any time. All that makes it even harder for investor relations practitioners to get beyond the conventional wisdom. So much of it represents the particular view of an investor or investor relations consultant, both with a profit motive. Or, the range of opinion on a particular subject only creates confusion. Investor relations people will benefit tremendously from having the information that spawns knowledge and confidence in planning and carrying out a results-producing program.

The following is a starter list of mysteries and items of conventional wisdom where more light will bring clearer understanding. The list of potential applications grows as knowledge expands.

1. Knowing the intricacies of each investment style and method, and then applying this knowledge to become an improved source of information with each of the company's institutional investors;

2. Refining the knowledge of investing methods unendingly as the basis of analysis in accurately targeting prospective institutions. We will never have the perfect list of institutional investor targets. This process of identifying them continues to progress, but remains inexact, because the information base is thin to begin with, because investing

methods continue to evolve, and institutions continue to change their basic approach. Some stick with one philosophy through thick and thin, but the trend is to ride with what seems to be working best. The zeal to be maximizing returns at all times is real and doesn't appear to be tapering off. We will always need to know more about investing styles and methods, so that we can follow them more closely as they evolve and are applied by investor after investor.

3. Knowing enough to track the continuing evolution of investing approaches and methods, be able to have a good sense of their relative use throughout the investment universe at any time, and predict the trends as styles move in and out of favor and new ones come into vogue. This knowledge can put investor relations professionals into the center of the company's share price management program. A sophisticated understanding of investing foundations and trends helps document the kinds of value-building activities that appeal to certain types of investors. Companies also gain more control in the make-up of their shareholder base.

4. Helping quantify the most popular ways being used by investors and analysts in valuing companies. This is a two-part proposition. One involves having a better appreciation of the relative use of such performance measurements as price/earnings ratio, price to book value, price to sales, discounted cash flow and the like. In addition to gaining access electronically to all the studies and speeches on trends in performance measurement, we can add first-hand knowledge as we grow as a source of computer-supplied information to investors and analysts. The second part of the proposition is to translate the measurement and valuation techniques of investors into corporate information. The value that investor relations people add to the information process rises commensurate with the depth and breadth of their knowledge and insight into investing practice. Discussion of the corporation's value drivers takes on more meaning. So does the advice given by investor relations people to corporate

executives on share price management strategies that will go over well with investors.

How does computer-driven information help open these doors to wisdom? The answer bears repeating, for emphasis. First and foremost, by creating "computer dialog" with investors and analysts. That's a step being taken only timidly at present. For it to blossom, cooperation will be needed between companies and the investment community. Investor relations people probably will have to be the aggressor, in asking to be educated by investors and analysts on their information needs beyond the surface. Edification would result, for example, in being shown the models in some detail, within proprietary boundaries. Replicating the models in software on both ends of the modem would facilitate information flow. Institutions and analysts are warming to the idea as they see the benefits in the form of better information. Institutions seem to be welcoming quality information directly from companies as they lean less on sell-side analysts. As relationships with individual institutions and analysts grow, questions concerning material disclosure, proprietary modeling and analytical methods, and the ability to continue adding value will become more important and sensitive.

Investor relations practitioners also can cut into the mountains of valuable information available electronically in making themselves experts on the capital markets, behavior of investors, and trends taking place. It serves as an unlimited source—everything from the results of consensus surveys on the direction of the market to in-depth, technically oriented articles explaining various investment practices. Searches of the vast computer database can yield streams of information and trigger innovative thinking based on greater knowledge. Investor relations people aren't even scratching the edge of the learning bonanza that awaits inside electronic retrieval and expands with each day.

Computers supply most of the macroeconomic intelligence that underpins investment decisions. Investors rely on data pouring through computer systems in studying and predicting the state of the economy domestically and in various parts of the world as the basis for such critical decisions as the stock/bond/cash mix of their portfolios, percentages to invest in equities of domestic and international companies and funds, and which industries and specific companies to favor. Consider the benefits to investor relations people with a grasp of that same information, namely the ability to see how economic factors affect investor decisions and anticipate the patterns of investing. Now, we're really talking about sophisticated communications: positioning the company as an investment based on having a strong sense of where it stands in the investing patterns and cycles of leading institutions and analysts.

The company can be aggressive in its communications, regardless of its situation. If the patterns and cycles are positive, the company can drive home its investment worthiness. If the company is in neutral with investors, it might get them moving by focusing on fundamental strengths that ride above the patterns. A negative scenario may be overstated, the company may be in the heap undeservedly, or, in the worse case, macroeconomics may have taken their toll. A clear understanding of the reasons gives the company a basis to communicate intelligently—in explaining why it should be analyzed favorably or in preparing investors for the comeback so they see it early.

Not to be forgotten in the recitation of market intelligence resources spawned by technological advancement is the array of investment universe listings used by companies for targeting institutions, brokers, and analysts. The ability to create computer software programs for assembling data into numerous usable formats for sale to hundreds of business enterprises is what enables vendors like CDA, Technimetrics, Vickers, CORTRAC and Research Services to provide these products at reasonable prices. Each day, it seems, enhancements are made that extend the capability—refining the information or customizing the lists even more. Companies may receive lists and labels overnight, but they were printed by computers. Or, they can take the names right from the vendor's computer database with a PC and a modem.

Shareholder Behavior

Computers are helping immensely in two key areas involving
shareholder behavior: keeping track of investor holdings and in
monitoring investor attitudes, especially now that shareholders
have an agenda and are actively pursuing it.

Shareholder identification, or *stock watch programs* as they have
come to be called, became somewhat the norm in the 1980s as companies worried about hostile takeovers or proxy contests for control. The systems were set up to facilitate contact with shareholders,
the trick being the ability to identify those investors holding their
shares through bank or brokerage accounts. Their identity is
mostly hidden behind the "Street" accounts. Proxy solicitation
firms streamlined their computer capabilities and contact networks
in finding the real holders and tracking changes in ownership by
keeping up with the buying and selling of shares.

Stock watch programs are two dimensional, the other use being in proactive investor communications. Comprehensive lists of
current shareholders—combining those registered with the company and those holding the shares in "Street name"—enable investor relations departments to be in direct contact with their major
investors and also provide an excellent market research tool in
profiling the shareholder base and analyzing their reasons for
holding shares. A number of investor relations consultancies have
joined the proxy solicitors in providing ongoing stock watch services. With takeover pressures lessened as the new decade was
beginning, stock watch programs handled through consultants
have declined somewhat, indicating that the fear motive is out-
weighing the proactive investor relations motive.

Some companies opted to internalize the process in the 1980s
and the trend continues, albeit modestly. To do this successfully
requires sophisticated software, the know-how in using it, strong
investment community contacts, and the time to be working those
contacts in discovering who holds the stock and keeping the list up
to date. However, it is those very activities that make investor relations a valuable function: building relationships and learning the

reasons for investor interest in the company. Meanwhile, the company has the security of knowing the contact lists are at the ready should hostility break out. Computers make the capability possible. They acquire, store, assemble, analyze, format, transmit, update, and report the data. Information sources that become inputs include the 13(f) filings, transfer sheets, depository trust reports, record shareholder lists, and market data gathered by contact efforts, stirred knowingly by a skilled and experienced investor relations professional.

Computers play several useful roles in helping companies keep tabs on shareholder activism and prepare themselves to handle the communications well in situations affecting them. The electronic databases are filled these days with valuable research to stay on top of the trends and dig into the specifics:

the prime, emerging and declining issues;

voting patterns on proposals in general and with each issue;

individuals and institutions or shareholder groups leading the charge and their particular interests; and

corporate attitudes, responses, and initiatives.

Companies are being more farsighted in planning their communications responses to certain issues. Electronic retrieval provides a rich research resource. Action plans, position papers, backgrounders, speech materials, statements, and constituency letters are being written and stored in the computer, along with contact lists, address labels, and related mobilization tools.

Market Behavior

How the markets behave has a big impact on a company's share price. Analysts believe that macroeconomic factors and market behavior together constitute about three-fourths of the stock price at any given time, leaving company fundamentals and communications influencing about 25 percent of the price. Of course, corporate performance and communication influence market behavior.

Continuous market watches are becoming an important part of the information-gathering network. The motivation is both defensive and offensive. Electronic data sources enable companies to track stock price, volume, and change, allowing them to measure liquidity and volatility. The numbers can serve as signals, measures, and barometers. Consistent levels indicate normal trading and interest. Unusual volume signals a buying or selling spurt, possibly triggered by an analyst recommendation, strong broker backing or flurry of activity by several institutions. It also could flag an accumulation of stock or rumors about a possible acquisition or takeover.

Companies are becoming much more interested in watching their stock behavior in order to make sure liquidity and volatility are properly disposed and balanced. Sufficient liquidity assures that there is enough stock available to handle order flow smoothly, bringing price changes that are consistent with amount of trading taking place. Volatility occurs when the stock is illiquid, pushing prices too far, too fast.

Market behavior also helps companies assess their relative valuation. Companies are comparing their share price, volume, change, liquidity, volatility, and price/earnings ratio against companies in their industry, peer group and the market as a whole, traditionally as measured by the S&P 500 index or other appropriate S&P barometer (the 400 industrials or utilities as examples). The data gives the company a clear indication of its relative standing as an equity investment. This understanding is useful in determining the types of investors that might be interested in buying shares and can even give some clues on timing. The company may be seen as a low or high P/E stock, for example, when compared against its industry or the market. Or, it might be moving into favor with the technocrats who are reading meaning into trading patterns, volume and price movement.

Companies are tracking the numbers every day, using their computers to compile charts for management that show industry, peer group and market comparisons.

General Information

Electronic databases are wondrous sources of information on an endless number of subjects. That makes them ideal for any corporate communications function. There is no reason for companies to limit the breadth and depth of their research and writing. The opportunities to gain knowledge leading to expertise on the domestic and global capital markets, economy, and the factors that influence them, the industries and markets served by our company, technologies vital to our industry are at our fingertips.

The increased knowledge will improve the quality of annual reports, white papers, video presentations and other communications materials, while enabling us to write executive speeches that truly say something new. It will expand the investor relations contribution to the corporation by yielding information that can be used in advising management on such critical policies and actions that affect share value as dividends, mergers, acquisitions, divestitures, share repurchases, ESOPs, shareholder rights proposals, and other governance-related issues.

The good news for investor relations practitioners is that the number and size of electronic data sources just grow and grow. They are very much in competition with each other, adding information and convenience by the day. Any list of services will be partial, made obsolete by time. With apologies to those missed, here's a list:

Dow Jones News Retrieval	Value Line
Quotron	Standard & Poor's
CableSoft	DowPhone
Mead Nexis/Lexis	INET
ABI/Inform	NewsNet
Bridge	Business Dateline
Investex	The Source
VuText	NewsFlash
Instinet	Dialog
CompuServe	Comtex

continued

Citicorp Global Report	PR Newswire
IBES	BusinessWire
First Call	Bridge
Telescan	Bloomberg
Track Data	Media General
Reuters	Burrelles
Compustat	Business Research
Bechtel	Zacks

With so much information flowing, it is critical for companies to know what is contained in these files in the databases. Investor relations people should be monitoring the content continuously. It's easy enough to do, using a PC and modem to tap into the various resources. Check at least the major ones that are most popular with investors, analysts and those brokers operating computers. The best way to determine which ones are used most is to ask several of your favorite analysts and portfolio managers. Compustat, Dow Jones, Quotron, Reuters, Bloomberg, Zacks, IBES, and Instinet will surely make the list. Inaccurate information in the files can be a real danger with the increase in quantitative-oriented investment modeling and the trend of money managers to bypass the brokerage analysts and go directly to the databases for research support. If the performance numbers on file are inaccurate for some reason, the company may not even make the list of investment candidates or it may be given a lower investment ranking than warranted based on the software formula. The old computer saw about "garbage in, garbage out" is true, and it can doom a company's investment chances with some firms.

Investors, analysts and corporations are about to have a brand-new information dissemination/receiving resource, with a name of its own no less—EDGAR. EDGAR is the child of the Securities and Exchange Commission, but this kid is going to have a lot to say. An acronym standing for *Electronic Data Gathering, Analysis, and Retrieval System*, EDGAR will function as the required disclosure filing method and resource base for public companies when it is completely operational in 1994. That's the year for completing the process of bringing all companies into the system. Companies were being added all through the second half of the 1980s; hundreds were filing all their disclosure documents electronically as the decade began—either by telephone lines, disks or magnetic tapes. EDGAR will pour forth a motherlode of information:

10-K, 10-Q (the SEC-required annual and quarterly reports) and 8-K reports;

13-D (indicating 5 percent holdings in a company) and other Williams Act filings;

various stock ownership reports, including Forms 3, 4, 144, and 13(f); and

proxy statements, prospectuses, and other registration materials.

Reference rooms and copying service offices also will be located in Washington, New York, and Chicago. The annual report will not be part of EDGAR's reservoir since it is not a required filing document.

Clearly, EDGAR is going to grow into a busy, vital contributor to the information process. Investors and analysts can obtain valuable financial and performance data with the touch of a computer key. EDGAR is sure to get a good workout once the filings are available; that's scheduled to start in 1991. Corporations aren't likely to be shy about taking advantage of the comprehensive database either. EDGAR stands ready to help companies learn more about each other. As such, it is being used in merger/acquisition research as well as in refining investor relations strategy and communications content by studying and comparing the basis of valuation of a number of peer companies.

STREAMLINING INFORMATION DISSEMINATION

Gone are the days when companies relied on the mails and messengers to get information to their intended audiences. The methods today: computer-to-computer links, facsimile through telephone lines, and electronic data transmission services.

The third of these three currently tops the popularity chart, but we're seeing more direct contact between computers. Electronic dissemination services are highly efficient; they're set up to send information to the audiences companies want to reach. Most companies have abandoned the old-fashioned methods of distribution, now releasing information or making statements electronically. Here's a quick review of the primary methods.

PR Newswire and BusinessWire relay releases, announcements and other information to both the media and investment community. Media lists can be tailored and expanded to reach virtually any outlet, and they're global. Investment lists include the sell and buy sides, and also cover the world. Information flows into these offices on electronic machines, similar to the Dow Jones broadtape and Reuters wire. Recipients value the information enough to watch the machines closely, sort the releases and announcements, getting them to the interested editor, reporter, analyst or portfolio manager. Stepping ahead technologically, both PR Newswire and Business-Wire materials are available on-line through computers, virtually as the stories run on the wires. Thus, analysts and investors can call up the information on their personal computer screens.

Companies have a number of other services available for media coverage. Media directories provide lists covering virtually every type of outlet and including the names of editors, beat reporters, columnists, news directors and other key personnel. Several provide release distribution. They handle reproduction and distribution of materials, using lists kept current and computerized.

Focusing on the buy and sell sides, companies are turning more and more to such services as First Call, Telescan, and Timed Release. First Call has gained wide respect, because of its stature with institutions. It was begun by a group of brokerage firms wanting to get their research into the hands of institutions. More than 20 sell-side firms now sponsor the service, reaching over 500 institutional firms worldwide, with the number rising. Information is sent via computer. Brokers transmit research reports and their "morning notes"—daily news flashes, sell/buy/hold opinion updates on companies, macroeconomic or industry trend data, whatever else is pertinent to the investing process. Companies pay an annual fee to participate, and can send releases, announcements, statements or comments on breaking developments. They also can be two-way participants in the system, receiving the same brokerage-based information going to institutions. The addition is an important piece of market intelligence, since companies not only are monitoring analyst comments on themselves, but also are watching industry and peer competitors.

Telescan reaches about 20,000 investors, including many individuals along with institutions and analysts. Its format offers companies the opportunity to broaden the information sent to the Street. Profiles, backgrounders and other materials can be put into the database as well as releases, announcements or comments. Each carries a notice or summary of the content, which is punched into the subscriber directory. Subscribers see the summary, call up the story on their screen, and print it out if they want a copy. The notice stays in the directory for a week, with companies allowed to store up to 26 stories in the database.

Timed Release sends corporate releases simultaneously to the media, analysts, investors, stock exchanges, and database terminals worldwide and around the clock. Companies hook up with the central distribution point through a modem. Undoubtedly, the number of electronic service options for reaching investors will continue to multiply.

Voice mail will increase in use as investors and analysts acquire the capability. Meanwhile, facsimile is the leading personalized electronic linkup between companies and the investment community. The communications is direct, between investor relations department and the specific brokerage analyst and institutional analyst and portfolio manager; where contacts are well established, they expect to be on the priority list to receive faxes of earnings releases and key announcements. Companies also are using facsimile distribution in expanding the contact loop, tailoring a release, for example, with a cover note tying the results to an institution's investing style. Technology that generates simultaneous faxing to multiple phone numbers is catching on fast.

Mailgrams are still used to send information; they signal importance, but aren't as fast as facsimile or computer transmission. Overnight services are employed to reach global points or send packages of information.

Quarterly earnings data leads the list of information being sent technologically. Releases are more revealing than ever before, often including a condensed balance sheet, business unit breakouts and other data. But technology as a communications tool is going well beyond earnings releases. The equity valuation process is enhanced by being able to take advantage of modern communications methods that are readily accepted by the audiences. In addition, the ability to send information quickly can be critical in seizing a situation that calls for using communication to take control or at least be heard.

ORGANIZING THE INVESTOR RELATIONS OFFICE

Computers are revolutionizing information and resource management in the investor relations office. The ability to enhance the quality of information, maximize the use of time, and save money by automating office administration is coming exactly when needed as investor relations professionals work to increase their output and value with their still small staffs and tightly controlled budgets.

Three main jobs are being done with computer assistance:

1. Managing information, focused on organizing, storing and facilitating the use of information.
2. Efficiently running the host of administrative tasks that make up the function, including keeping mailing lists; maintaining information files; producing, editing, customizing and reproducing publications, articles, releases, backgrounders, speeches, reports; preparing and duplicating letters and address labels; taking and recording calls; and even opening the "mail," when it comes electronically.

3. Analyzing information in planning and implementing the investor relations program, and in generating management reports related to the capital markets, stock price valuation and investor relations programming results.

Several software programs exist to help supply and format information, and run the investor relations function. Companies tend to be combining outside computer services and software programs with internal capability in creating the modern technology-based investor relations office. Some value-added software not only provides the information, but analyzes it as well. A list of the company's longer-term institutional holders is an example. Other software guides practitioners in setting up and maintaining the many files and activities that constitute the function—from target list compilation and address label production to copy preparation and report generation.

Management Information

It all begins with management information—what should be put into the investor relations database and how the system should be programmed to ensure highest productivity when in use. Let's take a look at a comprehensive working investor relations computer file system, by the numbers:

1. Shareholder identification and targeting information. It includes 13(f), depository trust, transfer sheet, record, beneficial ownership, and other research-related data that comes together in keeping shareholder lists current and in creating institutional target groups.
2. Stock trading and market data, including price, volume, change, volatility, and liquidity covering the company, industry, and peer groups, and the market. It enables the company to track stock performance against peer groups and the market.

3. Price/earnings ratios and consensus earnings forecasts for the company, peer groups, and market as a whole.

4. Investor, analyst, broker, and media profiles. These are invaluable in building relationships, handling phone or face-to-face conversations, and in preparing executives for interviews. As the phone call with an analyst begins, the investor relations person is studying the file, recalling what was covered in previous conversations, being reminded of favorite concerns or strengths, checking the date of the last research report and current recommendation. The profiles become the basis of invitation lists for financial meetings.

What is contained in the files will vary with each investor group and person. For example, the thrust with institutional holders will be size of holding, pattern of buying/selling transactions, whether their position was ever liquidated then begun again, key portfolio manager and analyst contacts within the firm, holdings in industry/peer companies, investing style and method, summaries of previous conversations.

With brokerage analysts, the file will cover position on the company, date of last recommendation, number and dates of recent research reports, summaries of reports, dates and content of conversations with investor relations and management people, likes and dislikes regarding the company, investing method utilized, attendance record at meetings, whether a member of the *Institutional Investor* magazine all-American team, employment history, any other industries followed.

A few companies try to keep broker profiles, concentrating on the loyal top producers. The dossier includes tracking periods of strong recommendation and the reasons at the time, fundamental reasons for favoring the company, types of customers, previous contacts and nature of conversation, meeting attendance record, time with the current firm and others in the broker's past.

Media profiles are geared toward improving relationships, preparing for interviews, making sure the company isn't about to be blindsided by questions inherent in a particular journalist's bias, and selecting the appropriate outlets and reporters for certain story ideas. Companies are building profiles on media outlets and individual reporters and editors; special software exists to help set up the database. The software can be programmed to help companies keep tabs on subjects being covered by each outlet and reporter; quality and accuracy of the coverage; media outlet or reporter depth of understanding and bias.

Profiles of each media outlet or reporter include:

a) lists and summaries of stories, in total and by various categories;

b) descriptions of how the stories were covered;

c) evaluation of the stories on the basis of accuracy, depth, and objectivity;

d) whether the company was interviewed, person being interviewed, an appraisal of the interview and its use in the coverage;

e) favored and unfavored kinds of stories;

f) particular bias involving business, the industry, company or certain executives; and

g) coverage of competitors or other companies in the community.

5. Mailing lists and labels. Computer wizardry allows these to be set up in numerous combinations, updated, changed, merged and otherwise manipulated in seconds.

6. All the communications materials that should be on file and at the ready. These include releases, backgrounders, position papers, speeches, blocks of speech material for use in future speeches, annual and quarterly report drafts, corporate profile, mission statement, key announcements and statements, commentary on any industry or community or financial

issues, letters, and anything else that may be needed as a reference or communications tool.

7. An electronic book of corporate financial data. It will include pro-forma financial statements, spread-sheet data, notes and other support material, SEC filings, and more.

8. Industry and peer group information. It can have operational (as in competitive intelligence), financial (as in acquisition defense or offense), and stock price valuation comparison purposes. In satisfying these various uses, the data will include in-depth, numbers-oriented operational and financial profiles, and such valuation-related information as stock price and trading statistics, earnings forecasts, analyst and institutional investor positions.

9. Macroeconomic and capital markets data.

10. Annual report planning and production schedule.

11. The annual meeting plan, with complete logistics detail.

12. The crisis communications plan.

13. Shareholder services software. Some companies are using computers to handle more of the shareholder services traditionally done by banks, such as securities registration and transfer, dividend paying/reinvestment, and record keeping.

14. Stock price valuation software. Increasingly, companies are using valuation software; packages have been developed by a number of consulting firms. The software helps companies calculate their intrinsic worth and fair value. In some companies, the valuation program is managed in the office of the chief financial executive, in others, by the investor relations officer. Whichever, investor relations people should be an integral part of the process. They must understand the valuation thoroughly, so they communicate it effectively.

15. Investing software. Investor relations people benefit from being able to see and work with the same software being used by investors. Basic purpose of the software is to generate

data for use in investment modeling and portfolio management. The packages can be expensive and considered a luxury, but they are a possible next step in refining investor relations wisdom.

Investor Relations Administration

Savings in time and steps to improve program quality and execution, and increase staff efficiency are the rewards of technology in the investor relations office. Computers help corporate investor relations departments do more things faster and better without having to hike up the size of the staff.

Key activities include calling up information and copy already on file; editing copy into new material which takes its place in the system; printing out letters and labels en masse quickly; and disseminating releases and other information broadly or selectively within minutes.

Analysis and Reporting

Because so much information can be pulled from the database easily and combined in myriad ways, computers are creating a new state of the art in analysis, while rewriting the techniques for generating reports as well as upgrading their quality severalfold.

The ability to analyze is unlimited; people need to discipline themselves in making sure the analyses have some use. The analysis can be as broad as comparing stock valuation and performance against an appropriate industry group or the S&P 500, and as specific as measuring transaction patterns for six selected companies among a group of institutional investors not holding shares in your company before contacting them.

Such also is the horizon for generating management reports. Computers seem to enjoy turning data into charts, graphs, and reports. What's important is to focus the charts, graphs and reports on information that draws management into the capital markets puzzle and investor relations process—valuation, the inner workings of Wall Street, what's happening to the stock and why, investor and market behavior, what investor relations is doing to communicate what's critical to improve the company's capital position.

16

Why a Proactive Approach Is Best in Media Relations

Media visibility can be a productive investor relations tool, but *media relations* is becoming a critical component of the corporate survival kit. Well-placed articles in leading business and financial publications can have a positive effect on stock prices and should be a serious piece in any investor relations program. However, there is a huge difference between efforts to make media placements and a hard-working, ongoing program to establish and maintain close, mutually respectful relationships with influential writers and editors. Increasingly, companies are doing the former, to their benefit, but few are doing the latter.

Across the range of communications activities that make up a well-rounded investor relations program, disagreement is widest on the role and value of media relations. Some companies are aggressive about it, others run away from it. Some companies see continuous and consistent media exposure as an integral part of improving stock price, others believe the damage that can be done by the media far outweighs any potential for benefit. Some companies work at controlling the media's coverage while others are convinced that any control is impossible.

These differences in attitude and activity often are closely aligned with the personalities and experiences of management. Corporate executives are inclined to be wary of the media. So are investor relations officers with financial backgrounds—people who, until now, have never had the responsibility of getting along well with the media and don't see the need for it. Investor relations practitioners with a communications/public relations upbringing appreciate that need.

The reluctance of senior executives to step into the media waters comes from ignorance and fear of embarrassment. Perhaps they have been burned previously; probably because they weren't properly prepared. Or, they watched associates get burned. Certainly, they see more negative stories than positive. And, they're not accepting the real and legitimate role of the media. Executives are accustomed to controlling risk and the behavior of others. They can only hope to influence these critical variables in a media situation.

In these times of heavy press weight, it makes no sense for a company to be unenlightened about how to conduct effective media relations. Even if the company isn't particularly aggressive about pursuing coverage in the everyday world of business, there is value in understanding how various media outlets operate and knowing some of their key people. Harm will not come from understanding the formats, story interests, approaches, and biases of each major print and broadcast outlet that may cross the company's path. Harm will not come from having quality working relationships with reporters, columnists, editors, and assignment directors at each of these outlets. The opportunity to secure a positive story, should it be useful or necessary, is enhanced. And, should push become shove, the company will fare better by having insight into the "agenda" of the inquiring newspaper, magazine, or TV station and be in a position to participate in the outcome if it has established some rapport with the reporter.

Exercising initiative in creating a high media presence and being prepared to handle communications in crisis situations—a product recall, environmental calamity, or hostile takeover bid are three contemporary, recurring examples—represent the two ends of the spectrum in media relations. In between is a potpourri of possible media encounter: the flow of regular releases, the occasional event (a plant opening or annual meeting), responding to requests for information, and invitations to take part with other companies in "roundup" stories that might cover an industry or subject with broad dimensions. Virtually all of these are fundamentally positive, by definition, and companies benefit from handling them professionally. Some of the roundup stories deal with issues, trends, or problems that can be controversial, but they often produce an opportunity for the company to stand out as a leader, offer an intelligent solution, or add meaningful comment to the debate. Still, many companies run away from the opportunity, anticipating that only bad can come from the inquiry.

Communications professionals can take the lead in helping their managements develop a reasonable attitude and sound procedure toward media relations. The task is tough: while communications people are being aided by the price companies are paying for mishandling crises, executives can't be faulted for shrinking back from the investigative zeal of journalists. Many managers remain skeptical, dismissing the pleas of public relations people as out of tune with corporate strategy or naive. Some executives even distrust their communications people, fearing misguided press loyalty or a heightened sense of cooperation that causes them to say too much.

Without question, the advice of communications professionals to top management must be wise. Not every media situation will call for a response A company can confront a "no-win" media reality. "Hatchet" jobs do result from a reporter's conviction that the story has to be told. Sometimes stories grow bigger, as each side in the controvery argues its case in print or over the air. Relative relevance flies out the window. The business/media relationship can be adversarial. The communications person has to know when to advise the company to stay out the controversy, or back off, and when to jump in because the company *is* involved, *will be* covered, and its comments are crucial to public opinion.

The media has a lot to say about what is and isn't a story. Everyone has to live with their judgment. But, it can be influenced, and being in a position to influence it can be critical. The additional voice (of the company) can cause a journalist to either realize that the subject isn't important enough to cover or to change the slant of the story in some way.

Occasionally, a company is "blessed" with a CEO who seems to understand, almost instinctively, the benefits of cooperating with the media; who knows when to call on them to help get a message across and when and how to be responsive to minimize damage, to get the company's side of the story across, or even to turn the likely public reaction positive by influencing coverage from the start. These CEOs become media favorites because they are available, articulate, and, oftentimes, colorful. The opportunity for the company to have more control of the outcome is heightened.

However, most senior executives question the value of an aggressive media relations program, possibly because they don't have confidence in their personality and aptitude in handling interviews well. For them, vast resources of evidence exist that can be tapped by communications professionals determined to document the value of a professional media relations program. In fact, assembling the documentation is well advised. It will take some work, but the effort should be illuminating. More documentation would benefit the communications practice; the material is there, but it needs to be organized and presented in a cohesive format. Its essence is academic research and case studies.

Documenting the value of media relations should cover its two major roles: producing evidence showing the benefits of media relations in accomplishing a certain objective such as bringing a company to the attention of investors or increasing broker following or the number of individual investors; and showing evidence of the results of media relations in a crisis.

Numerous academic studies have been done on the effect of media coverage. These studies have tended to be tied to specific events such as the impact of major corporate announcements on share price. Perhaps more valuable are the hundreds of case histories available for study. They are far ranging and cover both proactive media visibility build-ups and crisis communications. An excellent resource is the award-winning programs of the Public Relations Society of America, the International Association of Business Communicators, and other professional communications organizations.

INVESTOR RELATIONS ROLE IN MEDIA RELATIONS

Under continuous debate is the role of investor relations in a media program. Investor relations people are becoming increasingly uncomfortable dealing with the media. A big reason is the growing number of practitioners without experience in media contact who share the fears of the CEO about doing a poor job in the interview or being burned by the negative motivations of the reporters. More and more investor relations people have backgrounds in finance, law, strategic planning, or are former analysts, portfolio managers, traders, or brokers.

But discomfort doesn't change the fact that investor relations people are eminently qualified to handle media relations. They are qualified on the basis of the information they possess and in their ability to deal with the personalities of each group. The requisites of talking with analysts and investors are virtually the same as in talking with reporters and editors. Analysts and reporters alike are aggressive, egocentric, persistent, penetrating, and often negative in their questions.

By virtue of their access to information afforded by their job responsibilities and daily workings with analysts and portfolio managers, investor relations people have insight into corporate strategy and detailed knowledge of the financial structure and every operation of the company. Their knowledge is likely to be superior to that of public relations people who serve as the corporate spokesperson.

Investor relations people also are accustomed to explaining the intricacies and subtleties of the business. They do it daily with analysts and investors. Investor relations people have had to learn how to be adept in knowing what to say, how to say it, and how far to go in providing information and interpretation. They've gotten comfortable in dealing with Wall Street and investors, but many haven't transferred that comfort to dealing with reporters and editors. They argue that it's hard to shift mental gears when talking with an analyst versus a reporter, which suggests that companies are willing to provide more information to analysts than reporters.

That willingness probably stems from having a sharp focus on the value of a favorable analyst's report and being more relaxed about talking with someone whose words aren't going to be read by hundreds of thousands of people the next day. And, because the contact with an analyst or large institutional holder is frequent, over time, a relationship has grown.

By not taking on the media role, investor relations people can be doing their companies a disservice. The benefits that accrue from passing along investor relations wisdom to the business and financial press parallel those of a good analyst/investor contact program. Investor relations people are in an excellent position to increase the knowledge of journalists. Informed journalists are more likely to write informed stories. As a rule, the company fares better in a story written from a high level of well-rounded expertise. Media ignorance is a chief complaint of corporate management. Companies can change that. The opportunity to do so is greater today due to the rise in importance of business news. A metro daily that once had two business writers now may have 20, with reporters specializing in certain industries. Companies can help educate reporters, who have more incentive and time to learn.

The expertise of the business media is elevating its clout with readers and watchers. Companies should view that influence as an opportunity as much as a concern. Again, the stakes parallel analyst relations. The analyst can write a "sell" recommendation as well as a "buy." Investor relations people recognize that reality and work hard to keep the analyst informed. They're prepared to deal with the "sell" recommendation; its possibility doesn't cause companies to shy away from ever contacting a powerful analyst in the first place. Indeed, should the "sell" call come, the investor relations person will be working harder than ever to understand the basis of the recommendation and point out how the company is handling it.

There's no reason attitudes toward the media shouldn't be the same. There are opportunities for high-impact, widespread coverage that benefits the company tremendously. The potentially negative situations aren't likely to disappear if the company sandbags the reporter. It is the absence of a well-conceived, well-stated response that can do the damage. Often, investor relations people are best qualified to craft and deliver that response, engage in the inevitable conversation with the reporter that goes with it.

Just as relationships grow with analysts and investors, so can they blossom with reporters, and yes, involve investor relations people. The precautions will be similar; investor relations people are quite familar with them.

Companies tend to handle the investor relations role with the media in one of three ways:

1. Investor relations is the principal contact with the business and financial press while the public relations department handles relationships with the rest of the media;
2. Public relations handles all the contact, utilizing investor relations as a resource, either for information or in conducting phone conversations, and interviews; and
3. Public relations handles all the contact, with investor relations having virtually no participation.

The first is ideal, the second can work quite satisfactorily, and the third probably leaves the company missing opportunities for positive coverage or to articulate its case persuasively.

The argument for investor relations participation in media relations is not intended to denigrate the contribution of public relations people. Companies combining the function leave the question moot. Many companies have vested the corporate communications or public affairs responsibility in a senior officer. The position lends authority to the media relations function, paving the way for the media contact specialist to become an expert on the company. However, hundreds of corporations have separate investor and public relations functions, and in most of these companies, the investor relations person has built up more knowledge and is involved in more situations that call for discussing corporate strategies. Clearly, investor relations people are in a position to contribute to the media relations process, for the good of the company.

THE CASE FOR PROACTIVE MEDIA RELATIONS

The following is a vast oversimplification of corporate attitudes toward media relations, but it still has some validity. It goes like this. Smaller, younger companies are more aggressive about gaining attention through media stories. They're willing to take more risks, put themselves on the line to gain the coverage. They have little money available to spend on advertising. Bigger companies are conservative, risk-averse, and less inclined to take chances with media coverage. They prefer to control the content and placement of their messages through advertising.

This attitude among bigger companies seems to be changing. There is a growing recognition that a steady flow of essentially favorable media news and feature coverage can play a vital role in shaping and projecting a company's public image and reputation. This favored reputation has a positive ripple effect among a diversity of audiences—consumers/customers, politicians, community leaders, future employees, and most importantly, current and potential shareholders.

A number of huge, well-known business enterprises have deliberate programs to carve public reputations for being among the most respected and admired companies. The majority are consumer companies, with products that are highly visible. These companies recognize how products sell reputation and reputation sells products; they're capitalizing on their products to help forge that reputation, and marketing their enhanced image to sell more products. In turn, the popular products and respected reputations attract investors. The group taking this lead is not limited to consumer companies, however. The concept carries over to industrial and business service companies favorably influencing investors through good reputations resulting from high visibility, a record of citizenship and consistent financial performance.

The media coverage is being produced from planned, professional public relations programming. It's far more methodical than magical—the result of careful planning, good research, hard work, excellent execution, and follow-up. It starts with the company taking a proactive attitude, then finding or creating opportunity for visibility. It seems to be occurring in three ways: sponsoring events of community and national interest; lending support and executive expertise to major economic or social opportunities or issues; and providing useful or interesting information that is either edifying or entertaining.

Corporate sponsorship of events has grown enormously popular in the last decade. Most are community based; many involve athletics. Some produce national exposure; a handful of companies has taken on big-time sponsorship of such events as golf or tennis tourneys, stops on the auto racing circuit. But most are local or regional, frequently with a beneficiary (such as a hospital, a community improvement project, or a disease-related fund raiser). Runs, bike races, golf tournaments, music festivals, and art or food fairs are all very well received. The goodwill quotient is high; media coverage comes from the interest in the event.

More serious is the support of programs that help spur nationwide economic growth or resolve a social need by providing resources—financial, the collective knowledge of the company, or employees with specific expertise. A company's leadership in these roles often generates positive media focus.

Companies also are sharing information and even helping develop it through studies and surveys. American business is a vast reservoir of valuable information with most of it being filed in cabinets or computers. Companies also have the bulk of the country's resources to do more research and the analytical expertise to make it meaningful. In being more open with this information, companies can literally do a "world of good." The information itself can yield an unending stream of media coverage.

This kind of sharing of resources, people, and information also can lend a hand to corporations where it is crucially needed—with their own reputations. Companies have a long way to go in overcoming the negative image of big business. The surprising success of "Roger and Me," the movie about General Motors, is evidence of public attitudes toward large companies. Facility closings, employee layoffs, product quality problems, a perception of ducking environmental and other pressing social issues, and their sheer size do the biggest damage.

Institutions almost always fall out of favor in mature societies, and American business is the nation's biggest institutional group. That's all the more reason managements must be sensitive to the concerns of citizens and mindful of the role of the media in influencing public attitude. Executives need to recognize the role of the media, which is often adversarial in pointing out problems and seeking reform. There is a fundamental good behind its purpose. Collectively, business has done more "good" for society than probably any other institutional group. Companies certainly are a force for good: they provide products, services, jobs, income, technology, production, and foster human resources.

Companies would be better off showing their warts, not being so defensive, sharing their problems, and seeking help. In return, the media would be more interested in writing and talking about their progress, successes and participation in solving economic and social needs. These developments would be seen more in context with the human condition instead of being viewed suspiciously by journalists as attempts by otherwise close-mouthed companies to toot their own horn.

Companies can benefit from dealing with the media realistically. That means recognizing the media's role, and being active participants in their information/opinion gathering process. Rather than complaining about biased reporting and inaccuracy, companies can work to improve thoroughness, accuracy, and interpretation. Companies should challenge the media to be accurate and fair by being sources of comprehensive information and by improving accessibility to it. This plea isn't naive. The level of information given by companies could rise significantly and still be considered judicious.

Companies will have to restore the appetites of journalists for the information. Indeed, they are suspicious. Still, it shouldn't be difficult, once they see the value there. Yes, it will take some education in pointing out what's important to report for the benefit of the economy or solution of a problem. Take any issue—environmental, technological, marketing, employment—and bring together all the data, description, and analysis that has been done inside all the corporations of America. What an incredible wealth of information it would represent!

Companies are concerned that much of it would be proprietary? Now, *that's* naive. And harmful, to the extent it causes companies to hold back communicating what amounts to their real strengths, talents and contributions. What's truly proprietary doesn't have to be revealed. Companies are in control of the information. The level of coverage rarely, if ever, goes beyond what already is known within the industry itself.

There is a bottom line to all of this in the context of investor relations. Companies have no more powerful an ally or information dissemination tool than the media. No other source reaches as many people as quickly, or influences as many of them, as strongly. At the same time, companies have no more powerful threat than the media. The media can help build respect, admiration and confidence in a company. Or tear them down. A professional media relations program should be a top corporate priority.

COMPONENTS OF A MEDIA RELATIONS PROGRAM

Companies usually fall into media relations habits, set by their personality and experiences, rather than developing sound policy and procedure aimed at accentuating the benefits of proactive media visibility and getting a fair shake when the chips are down.

A programmed approach to media relations takes companies into six activities. They can be seen as layers, with the addition of each layer making the program that much stronger.

1. A general policy complete with a set of procedures. It guides the company, determines the parameters and players, and provides a basis for measuring results.
2. The research phase, where the company learns everything it can about each media outlet, reporter, and editor that might be part of the contact stream.

3. A contact process, which brings members of the press face to face with management and certain chosen experts within the company. These relationships are nurtured apart from the pressures of an event or story. They are developed through lunches, background briefings and the like.

4. An aggressive attitude about being helpful to the media. It is carried out in responding quickly and qualitatively to requests for information and in arranging interviews with company people who are sources of explanation, interpretation, commentary or insight on a particular subject. The effort works from the concept that being a media resource pays dividends. It does.

5. An ongoing proactive media visibility program. It pursues coverage, rather than waiting and hoping for the media to contact the company. It is based on being able to show reporters and editors the value of a story that includes coverage of the company.

6. A fully developed crisis communications plan. It anticipates the crisis and dictates how the company handles it, including the critical communications. It carefully lays out every aspect of the company's response by detailing activities, participants, and their assignments.

Setting Policy and Procedures

Let's take them one at a time. Policy and procedure precede any serious effort. They're important, because they formalize the process, give it some substance and stature within the corporate priority lineup. Companies are guided by policy and procedure; media relations should be included in this structure.

A written policy focuses management attention on the role and the importance of media relations. It gives shape to what can easily be a soft and wobbly function. It creates accountability for the media relations people, spells out management's participation, and puts executives on the line to fulfill their commitment.

The written policy should contain both broad and specific statements of goals and objectives. The overall purpose is to gain corporate acceptance of the legitimacy of the activity. Thus, the policy indicates the company's recognition of the value of media relations, a commitment to it, and an intent to conduct a planned, organized, and professional program. It also contains a statement on the benefits of good media relations in achieving fair and reasonable coverage. The specifics deal with such points as encouraging a high level of coverage by pursuing and responding to opportunities, and maintaining open communications with certain limitations. The policy also may describe the importance of business news in our society, the role of the press in reporting on it, and the responsibility of companies to participate in the information dissemination process. Word it carefully; some CEOs may have trouble accepting the statement, but if they do, it certainly is a step in the right direction.

Procedures cover the methods of working with the media and outline the boundaries in terms of subjects and information. They list what can and can't be discussed; designate spokespersons on corporate, business unit, plant and office levels; and describe procedures for gathering, sharing, and disseminating information. All of this should be quantified so that it leaves little room for deviation. The quantification is needed because the process can be complex. It is advisable, for example, to define who can and can't talk with certain media and what they can and can't discuss. A plant manager can talk with the local press, but not *The Wall Street Journal* or *Business Week*. Those calls should be referred to the corporate media relations, public relations, or investor relations departments, depending on company policy. In some cases, the person being called is the right person to answer the call, but procedure should still send the request through the proper channels. It keeps control over the media relations process and enables the specialist to coach the person about to be interviewed. A business reporter talking with a division president is an example.

Reporting procedures should be established, which gives the corporate media relations department a complete record of every media contact. The information also is vital in analyzing the program with an eye toward making it better. The records provide a file of interested media and interesting subjects. A smart, aggressive media relations specialist can use this data to expand existing interest, as well as fashion storylines and media targets.

Laying in the Critical Research

"Know thy friends and enemies." Hopefully, there won't be any enemies among the media. Skeptics, yes, and liberals with a sense of reform. Democrats, for the most part. Pursuing the truth. Veterans and youngsters. Experienced and inexperienced. Open and closed. Polite and abrasive. Confident about what they know and interested in learning. More interested in the story than its effect on the people. Always looking for reliable sources and resolute about protecting them. Intent on truth and accuracy. Seeking balance. Trying to verify statements. Suspicious. Manipulative and capable of being manipulated.

Friends? It's possible. But, mutually respectful professional associates is more practical. If friendships develop, reporters and editors tend to back away from story situations in the interests of maintaining their journalistic integrity.

Knowing every media outlet and key contact is basic to every facet of a media relations program—from being responsive to being proactive. The ability to maximize the opportunity, minimize the risk or turn it into positive coverage in each contact will be enhanced by having a clear and thorough understanding of the format, style, attitude, knowledge level, bias, and the likely purpose of the journalist and print or broadcast outlet he or she represents.

Research enriches the results in a proactive placement program. Companies learn the kinds of stories to pitch by studying the kinds of stories liked by each outlet or reporter. Companies learn how to present the story and what information to include by studying the favored approaches and prevalent points made in the story. Companies learn which media outlets and reporters or editors to approach with a specific story idea.

Research alerts companies on how best to handle media requests for information or interviews. The company can look at previous coverage, of itself and others, to see how the particular paper, magazine, TV station, and even reporter, handled the coverage. The research can be invaluable in guiding the company's response.

Companies serious about media relations are enlisting the computer in producing a thorough research base. A number of media relations software programs exist today to help companies compile and store the data. The software provides a complete book on media intelligence. It enables companies to:

set up and store the names of media outlets (complete with profiles organized under a range of classifications);

identify and profile specific reporters and editors;

provide lists of articles and "clips" of the stories;

show coverage of designated companies in the industry or community;

compare coverage among companies and with your company; and

report the information in any number of ways, utilizing graphic formats as an option.

With a PC and modem, the software can be supplemented with outside data retrieval that can include access to additional story clippings, names of media outlets and journalists.

Companies also can prepare and store media materials in the computer—releases, background papers, product descriptions, marketing positions, executive bios, copy blocks used in speeches, and cover letters. Any of these can be updated, edited, or tailored easily with the word processor.

Here is just a partial list of how this research can be used in an ongoing media relations program:

1. Determine how the media in general covers your industry, the companies in your community, your company specifically, and your company in comparison with any designated others;

2. Determine and compare the amount of coverage being given;

3. Determine and compare coverage of each individual media outlet;

4. Analyze the content of the coverage, in general, by each media outlet, for the industry or community, comparing your company with others, as to accuracy, thoroughness, fairness, knowledge, bias;

5. Analyze each reporter in terms of accuracy, thoroughness, fairness, knowledge, bias for your company, others in the industry/community, the industry as a whole, and on a company-by-company comparative basis;

6. Determine the coverage areas of greatest interest to the media as a group and by each outlet;

7. Use the research as the basis of suggesting storylines favorable to your company that fit into a media outlet's interest levels;

8. Use the research as the basis of correcting misperceptions and overcoming bias in a particular publication or station;

9. Use the research to quantify the media relations process in selling a more aggressive effort to senior executives by defining opportunities, proving to them that other companies are faring better because they're working harder at the process, in documenting problems, pinpointing media ignorance or bias, showing how more contact and education can be beneficial.

Getting to Know the Media

The next level involves starting to build relationships with key media people. There's a big advantage in already knowing the reporter as the phone conversation or interview is taking place—whether the storyline was suggested by the company as part of its proactive visibility program, or the call was initiated by the reporter and the subject is potentially delicate. The benefit of knowing the other person is mutual: company and journalist.

Information has to be the basis of the relationship-building. Time is of the essence for everyone. There should be a reason for each meeting, even when a story is not the objective. The reporters and editors are getting to know the corporate people as they are learning about the company and its plans, its industry, economic status of the community or nation. At the same time, the company is finding out how the reporter thinks, how much he or she knows, and is gaining valuable insight into the interests of the media outlet.

Companies benefit from including everyone who is likely to be talking with the media in the relationship-building process. The list of corporate contact candidates should include the chief executive officer, chairman (if not the CEO), president, executive vice presidents, chief financial officer (CFO), probably the second highest ranking financial executive, heads of the business units, and functions such as research and marketing, and any specialists with expertise that is recognized or deserves to be recognized. Of course, the investor relations or appropriate communications officer should be included as well.

There are a number of ways to structure the meetings—in terms of format, content, and participants. Ideally, the process is seen as ongoing, leaving the company room to introduce subjects and executives into it over time. The dynamics of change also factor in; managers and journalists are constantly on the move. Some companies prefer meeting with the media one to one. This approach usually indicates a highly active program and/or one in which the company is trying to exercise some control in the flow of information. It will take many meetings to cover the various executives and media people, but the potential to forge closer, more qualitative relationships is greater.

Others like to bring in groups of journalists, who may talk with one executive at a time, or several, picked either to discuss certain subjects or extend the range of contacts. Sessions can be freewheeling or devoted to specific topics as the company seeks to expand media knowledge in an organized way. Selections of executives and media people also are organized with care, consistent with the goals of the program to bring all the players in both loops into the process. Care must include making sure competitive media aren't afforded advantages in learning first about major developments.

Some companies hold briefings at scheduled times, allowing an open agenda or announcing the subjects, inviting the full media corps and, thus, giving them the option of participating.

Who should constitute the prime media group will depend on the company and its location. Companies need to be realistic in their expectations. Big companies with the potential to make news, be part of the coverage of major stories involving the economy or their industry or certain issues, or with worthwhile information to share can be more ambitious in setting their target group. If those companies are in or near New York, the list can logically include the leading business/financial publications, business editors of the wire services, news directors of the cable TV business shows. Companies in sizable metro areas can include the bureaus of these outlets.

Certainly, the core group for most companies, regardless of location, should include business writers covering their industry from the metro dailies; the business editors of those papers; any specialized business magazines or newspapers in their city; bureau chiefs or business writers of Dow Jones/*Wall Street Journal*, Reuters, *New York Times*, Associated Press, *Business Week*/McGraw Hill, Finanical News Network, Cable News Network and any other important business-news bureau/correspondent in town.

What to do about radio and television? The call probably belongs to the company. The broadcast media offer the potential for great good or harm. Trying to educate them can be strategically smart and highly beneficial. Keeping them uneducated can be dangerous. Business news coverage on radio is picking up. Most stations now have business shows, which cover the markets and company news, such as earnings, stock price changes, dividend increases, significant technology or product developments, new plants, licensing agreements or overseas joint ventures. Occasionally, television picks up on positive news, but it is more inclined to look for the downside in a local business story—a surprise earnings decline that sends the stock price spiraling lower, dividend cut that presumes tougher times, a plant closing that causes layoffs. Pre-established relationships may enable the company to get a few words in to help explain the situation more favorably than will be the result if the story relies on only the hard facts and perhaps a pessimistic quote from an analyst.

Built-in relationships also can produce proactive story coverage from broadcast media. Radio and television stations recognize the importance of the economic impact on society and are seeking ways to cover business and the economy intelligently and competitively with the press. As a result, they are becoming more receptive to story ideas from companies.

Sometimes, there's a fine line between business and general news. Technology breakthroughs in medicine, efforts to contain skyrocketing insurance costs, improved automotive safety, new environmental safeguards or solutions can have tremendous impact on society as well as on corporate fortunes. The broadcast media is just as interested in covering these stories as the print press.

Evidence of this is seen in the use of company-produced video releases, typically 60 to 90 seconds long covering a subject of wide consumer appeal that has a company hook, such as a technology breakthrough, marketing trend or approach to solving a problem. The releases must maintain editorial integrity and they tend to be used by stations in smaller markets, but do show up as well on the bigger stations.

Being Responsive to Requests

Companies stand to help themselves in two ways by cooperating with media requests for information: gain worthwhile exposure and chalk up a future favor. Trouble is, frequently, the request takes immediate hard work to fulfill, requires the resources of others in the company, or offers the potential of corporate discomfort.

Reporters looking for information or commentary more often than not are working under deadline pressure. The story typically takes one of three turns:

1. It concerns the company—questions raised from a corporate press release or efforts to learn the possible impact on the company of some significant industry development, regulatory/legislative change, or startling economic news;

2. The company is being asked to lend expertise or comment on a growing issue, scientific progress, or continuing trend, such as new approaches to dealing with the high cost of health insurance, potential efficacy of a burgeoning but unproven medical discovery, or the benefits of management incentive compensation packages tied to stock price gains.

3. The company is being asked to participate in a roundup story on a subject that can be as serious as the effect of Japanese investing in America or as light as employee reaction to new office fashions.

The questions can call for all manner of response—facts that are simple and complex, explanations, background, prediction, commentary, and sometimes, a good colorful quote that enlivens the story. Companies are in a position to help the reporters and, as a result, themselves. The reporters want to make the story on the company as complete as possible. They recognize that the company's expertise can add value to the trend or issues story. They want their contribution to the roundup story to be good enough to be included in the piece. They remember the companies that came through. Companies develop reputations for being responsive and a reliable resource. The relationship benefits from the cooperation.

Companies intent on maintaining good media relations are willing to work hard to produce the information, do some research on the spot and think through how to shape the answer for a reporter or prepare a meaningful piece of copy, convince the appropriate expert within the company to conduct a phone or person-to-person interview. Companies with proactive attitudes and programmed approaches have a cadre of experts ready to handle the interviews, including investor relations people.

Efforts produce rewards, not only in strengthening media ties, but in the resultant coverage. By taking part in industry, trend, issues and national stories, companies enhance their reputation as business leaders and document their valued knowledge. The frequent exposure helps them win a bigger share of mind.

The tricky part of the whole process is the story that touches a nerve. Proactive companies don't disappear in these times. They work to give answers that are as useful as possible for the situation. Often, the effort to be responsive brings forth some new thinking on the issue, or enables the company to explain itself credibly. In most situations, companies fare better when they're willing to talk about the problem, why and how it occurred and what they're doing to deal with it, rather than let others, including their adversaries, speak for them.

Companies with qualitative media relations crafted by being available, open, and cooperative are going to find reporters and editors more receptive to story ideas and more open to their arguments in a troublesome situation, more willing to include or even emphasize their points of view and explanations in actual coverage.

Conducting a Proactive Program

A steady flow of favorable business press coverage can have a positive effect on a company's stock price multiple. Doubters argue against that idea, but there is growing conviction among investor relations practitioners of its factuality and sufficient evidence from academic studies to make proactive media exposure a basic part of the investor relations strategy. The appearance of a major article in leading business magazine touting a new technology or laying out prospects for improved financial performance can move investors to action immediately. The overall impact can be even greater for smaller companies, who still essentially are undiscovered by investors.

Media influence on investors is increasing, partially because of their desire to rely on themselves for research and analysis, and partially because of the improved quality of the stories. Indeed, many of them constitute an investment analysis, frequently combining the professional opinions of several respected industry analysts. The article can be as valuable as an analyst report, while reaching thousands more potential investors on a very timely basis.

Among the academic studies is recent work by Dr. James A. Danowski, associate professor and director of graduate studies for the University of Illinois at Chicago. Dr. Danowski has documented that stock price does react to media coverage through studies that involve hundreds of companies. His work suggests extensive market inefficiency; that not all relevant information already is discounted in the stock price. There are countless examples of stock price reacting—favorably and unfavorably—to corporate news or major business articles. The occurrence is relatively common.

Before launching an aggressive media placement program, companies should know everything they can about every media outlet, and the reporter and editor to be contacted. Research is the fuel that will make the program run. The objective is to present story ideas that appeal to the writers and editors by knowing their likes and dislikes, and by knowing how to build the backup information and suggesting people for interviews that will bring the story to life.

What appeals to the business press? The analysis begins by understanding the key elements that run through nearly every significant story: change, discovery, tension, conflict, personality. Some combination of these key ingredients is sought. Notice how many stories involve real people and are written to bring forth the personalities—ambition, intelligence, special talents, dishonesty, success, the meteoric rise then fall from grace, or the ability to generate wealth.

The quick response from investor relations people is that there are few positive storylines in these scenarios. Hardly. There are the classic underdog and turnaround stories. Winning against the odds is a favorite. Success comes in taking command of a market through a smart strategy, compiling a string of financial performance advances, and building a record of strong management as seen in a superior team of executives or proven succession program. Discovery often comes in technology, creating a new product idea or overcoming technological odds—a true breakthrough. Tension and conflict are common in many of these situations—among executives or scientists within the company, in risking marketshare while the change is taking place, in bucking conventional wisdom or racing the competition. Communications people need to be imaginative in drawing it out, and companies need to be willing to discuss it, recognizing that it's a real part of the story.

There are many other exciting storylines:

taking a position on an issue;

picking up on a trend early, being able to produce evidence showing its validity and articulating the company's influence in it;

finding an approach to solving a well-recognized problem;

innovative ideas involving important corporate functions, such as employee relations;

sharing what the company is learning about a perceived problem, such as an environmental concern;

looking for good news in apparent bad news.

The latter can be especially beneficial to a company, because it can change an opinion or perception, or at least cause the audience to look beyond the present and be more optimistic about the future. Examples: product developments to stop the erosion in marketshare; significant cost-control programs that are restoring competitiveness. Be prepared to document the turnaround.

In sum, communications and investor relations practitioners activating their creative juices in finding storylines should look both at the numbers and beyond the numbers. The numbers provide investment analysis-type stories. Beyond the numbers come the stories that hit at the culture, heart and soul of the company—

what makes it tick. The real challenge and reward for the company's communications people are in discovering the essence, depth, and subtleties found inside the company and then figuring out how to capture them in words.

Best way to approach a particular media outlet with a story idea will depend on the company's relationship with the editor or reporter. If it's close, the story idea can be discussed in a meeting or on the telephone. In most cases, however, the most effective starting point is an outline or "treatment" of the idea, occupying one or two pages. It can be a letter, or sent with a short cover letter. It should contain a concise description of the theme and include proof of its value. The journalists need to be assured that the story will grow, not disappear, as material and evidence are built from research and interviews. Appropriate people to interview also should be identified. Backup material should be ready for presentation. This can include a backgrounder, written to help "sell" the subject, copies of reports indicating internal research and study, any industry or outside data that lends credibility to the idea. Be wary of press clippings; they may convince the editor that the idea isn't unique. Indeed, don't try to peddle a used story. And, offer the idea exclusively.

Another question for companies is who to contact inside a certain media outlet. Again, the answer depends on the outlet, but there is a logical path and some protocol. First person in the line is the reporter covering your company by virtue of having been assigned it as part of his or her "beat." Metro dailies and certain business magazines have divided the business world into beats. As business has moved into the spotlight, these publications have become large enough to have staffs of reporters. A beat may be an industry, several industries or group of companies organized in some logical fashion. A story taken to the business editor will probably be bucked back to the beat reporter.

National outlets raise the question of whether to contact the local bureau chief in the headquarters city of the company or approach the appropriate editor in charge of the section the storyline fits. Perhaps, the story involves a turnaround, unique corporate strategy, marketing success, or global expansion. The bureau chief should be tied in, either receiving the initial contact, or a copy of the story treatment, so indicated in the cover letter.

What if you have a "friend" at the targeted publication? Use the relationship to determine the best person to contact. Perhaps, he or she will put in a good word about the story or your credibility as a worthy resource.

On the broadcast side, there are two key contacts, depending on the avenue being taken. For regular programs, such as interview or talk shows, the producers book the guests. When seeking coverage on the news programs, the contact is the news or assignment desk.

Vital in any proactive media placement program that covers the business/financial press and broadcast outlets are close analyst ties. Reporters rely on brokerage (and buy side) analysts and investment managers for information, background, insight, commentary and opinion on individual companies as well as industries and a host of macro factors that might influence corporate performance or the outcome of a trend or development. Good analyst relations are integral in good media relations. Companies should be prepared to give a reporter the names of certain analysts as the storyline is being suggested.

Helping companies pursue aggressive media exposure is proving to be a lucrative business for public relations and investor relations agencies. Dozens of firms emphasize it, several have built their businesses on media programs. Their stock in trade focuses on establishing and maintaining contact networks, knowing the kinds of stories each outlet and reporter prefers, and knowing how to present the story ideas.

Companies also should be aggressive about achieving regular coverage in their trade publications. These magazines are an information resource for analysts covering the industry. They use the information in deciding which companies to cover and in making investment recommendations. They also can draw important perceptions in evaluating industry leadership by the amount of coverage a company garners in the trade press. The absence of steady exposure can subtract from a company's genuine place at the top of the industry.

Communications in a Crisis

Crises produce an ultimate test for a company and its communications capabilities. In certain crises, how a company handles the communications can determine the outcome. Even where communications isn't "make or break," it can create or change attitudes toward the company—for better or worse—for a long time to come.

Crises also can have a severe effect on stock price, and thus, carry weighty investor relations implications. The crisis doesn't have to involve a hostile takeover bid to create that impact; it can involve product safety or a recall, a serious accident, environmental suit, or any of the many business and social issues of the day.

Companies need to be prepared to handle crises—the situation itself and the communications. A written plan, with comprehensive set of procedures, is recommended. Here are some of the elements that should be considered for inclusion in the plan.

Designate a Crisis Management Team

It should include the chief executive officer, communications officer and chief counsel, investor relations and strategic planning officers (or their alternates), key operating people who would be involved directly in dealing with the situation, probably the chief financial officer or alternate, and representatives from outside communications, public affairs, and legal consultancies.

Conduct Thorough Research

Conduct research in order to identify and build an information base on issues that can impact the company. Being able to see, dissect and understand issues in advance prepares a company to deal with them intelligently should and when they arrive. Some issues are unavoidable, others can be avoided, tempered, resolved or at least debated reasonably by early action. Issues left unattended often boil into crises. Those of highest concern to society currently generally involve safety, the environment, and fair treatment.

While the research itself can be housed in the public affairs or investor relations department, the company benefits from having the highest number of people involved in the process. It serves to increase support for corporate action. Information and expertise on an issue can be far-ranging, covering scientific, marketing/sales, personnel, accounting/finance, legal, and other functions within the company.

Identify and Plan for Events-related Crises

Crises topping the priority scale will depend on the company and its industry. Plant safety is number one in industries working with potentially dangerous materials or equipment, for example. A company list of emergencies likely will include:

a) fires and explosions;

b) plant accidents;

c) injuries to employees or members of the community;

d) transportation accidents;

e) product safety, involving precautions, injury or harm, warning and recall;

f) environmental accidents and warnings, company alerts to the community, charges and regulatory/court actions;

g) natural disasters, such as tornados, hurricanes, or earthquakes;

h) strikes or walkouts;

i) threats against the company or any employee;

j) incidents on company property involving employees or others using the facilities; and

k) incidents involving employees away from company facilities.

The plan should cover every conceivable action that could be required in the event of an emergency or building of a crisis and spell out assignments for every person involved. It also should encompass every location, domestically and worldwide. Thoroughness is critical. Events happen fast, putting a premium on time and action, while creating pressures in handling the situation effectively. Plans should include procedures for making contact with participants, list work and home phone numbers. Review and practice sessions are advised.

Develop a Comprehensive Communications Plan
It has two parts: procedures for gathering the information and for disseminating it. A resource team helps get all the essential information together. In the case of an emergency, the members may be at one location—the site of the event. In a crisis, for example a product recall, they can be throughout the world. They can include plant and production people, marketing and sales employees, security personnel, communications professionals, industry and other outsiders with knowledge and expertise on the situation. The focus is on facts and much more—reaction and comments, background information, proposed ways of handling it, and experiences with similar crises in the past.

Information dissemination becomes crucial. How companies handle communications may influence the outcome, but it clearly will affect attitudes toward the company. In many crises, how the company behaves and presents itself in the first few days leaves lasting favorable or unfavorable impressions with the public. They're looking for companies to be concerned, honest, forthright, willing to accept appropriate responsibility, keenly interested in resolving the issue.

Stonewalling the media and public starts the process off badly. Both could become negatively disposed, unnecessarily. The media's job is to get all the information they can on the story. Bias forms from a lack of cooperation. Liberalism may be lurking in the background. Companies can keep it from igniting in individual reporters. The public, of course, is a tougher case. Big business has to battle bias, but companies certainly can win support from large segments of the public by being open, forthright and action oriented. Johnson & Johnson showed that in its handling of the Tylenol package tampering crisis.

Ideal responses are key. If explanations are available right away, they should be discussed openly along with actions to take care of the problem. If investigations are required, they should be announced and launched immediately. If help is needed, it should be started, by company initiative. The four things a company should avoid are inaction, appearing to be unwilling to spend money to correct the situation, trying to duck the blame, and showing insensitivity to any victims. The three things they should do are launch help immediately, investigate the cause, and indicate they'll do whatever needs to be done.

Making decisions and communicating them quickly put the company in an aggressive mode, rather than reactive, defensive or silent. If possible, the first stories covering the event should include some action-driven corporate response. The tone is set. The media are likely to be looking for company comment and information. The public has favorable expectations from the company, even though something negative has happened. None of this dismisses the severity of a crisis. The more severe, the more that is expected of the company.

Lawyers will be concerned with indicating guilt. Companies certainly can take actions that ease or correct a real situation in the best interests of society without those actions indicating anything other than concern. The company is involved in what is happening. The actions enhance the communication process; it is much better to communicate facts on what the company is doing than try to respond to inaction and speculation.

Internally, the crisis communications plan designates spokespersons. One is ideal, if the situation allows one person to handle all the inquiries. But that may be impractical in the rush of calls and need to communicate to a diversity of audiences virtually simultaneously. With multiple spokespersons, companies must be careful to coordinate what they are saying. Consistency is critical. As much of what they say as possible should be on paper—releases, statements, concise backgrounders.

Companies with foresight have taken to writing positions, background pieces and parts of statements on various issues in advance. While emergencies and crises can't be predicted or even anticipated, the kinds that could occur can be researched, with the company planning in advance how it would handle them. Some of that response can be committed to paper. All the material can be put into the computer, available to company spokespersons online as part of a communications package.

The briefings, backgrounders and statements enable various spokespersons to be consistent in what they say: public relations people with the media, investor relations with analysts and investors, sales representatives with customers, public affairs with government and community leaders, personnel with employees, the CEO with industry and other business executives, the CFO with bankers and creditors.

The crisis communications plan also should give guidance on information dissemination methods—conditions and times for holding press conferences/briefings, sending out releases/statements. It sets forth policy on some potential sticky choices—whether to allow cameras into a plant or permit employee interviews, as examples. The situations can be tricky: a company can forbid photography or interviews inside its facilities, but not outside. Companies have some control inside, none outside.

When a crisis hits, media relations is suddenly paramount. If contacts don't exist, the company can be in for a rough ride. The lack of contact becomes more of a disadvantage to the company than the media. The media can draw upon electronic databases and information files; reporters can interview analysts, fund managers, other companies in the industry. The company becomes another source, rather than a special source. There is limited personal knowledge and experience with executives, probably no rapport with the spokesperson that would have created additional background, insight, understanding, or favorably disposed the reporter to look more closely at the company's side.

Hostile takeover bids produce different sets of circumstances, but offer equally difficult media-relations challenges, with the company's independence hanging in the balance. Economics almost always tilt that balance, with trust being a pivotal factor in the economic decision. Investors will take the best deal, as long as they trust the people making it. The job of the company is to convince shareholders to keep their shares, trusting the ability of the incumbent management to provide the best economic package over time. Creating distrust of the insurgents may be a strong communications theme as well. The job of the bidder is to convince shareholders that the premium is their best return in a cash tender offer or that a new management team will produce better value in a proxy contest for control. Creating distrust of present management may be a strong communications theme as well.

Those who strategize and study takeovers say that media coverage can determine the outcome. And the first few days are likely to make the difference. Here's one scenario, that was played out over and over in the 1980s as takeover wave followed wave. A 5 percent stake in the company is announced. The bid is rumored, hinted at or the intention to make a takeover run is announced. Institutions and arbitragers buy shares en masse because they're confident the company now is in play and eventually will be taken over. The stock price jumps higher. Shareholders sell, for the gains in the price run-up. The company's shareholder base changes dramatically. The company is lost.

Here's a scenario played out less often. The company is put in play. Buying and selling of shares is less pronounced. Stock price shows only a little volatility. The reasons? Institutions and arbitragers are less confident the takeover will go through. Institutional and individual shareholders believe that management is doing a good job, which is reflected in a higher share price that is seen as representing fair value. There appears to be a preference for incumbent management to continue running the company.

Communications strategy at the time of the bid (or indication) focuses on management performance. Valuation is the theme. Information provided the media proactively and in response to questions stays concentrated on performance. To carry that off, the company has to clearly understand its valuation and be prepared to describe it at a moment's notice. Indeed, valuation should be incorporated into a communications format so that it can be discussed easily whenever the situation calls for it. In the takeover threat, the company has to be geared up to communicate both verbally and in print with key journalists, analysts, institutions, brokers, and shareholders. The methods will include interviews, press conferences, phone conversations, meetings, faxed statements, electronic mail, and overnight delivery of background material. Taking the lead in talking with the media should be the CEO. But, in focusing the information on valuation, the possibilities are excellent that investor relations people also are talking directly with reporters and columnists. Takeovers, prominent in the 1980s, and proxy contests, likely to be the mode of choice in control contests in the 1990s, are covered extensively in Chapter 6.

SOME TIPS ON GOOD MEDIA RELATIONS

Here is a random list of ideas designed to help companies maintain productive media relationships.

1. Consider coaching for executives, managers and experts inside the company that have or can have regular contact with the media. The coaching can have two dimensions: preparing people to be effective in proactive and responsive media interviews; and preparing them to deal with adversarial situations. Trainers help executives organize and present information and ideas clearly and succinctly, overcome discomfort in interviews by preparation and practice, and by knowing more about the methods and motives of the interviewers.

   Executives are taught how to maintain or take some control in the interview, how to answer questions, how to make the information points they wish to express, how to give short answers that are hard to edit into a different context, how to answer tough questions. Typically, role playing occurs. Print and broadcast interviews are simulated, videotaped, played back, critiqued, and repeated to make executives increasingly comfortable in the various situations. A number of specialist firms provide media coaching.

2. Make sure anyone talking with the media understands the meaning and differences between "off the record," "not for attribution," "for background only" and other phrases executives are inclined to use as they get into media interviews. "Off the record" means the information cannot be used. It is risky to go off the record. Reporters can use the information if they find someone else who will say it. If the information is valuable, the reporter may pursue another source. Reporters don't like being told something is off the record. It is better for the person being interviewed to avoid the information altogether.

   "Not for attribution" means the information may be used but not attributed to the person providing it. You must be sure that applies to the company as well as the person giving the information. "Background" has a similar meaning; the information can be used but not attributed to the source. But, be sure the reporter is following the same definition before you speak. A phrase sometimes used is "deep background." Be wary of it. The accepted definition seems to be "off the record." Managers often find themselves in the middle of an interview using phrases like "just between us" or "you can't use this, but . . ." Coach executives not to do this. The phrases carry no weight with reporters.

   Sometimes, in the spirit of cooperation, the person being interviewed gives information and is unsure of its accuracy. It's okay to ask the reporter to check back before using the information. At that time, the company can correct any errors or misunderstandings, but not ask that the information be taken out of the story. And don't ask a reporter to read something back before it's printed or broadcast. They won't do it and the company is marked as amateurish.

3. Work at being a source. You can be helpful based on your knowledge of the industry, the economy in the community,

other companies and your own company. The process builds and strengthens relationships and creates a better framework for presenting your stories or arguments.

4. Work at educating your management on the role and job of the media. Get them to understand and appreciate the value of a story that is positive on balance. Get them to recognize that the more involved the company gets in the issues and needs of the day, the more visible and defined will be its reputation. Try to get managers away from the feeling that relationships with journalists are adversarial by definition. Working together is the course of action that pays off.

5. Be selective in attitudes toward journalists. Evaluate them individually. Each is different, in personality, experience, skill level, energy, and ambition.

6. Don't let the lawyers set communications and media relations policy and style. Most will put a muzzle on the process. Be gutsy if necessary to show the value of progressive media relations. Arm the arguments with evidence.

7. Don't stonewall a reporter. Say as much as you can and explain why you can't say any more.

8. Be available to respond to questions after issuing a release. Nothing is more irritating to a reporter than to receive a release, have questions, only to call and discover the company is out to lunch. It happens too often. Include your home phone number on releases. Disseminate releases early in the day. Don't send out good news at the wrong time (late in the day, especially Fridays) and don't try to hide bad news by releasing it at times that make it difficult for reporters to make deadlines. Significant news can't be ditched. The reporters will only react negatively to the subterfuge. Use good release dissemination methods. The wire services have become the standard method and are quite reliable, namely the PR Newswire, BusinessWire, and various regional services. Facsimile, electronic mail, and First Call reach targets effectively. Messenger services are virtually obsolete.

9. Don't be overly aggressive about the use of releases and press kits. Public relations people, especially agencies, are flooding the media with materials of little value. Companies can develop reputations for sending out junk with certain journalists. It is important to exercise discretion both in terms of subjects for releases and distribution lists; they should be targeted. Press kits represent a long odds game; seldom do they motivate a reporter to run a story or arrange an interview.

17

Debt Relations a Growing Part of the Job

What do the terms "investor relations" and "the World Series" have in common? They're both inclined to overdescribe their boundaries. But, just as major league baseball now includes teams from Canada as well as the United States, investor relations is expanding to include debtholders and analysts as well as equity investors and analysts.

Investor relations has grown up as an equity caretaker function, while the debt side of the equation has been the traditional province of the finance department, guided by the treasurer and the chief financial officer. Bondholders and debt analysts mainly talk with the treasurer or CFO. The relationships are a natural part of the treasury function, which includes rating agency presentations, aranging lines of credit, and securing short- and long-term debt.

While equity and debt relations seem to be separate in most companies, some merging of the activities has been taking place in recent years. It has been happening in part because of the growing tendency of companies to have people with financial backgrounds responsible for investor relations and place the function in the finance department. Increasingly, investor relations people are bringing stronger financial credentials to their range of assignments. In some companies, the function is combined with treasury or pension fund management.

The second reason is senior management's growing recognition of the communications value supplied by the investor relations function. The cost of capital and competition for it, now truly worldwide, raise the role of communications in persuading bankers, rating agencies, and investors to make commitments and offer the best deals. Investor relations people are participating more and more in rating agency presentations, providing solid feedback on investor attitudes and confidence levels toward the company, helping organize the material and put the words together.

The surge in debt financing in the late 1980s put even more emphasis on communications. Debt moved into favor, for a number of reasons. It was seen as a smart choice because of its lower cost in capital raising. Debt was preferred over equity by many companies in financing acquisitions and funding other capital expansion programs that required additional capital. It was used heavily in financing restructurings as companies sought escape from hostile acquisitions. It was used extensively, of course, in financing takeovers. It was the chief financing device in a recapitalization or leveraged management buyout. High-yield (junk) debt figured in many of these situations, especially the recaps, LBOs and hostile changes in control. In all these situations, the added benefit of debt was rationalized as an incentive boost for corporate officers to manage their businesses more aggressively and effectively in meeting the payback and interest burden.

Because so many investment opportunities were on the table, institutions investing in bonds became more aggressive in their research. And, lower-rated, higher-return, higher-risk (junk) bonds had burst upon the scene. The analytical community grew in size and importance, with cores of analysts specializing separately in investment and high yield grades of bonds.

As a result, communications between companies and their bondholders and debt analysts clearly has grown, with the investor relations function becoming more involved. Contact levels are higher in both public and private companies. More conservative by nature, bondholders seek reassurance that their investments are safe and expected yields intact, especially when warning flags are flying as they have been with heavy indebtedness pulling down a number of companies.

In many now private companies, the investor contact function has not disappeared; its emphasis has switched from equity to debt holders and from equity to debt analysts. Investor relations people continue to operate, handling the contacts and communications.

The communications task has intensified in companies troubled by what turns out to be overleveraging as their economic fortunes sour. The debt burden proves to be too much, leading to restructuring the debt or recapitalizing the company altogether. These situations call for bondholder approval, triggering a proxy solicitation campaign. In some companies, the bondholders have been the aggressor, forming committees and taking the initiative in proposing plans that are more favorable to them. Or, the committees insist on evaluating the company's offer. Both situations challenge corporate communication and investor relationships. Bondholder and analyst communication can be onging during these times.

POSITIONING EQUITY AND DEBT RELATIONS

As companies move forward, the question of how to position debt and equity relations is taking on more meaning. The objective should be to strive for parity in terms of information flow and cooperation, investor relations experts agree. Companies should try to build relationships on both sides, based on fair and equal treatment.

The rationale for this behavior is easy to make. It involves the value of keeping debt investors and analysts positive about the company's prospects and it involves the cost of capital. Real opportunities exist to affect the cost of capital. Confidence in the company influences bond ratings favorably and shaves basis points in new offerings. These can result in savings totalling millions of dollars. Just as important is trying to prevent bondholders from getting short-shrift in investment deals—earning a lower return than anticipated or even losing money if performance turns down or recapitalizations occur that favor equity holders.

Some companies are defining investor relations broadly, tying it into a capital structure approach to the markets. The capital structure includes equity, debt and retained earnings; investor relations is a communications function that covers both the debt and equity sides. The modern corporate capital structure is flexible, riding with hard-nosed calculations on the best deals that can be made domestically and globally in terms of availability of funds and cost. At any time, the emphasis between equity and debt is shifting.

In this environment, it makes sense to combine, or at least, coordinate the communications and relationship-building activities among these two investor groups. They're overlapping more and more. Debt and equity holders often are the same investors, especially among institutions. And debt holders may become equity holders in the future as companies restructure their debt, recapitalize or "go public" again, or conduct massive stock offerings. Companies take advantage of lower yields on their bonds to retire them, easing or eliminating the interest/principal cash flow burden. It becomes a smart economic decision in the capital structure management. While debt payback can be a management incentive, too much leveraging can drag the company into bankruptcy, destructive restructuring or set it up as a certain takeover victim. Healthy public companies can be expected to retire debt in the future, and perhaps issue new stock to raise capital. And, any number of companies privatized by leveraged management buyouts in the 1980s are virtually certain to be taking the same route. Some already have. Experts see the 1990s as a period of renewed stock offerings.

In the broadened capital structure context, the question becomes who handles the contact. Tradition, "turf," organizational structure, and qualifications all play a part. Traditionally, debt relations has been a finance department responsibility, handling the "banking relationships." It takes certain qualifications to be able to build the contacts, most notable having a proper financial background. The traditional investor relations person with a communications/public relations background has been seen as unprepared for the role. That picture is changing, however, as the investor relations function is structured within the finance department, run by people with finance credentials.

HOW PROACTIVE SHOULD DEBT RELATIONS BE?

The other merger that needs to be fashioned involves the degree of aggressiveness the company takes in relationships with debt analysts and institutional debt holders. Investor relations people working the equity side have gotten into the marketing mindset; treasury people dealing with banking, bond brokerage and investor contacts tend to be more responsive than proactive. Investor relations is more "service driven." Treasury people are used to being sold on deals by the bankers.

Certainly, fixed income analysts and institutional bond investors desire a strong corporate information base. The debt analyst splinter group has been vocal in its continuing efforts to encourage companies to be more forthcoming. Institutions have picked up the charge as bond issues increase and risks rise. The high-return potential of bonds is a stong investor incentive; the return/risk equation has magnified the importance of quality research and analysis.

Chief contact for debt analysts and investors has been the treasury function—treasurer, assistant treasurer with specific responsibility, or the chief financial officer. In most companies, they take the call, answer the questions, respond to the sales pitches, initiate the contacts when the company is getting ready to enter the market with a bond issue.

While analysts and investors would like to see companies be more open with information, they're also inclined to respect the knowledge of financial officers more than investor relations professionals. However, this too is changing as investor relations people demonstrate both their technical and strategic knowledge of the company. The change also is being encouraged by institutions investing heavily in the many debt offerings (both high grade and high yield) of companies during the late 1980s. Institutions started calling their investor relations contacts for debt issue information, or they secured the names of the corporate contact from equity analysts or portfolio managers inside their firms.

Analysts and institutions are mainly concerned about the quality of information, not so much the source. They're getting comfortable talking about the debt side with investor relations professionals they respect and trust.

How aggressive a company wants to be is another matter. And, here is where the investor relations marketing approach can clash with corporate priorities. The wisdom of being proactive goes with the strategy of using the debt markets regularly. Companies issuing debt fairly frequently are well advised to be building analyst and bond investor relationships. Companies with just one or two issues, unlikely to tap the market again, would just as soon see the prices decline so they can buy back the bonds at lower cost. Either way, companies benefit from being seen by debt analysts and investors as cooperative with information.

More companies, however, are taking it another step, putting together proactive debt relations programs. They involve meeting with the fixed income analysts group or sponsoring their own meetings just for debt analysts, inviting them to regular presentations. The evidence that companies are working harder to establish quality relationships is seen in the growing number of one-to-one meetings. And, they're preparing materials geared to the bond side.

Help is available in identifying those institutions investing substantially in bonds. CDA, Technimetrics, and CORTRAC all offer lists of institutional bondholders. Companies can obtain lists that identify their institutional bondholders, those of their industry or peer group, or they can order lists that show the various bonds held by individual institutions. Typically, the information includes the type of bond, coupon, years to maturity, duration, rating, sector, dates and sizes of transactions, phone numbers, as well as names and numbers of the firm's fixed income analysts and portfolio managers.

With this data, companies can target appropriate institutions, identifying their own holders, creating lists of investors in their industry or peer group, and holders of certain types of bonds.

What kind of information is important to bond analysts and investors? Cash is critical. Analysts are more concerned about the ability of the company to generate enough cash to cover the debt and still continue to expand the business. The information base is more quantitative. It involves thoroughly understanding the financial picture and covenants of the bond issue. Strategies to stay healthy and grow are important, but today's bottom line is crucial.

Evaluating the bond issue, analysts and institutions are studying terms of the indenture and the company's ability to meet them in the future; basis points of the issue compared with the Treasury curve; historical trends in ratios and spreads; use of the proceeds and cash to be generated from the asset purchased or improved by the capital raised from the bonds; depreciation schedule; overhead costs; breakout of reportable segments and other financial detail that explains the part of the business affected by the capital investment.

18

Material Disclosure: The Delicate Role of Investor Relations

Investor relations people literally are stepping through a quagmire when dealing with the shifting issue of non-public material information. What makes the terrain so squishy is the unsettled state of the issue, leaving the aftermath of events to decide whether a company, its employees, or market participants acted properly. Mucking around in the swamp, trying to find high ground are the regulators, Congress, and the courts, as well as companies, lawyers, analysts, traders, brokers, and investors.

The issue involves disclosure of material information—when and how. The problem starts with a definition of what is material; turns out it defies simple declaration. There is a starter definiton, framed by the Securities and Exchange Commission and refined by court interpretation and pronouncement. The SEC says information is material when it influences an investor to make a buy, sell, or hold decision. Disclosing and failing to disclose this vital information both come into the realm of materiality. The courts have said information is material if there is "substantial likelihood" that a "reasonable investor" would consider it important in "the total mix" of information.

While it may be difficult to know at times whether certain information is material, the rules on what to do when revealing the facts to one person or a small group of people are clear. Selective disclosure is verboten. Letting something material slip to one person means that the information must be released immediately to the investing public. That's done in a proscribed matter; a news release that is provided to key outlets, including Dow Jones, Reuters, Associated Press, United Press International, *The New York Times*, and daily papers in the home city of the company at minimum. Sometimes, an interview can satisfy the requirements if it produces a story running on an influential wire, such as the Dow Jones Broadtape, that reaches across the media and investment community.

Questions about materiality show up mostly in situations involving mergers, acquisitions, takeovers, and in contact with analysts, brokers, and investors who are looking for an information edge. Investor relations practitioners must be aware at all times of the possibility of being thrust into a material information discussion. In the daily dealings with professionals, especially analysts, the issue can be subtle; it sneaks up on the investor relations person in the middle of what appears to be a casual phone conversation. Suddenly, the complete answer to a question could cause the investor relations person to cross the line. In mergers and acquisitions (M&A) activity, the question can burst upon the investor relations person. Rumors in the marketplace bring a phone call from the exchange, *Wall Street Journal,* Reuters, a couple of analysts, or major institutional investors. There is pressure to respond quickly. Investor relations people must be thinking and deliberate every second. The desire to always give a reporter or analyst a good answer can trip us up. Most of the mistakes made in recent years have resulted from being caught off guard, perhaps being too quick to comment or not having a guiding policy that kicks in almost automatically. That's why preparedness is so important.

The materiality issue applies mainly to three situations. They are:

1. Timing in announcing a merger, acquisition, or involvement in a hostile contest for corporate control. With M&A activity, the time-honored "bright line" test of making the announcement when an agreement in principle was reached has been weakened, if not rendered obsolete, by a more recent U.S. Supreme Court ruling.

2. Responding to rumors that are affecting stock trading and price. The burning incidents focus on merger, acquisition or takeover rumors.

3. Working with investment professionals, especially sell-side analysts who are seeking to gain an advantage in forecasting corporate performance as a precursor to higher or lower valuation and stock price. Thorny is the question of what companies should do when they confront material changes, are asked to comment on analyst estimates of future earnings or find those forecasts to be overly optimistic or pessimistic.

Disclosure has been the trickiest element of the investor relations responsibility ever since institutional investment in stocks magnified and acquisition activity became a bigger part of corporate strategy (friendly and hostile) over 30 years ago. However, it intensified in the 1980s, influenced by the long bull run in stocks that encouraged the endless pursuit of higher returns virtually among all the players—institutions looking to find high flyers early among stocks and capture the premiums in M&A deals; brokerage analysts collecting substantial commissions from the success of their investing and acquisition recommendations; and the new breed of corporate raiders and their financing partners.

The drive for huge and excess returns and fees got out of hand, with a few investors succumbing to the temptations of using inside information to whittle an advantage. Some dealmakers were accused of being part of the problem, conspiring in selectively leaking information on companies about to be put in play or acquired. Scandals rocked the financial services industry, leading to tougher enforcement, severer penalties, convictions and imprisonment, and the inevitable Congressional study. Out of the mess came new vigor in policing the proper handling of non-public material information. Investor relations was front and center.

HOW WE GOT HERE

Required disclosure is imbedded in the Securities Acts of 1933 and 1934. Enforcement is within the jurisdiction of the Securities and Exchange Commission, which was established at the same time. The acts are very thorough in laying out structured disclosure requirements, with the 1933 act covering various registration documents dealing with the offering and sale of securities, and the 1934 act aimed at protecting investors against price "manipulation" in the markets after the securities are issued.

Less precise are the acts in seeking to control unstructured disclosure—releases, responses to rumors, and relationships with analysts and investors. These are covered under antifraud Rule 10b-5 of the 1934 act, now widely interpreted by circuit courts, state supreme courts, and the U.S. Supreme Court. What is shaping current corporate behavior in announcing mergers/acquisitions, handling rumors, and working with analysts is the body of court precedents and a number of line items in the acts that literally serve as exceptions to the absence of any general duty to disclose beyond the registration, proxy and tender offer filings and the 10-K, 10-Q, and 8-K reports. One of these line item exceptions is a prohibition against a company trading in its own shares while possessing non-public material information. The company either has to refrain from trading or release the news. Another is the mandate to update or correct prior disclosures that still constitute the last word, in ensuring that investors aren't misled. The courts have reinforced the duty to correct or update information in case after case. In interpreting the acts, the SEC also admonishes companies to be accurate and complete in their releases, statements and comments.

Court cases serving as milestones in the build-up of current practice date to 1968 when the *Texas Gulf Sulphur* decision put investor relations people on notice that disclosure was a major concern of the regulators of the financial markets. It was the SEC that sued the company for violation of Rule 10b-5, claiming it made false, misleading, and incomplete statements concerning drilling operations and that executives were in possession of material information while trading in the stock. The circuit court upheld the SEC position.

Court decisions since have dealt with the parallel but sometimes melding issues of non-public material information involving mergers, acquisitions or rumors, and analyst relations. The famous *TSC Industries v. Northway, Inc.* case in 1976 became the precedent-setter in creating a general standard of materiality. The U.S. Supreme Court held that information is material if it would motivate an investor to take action. The standard was reinforced 12 years later in the *Basic Inc. v. Levinson* case when the court ruled that materiality existed "if there is a substantial likelihood that a reasonable investor would consider it important in making an investment decision." On the flip side, "substantial likelihood" must exist and omitting the facts that a "reasonable investor" would consider significant in the "total mix" of information becomes a material situation. The two cases show the range in applying the materiality standard: the *Northway* situation involved proxy materials, while *Basic* spokespersons denied the existence of merger discussions that indeed were taking place. The courts have applied the *Northway* materiality definition in a host of rulings right through the *Basic* case.

M&A and Rumors

Key cases in reaching the current status of handling mergers/acquisitions and rumors involving them are the *Heublein, Carnation,* and *Basic* court decisions. The *Heublein* and *Carnation* cases established the "bright line test" for timing in announcing a merger or acquisition; the *Basic* ruling took it away. A *Heublein* spokesperson (*Greenfield v. Heublein* in 1984) said the company wasn't aware of developments that would account for market activity in the stock even though merger discussions were occurring. A *Carnation* spokesperson (1985) indicated there were no corporate developments in response to inquiry as stock price rose on rumors. The spokesperson didn't know merger negotiations were underway.

With *Heublein*, the circuit court ruled that companies don't have a duty to disclose until price and post-merger structure are determined, namely until an agreement in principle is reached. It became the bright line test. No legal action was brought against *Carnation*, showing that the bright line test was in force, but the SEC filed a special report, fundamentally disagreeing with both the *Heublein* and *Carnation* outcomes. The commission was concerned that corporate statements indicating nothing is going on could mislead investors.

The bright line test was washed away in the 1988 U.S. Supreme Court ruling in *Basic v. Levinson*. The decision squares with the SEC position. In *Basic*, the court stated that preliminary merger or acquisition negotiations could be material under certain circumstances. *Basic* spokespersons denied merger discussions three times over 13 months amidst rumors and stock activity. The suit followed the merger.

New precedent and reinforcement of previous precedent mark the decision. It reaffirms a duty to disclose information in certain situations under the antifraud provisions of the federal securities acts. The court confirmed the standard of materiality in its statement that there was a "substantial likelihood" that a "reasonable investor" would find the information important in the "total mix."

In deciding whether disclosure should be made before an agreement in principle is reached, the court applied the "probability/magnitude test." The court offers guidelines in determining the probability and magnitude of a prospective merger: whether senior management, the board and investment bankers are involved in the discussion indicates probability, while magnitude factors can include the size of the two companies and potential premiums over market value. The bigger the companies and the bigger the premiums, the greater is the magnitude, according to the court.

In a very real sense, the decision is unsettling, because it throws the questions of whether and when preliminary merger negotiations are material into a case-by-case situation, determined by the probability and magnitude equation each time.

Vanquished with the *Basic* decision is the rationale supported previously by the courts in allowing silence until an agreement in principle is signed. Three arguments were dismissed. First, quick-draw investors could be hurt if the deal fell through. To quote the court: The argument assumes investors are "nit wits, unable to appreciate—even when told—that mergers are risky propositions until the closing." Second, early or premature announcement could kill the deal or spoil the terms by taking away the wraps of secrecy. The court said it flies in the face of the definition of materiality.

However, the court suggested the validity of companies making "no comment" in preserving the secrecy of the negotiation process. "Silence, absent a duty to disclose, is not misleading," the court said. That duty would come into play judgmentally if rumors were triggering trading, and by court precedent if the company had previously said anything other than "no comment."

And, third, the court rejected the notion of the bright line test as a clearly defined and thus somewhat comfortable start point for materiality to click in. It's too easy, the court said, versus wrestling with the tougher, more complex and much fairer process that involves exercising judgment in considering the various circumstances.

Lawyers analyzing the fallout of the *Basic* decisions are especially interested in the *fraud-on-the-market theory*. Fraud can occur through failure to disclose what a reasonable investor would consider to be material, or in making misstatements, whether as an announcement or response. The fraud-on-the-market theory opens the door to class action legal suits. Cases can be built on the argument that the market as a whole was frauded. Attorneys note that the *Basic* decision was handed down at a time when there was great sensitivity to insider trading; the scandals were in full bloom.

The courts also have dealt with what they see as full and fair disclosure for companies venturing beyond the "no comment" response. *The Texas Gulf Sulphur* ruling sent a strong message to companies that their communications not be false, misleading, or incomplete. Accuracy when volunteering information is demanded as a result of the *Carnation* decision. The *First Virginia Bank Shares v. Benson* (1977) judgment demands completeness in voluntary disclosure. The duty to correct earlier misstatements or those turned stale by time was articulated in the *Ross v. A. H. Robbins Co.* ruling in 1979. A number of decisions spell out the duty to correct third party misstatements that can be traced to the company.

According to the courts, mum can be the word on rumors as long as they don't originate with the company. The ruling dates to the 1969 second circuit court decision involving *Electronic Specialty Co. v. International Controls Corp.*: "While a company may choose to correct a misstatement in the press not attributable to it, . . . we find nothing in the securities legislation requiring it to do so." The ruling was reinforced in the *Basic* decision. The standard corporate statement is "the company has a policy to not comment on market rumors."

However, rumors that spark unusual market activity that appears to be prompted by information leaks are especially troublesome to the SEC. The commission has commented a number of times on situations where leaks are the virtual certain cause of increased trading. It believes that "disclosure of material developments should occur where an issuer (company) is aware that persons with access to the information are trading on the information." The SEC cites delays by Sharon Steel Corp. in announcing its interest as a possible suitor of Reliance Electric Company after it became the subject of a tender offer. Sharon Steel shares experienced increased volume and share price before the corporation made its announcement after being "prodded" by its exchange to do so, the SEC notes.

The commission called Sharon Steel's disclosure belated. "Sharon Steel was aware that some investors knew about the Reliance shares; indeed, several brokers had called specifically to confirm

Sharon Steel's ownership of the shares. Sharon Steel also knew from the unusual market activity that investors were actually trading on the information. Under these circumstances . . . Sharon Steel should have quickly disclosed its ownership interest in Reliance."

But, the *Heublein* case did little to strengthen the SEC argument when the U.S. Supreme Court ruled there is no duty to disclose if the company sees no indication of leaks even though it is aware of material information and unusual stock trading. The key phrase: the company isn't aware of any leaks. The SEC did get some help in the *Basic* ruling of the U.S. Supreme Court. Companies need to be careful of their wording, if they choose to comment on trading activity, as pointed out in the *Basic v. Levinson* opinion. The SEC comments that statements indicating management knows of no reason for the stock activity, such as leaks of merger discussions or substantial holdings in a company, can be "misleading because the natural reading of such a statement would be that management knows of no developments (and not merely of no leaks of developments) that could account for the activity."

Dealing with Analysts, Brokers, and Investors

More subtle, pervasive, and critical to corporate success in the long run (and potentially dangerous from a legal liability standpoint) are the material disclosure situations that investor relations people may encounter every day as they talk with brokerage and institutional analysts, portfolio managers, and individual investors, brokers, traders, business associates, and even friends and relatives.

The interest and payoff for all the players is in being proactive: companies in marketing their investable characteristics; the sell side (analysts and brokers) in piecing together the puzzle in figuring out the best timing for stock actions; and investors in their continuing quest to buy low and sell high. In its role, the SEC has walked a tightrope in encouraging information flow that vents the individual talents and intelligence of professional investors, while policing the markets and arresting the abusers. The SEC has repeated its desire to maintain a healthy level of professional analysis and sophisticated investing.

It also has gone full circle in trying to make companies comfortable in projecting future earnings, both in required filings and voluntarily. At first, projections were opposed by the SEC; now they're allowed, backed by "safe harbor" provisions designed to keep companies free from liability as long as the projections are reasonably based and well presented. That doesn't mean companies can't be sued for making projections that never reach reality, but the safe habor provides a basis for a strong defense. Companies choosing to make projections are under the gun to keep the markets current on the information underpinning the forecasts. Regular updates are in order, whether the news is positive or negative. The courts also are strict with companies painting a rosy picture of the future in defending against a takeover. The courts warn target companies (*Starkman v. Marathon Oil*, 1985) to be certain that buoyant earnings projections or asset appraisals based on future economic or corporate events be "virtually as certain as hard facts."

The SEC has been aided by the courts in policing the markets as well. Companies were warned to exercise great care in dealing with analysts who are putting together their information "mosaics" by combining data from various sources. Information becomes material on the basis of each analyst's skill and experience in assembling pieces of data in making investment recommendations and decisions. Circuit court judge Irving Kaufman in his opinion in the 1977 *SEC v. Bausch & Lomb* ruling, described the trouble companies can get into when talking with an analyst. He likened a conversation with an analyst to a "fencing match conducted on a tightrope." The corporate spokesperson is "compelled to parry often incisive questions while teetering on a fine line between data properly conveyed and material inside information that may not be revealed without simultaneously disclosing it to the public. Exhorted by the Securities and Exchange Commission and the various stock exchanges to divulge tidbits of non-public, non-material information, which may assume heightened significance when woven by the skilled analyst into the matrix of knowledge obtained elsewhere, the corporate representative will incur severe consequences if he discusses areas which are later deemed material."

Companies can be charged as "tippers" for selective material disclosure to analysts, brokers or investors, incurring SEC sanctions and civil liability in investor lawsuits.

But neither are the analysts, brokers, traders, investors and press free from harm. Direct help in curbing insider trading violations came in 1988 when the U.S. Supreme Court upheld a lower court conviction of former reporter R. Foster Winans on mail and wire fraud and by not overturning the prior securities fraud conviction. The ruling gave the SEC ammunition in pursuing insider trading violations on the basis of "misappropriation" of inside information.

The "personal benefits test" came out of the celebrated (Raymond) *Dirks v. SEC* case (1983). Companies, employees, analysts, brokers, traders, investors and others dealing with inside information are liable for the consequences if they have breached a duty to shareholders and the markets, in effect, failing the personal benefits test. In the *Dirks* case, the U.S. Supreme Court ruled that analysts aren't liable for using inside information if they don't realize it was given out with the intent of benefitting the provider. The ruling means that analysts aren't obligated to keep the information under wraps or not use it in trading as long as it wasn't wrongfully obtained.

At the same time, the Association for Investment Management and Research, in its handbook on practice and behavior, is firm in saying that analysts can't use non-public material information, and further, they should let companies know when it is given out, suggesting that public disclosure be made. The SEC has always encouraged brokerage firms to have policies and procedures that protect the integrity of the legitimate process of gathering and analyzing information by market professionals.

OUTSIDERS ALSO MUST BE CAREFUL

Outsiders become insiders as they join the information circle, consult with client companies, and produce or reproduce information. This means the list of outsiders with insider responsibility and liability includes investor and public relations consultants, printers, lawyers, accountants, investment and commercial bankers.

Investor relations consultants are most likely to be moving into the potential risk arena in the materials they create for companies and in analyst/investor contact. The SEC has investigated several situations in the past, censuring firms and ordering them to discontinue certain activities involving the dissemination of information. While firms are recognized to not be "guarantors" of information, they shouldn't see themselves simply as "publicists or communicators," the SEC says, "with no attendant responsibility whatsoever for the contents of such information." Firms disseminating information on companies that "they know or should have reason to know is materially false or misleading, in connection with the purchase and sale of the securities, may render themselves liable for violation of the federal securities laws."

The SEC has cited written materials resembling brokerage reports or fact sheets; investors can mistake these for the real thing. Agencies and companies should identify these pieces as company-sponsored and include "disclaimers" of their role in providing investment advice.

EXCHANGES PUSH FOR DISCLOSURE

While federal securities laws don't impose a general duty to disclose or a specific obligation to respond in kind to rumors, the New York, American, and some of the regional exchanges as well as the National Association of Securities Dealers (NASD) are more aggressive in their admonitions to companies to communicate.

The New York Stock Exchange says its listed companies are "expected to release quickly to the public any news or information which might reasonably be expected to materially alter the market for its securities." The manual also calls for companies "to act promptly to dispel unfounded rumors which result in unusual market activity or price variations." The exchange tries to help companies decide when disclosure is absolutely necessary. It can be delayed for good business reasons, but not beyond the time its confidentiality can no longer be maintained.

The American Stock Exchange follows similar thinking. Its manual tells companies they have a duty to disclose "information necessary to make an informed investment decision even when, as is frequently the case, the disclosure entailed must be more prompt and comprehensive than is required by the securities laws." Getting around the mandate calls for "exceptional circumstances."

AMEX helps companies recognize material occurrences by listing a host of them—merger, acquisition, joint venture, earnings, dividends, stock split, stock dividend, gaining or losing a major piece of business.

NASD orders companies to disclose material information "promptly" and it doesn't provide an opportunity to delay release to preserve any business dealings. A number of regional exchanges, including Boston and the Midwest, also have general duties to disclose material information.

While the exchanges and NASD clearly state their tougher requirements, there is virtually no record of companies being disciplined for non-compliance. The rules are there, minus government or private rights of action force.

ESTABLISHING A COMMUNICATIONS ATTITUDE, POLICY, AND PRACTICE

Most companies grapple with the questions of whether to be proactive or reactive, open or safe when considering the delicateness of disclosure. Companies with an aggressive communications bent tend to go cautiously, leaning on the legal guidelines. Normally close-mouthed companies clam up altogether.

In taking a realistic approach toward disclosure, companies are adopting the attitude that being smart is the best policy. A smart policy tries to achieve the difficult balance of being open and forthcoming while knowing when to say nothing. It also incorporates knowing just what to say when "talking." Companies that get into trouble most often do it by saying the wrong thing, rather than waiting too long to communicate or saying nothing.

Picking the spots in deciding when and when not to communicate isn't necessarily being inconsistent. Its purpose is more in line with being strategic in the best interests of the business. That may call for a thorough description of the benefits of an acquisition in expanding the core business to enhance value. It surely calls for close relations with analysts based on comprehensive information that heightens their ability to estimate earnings accurately. The policy also includes not commenting on mergers or acquisitions until the deal is a virtual lock, or on market rumors or analyst earnings estimates. The company makes sure that analysts and investors are well aware of the policy. They're also well informed, prepared and comfortable in making their own judgments and investment decisions.

The policy has clear exceptions—should false rumors be causing active trading or an analyst estimate that is so out of line it violates the practice of good disclosure. These become managable situations within the context of consistent communications.

Companies taking this attitude and following this approach believe that a strong and effective investor relations program helps avoid disclosure problems. The key is maintaining a highly informed marketplace. M&A activity doesn't jolt the market; the events are taken in stride in the context of the company's well-known strategies for growth. Analyst estimates are within a reasonable range. Relationships between analysts and the investor relations people are highly professional, based on information that falls within certain parameters understood by all the analysts. These parameters define the boundaries beyond which lies material information. An analyst stepping out of the estimate range does so knowlingly. Institutions recognize it; so does the company.

The analyst has gone on his or her own; the company has no responsibility.

Granted, that's an ideal situation, but many companies have achieved it and have been able to maintain it, largely through the communications process. These companies have done acquisitions without driving the marketplace into a frenzy. They haven't had an analyst go over the edge. And, they have no reason to change the status quo.

The test, of course, comes when revenues slow or earnings soften, and the company faces the prospect of a downturn. Earnings or other negative surprises are anathema to analysts and investors, and thus, to investor relations practitioners as well. They are to be avoided. How? By keeping analysts and investors informed so they can track the trends accurately. That process involves providing the basic information and helping analysts stay tuned into the conditions that affect performance. Armed with information, the analysts should be able to see when the slope is curving down as well as up. There's plenty of precedent for analysts predicting declines or earnings that are lower than even the company expects. A running dialogue based on an information level that is sufficient and available consistently will avoid the risk, need or inadvertent disclosure of something material. Let the analysts maintain their mosaics. The only time the analysts should be surprised is when the company is genuinely surprised.

Companies need to be sure that fear of making a mistake doesn't detract from conducting a proactive, marketing-driven investor relations program. Fear and ultra conservatism can slam the door on productive analyst, investor and broker relations. It can reduce the quality of Street feedback that helps companies evaluate rumors and performance projections in deciding how best to handle them.

Clearly stated and understood policy and procedures make a disclosure program work. Policy and procedure are interwoven; the latter fulfills the former. Basic tenets of the policy should be written out, but not be so verbose as to keep lawyers awake at night worrying about helping litigants fatten their case.

In being thorough in covering the policy matters and procedural points, the following serves as a checklist for consideration:

1. Operate a team approach to disclosure. The team should cover the range of expertise needed to write the best policy and procedures and reach the best conclusion when a disclosure question arises. It probably includes legal, financial, investor relations, and corporate communications people in addition to the final arbiter, the CEO or CFO.

2. Establish and follow an internal review process that makes sure material disclosure is made properly or avoided, depending on the situation. The review should cover releases, speeches, financial presentations, statements, announcements, copy for reports, brochures, videos, and any other materials.

3. Maintain confidentiality by adhering to the toughest standards. Minimize the number of persons with a "need to know" and drill them on the importance of secrecy. It's easy for carelessness to creep in: several secretaries typing drafts of an earnings release, too many people on the approval list, several people in the mail room seeing the release before it is distributed. Keep filing cabinents containing material information locked and limit computer access to the need-to-know group. The objective is to do everything possible to prevent leaks.

4. Control the availability and use of material information by centralizing it. This can involve several aspects. Some companies have a central repository. Data General, for example, produces an internal report quarterly that contains the information employees can make public. The control process also can designate the people who prepare the information. This serves to limit the number of people in the need-to-know position. And, it certainly includes designating spokespersons. The company may have one or several, depending on its size and organizational structure. The investor rela-

tions professionals, the CFO and CEO for example, may be authorized to talk with the investment community, while the corporate communications group handles media contacts. All requests for information funnel into these departments.

5. Be sure everyone in the company understands and practices the policies and procedures. Manuals and meetings help guarantee compliance. Periodic reminders are a good idea. New employees should be given the word.

6. Some statements should be included in the policy that leave no doubt about how to behave. They might include such things "as it is the policy of the company to release material information in a timely manner, to not reveal material information beyond that covered in releases and other official communications, to maintain the strictest confidentiality, and follow procedures that ensure it."

7. Make sure analysts, portfolio managers, brokers, and the media are aware of the company's policies and procedures. It will help smooth the communications process.

8. Review releases and other public statements periodically to make sure they still constitute the company's position on the subject. Companies don't want to miss a requirement to update or correct previous communications that may no longer be the official word.

9. Check coverage of releases and announcements as well as what appears in the various computer databases. This has three values: inaccuracies can be corrected; the company can analyze how it is being treated by the media; and it can develop a better understanding of the body of information out there that is fostering knowledge and opinion.

10. Brief executives about to meet with analysts, brokers, investors or the press. Cover the whole concept of materiality carefully. Discuss any matters that can't be mentioned or described.

HOW COMPANIES ARE HANDLING VARIOUS DISCLOSURE SITUATIONS

Ideally, companies are able to control leaks so they can announce mergers or acquisitions when the deals are firm. At the same time, their relationships with analysts move along smoothly, with mosaics built from combining lots of pieces of non-material information into material forecasts of performance that fall within the bounds of realism.

It's when a company's stock begins to trade outside of its usual patterns, probably causing more than normal price movement, that the exchanges, SEC, investors, analysts and brokers become keenly interested. Is the increased action based on insider material information? Are rumors flying? It's easy to pick up on the rumors. The company gets one or several phone calls—probably from the exchange, a reporter, leading industry analyst, major institutional investor. The exchange is looking for an answer. It may want a press release. It might halt trading if the pace is brisk enough.

First thing to do is track the source of the activity. It could be a new research report or recommendation from an influential analyst—buy or sell. One or several big holders may have decided it is time to take or leave substantial positions in the stock. Or, indeed, there may be rumors about a possible merger, acquisition or takeover, with the company being the acquirer or acquiree. The trading can be buy or sell.

If stock recommendations or investor actions are pushing up the activity level, it makes sense to say so. Rumors are a far more complex situation. The company should investigate their origin. It can invoke its general "no comment" policy or variation, namely its policy of not commenting on market rumors. The courts have said it's always okay to have no comment. However, they also have said comment is in order when rumors can be traced to the company. It's a virtual bet that leaks about a merger or acquisition that are accurate have begun with someone associated with the deal, either inside or part of the consulting team.

If the rumors are true and can be traced to the company, it is advised to issue a release, which can characterize discussions accurately, for example, being in their preliminary stage without a deal being struck. There are numerous examples of companies taking this action. If the rumors are true but haven't been leaked by internal or advisory sources, the company can choose not to comment or it may decide to say that preliminary discussions are underway and either identify or not name the other company. Many investor relations people favor this option in the interests of fair and open communication, especially when heavy trading is taking place. They argue that stonewalling the press, analysts or investors is not good for relationships. False rumors should be wiped away. The company can issue a release saying that there is no M&A activity currently taking place.

Companies also have the choice of making other comments. They can say they know of no reason for the market activity, they can say there are no corporate developments to account for the activity, they can deny the existence of any activity, or they can describe precisely what is taking place. When volunteering information, the courts and antifraud provisions of the securities laws mandate that companies be accurate, complete, not mislead investors and update/correct any prior statements that no longer are accurate or complete. Companies must be sure they're right when they say there are no developments or they're not aware of any negotiations or developments that might be affecting stock activity and price.

Here is a checklist of times when companies may be obligated to make affirmative disclosures, provided by attorney Harvey L. Pitt, partner with Fried, Frank, Harris, Schriver & Jacobson at a conference of the National Investor Relations Institute in 1988 after the U.S. Supreme Court ruled on the *Basic Inc. v. Levinson* case.

1. There is an SEC line item requirement, proscribed under the federal securities laws. These mainly involve registration and proxy statements, 10-K, 10-Q and 8-K reports, tender offer filings, and the management discussion and analysis in the annual report.

2. There are rumors or leaks. Depending on the source and severity, the company may have an obligation to respond.

3. There are prior statements that need to updated.

4. The company decides to buy or sell stock.

5. The company chooses to speak because it wants to clarify the issue or make a definitive statement that it believes is beneficial. The statement must be complete and accurate.

6. Exchange regulations encourage and mandate disclosure. The specific situation will determine whether disclosure is truly required and when it must be done.

7. There is a need to respond to an exchange inquiry into unusual stock trading. The company can say it is planning to put out a press release or not to comment. And, whatever it says must be the truth.

Lastly is the question of how companies deal with analysts who are working through their mosaics, estimating earnings and making other comments in reports or recommendations that are material. Lawyers advise companies and their investor relations people not to read, edit, approve, or comment on analyst reports, before they are issued (or afterward for that matter), and not to confirm or comment on analyst estimates of earnings or other material numbers or statements.

Is there ever a time to help an analyst whose projections are way off the mark? Companies need to analyze the situation carefully, in determining why the analyst is not in synch. It may be by his or her choice, with full knowledge and understanding of the fundamentals, industry and economic trends, company position and prospects. Or, something may be missing in the mosaic. Investor relations people can handle the situation by discussing the factors and conditions that lead to the conclusion without commenting on the estimate itself. At that point, it's up to the analyst to stay or change his or her forecast.

Of course, investor relations people are warned against selective disclosure of material information. Should it occur—

intentionally or otherwise—lawyers strongly advise the company to issue a release immediately. When involving a possible merger, the stakes can be high, causing the mistake to ruin the deal.

How does the company make sure the investor relations spokespersons are able to distinguish between material and non-material information at all times, even in the middle of a phone conversation? The fundamental answer is making sure the investor relations people are tied into the information stream at the highest level. Trust is part of that proposition. And so is confidence in the abilities of investor relations professionals to handle investment community contacts effectively on all counts, including material disclosure. Strengthening the process is continuous discussion among senior executives and investor relations spokespersons to clarify where the material information lines are being drawn at any time.

DISCLOSURE WHILE IN REGISTRATION

Disclosure can be a factor while companies are in the registration period for securities—whether "going public," namely making an *initial public offering* (IPO), or issuing additional stock (a secondary offering). The time has come to be called "the silence period," because companies have to be careful not to tout themselves while their securities are being prepared for sale or being sold. The line between regular communications and being too promotional is a thin one; lawyers urge caution.

Essentially, communications should be consistent with the company's regular pattern. That means normal advertising, distribution of brochures and other sales promotion materials, releases on business developments and financial results, shareholder reports, meetings that previously were scheduled. To be avoided are such aggressive communications as bullish projections of the sales success of new products, forecasts of sales and earnings, opinions on valuation and the future performance of value drivers. Lawyers suggest using what can be published in the registration statements as a rule of thumb in what can be covered in releases, meetings and conversations with the investment community and others.

The registration period is considered to start when the company gets serious about the offering, measured as the time the discussions with underwriters are meaningful and the offering is a virtual certainty. The waiting period begins with the filing of the registration statement and doesn't end until the effective date, which is the time the SEC says the shares can be sold. That typically occurs with the filing of the final registration documents. The post-effective period runs 90 days for initial public offerings and 40 days for companies making previous offerings.

"Due diligence" meetings and road show presentations make up the bulk of the selling effort. These occur following the effective date of the registration. The due diligence process enables the principal underwriters, including the syndicate, to satisfy themselves on the quality of the offering. The process has grown to include the road show, where management describes the company, its strengths and strategies to prospective investors. In these various presentations, companies need to be careful about what they say; the content of the prospectus is seen as a general guideline.

Investor Relations: A Career or Preparation for Moving On-High

Over the last 25 years, investor relations has grown from a step-child to a mature, productive, contributing adult. While in some companies, investor relations is still trying to find its place organizationally, its rightful role is being better understood and utilized. And, as in any family of bright, open, inquisitive people, the now grown-up child is helping educate its parents on some important modern ways.

Investor relations belongs within the circle of key corporate disciplines. What it brings is just as valuable as the other functions up there; so is its worth in protecting against the risks to survival and growth. As the capital markets have become more institutionalized and globalized, the processes of raising capital at low cost and maintaining good relationships with investors and lenders have become more complex, opportunistic, and dangerous.

The professionalization of equity investing—stocks are still the basic "product" of investor relations people—has brought with it increased demands for quality information, opportunities to lower the cost of capital through strategic marketing of shares, the high-stakes plays of investors whose actions can create volume and price volatility, investor participation in corporate decision making, threat or loss of control of the assets that make up the enterprise. Qualified and well-respected investor relations people are in the middle of these and many other opportunities and challenges that relate to capital formation and corporate survival and growth, gathering and analyzing market intelligence, recommending strategic actions, and communicating information designed to help accomplish broad and specific financial and operating objectives.

As the equity market and its investors have become more sophisticated, so has the investor relations function and its practitioners. The need to have command of finance, economics and the capital markets system as well as the traditional communications and management skills has broadened the prerequisites of the investor relations professional. People with finance, management, planning, legal and investment backgrounds now constitute more than half of the corporate practitioners, as judged by a 1989 membership survey of the National Investor Relations Institute (NIRI). While the NIRI membership doesn't include the entire profession, it does constitute a broad cross section and valid sampling.

Well under half of the survey respondents have a communications or public relations background, while nearly four in 10 of the corporate practitioners are trained and experienced in finance-based functions, and about 10 percent of those on the corporate side are former analysts, brokers or traders. Interestingly, just 43 percent of the respondents running or working for consulting firms did their basic training in public relations or communications.

As investor relations continues to gain stature as a bonafide senior executive discipline, the emerging challenge of the profession and its professionals is to master and meld the multi-dimensional attributes that make up the total responsibility. More and more professionals are becoming proficient across the spectrum of skills, embracing finance, communications, management, and a working knowledge of the global capital markets. They include representatives of the various training grounds; there isn't a proscribed path to the top, even though finance and business MBA backgrounds seem to offer an edge in the current environment of financially driven managements and complex capital markets.

The NIRI survey sends a clear signal toward favoring a financial background. A third of the corporate respondents indicated they report to the chief financial officer, another 11 percent to the treasurer, and just nine percent to the communications officer. It's also a good bet that most of the investor relations heads reporting through a finance function have finance backgrounds. These companies are inclined to have the investor relations officer utilize the public relations/corporate communications department as a professional resource in preparing reports, releases, and other materials.

Many companies separate the functions altogether, with the public relations department being responsible for the annual and quarterly reports, earnings releases, writing speeches, and the like. These arrangements may or may not maximize effectiveness. The situation sets up the not-always-guaranteed need for close, professional cooperation and coordination.

Mixed signals float up from the NIRI survey in trying to determine whether senior management is ready to welcome investor relations onto the executive floor. Two measures are cited. The first is reporting relationships: 13 percent of the corporate respondents report to the chairman, nine percent to the president, and five percent to the chief executive officer. So, while 44 percent report through finance, 27 percent report to the chairman, president or CEO. The second is job titles; to the extent they reflect responsibility, there's work to be done. Just 18 percent of the survey respondents are vice presidents, either of investor relations or corporate communications with investor relations duties. Some 45 percent have the title of director or manager of investor relations (32 percent) or public relations/corporate communications (13 percent). Six percent are either the CFO or treasurer, no doubt of smaller companies where investor relations is part of the job. A sizable 27 percent covers a wide variety of other titles, with numerous reporting relationships, indicating that too many managements still don't understand how to evaluate and structure investor relations or aren't committed to it. Investor relations people shouldn't be reporting to the advertising or personnel departments, for example. That becomes something investor relations people have to hide from brokerage analysts and institutional investors because it's a dead giveaway.

INVESTOR RELATIONS AS A ROTATIONAL POSITION

Some companies are using the investor relations position as a valuable stop on the way to the top for executive prospects. In fact, the number of companies doing this seems to be growing, motivated mainly by the desire to give real comers some tough firing line experience. Most of the people filling these assignments have MBAs in finance or business, financial or operating backgrounds. Very few people moving through investor relations in a rotational mode have a public relations or communications upbringing.

The concept has to be encouraging and discouraging to the investor relations profession. Whether practitioners are encouraged or discouraged depends on where they're coming from and aspiring to go. It tells career-driven practitioners that these companies see the investor relations job as upper middle management at best and as more of a learning opportunity than a critical, lifetime, highly valued activity.

However, it is easy to speculate that most career-minded investor relations executives have communications and public relations backgrounds, and they're not likely to be involved in the rotational process. Their challenge is to be continually educating corporate executives on the higher role and value of investor relations, at their companies and in general. Their most practical career opportunities involve elevating investor relations or moving into officer positions in corporate communications, public affairs or corporate relations.

The rotational format gives executives with bigger ambitions excellent experience. It's also easy to speculate that today's investor relations practitioners with accounting or finance degrees, MBAs, previous jobs in operations, experience as analysts or brokers are very willing to advance beyond investor relations into such senior positions as chief investment officer, treasurer or chief financial officer. Beyond that lies the executive suite.

Investor relations stands to gain from the rotational concept down the road, as well. Executive understanding and appreciation of the function's role and value should grow as the number of senior officers who are former investor relations directors increases.

There is some risk for companies in the rotational concept, even though they are selecting smart, motivated, executive-caliber people for the job. Learning mistakes can hurt the company. The company's reputation with analysts and investors can be tarnished and take a long time to restore. Many analysts and institutional investors are skeptical about companies continually changing the investor relations face. It can take years for investor relations people to be effective, and just as they're reaching that point, they're gone. There's no assurance the replacement will be as good. But there are compensating factors. Analysts and portfolio managers like the idea of being given people with operational and financial experience to work with; they're seen as being fundamentally more qualified to serve as information resources than people with journalism or communications backgrounds.

However, the bottom line never changes: the analysts, investors, and brokers judge each investor relations practitioner on his or her worth in day-to-day interface.

Executive recruiters advise investor relations professionals to be open and enthusiastic about the prospects of promotion. They see investor relations as an excellent learning and personal growth experience that helps prepare people for higher positions.

ELEVATING INVESTOR RELATIONS

It takes two essential elements for investor relations to rise to the top: the support of the company and skills of the practitioner. They blend differently at each company. Some senior executives are aggressive in wanting to maximize share value and price; they seek effective investor relations resources. Some managements are open, recognizing the need and value of investor relations, creating an environment that gives investor relations people the opportunity to function effectively. Some managements believe that anything beyond required disclosure is touting the stock and are uncomfortable with efforts that are the least bit proactive. Their numbers are declining in the face of global competition for capital and institutionalization of the markets. Some executives are skeptical about the trade-off between giving away too much information and its value in raising share price.

Investor relations practitioners can make a big difference in how successful the function becomes in any corporation. The opportunity is there with any executive corps that is at all open, receptive, and striving to stay current and manage the various dynamics that are driving the company. The global capital markets certainly constitute one of those drivers. Investor relations people's ability to show their managements the proper role and value of the function is just as vital as their ability to build meaningful relationships with the investment community.

What's needed are personal attributes and skills that enable investor relations people to be persuasive with management, combined with the ability to practice investor relations at its most sophisticated and productive levels. The best way for investor relations people to help management fully appreciate the function is by quantifying the process and demonstrating its value day after day. Performance should be the base measure, with that performance quantified in ways that executives accept as important. To elevate the function and for their own good, investor relations people must be able to articulate those performance measurements and results.

Companies advancing the state of the investor relations practice are blessed with enlightened managements and talented investor relations resource teams. Investor relations people who are making progress in educating management and increasing the role of the function should be encouraged and motivated to continue. Investor relations people confronting little success in helping management see the value of the activity should be examining the reasons as accurately as they can. It still may be possible to open the door. You may have to broaden yourself, try new ideas, get the advice of well-respected, proven, outside resources. After a reasonable time, if you're convinced that you have done the best you can, expanding your own skills and utilizing the best resources that you were allowed to muster, it's appropriate to move to another company. The effort didn't succeed, perhaps because the timing wasn't right, or there wasn't sufficient rapport to make the marriage work. Someone else may be able to show management the way, or the company may never learn.

In building management support, the smartest thing the investor relations officer can do is create a clear understanding from the start of the role of the function and how it will be measured. It puts the investor relations head on the block to be accountable. It sets up the basis for quantifying investor relations. That's exactly what you want if the function is going to grow in value and stature. Management and investor relations should be in complete agreement on the principal goals, objectives and methods of measuring progress and results. These objectives should tie to the capital formation process and the strategic priorities of the company. For example, Bausch & Lomb has these five objectives: maximize equity valuation, minimize the cost of capital, promote trading liquidity, develop and consult on methods of creating value, and contribute to attaining the overall business and strategic goals of the company.

Progress and results should be reviewed regularly with senior management—annually, semiannually, or quarterly. Include presentations to the board to increase the directors' knowledge and appreciation of investor relations.

Three potentially highly useful roles provide the pathway for investor relations people to quantify their value, based on performance:

1. As an information resource, to both the company and investment community;

2. In building and maintaining vital "Wall Street" relationships; and

3. In serving as a strategic advisor to management.

Out of these flow all the investor relations activities that are important today and are likely to be even more so in the future as the global business competition tightens and investment circles shrink. All three can affect share price. Thus, investor relations people can play a key role in share price determination.

The three frequently work in unison. Information drives investment decision making and is the basis of strong analyst, investor and broker relationships. Those relationships give investor relations professionals the kind of valuable information that enables them to advise management on such planned moves as acquisitions, divestitures, partial public offerings of a subsidiary, dividend policy changes, and write-offs. Anticipating market reaction to major moves is critical in deciding whether and how to make them. Investor relations people are the quintessential link between their companies and the investment community. Previous chapters have explored all of these activities in detail.

Understanding and communicating equity valuation is today's lesson behind information flow and relationships with investment professionals. Valuation will continue to be the basis of sophisticated investor communication for some time to come. It is being shown as the company's best subject for getting on the institutional wavelength. Thus, it can quantify the role and value of the investor relations function.

Maintaining good "Wall Street" rapport takes on added importance daily as institutional influence on companies grows and pressure on brokerage analysts to increase income for their firms mounts. These relationships are tough to establish and nurture, because of the personalities of the players and seriousness of the investing process. Institutional equity stakes in companies often are huge and the impact of a buy/sell decision can be substantial. Institutions still will decide the outcome of most proxy votes, whether the issue involves governance or control of the corporate assets.

Investment community impact weighs heavily on corporations. It affects their cost of capital, ability to live out long-term strategies and programs, and amount of independence executives have to manage the company. Investor relations people are the keepers of investment community relationships.

There are other ways investor relations can contribute to corporate success.

1. It brings an outside perspective. Companies can become too ingrown and myopic in their attitudes and views, cutting themselves off from the benefits of outside thinking and knowledge. Feedback of investors and analysts, even when critical, can be constructive. And, few audiences are more direct and demanding than investors.

2. It sorts through the masses of information available in this computer age to help senior officers focus on what's important. Serving the information needs of the CEO, president and other top officers should be a priority of the investor relations director.

3. It helps bolster the confidence of senior executives so they can perform more effectively. They are the beneficiary when investor relations people are taking care of the contacts with institutional investors and analysts. An important weight is lifted from management's shoulders. There's a sense of comfort and confidence-building in knowing that responsibility is in good hands and under control. Positive "Wall Street" feedback also makes management more aggressive.

4. It enhances the company's image to improve business. Reputation can help win a new contract, make the difference in being the first choice of a coveted business partner, or create the right climate for arguing victoriously on an regulatory or legal issue.

5. It can work at attracting shareholders who are more interested in profiting from the long-term growth of the company than turning a return in the current quarter. In the final analysis, this may be the real contribution of investor relations, if it can succeed in identifying patient investors and presenting them with the investing merits of the company.

MAKING INVESTOR RELATIONS A CAREER OR STEPPING STONE

No job offers more opportunity to learn and know more than investor relations. Even the CEO isn't required to know as much about as many aspects of the company, industry, product markets, capital markets, domestic economy, and the factors that drive it, and ditto numerous other economies around the world as well as the global economy as a whole.

It's quite a challenge, and opportunity. The investor relations person with the intellectual capacity and curiosity, training, energy, personality, experience, and range of skills to master the challenge can certainly take advantage of the opportunity. You can use this extensive package of credentials to be among the most effective and valuable investor relations people in the profession, proving that to your company or clients, or moving on to greener pastures if the present opportunities don't match your abilities to contribute. Or, you can use them in moving into other, often higher positions, hopefully, all at officer levels—the corporate communications, public affairs, pension management, treasurer, chief financial officer, and the chief administrative officer.

The chief executive officer? Absolutely. The broad range of skills and wide knowledge only raise your qualifications. Former investor relations directors have made it to the executive suite, and the number is sure to increase as companies rotate their stars through the investor relations office.

Outstanding investor relations people are accomplished writers and editors; make excellent verbal presentations; have persuasive personalities; are equally adept at understanding the theory and practice of communications, the principles and inner workings of finance and accounting, and the macro and micro economic factors that are driving the domestic and global economies; and are effective in building relationships with a cross section of constituents, including executive associates, rank-and-file employees, technical specialists, security analysts, institutional and individual shareholders, brokers, reporters and editors, lawyers, investment bankers, printers, and computer researchers.

What distinguishes the outstanding investor relations practitioner from the pack? Here are some of the qualities and characteristics.

1. Proven credibility with both the investment community and the company's executives.

2. Ability to deal with the pressures. They come from all directions—inside and outside the company. They're subtle and dramatic. The investor relations officer may have 10 seconds and one line of opportunity to state the company's case with the media or effectively answer an analyst's question without crossing the line of materiality. How they deal with the daily inquiries adds up to a pattern of success or failure. And, all the while, many eyes are watching. The investor relations job is highly visible inside the company, often conducted in a fish bowl.

3. Functioning as an information resource. Investor relations people can establish themselves as the repository of information and counsel throughout the corporation.

4. Operating from a senior management perspective. Investor relations people explode their chances for success when they embrace the mindset of the CEO and other top officers.

5. Thinking independently. While in synch with management goals, investor relations people still must maintain their independent intellectual status. That's how they bring new ideas, fresh solutions, and outside resources to a situation.

6. The personality and intellectual capacity to maintain a broad range of productive relationships. It's critical in the investor relations job. The practitioner must be comfortable in developing close contacts with what amounts to the most diverse range of constituents any executive in the company will encounter—from "Wall Street" to government, employees to social activists.

7. The intelligence, energy, motivation and curiosity to master several diverse disciplines—communications, marketing, finance, the capital markets, management, economics, and many more.

8. Being opportunistic. Investor relations people need to be ready to jump at any chance to demonstrate their value. The company will be the chief beneficiary when the situation enables investor relations practitioners to bring forth a special insight or capitalize on certain skills.

9. Ability to maximize financial and human resources. Investor relations people benefit from surrounding themselves with the best talent, whether gathered internally, from outside, or in combination. Efficient use of the budget is always laudatory. Companies entered the 1990s especially interested in getting maximum mileage from mininum dollars. Virtuous is the talent to stretch resources without sacrificing quality.

10. Possessing a host of personal attributes—good listener, self-assured, well-read, intellectually curious, common sense, verbally expressive, keenly interested in the career potential of the position.

11. Ongoing enthusiasm for self-improvement. It can take many forms—advanced degree; university classes in courses that expand knowledge; broadening your capability to operate effectively in related functions; leadership in industry, professional or community activities; professional networking and contact building.

Above all, investor relations people shouldn't allow themselves to be held back; it's too much of a waste of a valued resource.

Index

A

ABI/Inform, 333
Accumulation phase, of life cycle, 226
Active investors, 5, 224
  specialized styles, 63-64
    sector rotators, 64
    value buyers, 63
  styles, 61-66
    core manager, 62
    quantitative style, 62
  valuation methods, 64-66
  See also Passive investors
Activism, 37-38, 117
  corporations' view of, 129-35
  current climate/trends, 126-27
  growth in, 124-29
  and public pension plans, 119
  takeovers as trigger for, 118-21
ADP, *See* Automated Data Processing
ADRs, *See* American Depository Receipts
Adventurers, investment style, 225
Affinity groups, 27, 227-33
AIMR, *See* Association for Investment Management and Research
Alcar Group, 171
Alcar value-creation model, 172-74
Alternate value, 185
American Association of Individual Investors, 18-19
American Depository Receipts (ADRs), 245
American Stock Exchange (AMEX), 206, 248
AMEX Clubs, 237, 309

Analyst priority plan, 200
Analysts, role of, 49-53
Analyst societies, 202
Annual meetings, 312-17
Annual reports, 4, 29, 49, 74, 141, 144, 156-57, 259-96, 333
  aggressive use of, 265-66
  contents of, 262-63, 264
  educational value of, 266
  main sections, 268-78
    corporate profile, 278
    cover, 277
    financial statement/footnotes, 271-73
    investor information page, 278
    letter to shareholders, 268-71
    management discussion/analysis, 274-77
    operations review, 273-74
  marketing, 286-87
  packaging of, 264
  positioning, 262-67
  preparation/production of, 279-84
    creative team, 279-80
    design/writing of, 280-84
    production schedule, 279-80
  and 10K report, 260-62
  theme of, 265
  value of, 290-94
  See also Employee annual reports; Interim reports; Mini annual reports; Summary reports
Anti-takeover measures, 37, 94, 119, 123
  See also Takeovers

APT, *See* Arbitrage pricing theory
Arbitrage pricing theory (APT), 47-48
Article reprints, 259
Asset allocation, 53-54
Asset value, 64
Associated Press (AP), 362, 390
Association for Investment Management
   and Research (AIMR), 198, 199, 218, 270,
   290, 304, 307-8, 399
Audience base, of investor relations pro-
   grams, 149
Audience groups, 30-31
Audio-visual presentations, 294-96, 318
Automated Data Processing (ADP), 231

B

Balance sheet analysis, 206
Ball, David, 130-31
Banks, 15
Bank trusts, 12
Basic Inc. v. Levinson, 394-95, 407
Bear raids, 70
Bechtel service, 334
Bell Atlantic Corporation, 310-11
Bernard L. Madoff Investment Securities, 190
Beta, 48, 69
Better Investing (NAIC), 239
Bloomberg service, 334
Boesky, Ivan, 97
Book value, 176, 177, 182
Bottom-up investors, 61-62
Bridge service, 333, 334
British market, and international investors,
   252
Broadcast media, 362-63
   contacts, 369
Brokerage analysts:
   analyst societies, 202
   building relationships with, 196-210
   importance of information to, 143-44
   meeting forums for, 303-7
   personal meetings with, 201
   pre-contact research, 198-203
   studying writings of, 201
   working with, 203-10
Brokerage commissions, *See* Commissions
Brokerage firms, 24-25, 223
   attitudes toward stock investing, 80-82
   new products, 79
   regional brokerage firms, 299-301

Broker communications, 238
Broker contact programs, reaching individu-
   als through, 233-39
Bullseye Service, CDA Investment Technolo-
   gies, 292-93
Burrelles, 334
Business Dateline, 333
Business Research, 334
Business Roundtable position paper, 133
Business Week, 357, 362
BusinessWire, 288, 304, 334, 336
Bust-up value, 185, 186
Buy-side analysts, 50, 55
   and field trips, 313
   meeting forums for, 305
   and quarterly reports, 289
   See also Sell-side analysts
Buy-side/sell-side relationships:
   building, 189-218
   building brokerage analyst relationships,
     196-210
   evolution of, 191-92
   redefinition of, 195-96

C

Cable News Network, 362
CableSoft, 333
California Public Employees' Retirement
   System (CalPERS), 74, 127-29, 132-33
Call-outs, annual reports, 284
Capital asset pricing model (CAPM), 47
Capital markets, 43-76
   analysts, role of, 49-53
   asset allocation, 53-54
   economics basis to process, 45-47
   equity investment strategies/styles, 54-66
   foremost role of, 43
   futures/options, 66-69
   globalization of, 242
   indexing, 74-76
   institutional behavior, trends in, 71-74
   need to understand, 8
   risk/return calculations, 47-49
   secondary role of, 43-44
   short selling, 69-71
   staying astride of, 7
   trends/patterns of, 9
Capital structure ratio, 207
Carnation case, 393-94
Cash management accounts, 81

CDA Investment Technologies, 199, 292, 301, 329, 386
Celebrities, investment style, 225
Charts, annual reports, 283, 284
Chief executives (CEOs):
  as information resource, 195
  special letters from, 293
Citicorp Global Report, 334
COBO lists, *See* Consenting beneficial owner (COBO) lists
Collectibles, 81
Commissions, 13, 56, 80-81
Commodities contracts, 82
Communications:
  and affinity groups, 228-29
  broker communications, 238
  crisis communications, 370-76
  establishing attitude/policy/practice, 401-5
  inconsistency in, 22
  skills, 8-9, 38
  style/tone/language of, 142
  and takeover defense strategy, 105-6, 107, 109
  vehicles:
    for marketing, 141
    selecting, 216
    using, 154-58
  See also Crisis communications
Communications plan, developing, 372-76
CompuServe, 333
Compustat, 193, 325, 334
Computer-generated data, reliance on information, 144
Computers, 55-56, 62, 309-10
  and market behavior, 331-32
  and shareholder behavior, 330-31
  See also Technology
Computer-to-computer links, 335-38
Comtex, 333
Consenting beneficial owner (COBO) lists, 231
Consultants, 6, 104-5, 238, 400
  primary role of, 168
"Control shares" provision, 94
Core manager, 62
Corporate advertising, for marketing annual reports, 287
Corporate governance:
  institutional involvement in, 36-38, 117-35

key issues, 122-24
responsibility in takeovers, 112-14
Corporate and Industry Research Reports (CIRR), 305
Corporate profile, annual reports, 278
Corporate trust accounts, 12
CORTRAC, 199, 329, 386
Cost of capital, 72, 172
Cost-reduction programs, and raised corporate securities' values, 184
Cover, annual reports, 277
Coverage targets, 24-25
Creating Shareholder Value (Rappaport), 171
Crisis communications, 370-76
  communications plan, developing, 372-76
  crisis management team, designating, 370
  events-related crises, identifying/planning for, 371-72
  research, conducting, 370-71
  See also Communications
CTS v. Dynamics, 96

D
Danowski, Dr. James A., 366
Databases:
  and market intelligence, 325-29
  See also Technology
DataStar, 305
DCF, *See* Discounted cash flow
Debt, 10-11, 40-41
Debt/equity ratio, 207
Debt relations, 381-87
  positioning equity and, 383-85
  proactive debt relations, 385-87
Delaware takeover protection laws, 123-24
Delivery systems, 4
Demographics, and psychology, 223-27
Design, of annual report, 280-84
Dialog service, 305, 333
Direct contact, 4, 29
  as measure of investor relations program, 164
Direct mail, 232-34, 309
  See also Mailings
Directors, responsibility in takeovers, 112-14
Directory of Pension Funds and Their Investment Managers, 14-16, 199, 212
Dirks v. SEC, 399
Disclosure, 38-41

Discounted cash flow (DCF), 64, 65-66, 174, 182, 266
Distributing information, methods of, 29-31
Divestitures, and raised corporate securities' values, 184
Dividend discount models, 64-65
Dividend income, 173-74, 193
Dividend mailers, 259
Dividend payout ratios, 208
Dividend Policy, Growth and the Valuation of Shares (Miller/Modigliani), 64
Dividend reinvestment plans (DRPs), 27, 227-28
    advantages of, 228
Dividends, 173, 176, 208
Dividend stuffers, 294
Dow Jones, 288, 304-5, 325, 362, 390
Dow Jones Industrial Average, 205
Dow Jones News Retrieval, 305, 333
DowPhone, 333
DRPs, *See* Dividend reinvestment plans
Due diligence meetings, 410
Dynamic asset allocation, 54
Dynamic hedging, 69

E
Earnings momentum, 63, 193
Earning sources, 209
Earnings per share (EPS), 174, 176, 182
Economic indicators of performance, 204
EDGAR, *See* Electronic Data Gathering, Analysis, and Retrieval System (EDGAR)
800 telephone number, 229, 240, 278, 294-96
Electronic communication, emergence of, 294-96
Electronic Data Gathering, Analysis, and Retrieval System (EDGAR), 334-35
Electronic data retrieval, 157, 194, 295, 331
Electronic data services, 193
Electronic distribution of printed information, 29
Electronic information dissemination, 157, 335-38
Electronic Specialty Co. v. International Controls Corp., 396
Ellis, Charles D., 217
Employee annual reports, 284, 286
Employee Retirement Income Security Act (ERISA), 118, 130-32

Employee stock ownership plans (ESOPs), 227-28, 231
Enhance index funds, 68
EPS, *See* Earnings per share (EPS)
Equities markets, institutionalization of, 14
Equity commissions, 13
    decline in, 80-81
Equity investment strategies/styles, 54-66
Equity research/analysis, 12-13
ERISA, *See* Employee Retirement Income Security Act
ESOPs, *See* Employee stock ownership plans
Events-related crises, identifying/planning for, 371-72
Execution stage, of investor relations programs, 149
Exotics, investments in, 81-82

F
Facsimile distribution, 141, 157, 335-38
Fact books and sheets, 4, 29, 30, 141, 155-56, 259
    definition, 291-92
    specifications, 238-39
    value of, 291-92
Farm land investments, 81
Field trips, 312-17
    budget, 314
    contacts with attendees, 314-15
    definition, 312-13
    invitations to media, 316-17
    letters of invitation, 315
    mementos, 316
    menu selection, 315-16
    payoff for audience, 313-14
    planning, 314
    presentations, taping, 315
    purpose of, 313
Financial advertising, for marketing annual reports, 287
Financial Analysts Federation, 199
Financial information, 151, 209
Financial meetings, winnowing contacts from, 156
Financial News Network, 295-96, 362
Financial planners, 12, 17-18, 223
Financial statement, annual report, 271-73
First Call, 157, 194, 288, 305, 325, 334, 336
First Virginia Bank Shares v. Benson, 396

Fixed annuities, 81
Footnotes, annual report, 271-73
Foreign investors, 244
   influence on West German market, 252
401(k) plans, 81
403(b) plans, 81
Fraud-on-the-market theory, 395-96
"Free" cash, 65
French market, and international investors, 252-53
Fundamental analysis, 74-76, 182, 204-5
   basic components of, 204
   and valuation, 180-81
Futures contracts, 66-69, 82

G
Georgeson & Company, 121, 132
Global investing, 48
Global investor relations program, putting together, 33-34
Global portfolios, 61-62, 72
Global stock market, 11
Golden parachutes, 124
Graphs, annual reports, 283, 284
Greenfield v. Heublin, 393-94
Greenmail settlement, 119
Guardians, investment style, 225

H
Hambrecht & Quist, 301
Handout materials, 318
Headlines, annual reports, 284
Hostile takeovers, *See* Takeovers

I
IBES, 334
Icahn, Carl, 97
Income statement, 206
Independent Election Corporation of America (IECA), 231
Index arbitrage, 60
Index funds, 57-58
   forms of, 59-60
Indexing, 58-59, 71-73, 74-76, 193-94
   disadvantages of, 75
   and fundamental analysis, 74-76
Individual investors:
   emphasizing, 77-85
   investing approaches, 16-19

leading back, 82-85
   marketing to, 219-40
   media influence on, 366
Individual retirement accounts (IRAs), 77, 81
INET, 333
Information base:
   of investor relations programs, 149-51
      financial information, 151
      operating information, 150-51
      strategic information, 150
Information flow:
   as measure of investor relations program, 165
   and valuation, 180
   value in investing process, 143-49
Information resources, institutions evaluating companies as, 194-96
Initial public offering (IPO), 409
Insider trading, 96
Instinet, 190, 333
Institute of Chartered Financial Analysts, 199
Institutional behavior, trends in, 71-74
Institutional Investor, 14-16, 155, 212, 239
Institutional investors:
   concentrating on leading market influentials, 217
   current holders, starting with, 214-15
   directly influencing, 210-18
   finding "desirable" shareholders, 213-14
   globalization of, 244-47
   predicting response from, 216
   selecting communications vehicles, 216
   and takeovers, 91
   taking a broad approach with, 217-18
   using research to target, 212-13
Institutionalization, 8, 78
   of equities markets, 14
Institutional momentum, 80
Institutional Research Network (IRN), 295-96, 304
   formats, 296
Insurance companies, 15
Integrated asset allocation, 54
Interim reports, 4, 29, 74, 141, 144, 259
   value of, 290-94
   See also Annual reports; Mini annual reports; Summary reports
International investor relations program:
   assembling, 247-49

commitment of American companies,
    254-55
and local market research, 251-52
meeting formats, 255-57
International Monetary Market, Chicago
    Mercantile Exchange, 245
International portfolios, *See* Global portfolios
Intrinsic value, 185, 186
Investex, 305, 333
Investment bankers:
    and takeover defense strategy, 108
    and takeovers, 98
Investment Company Institute (ICI), 16, 79
Investment goals, and portfolio manage-
    ment, 226
Investment management firms, 15, 17
Investor club programs, 227
Investor feedback, as measure of investor re-
    lations program, 165
Investor information page, annual reports,
    278
Investor newsletters, 29, 141, 229, 259, 293-94
Investor relations:
    as a rotational position, 414-15
    as career/stepping stone, 411-22
    contribution to corporate success, 419
    elevating, 415-19
    external/market forces impacting, 35-41
        debt, 40-41
        disclosure, 38-40
        institutional involvement in corporate
            governance, 36-38
        takeovers/proxy contests, 35-36
    genesis of, 3-6
    globalization of, 241-60
    marketing, 139-66
        case histories, 158-63
    mediator role, 38
    monies, use of, 5
    ongoing task of, 6
    and principles of finance, 3
    purpose of, 142-45
    and takeovers, 100-106
    trend in, 155
    value of, 145-48
Investor relations consultants, 6
Investor relations office:
    organizing, 338-44
        administration, 343
        analysis/reporting, 343-44

management information, 339-43
    software programs, 339
Investor relations professionals:
    ability to function as information sources,
        143
    basic duties of, 148-49
    as information sources, 246-47
    and investor clubs, 232
    qualities/characteristics of, 421-22
    and research, 153, 198
Investor relations program:
    assembling, 247-49
    basic structure of, 149-51
    building/maintaining market relations, 23-
        27
        increasing analyst coverage, 23-25
        reaching individuals, 26-27
        reaching institutions, 25-26
    conducting benchmark attitudinal/knowl-
        edge, research , 23
    distributing information, methods of, 29-31
    global investor relations program, putting
        together, 33-34
    information process, 27-29
    measuring, 41, 163-66
    media relations, value of, 34-35
    setting objectives, 21-23
    technology, use of, 32-33
Investors' Daily, 295, 305
IPO, *See* Initial public offering (IPO)
IRAS, *See* Individual retirement accounts
IRN, *See* Institutional Research Network

J
Japanese market, and international investors,
    253

K
Keogh plans, 77, 81
Knowledge base, building, 143

L
Language, of communications, 142
Lawyers, and takeover defense strategy, 108
LBOs, *See* Leveraged buyouts (LBOs)
"Lead steer" theory, 182, 217
Leverage buyout (LBO) specialists, 98
Leveraged buyouts (LBOs), 98-99, 112
    price in, 186
Lexis/Nexis service, 305, 333

Life cycle, phases of, 225-26
Life insurance, 81
Liquidity, 226, 332
Liquidity ratio, 207
Lockheed Corporation, 120-21
Lotus One Source, 325
Lowes Corporation, 287

M

Macroeconomic factors, 204
Macro risks, 48
Mailings, 29, 140, 141, 155-56, 229
Management Discussion and Analysis of Financial Conditions and Results of Operations (MD&A), 274-77, 290, 390, 402
Management quality, 209-10
Market behavior, and computers, 331-32
Market indexation, 205
Marketing, 139-66
    annual reports, 286-87
    communications programs to support, 239-40
    components of, 4
    to individual/retail brokers, 219-40
Marketing approaches, 221-23
Marketing skills, 8-9
Market intelligence, 325-29
Material disclosure, 38-41, 389-410
    dealing with analysts/brokers/investors, 397-99
    establishing communications attitude/policy/practice, 401-5
    exchanges' push for, 400-401
    handling disclosure situations, 406-9
    history of, 392-99
    outsiders, 400
    while in registration, 409-10
MD&A, See Management Discussion and Analysis of Financial Conditions and Results of Operations
Mead Data Exchange, 305
Measure of volatility, 48
Media, and field trips, 316-17
Media directories, 336
Media exposure, 29, 141
Media General, 334
Media outlets, approaching, 368
Media relations, 345-79
    guidelines, 376-79
    investor relations role in, 349-52

media relations program, 355-76
    conducting a proactive program, 365-69
    crisis communications, 370-76
    getting to know the media, 360-63
    reporting procedures, 357-58
    research, 358-60
    responding to requests, 363-65
    setting policy/procedures, 356-58
    proactive media relations, case for, 352-55
    value of, 34-35, 348-49
Media relations software programs, 359
Meetings, 297-321
    annual meetings, 312-17
    attendee profiles, 319
    with brokers, 302
    for buy-side analysts, 305
    field trips and annual meetings, 312-17
    formats, 30-31
        international investor relations program, 255-57
    getting the most out of, 317-21
    hosting, 236-37
    ideas for improving quality of, 319-21
    and the media, 361-62
    organizing, 298-303
    planning, 298-99
    plotting forums for, 303-10
        brokerage analysts, 303-7
        brokers, 308-10
        institutions, 307-8
    programmed approach to, 310-12
    with regional brokerage firms, 300-301
    with sell-side analysts, 299-300
    with shareholders, 310-12
Merger and acquisition activities, and valuation, 185
Mini annual reports, 284-86, 287
Mitchell consulting group, 181-82
Momentum, 62, 80
    earnings momentum, 63
Money managers, 15
Money market accounts, 77, 78
Moody's reports, 293
Morgan Stanley Capital International Europe, Australia, and Far East (EAFE) index, 58, 244-45
Mortgage-backed securities, 81
Mutual funds, 17, 77, 79-80, 84
    growth of, 79

N

National Association of Investors Corpora-
tions (NAIC), 18-19, 232-33, 293
  Better Investing, 239
National Association of Securities Dealers
(NASD), 70, 206
National Investor Relations Institute (NIRI):
  annual directory, 237-38
  membership survey, 412-13
  position paper, 134
National media outlets, approaching, 368-69
Nelson's Directory of Investment Managers, 199,
  212
NewsFlash, 333
Newsletters, 4, 29, 141, 229, 259, 293-94
NewsNet, 305, 333
News releases, 141, 157
New stockholders, average portfolio size, 18
New York Society of Security Analysts
(NYSSA), 304
New York Stock Exchange:
  industrial, utility, transportation, and com-
    posite indexes, 205
  survey of individuals, 233
New York Times, 155, 362, 390
NIRI, *See* National Investor Relations Insti-
  tute (NIRI)
Non-objecting beneficial owner (NOBO)
  lists, 231, 311

O

Ongoing measurement process, of investor
  relations programs, 149
On-line data retrieval, 157, 194
Operating information, 150-51, 209
Operations review, annual reports, 273-74
Options, 66-69, 81
Orientation brochure, 294
Outside services, 323-44
Overhead transparencies, 29, 296, 318

P

Passive investors, 57-61, 224
  and stock index futures, 68
  See also Active investors
Passive management, 58
Payout ratio, 207
Pension plans, 72-73, 194
Pensions & Investments, 14, 72, 73, 155,
  212, 239

Pension World, 155, 239
P/E ratio, *See* Price/earnings (P/E) ratio Per-
  formance:
  economic indicators of, 204
  and passive management, 58
Pergamon Infoline, 305
Personality, influence on investments, 224-25
Phelan, John, 83
Pickens, T. Boone, 97, 124
Pitt, Harvey L., 407
Poison pills, 37, 93, 97, 119-20
  and takeover premium, 121-22
Portfolio insurance, 96
Portfolio management, 48-49, 51, 80
  and computers, 55-56
  and investment goals/liquidity/taxes, 226
  options/futures, uses in, 66-68
Portfolio managers, classifications of, 224-25
Pre-contact research, 198-203
Presentations:
  contents, 318
  formats, 256
  taping, 315
Press relations, *See* Media relations
Price/earnings (P/E) ratio, 65, 174, 193,
  207-8, 332
Printed informations, electronic distribution
  of, 29
PR Newswire, 288, 334, 336
Proactive debt relations, 385-87
Production schedule, annual reports,
  279-80
Professional management, 17
Profit sharing plans, 81
Program trading, 96
Proxy contests:
  impact on investor relations, 35-36
  revival of, 120-21
Proxy solicitors, and takeover defense strat-
  egy, 108
Psychology, and demographics, 223-27
Public pension plans, 72-73, 194
  and activism, 119

Q

Quantitative style of investing, 62
Quarterly reports, 229-30
  electronic transmission of, 338
  positioning, 288-90
Quotron, 304-5, 325, 333

R

Radio stations, and media relations program, 362-63
Raiders, *See* Takeovers
Rappaport, Alfred, 171
Ratios, 207
Real estate investments, 81
Recapitalizations, 98-99
Recap specialists, 98
Reconstructed proxy system, 126
Regional brokerage firms, 299-301
Registered Representative magazine, 81, 233, 239, 287, 292
Research, 12-13, 23, 150, 175-76
  and affinity groups, 235-36
  brokerage research, 191-92
  and globalization, 242-43
  media relations program, 358-60
  purpose of, 153-54
  sell-side research, 192-94
  using to target institutional investors, 212-13
  working with, 151-54
Research Services, 292, 329
Research Video, 295
Restructuring, 88, 98
  evolution of, 184-85
Retail brokers, 12, 17-18, 24
  marketing to, 219-40
  See also Brokerage firms
Retail equity commissions, 13
Return on equity, 176, 177
Return on investment, 171-72
  calculations, 47-49
Reuters wire, 288, 299, 304, 334, 336, 362, 390
Revenues, 176, 177, 182
RICO federal racketeering statutes, 71
Risk, 226
  calculations, 47-49
  and options/futures, 67
Risk/reward formula, 45-46
Road show presentations, 410
ROE, *See* Return on equity
ROI, *See* Return on investment
Russell 1000, 2000, 3000, 57

S

Savings associations, 15
SEC, *See* Securities and Exchange Commission

Sector rotators, 64
Securities Act:
  and material disclosure, 392
  Rule 10b-5, 70-71
  Rule 144a, 245-46
  Rule 14(a)8, 123
Securities and Exchange Commission (SEC), 38-39, 70, 121, 124, 125, 127, 151-52, 246, 260, 290, 389, 392, 399, 400
Securities Industry Association (SIA), 10, 17, 77, 82-84, 243
Selling short, *See* Short selling
Sell-side analysts, 49-50, 55
  and field trips, 313
  identification of, 299-300
  and quarterly reports, 289
  See also Buy-side analysts
Sell-side research, 192-94
Serious stock investors, investing approach, 18-19
Shareholder behavior, and computers, 330-31
Shareholder identification program, 105
Shareholder meetings, 230
Shareholders' letters, 260, 261, 268-71
  contents of, 270-71
  writing, 269
Shareholder value, 167
Shareholder value consultants, 6
Share price management, 167, 177-81
Sharon Steel Corp., 396-97
Short selling, 69-71
SIA, *See* Securities Industry Association
Silence period, 409
Simons, Harold, 120-21
Slide shows, 29, 296, 318
Smithburg, William D., 266-67
The Source, 333
Specialized knowledge, 144
Special letters, from CEOs, 293
Staggered boards, 93, 123
Staggered election of directors, as takeover deterrent, 37
Standard & Poor's 500 Index, 57, 92, 194, 205, 245, 332
Standard & Poor's 500 Index Directory, 239
Standard deviation, 48, 224
Stein Roe asset-value investing model, 172
Stern, Joel, 182, 217
Stockbroker clubs, 236

Stockbrokers' Society, 309
Stock index funds, 68
Stock index futures, 67
Stock price:
    market-wide movements in, 205-6
    as measure of investor relations program,
      164
Stocks, 80-82
    classifications, 51-52
    direct investment by individuals, competi-
      tion for, 78-79
    volatility of, 54
Stock watch programs, 330-31
Straight arrows, investment style, 225
Strategic asset allocation, 54
Strategic information, 150, 209
"Street name" shareholders, 231, 330
Style, of communications, 142
Subheads, annual reports, 284
Summary reports, 284-86
Surveys, 230-31
    and annual reports, 261
Synthetic instruments, 69

T
Tactical asset allocation, 54
Tailored-share purchase plans, 27
Takeover defense programs:
    and investor relations, 101-5
    role in, 106-12
Takeovers, 87-115, 185, 330
    deterrents to, 37, 96-99
    director responsibility in, 112-14
    future of, 114-15
    impact on investor relations, 35-36
    legislation, 95-96
    in 1980s, 90-92
    opposition to, 92-96
    price in, 186
    as trigger for activism, 118-21
Tax planning, 226
Technical analysis, 61-62
Technimetrics, 23, 199, 292, 301, 329, 386
Technology, 323-44
    general information gathered by, 333-35
    and globalization, 242-43
    investor relations office, organizing,
      338-44
    market behavior analyzed by, 331-32

and market intelligence, 325-29
    roles of, 324
    shareholder behavior, 330-31
    streamlining information dissemination,
      335-38
    use of, 32-33
Teleconferencing, 294-96, 305
Telescan, 157, 194, 288, 325, 334, 336-37
Television stations, and media relations pro-
      gram, 362-63
10K/10Q reports, 4, 29, 30, 49, 74, 144, 157,
      259, 278, 392, 407
    and annual report, 260-62
    value of, 290-94
Texas Gulf Sulphur ruling, 396
Thrift plans, 81
Timed Release, 336-37
Time-Warner merger, 95, 114
Tone, of communications, 142
Top-down investors, 61
Track Data, 334
Traders, as investor relations contacts, 12
Treasury bills, 17, 77, 78, 81
Treasury bonds, 17
Treasury notes, 17, 81
Trust Universe Comparison Service (TUCS)
    fund indexes, 58
TSC Industries v. Northway, Inc., 393-94
Typesetting, annual reports, 283-84

U
Underpriced stocks, and bottom-up inves-
      tors, 62
United Press International, 390
United Shareholders Association (USA), 124

V
"Valdez Principles," 125-26
Valuation, 28, 51, 146-48, 150, 157, 163, 166
    arguments for, 170-71
    as basis of investor relations practice,
      167-87
    as basis of strategic corporate action,
      175-76
    definition, 167-68
    electronic transmission of data, 338
    executive attention to, 178
    influence of investor relations on, 146
    investor relations responsibilities, 168-69

as measure of investor relations program, 164
measuring, 174
methods, 64-66, 171-74
negative views of, 169-70
share price management, 177-81
value drivers show in investment behavior, 175-77
Value, of investor relations, 145-48
Value buyers, 63
Value creation, as ongoing process, 184-87
Value-enhancing programs, 219
scientific process for, 181-82
Value gap, 179
Value Line, 333
Value-raising moves, investor reaction to, 183-84
Variable annuities, 81
Vickers, 199, 301, 329
Video presentations, 4, 29, 259, 294-96, 305, 318, 333
Voice mail, 337

Volatility, 51, 69, 332
measure of, 48
of stocks, 54
VuText, 333

W
Wall Street Journal, 155, 362, 375, 390
Wall Street Transcript, 295
Wealthy investors, investing approach, 18-19
White papers, 29, 259, 294, 333
Wilcox, John C., 132
Williams Act, 95
Wilshire 5000 Index, 57
Winans, R. Foster, 399
Writing:
annual reports, 280-84
shareholders' letters, 269
Written policy, media relations program, 356-57

Z
Zacks database, 193, 325, 334